LATER LIFE
The Realities of Aging

THIRD EDITION

HAROLD G. COX

Indiana State University

PRENTICE HALL, Englewood Cliffs, New Jersey 07632

Library of Congress Cataloging-in-Publication Data

Cox, Harold
    Later life : the realities of aging / Harold G. Cox. -- 3rd. ed.
        p.   cm.
    Includes bibliographical references and index.
    ISBN 0-13-524091-3
    1. Aged--United States--Social conditions.   2. Gerontology--United
States.   3. Aged--United States--Psychology.   I. Title.
HQ1064.U5C64 1992
305.26'0973--dc20   92-6957
                                                               CIP

Acquisitions editor: Nancy Roberts
Editorial/production supervision and
   interior design: Serena Hoffman
Cover design: Ray Lundgren Graphics
Prepress buyer: Kelly Behr
Manufacturing buyer: Mary Ann Gloriande
Copy editor: Nancy Savio-Marcello

© 1993, 1988, 1984 by Prentice-Hall, Inc.
A Simon & Schuster Company
Englewood Cliffs, NJ 07632

Printed in the United States of America
10 9 8 7 6 5 4 3 2 1

ISBN 0-13-524091-3

PRENTICE-HALL INTERNATIONAL (UK) LIMITED, *London*
PRENTICE-HALL OF AUSTRALIA PTY. LIMITED, *Sydney*
PRENTICE-HALL CANADA INC., *Toronto*
PRENTICE-HALL HISPANOAMERICANA, S.A., *Mexico*
PRENTICE-HALL OF INDIA PRIVATE LIMITED, *New Delhi*
PRENTICE-HALL OF JAPAN, INC., *Tokyo*
SIMON & SCHUSTER ASIA PTE. LTD., *Singapore*
Editora PRENTICE-HALL DO BRASIL, LTDA., *Rio de Janeiro*

Contents

Part II: The Individual
and The Social System

Part III: Adjustment Patterns
and Changing Lifestyles in Old Age

*Part IV: Societal Issues Confronting
Older Americans*

Preface

The demographic revolution in modern industrial nations seems to have occurred because of a decline in the crude birthrate combined with an improved medical technology's capacity to save and prolong life. The result, in all of the industrially developed nations, has been the same—a growing number and percentage of the population living to age 65 and beyond. Moreover, Donald Cowgill is projecting an ever-increasing expansion of the older population in the underdeveloped nations as well.[1] Barring unforeseen demographic changes in the near future, the number of older persons in Western Europe and the United States will continue to grow and constitute an ever-larger percentage of the population. The elderly in the United States have grown from approximately 3 million in 1900, composing less than 4 percent of the population, to 31.0 million in 1989, approximately 12.5 percent of the population. This shift in the age composition of the American population has resulted in a growing public awareness of the problems, potentials, and realities of aging. Persons in their middle years almost uniformly expect to live to retirement age and beyond. There is widespread interest in the quality of life of older Americans, expressed both by those approaching retirement and those already there. This widespread interest and concern about the lives of older Americans has produced innumerable articles and editorials from the popular press, increased interest and research by the scientific community, and the implementation of numerous government-sponsored service delivery programs for older Americans.

This book attempts to integrate material from this proliferating body of research and writing into a meaningful discussion of the major trends and developments in the field we call gerontology. Reflecting the interdisciplinary nature of the subject, the book includes material from psychology, sociology, social work, anthropology, the biological sciences, medicine, and psychiatry. I have attempted to favor neither the medical model, which sees old age as a process of deterioration, disease, and progressive decline, nor the more recent and popular human development model, which sees old age as a period of further growth, develop-

---

1. Donald Cowgill, *Aging Around the World* (Belmont, Calif.: Wadsworth, 1986).

ment, and new experiences. While the later years are a further development of the individual's life history and offer opportunities for growth and new experiences, ultimately all people suffer certain health losses and die. Thus, I have tried to present the later phase of the life cycle as realistically as possible.

The interdisciplinary nature of the gerontology tends to make texts on this subject eclectic. But in this book—written from a social science perspective—I utilize a symbolic interaction frame of reference. In this way the reader is provided with a single theoretical approach to the behavioral aspects of aging.

Writing a text, much like teaching a class, involves synthesizing and organizing a variety of materials into an understandable, interesting, and challenging presentation of the facts. In the case of the textbook, the product should be interesting, understandable, intellectually challenging, and applicable to one's own life. Only you, the reader, can judge whether I have met these standards. I hope that I have. In any event, in writing a text an author inevitably learns much more than any future reader of it. His or her attempts to synthesize, organize, and present the material inevitably begin with a clear understanding of it. Thus I have already gained much, since in writing this book I have increased my knowledge of, sensitivity to, and comprehension of the realities of later life.

I would like to thank all of my colleagues and friends at Indiana State University who helped and supported me as I prepared this manuscript; my students who raised questions, challenged my ideas, and thereby increased my understanding of the subject; Doris Panagouleas for her careful and diligent work in preparing the manuscript, Bela J. Bogner, Wright State University, Ernestine H. Thompson, Augusta College, and Franklin N. Arnhoff, University of Virginia, for reviewing the manuscript; and my wife for always supporting and understanding my work, however successful or unsuccessful it might be.

Harold G. Cox

1

Emergence and Scope of Gerontology

THE ADVENT OF GERONTOLOGY

Throughout the history of the human species, men and women have clung to life and used every means available to live as long as possible. A theme running through historical records in different time periods and different cultures has been the search for a way to reverse the aging process. The search for an elixir or fountain of youth was almost universal. Leonard Breen (1970) observed that "Special foods to be eaten, special relationships to be cultivated, surgery which might be undertaken, special waters or other liquids to be ingested all were thought to be solutions by some."[1] It was, however, not until the twentieth century that the understanding and study of the aging process left the area of witchcraft and folklore and became a legitimate subject of a number of different scientific disciplines.

Moreover, during the past 20 years aging and the field of gerontology have become the focus of extensive concern, discussion, editorializing, and political action. Aging has arrived as an issue and object of study; people are examining what it means to be old in America.

What accounts for this burst of interest? A number of factors might explain it—factors stemming both from individual experience and from the experience of society as a whole. The increasing number of people and the percentage of our population living to age 65 and beyond have made the problems of aging more widespread, more visible, and ultimately more widely known. And because of this increased longevity, almost all of us at one time or another have had the experience of helping an aging relative adjust and survive under changing life circumstances.

When only a small proportion of older people experience poverty, illness, or social isolation, we may not be aware of their problems. But as the number of older people living under these conditions grows, a challenge is directly posed to our social service systems and the problem "takes off." It becomes acute enough to be discussed and debated by politicians, the media, and other concerned individuals and groups. One definite effect emerges: a growing consciousness of— and sensitivity to—the problems of older people.

1

As the number of older persons has grown and public awareness of problems of the aged has increased, government delivery systems for older Americans have developed, providing services such as food, employment, information, homemaking, and counseling. New paraprofessional and professional occupations deal with the problems of older people, and political action and legislation have been initiated on their behalf. Significantly, the academic community has recognized aging as a legitimate area of study.

Before this surge of interest, physicians, health practitioners, and behavioral scientists often avoided the study of aging. Perhaps concern with the illnesses and problems of younger persons seemed more directly related to a humane cause: Young people have all their lives before them, and those who help them rightly feel that they are contributing to the future of society.

Older people, on the other hand, have most of their mortal lives behind them. Their medical, psychiatric, and social problems are often more difficult to deal with because they are frequently complex and interrelated. Whereas the communicable diseases of the young can often be entirely cured, many of the chronic medical problems of later life cannot. At best, the illnesses of the aged can be controlled, and a bad situation will not get worse; at worst, illnesses may resist treatment, resulting in disability and death. It is easy to understand why doctors would find more satisfaction in curing a disease than in stopping it from accelerating. But whatever the reason, older people have not received as much attention as younger people from health and other professionals.

In much the same way, psychology, sociology, and social work have not devoted as much research and attention to the problems of older persons as they have to those of younger people. Since scientists are subject to the same latent fears about aging and death that trouble the general population, they frequently find the study of aging uncongenial, if not depressing. Paying attention to aging processes reminds researchers that someday they too will grow old and die. As a result, the subject of aging has not received the attention it demands from scientists.

This neglect of the problems of aging appears to be over. Aging has become a legitimate subject of study, and the relevant professions as well as the public are becoming increasingly sensitive to its issues and problems. Individually, there are both personal and objective reasons for looking carefully at the later part of the life cycle. First, because all of us hope to live long lives, the better we understand this phase of the life cycle the better we can anticipate our future lives and the experiences we will confront at that time. Whereas courses in child development may help us understand our children, courses in gerontology should help us understand our future selves. Second, even if we are not interested in our current and future selves, understanding the life course, including both the problems and the potentials of later life, should prove invaluable as we attempt to understand and share the lives of our older relatives and friends. Finally, anyone who is sensitive and alert to the surrounding world cannot help but be intrigued by the explosion of scientific research and information that is both prolonging life and improving the quality of the lives of older persons. From organ transplants to senior services, from hospice programs to the debate over euthanasia, from exercise programs to living wills, the field of gerontology appears to be at the forefront of a proliferation of new knowledge and understanding of the human condition.

The remainder of this chapter will provide you with an overview of the demographic trends that reveal the dramatic rise in the number of persons 65 years and older in the population. We will also introduce some of the major problems of this group, as well as common public perceptions of the lives of older persons.

DEMOGRAPHIC TRENDS

In 1900 there were 3.1 million Americans over age 65, constituting approximately 4 percent (1 in 25) of the total population. In 1970, 20 million Americans were over age 65—approximately 10 percent (1 in 10) of the population.[2] In 1980 there were 25.5 million Americans over 65, or approximately 11 percent (1 in 9) of the population. Demographers estimate that by the year 2000, more than 36 million Americans will be over 65 and comprise 13 percent of the population; by the year 2030, more than 64 million Americans will be 65 and over and comprise between 19 and 20 percent of the total population. If the demographic projections are correct, 1 in 5 persons in the population would be over 65 in 2030. (See Figure 1–1.)

These figures are based on the current birthrate. Should the birthrate suddenly rise, the percentage of the total population over age 65 would drop

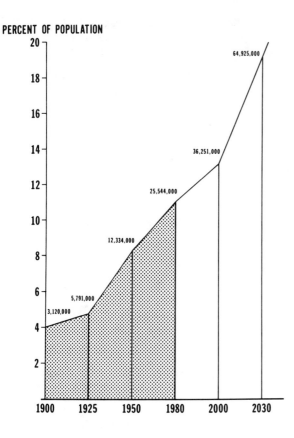

PERCENT OF POPULATION

FIGURE 1–1
U.S. Population Age 65 and Older,
1900–2030

*Note: 1985–2030 figures are projections.
Source: U.S. Bureau of the Census, Social Security Administration

slightly. The long-range trend in the birthrate has been downward, however, and no one is predicting any dramatic reversals in the next 30 years. Any further drop in the birthrate would make the 65+ group an even larger percentage of the population.

The population of the 65+ age group has grown by 3 to 4 million per decade since 1940. Growth during the 1970s exceeded earlier projections, climbing at an annual increment of 460,000. Every day approximately 5000 persons reach their 65th birthday. Every day 3600 persons in the same age group die. This means an increase of 1400 persons in the 65+ group each day. Figure 1–2 reveals how much more rapidly this age group has grown compared with the total population from 1900 until 1975.

Not only are more people living to 65, but once they reach that age they live longer. In 1900, fewer than 1 million Americans were 75 and older and approximately 100,000 were 85 and older. In 1980 there were 9.5 million persons 75 and older and 2.3 million 85 and older. While the 65-and-older group has increased approximately eightfold since 1900, the population 85 and older has grown 22 times. Moreover, the 85+ group is projected to grow more rapidly than the 65+ age group until about 2010, when cohorts born in the baby boom of the 1940s and 1950s begin to retire (see Figure 1–3).[3] Since it is the 85+ group that makes the greatest demand for services, one can easily foresee the impact of the growth of this age group on the resources of federal, state, and local governments.

The changing age composition of the American population is best illustrated in Figure 1–4. In 1900, 4 percent of the population was 65 and over while persons 19 and younger made up 44 percent of the population. By 1980 the

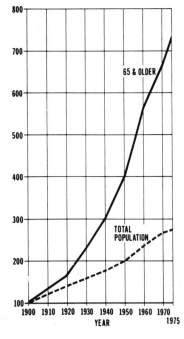

FIGURE 1–2
Rate of Increase 65 and Older versus Total U.S. Population, 1900–1975 (1900 = 100)
Source: U.S. Bureau of the Census

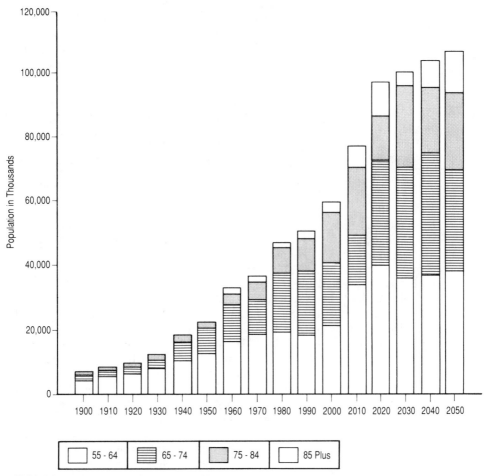

FIGURE 1–3   Population 55 Years and Over by Age, 1900–2050

Source: U.S. Census of Population, 1890–1980, and projections of the population of the United States, 1983–2080. *Current Population Reports,* Series P-25, No. 952, middle series.

proportion of 65+ persons had increased to 11 percent and that of the younger group had decreased to 32 percent. The U.S. Bureau of the Census predicts that by the middle of the next century the proportions of young persons and elderly will be almost equal, the young constituting 23 percent of the population and the elderly 22 percent.[4]

Louis Harris and Associates (1975) believe that there are three basic reasons for the current growth of America's older population. First, the large number of people born when the birthrate was high are now reaching age 65. Second, the many young adults who immigrated to the United States during World War II are also reaching 65. Finally, improvements in medical technology have created a dramatic increase in life expectancy.

Since 1900 life expectancy at birth has increased and the differential life

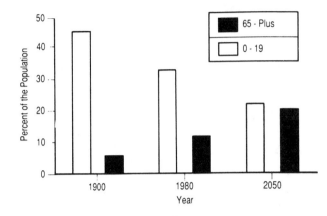

FIGURE 1–4
Actual and Projected Change in Distribution of Children and 65 + Persons in the Population, 1900–2050

Source: U.S. Bureau of the Census, *Current Population Reports*, Series P-25, No. 952; and Census of the Population, 1900.

expectancy of men and women has grown. In 1900 life expectancy for women in the United States was 48.3 years and for men 46.3 years. By 1985 life expectancy for females was 78.3 years and for males 71.3 years. While life expectancy generally increased by 27 years during this period, the sex difference in life expectancy increased from 2 to 7 years in favor of women. In 1985 white females had the highest life expectancy (78.9 years), followed by black females (73.6 years), white males (72.0 years), and black males (65.5 years). (See Table 1–1.)

The last few years have seen a slight decrease in the difference between female and male longevity. In 1988 the male–female difference in life expectancy was 6.8 years, in 1980 it was 7.6 years, and in 1970 it was 7.8 years.[5]

Life expectancy at birth is the average number of years a person can expect to live from the time of birth. For every child who dies in the first few months of life, others must live to a very advanced age if the entire population is to have an average life expectancy of approximately 74.9 years. Since people obviously die at any age in life, those who reach age 65 are a select group who have presumably survived many health problems and other obstacles along the way. Currently, those arriving at age 65 can expect to live approximately 16.9 years more.

Between 1900 and 1950 the increase in life expectancy came about primarily because of a decrease in mortality among the younger age groups. Stated simply, larger numbers of persons reached the older ages, but once there they did not live much longer than the previous generation had. Since 1950, however, life expectancy at the older ages has increased more rapidly than life expectancy at birth. Between 1900 and 1980 life expectancy for the 65 + group increased by 2.7 years for elderly men and by 6.4 years for elderly women.

Moreover, gains in life expectancy for the older age groups are expected to continue for some time. Table 1–2 indicates projected improvements for the 65- and 85-year-old males and females for the next 50 years. In 2040, when the first baby boomers reach 85, their life expectancy is projected to be another 6.3 years for males and 8.5 years for females.[6]

Formerly, the diseases that took large numbers of younger people's lives were communicable diseases—those traceable to viruses or bacteria. Medical science, in working to immunize the population against such diseases as smallpox, diphtheria, measles, and mumps, has done much to control the kinds of diseases that kill younger people. Older Americans are affected less by acute communicable diseases and more by chronic conditions and the deterioration of vital organs.

TABLE 1–1   Life Expectancy at Birth and at Age 65, by Race and Sex, 1900, 1950, 1975, and 1985

Age, Sex, and Race	1900*	1950	1975	1985**
Life expectancy at birth				
Total	47.3	68.2	72.6	74.9
Men	46.3	65.6	68.8	71.3
Women	48.3	71.1	76.6	78.3
White	47.6	69.1	73.4	75.4
Men	46.6	66.5	69.5	72.0
Women	48.7	72.2	77.3	78.9
Non-White	33.0	60.8	66.8	69.6
Men	32.5	59.1	62.4	65.5
Women	33.5	62.9	71.3	73.6
Life expectancy at age 65				
Total	11.9	13.9	16.1	16.9
Men	11.5	12.8	13.8	14.8
Women	12.2	15.0	18.1	18.6
White	—	—	16.1	17.0
Men	11.5	12.8	13.8	14.8
Women	12.2	15.1	18.2	18.8
Non-white	—	—	15.0	15.5
Men	10.4	12.5	13.1	13.6
Women	11.4	14.5	16.7	16.9

*Death registration area only

**Provisional

Source: National Center for Health Statistics

The major health problems of older persons are related to circulatory failure. This can include heart attacks, hardening of the arteries, or cerebrovascular diseases (strokes). A second major cause of death in the older population is cancer—a breakdown in body chemistry in which malignant cells divide and redivide abnormally fast. Both heart disease and cancer have been more serious for men than for women.

Chronic conditions among old people are a primary cause of disability in old age. Some of the chronic conditions can lead to the individual's death but many

TABLE 1–2   Life Expectancy at Ages 65 and 85 by Sex, Projections 1990, 2000, 2020, and 2040.

Year	Males		Females	
	At age 65	At age 85	At age 65	At age 85
1990	15.1	5.4	19.1	6.8
2000	15.7	5.7	19.8	7.3
2020	16.4	6.1	20.7	7.9
2040	17.1	6.3	21.5	8.5

Source: Office of the Actuary, Social Security Administration

do not. Table 1–3 indicates the major chronic conditions experienced by older persons. Four out of five older persons have at least one chronic condition and many have more than one. The most common of these diseases are arthritis, hypertension, heart disease, and hearing impairments. These four conditions together account for approximately 60 percent of all the chronic diseases reported by the community-based elderly.[7]

George Maddox (1982) has criticized medicine's neglect of the problems of aging. He contends that the United States spends much more money on spectacular medical achievements such as heart transplants and artificial kidney treatment than on preventive care, especially for older people. Maddox also argues that we do not care for older Americans until they are so sick that they require hospitalization, which only raises the cost of treatment.[8]

Gerontologists believe that there are two general strategies for increasing life expectancy. One is to conquer disease. They believe that if death from cardiovascular disease and malignancy were eliminated, life expectancy could be increased by 5 to 15 years. The second strategy is to alter the biological processes that are thought to promote aging while being independent of disease. This would require research into the biochemistry of aging people to discover the factors controlling the rate of aging. Gerontologists hope that medical science can eventually control that rate, rather than focusing primarily on controlling disease.[9]

Pressure from such critics as Maddox may encourage medical science to attempt to control the diseases of later life as well as the rate at which people age. Once the resources of the medical profession are directed toward the problems of aging, the results could be impressive. Although no fountain of youth would spring up, a further increase in the life expectancy of older Americans might reasonably be anticipated.

Although the number of persons arriving at age 65 is expected to increase for the foreseeable future, the increase should prove gradual rather than dramatic between now and the year 2010. The reason for this is the low birthrate during the 1930s. Since the people born in that decade will be retiring between now and the year 2010, the increase will be gradual. Also, the *dependency ratio* will probably not change appreciably in the next 20 years (see Figure 1–5). The dependency ratio is the ratio of those in the work force to those out of the work force. Thus most people under 18 and over 65 are out of the work force and

TABLE 1–3   Selected Chronic Conditions of the Population 65 and Over by Sex, 1986

Condition	Males	Females
	(per thousand persons)	
Arthritis	358.6	565.8
Cataracts and other visual impairments	242.0	301.0
Hearing impairment	371.0	242.7
Orthopedic impairment	137.4	197.5
Heart disease	295.5	263.3
Hypertension	329.5	440.0
Cerebrovascular disease	66.0	65.7
Diabetes	99.2	97.6

Source: National Center for Health Statistics

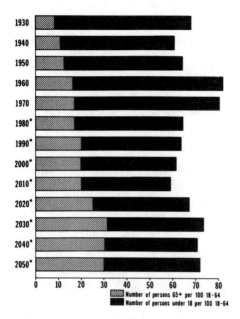

1930
1940
1950
1960
1970
1980*
1990*
2000*
2010*
2020*
2030*
2040*
2050*

0   10   20   30   40   50   60   70   80

▨ Number of persons 65+ per 100 18-64
■ Number of persons under 18 per 100 18-64

FIGURE 1–5
Number of Persons Aged 65 and Older and Under 18 per 100 Persons Aged 18–64, 1930–1980 and Projections to 2050
Source: U.S. Bureau of the Census

depend on those between 19 and 64 to produce the goods and services they need. Since those born in the baby boom following World War II are now part of the labor force, they are in effect keeping the dependency ratio lower than it would otherwise be. The competition for jobs among this large group is presently creating difficulties for many. The major problem, however, is expected in the year 2010 and thereafter, when these baby boomers begin to retire. Proportionately fewer people will be available to support them then, which means the dependency ratio should increase dramatically. One can only imagine the changes this may entail in production, taxation, and the support system for older Americans. There is an additional question: Will taxpayers in their working years be willing to be taxed heavily to support this large group of retirees?

Aging by Sex Ratio

Currently, six out of every ten older Americans are women. This is a result of the longer life expectancy of women. This was not always the case, however. As recently as 50 years ago there were equal numbers of older men and women. After 1930, women began surviving longer than men as pregnancy and childbirth-related deaths and mortality from infectious diseases dropped rapidly.[10]

As Table 1–4 indicates, projections of the sex ratio (the number of females per 100 males) will change little for the 65 and above group. In 1985 the sex ratio was 147 (there were 147 women for every 100 men). Demographic projections indicate only minor fluctuations in this figure between now and the year 2050, at which time the sex ratio is expected to be 145. During the same time period, however, the gap in the number of women 85 years old and over per 100 comparably aged men will widen. Demographers predict that it will peak in the year 2010 at 266 when women will comprise more than 72 percent of the oldest-old population.[11]

At any age in life, men are more likely to die than women. The higher mortality of men accounts for the faster growth of the older female population. Between 1980 and 1985, men 65 and over increased by just over 50 percent while the number of women increased by 86 percent. The excess of male mortality can be seen for the oldest age groups. Men 85 years of age and over account for only 7 percent of the elderly male population, but among women those 85 and over account for 11 percent of the elderly female population.[12]

Aging by Race

According to the 1980 census, 11.2 percent of the total white population is 65 and over versus only 7.8 percent of the black population. Of the 23 million persons 65 and over, 90 percent were white, 8.2 percent were black, and 2 percent were "other races."

Blacks' higher birthrate keeps their percentage of the 65+ group lower than might be expected. Another factor is that life expectancy for blacks is lower than that for whites. This may be explained in part by discrimination, which has kept blacks in the lower class and burdened them with a poor diet and less-than-adequate medical attention. Discrimination may also force blacks into high-risk occupations.

The nations' attempts to end racial discrimination may be having some effect on black longevity, however. In 1940 life expectancy at birth was 11 years longer for whites than for blacks. In 1983 the difference was 5.6 years. From 1981 to 1983 the black population showed an increase in life expectancy of nine tenths of a year—more than twice that of the white population.[13]

Comparisons of the sex ratios of blacks and whites find the black sex ratio a little more balanced. Whites currently have 69 men per 100 women at age 65;

TABLE 1–4 Number of Elderly 65 and Over, 85 and Over, by Sex and the Sex Ratio: 1960–1985, Projections 1990–2050

Year	65 and over			85 and over		
	Male	Female	Sex Ratio*	Male	Female	Sex Ratio*
1960	7,525	9,120	121	365	575	158
1970	8,441	11,716	139	556	1,055	190
1980	10,366	15,338	148	668	1,582	230
1985	11,535	17,000	147	773	1,934	250
Projections**						
1990	12,638	19,059	151	919	2,393	260
2000	13,763	21,159	154	1,350	3,576	265
2010	15,609	23,588	151	1,791	4,761	266
2020	21,211	30,211	142	1,942	5,139	265
2030	26,934	37,645	140	2,471	6,140	248
2040	27,430	39,985	146	3,804	9,030	237
2050	27,477	39,934	145	4,786	11,247	235

*Number of females per 100 males

**Projections assume middle level fertility (ultimate number of births per woman of 1.9; mortality (ultimate life expectancy in 2050 of 80.1 years); and net immigration (450,000 per year).

Source: U.S. Bureau of the Census

blacks have 73 per 100. It could be argued that racial discrimination leads to a poorer diet and less adequate health care for black women than for white women, thereby bringing the numbers of the former into closer correspondence with those of black men.

Aging by Marital Status

The individual's ability to cope with life changes and the inevitable losses of the later years often depends on his or her marital status and living arrangements.

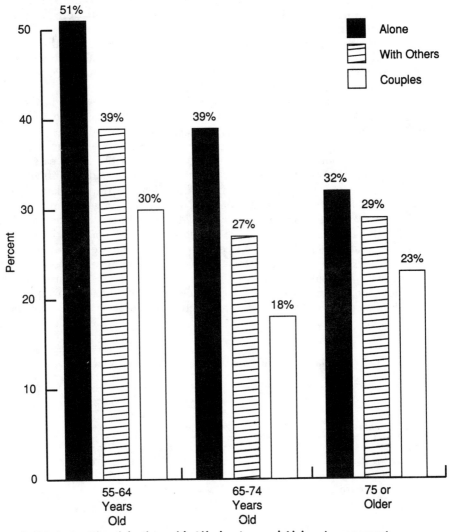

FIGURE 1–6 Dissatisfaction with Life by Age and Living Arrangement

Source: Beth J. Soldo and Emily M. Agree, "America's Elderly," *Population Bulletin*, 43, no. 3 (Washington, D.C.: Population Reference Bureau, 1988), 24.

As Figure 1–6 indicates for the 55 to 64 age group, the 65 to 74 age group, and the 75+ age group, the most unhappy and dissatisfied persons are those living alone. Looking at just the 55 to 64 age group, we see that 51 percent of those living alone are dissatisfied with life, 39 percent of those living with someone other than a spouse are dissatisfied with life, and 30 percent of those living with a marital partner are dissatisfied with life. The pattern for all three older age groups is the same. The married couples are the least dissatisfied with their lives, those living with someone other than a spouse are somewhat more dissatisfied, and those living alone are the most dissatisfied.

If being married makes you more satisfied with your life in the later years, then men have an advantage over women. As Table 1–5 indicates, about 80 percent of men 65 to 74 are married compared to only 51 percent of the women who are married in this age group. While only 9 percent of the 65-to-74-year-old men are widowed, approximately 37 percent of the women in this age group are widowed. At age 75 we see that 66 percent of the men are married and only 22 percent of the women. At 75+, about 24 percent of the men are widowed but 67 percent of the women are widowed. (See Table 1–5.)

It is clear that if older persons find being married and living with a spouse the desired state, the figures favor men. This is in part due to the fact that women outlive men by approximately seven years. That means there are more older women than there are older men. Therefore, following the death of a partner or a divorce a man who wants to remarry in the later years can easily do so. A woman wanting to remarry in later life may find it difficult to find an available partner. Moreover, a compounding factor to the unbalanced sex ratio in the later years is the fact that men tend to marry younger women at any age in life, and these age differences become wider as men reach middle and older age. It has also been argued that men in middle and older age with secure incomes have generally been able to find younger women who are willing to marry them.

Because of the above factors, older men are considerably more likely to be living with a spouse at present than are older women. Because of their much greater risk of widowhood and the reduced opportunity to remarry following the death of a spouse, older women are much more likely to be living alone than are older men.

TABLE 1–5 Marital Status of Population 65 and Over by Sex, 1987

Marital Status	Males		Females	
	65–74	75+	65–74	75+
	(in thousands and by percent)			
Total	7,608	3,970	9,624	6,773
Never married	4.7	4.3	4.8	6.4
Married, spouse present	79.7	65.9	51.0	22.4
Married, spouse absent	0.7	1.9	0.8	0.9
Widowed	9.0	23.6	36.7	67.0
Separated	1.1	1.0	1.2	0.6
Divorced	4.8	3.3	5.5	2.7

Source: U.S. Bureau of the Census

THE PROBLEMS OF AGING

Now that we have reviewed the demographic trends involved in the rise in the number of persons reaching age 65 and the tendency for this age group to live longer than their predecessors, let's examine some of the major problems that confront them.

Aging is an inevitable and lifelong process. During the time it took you to read the first sentence in this paragraph, you aged. Being "old," "aged," a "senior citizen" is a stage of aging. In 1935 the United States government set 65 as the age at which one was allowed to begin drawing social security checks, effectively making this the age of retirement. Sixty-five, however, was an arbitrary choice. It could just as easily have been 60 or 70. In actuality aging is a continuum, with conception at one end and death at the other. However, for the purposes of much of this text we will think of 65 as the beginning of older age, realizing, of course, that this is essentially a social definition.

Social Problems

At age 65 older Americans are often confronted with a series of developmental and adjustment problems. Most companies provide strong inducements for their workers to retire at 65 or before. With retirement comes less income and the loss of the status, privilege, and power associated with one's position in the occupational hierarchy. A major reorganization of one's activities is required, since the nine-to-five workday is now meaningless. Those who have shaped their identities and personalities to the demands of their occupational roles can expect a changing definition of self. And there can be a considerable degree of social isolation if new activities are not found to replace work-related activities. Finally, there is often a search for new identity, meaning, and value in one's life.

The major reorganization of one's life that must take place at retirement entails numerous adjustments. This reorganization can be viewed in the light of both gerontology and geriatrics. *Gerontology* studies the social, economic, political, and related social aspects of aging; *geriatrics* is a branch of medicine that deals with the problems and diseases of old age.

Like certain philosophers, students of aging have had difficulty with the dualism of the mind–body problem. Events in one's social life, such as the loss of a lifelong marital partner, can lead to a loss of the will to live and the onset of a series of physical and medical problems. Conversely, physical disabilities such as diabetes, prostate trouble, and arthritis may diminish one's capabilities as a husband or wife and so alter one's social world. The physical and social adjustments of older Americans are often difficult to separate.

Growing older is commonly experienced physiologically as a progressive decline in organic functions and psychologically as a progressive loss of sensory and cognitive capacities. These losses, however, are quite different for each individual; there is no predictable pattern. For one person, aging may bring a form of diabetes (for example, excessive amounts of blood sugar) that if not curbed can lead to blindness or the loss of limbs. For another person, aging may bring hardening of the arteries, a slowing of the blood flow to the brain, occasional forgetfulness, and the onset of senility.

Although the pattern is not predictable, as a general rule older people require more medical attention than younger people because they are more vulnerable to ill health. However, we should not forget that many older persons live healthy lives into extreme age, and some remain in good health almost until death. *Old age is not inevitably a period of poor health.* According to studies by Richard Kalish (1975), variability in the aging process can be seen by comparing 3-year-olds with 75-year-olds. Biologically, 3-year-olds are all likely to be going through approximately the same stage of development at approximately the same speed. At age 75, individuals vary much more in biological and behavioral functioning than do 3-year-olds or even young adults.[14]

Medical Problems

Leslie Libow (1977), medical director and chief of geriatric medicine at the Jewish Institute for Geriatric Care, has summarized what he considers to be some of the most common medical problems of older Americans.

1. *Mobility:* Twenty percent of persons over 65 have some problem in walking. Although only 5 percent of these are homebound, most use canes, walkers, or wheelchairs to get about.

2. *Brain:* From 5 to 15 percent of the population over 65 experience serious problems in thinking—most often identified as senility.

3. *Stroke:* This is the most common physical reason for older persons to be placed in nursing homes. Approximately two thirds of older people suffering from strokes are expected to have a complete or partial recovery; the remaining one third will survive but not be ambulatory.

4. *Heart:* Fifty percent of older people in nursing homes have a serious heart problem. The figures for the total population are not known.

5. *Prostate:* Prostate disease is very common among older men. Fortunately it is operable, with less than 1 percent mortality from surgery. There is much confusion about the effects of this operation, and patients should understand that it does *not* entail the loss of sexual functioning.

6. *Bowels:* Constipation and changes in regularity are common in later life. Excessive self-concern can result in an obsession with these problems. They are easily avoided: Doctors recommend a proper diet, including fruits and other fibrous foods.

7. *Bones:* Aging bones weaken and break more easily. As a rule, blacks experience fewer fractures than whites, and men fewer than women. Increased physical activity (walking, dancing, jogging, bicycling) is believed to be the best way to reduce fractures. Dietary changes are also held to be helpful.

8. *Breast:* Breast cancer is a concern of women. Middle-age women are somewhat more likely to have it than older women.

9. *Eyes:* Cataracts are common but almost always surgically treatable. Glaucoma, though not as treatable, is usually manageable. The only eye change considered normal in aging is a tendency toward farsightedness.

10. *Arthritis:* This is one of the most common problems in later life, with no known medical cure.

11. *Nutrition:* Signs in older people may include cracked lips, which indicate a vitamin-B deficiency; excessively dry skin; and anemia. Obesity caused by high-calorie diets is common, and heavy consumption of fats is held to contribute to hardening of the arteries. Malnutrition may result from poverty, inaccessibility of grocery stores, or lack of incentive to eat.[15]

That physiological decline is a problem for older people can be seen in a study by Harold Cox, Gurmeet Sekhon, and Charles Norman (1978) in western Indiana. The researchers asked a random sample of persons 65 and above about the degree of difficulty experienced in performing daily activities. Most younger persons, in examining Table 1–6, find the percentage of older persons who have difficulty doing routine tasks somewhat surprising. The losses of old age are real.

Moreover, as people age they are more likely to experience severe limitations to their daily activities. The risk of functional disability increases rapidly after age 65 (see Figure 1–7). Whereas less than 10 percent of those age 65 to 74 experience severe limitations to their daily activities, nearly half of those 85 and over experience such limitations. At all ages walking is the most common problem while eating is the activity least likely to pose a problem.

Social and Psychological Problems

Professionals are often challenged in their diagnosis of the psychological problems of aging and in fact it is difficult to distinguish whether certain problems are the result of a physical condition, such as hardening of the arteries (with related malfunction of the brain, perhaps occasioning bizarre behavior), or the result of depression.

Mrs. Jones retired at age 65 in good health and with no particular physical or emotional problems. By age 75, however, she had begun to experience a hearing loss and a heart problem accompanied by poor circulation that resulted in her having considerably less energy. Because of these difficulties she now stayed home most of the time, interacting with others much less frequently than she had

TABLE 1–6 Limitations in Daily Activities of Persons 65 +

Difficulty	Yes	No
Getting up and down stairs	40%	60%
Washing and bathing	20	80
Dressing	15	85
Getting out of the house	19	81
Watching TV	6	94
Using the telephone	25	75
Cooking	19	81
Cleaning the house	30	70
Maintaining the house	45	55
Getting around the house	20	80
Doing the laundry	30	70

Source: Harold Cox, Gurmeet Sekhon, and Charles Norman, "Social Characteristics of the Elderly in Indiana," *Proceedings/Indiana Academy of Social Sciences* (1978), p. 190.

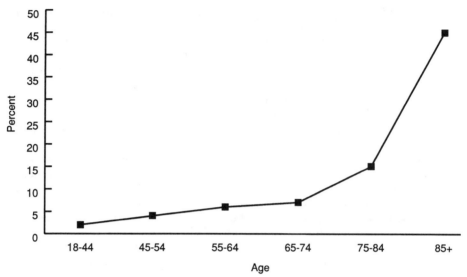

**FIGURE 1–7 Percent of Civilian Noninstitutionalized Population with Severe
Limitation of Activities of Daily Living, by Age, 1979**
Source: U.S. National Center for Health Statistics, 1987b, *Health Statistics on Older Persons,
1986,* pp. 2, 33.

in the past; she began experiencing periodic depression. Thus, a route can sometimes be traced from biological problems to social and emotional ones.

Several problems confronted by older Americans seem to be related to
social isolation and loneliness. Many older persons find that their health no
longer allows them to drive. This inevitably limits their movement in the community. In extreme cases they become homebound, rarely leaving the house or
apartment without assistance. Reed Larson, Jiri Zuzanek, and Roger Mannell
(1985) studied the consequences of being alone on the morale and lives of older
persons. In the process, they examined the importance of daily companionship.
In their words, "How dependent is the emotional state for older adults upon
continued sharing, reacting, loving and joking?"[16] Their findings indicate different
patterns of need for the married and unmarried in later life. Married couples are
usually not as socially isolated as singles, and lack of companionship does not
appear to be a significant problem for them. Many seem to cherish the opportunity to be alone. Their marriage gives them daily companionship, and they
appear to have arrived at a good balance between being with others and being
alone. They apparently enjoy periods of being alone in their daily lives and
activities. The unmarried, however—particularly those who live by themselves—
report that the absence of a daily companion is a legitimate concern. They spend
more time alone and appreciate it less. When alone they are more likely than
married couples to report feeling drowsy, passive, tired, and bored. These very
feelings may be the predecessors of depression. Isolation and boredom among the
elderly may lead to alcohol and drug abuse. Whatever the reasons, it would
appear that older married couples are better able to maintain a balance between
social activities and being alone. Single persons have greater difficulty arriving at

this balance and often complain of a need for companionship. The importance of confidants and intimate friends in the lives of the elderly is discussed in a later chapter.

Paranoia in old age is not uncommon, according to Frederick Charatan (1977). Those experiencing this disorder believe that they are the object of hostile attention from others. Older people suffering from paranoia, although perfectly normal in every other way, have gone so far as to believe they were being spied on by the FBI or Communists.

Undue depression is another common problem of older people, according to Charatan (1977). Many have experienced a series of losses and feel they can look forward only to still further losses. Depression in older age is twice as common in women as in men and usually follows immediately upon some loss. The most difficult loss for older persons is that of a spouse, and statistics show that bereavement in later years increases survivor mortality, often labeled the *broken-heart syndrome*. Men experience depression especially following retirement. The *retirement syndrome* is a depressive illness identified by psychiatrists.

The physiological, psychological, and social problems of older people are genuine experiences that must ultimately be dealt with. Although we regard aging as a lifelong process for all of us, the problems confronted at the later end of the life cycle seem somehow more serious and foreboding than those of earlier life. Unfortunately, for older persons these problems sometimes occur one after another, forming a complex tangle. Often, too, they occur when people seem to have the fewest resources for coping with them. Yet even though more than three fourths of the older population suffer from at least one long-term deteriorating condition, most learn to adjust to their disabilities and to find continuing satisfaction in life.

PUBLIC PERCEPTIONS OF OLDER PERSONS

Perhaps the major social problem confronting older Americans today is how they are viewed by the general population. Students of symbolic interactions have long argued that the most crucial determinant of our well-being at any age in life is how we are defined and categorized by others in our social environment. It takes a very strong and determined person to resist the social definition—handsome or ugly, intelligent or stupid, bold or timid, or any other label—placed on him or her by others and to carve out a new image. Most people behave the way others in their social world expect them to behave. The problem for older persons is that they are often seen in negative and stereotypic terms by other age groups.

Stereotypes

The word *stereotype* comes from a Greek word meaning "hard core." Today, the word has come to mean "the most frequent combination of traits assigned by one group to another." As a perception of an individual or a group, a stereotype is frequently rigid and biased as well as negative if not derogatory. Categorizing and stereotyping those around us—and making assumptions about their motives and future behavior—allows us to live in a complex world without having to deal with the wealth of details characterizing each individual. Thus, one who reduces all older people to a stereotype saves the time and energy it would take to respond to each of them individually. While this process may allow us to coexist with large numbers of other persons with a minimum of effort, it is most often unfair to the individual or group that is stereotyped. Very frequently, stereotypes of any group different from ourselves tend to be based on the least desirable traits possessed by some members of the group. Stereotypes of older persons are no different: These people are often thought of as feeble, senile, and destitute since this is the plight of the least fortunate among them.

Gerontologists have coined the term *ageism* to refer to a biased conception of someone based on his or her advanced chronological age. Like racism or sexism, ageism is an unduly negative view of all members of a group—in this case, older persons. Hendricks and Hendricks (1981) observe that part of the myth implicit in ageism is the view that older persons are somehow different from our present and future selves and therefore not subject to the same desires, fears, and concerns we have. We might consider whether we ourselves do not share many of the fears, desires, and concerns of older people.

Perhaps the most stereotypic view of the 65+ group in America is that all old people are alike; indeed, this kind of thinking lies at the heart of all stereotypes. But in fact there is considerable difference in the health of any two 65-year-olds, because of illness, lifestyle, or previous occupational pressures. Nor are older people's health and energy correlated strictly with their age. Mrs. Sampson, for example, regularly volunteers to help people at the community senior-citizen center, most of whom are younger than she. Grant Youmans (1977) speaks frequently of the different problems experienced by the "young old" and the "old old."

Similarly, older Americans retire as members of the working class, middle class, or upper class. Retirement incomes, previous experiences, and preferred lifestyles of the different social classes vary greatly, to say the least. Having a winter home in Florida and a summer cottage on a lake in Canada is quite different from living year-round in a small slum-district apartment in the heart of Detroit. We should keep these distinctions in mind when talking about the problems of older people.

Another stereotypic view of older persons is that they are isolated. For some older Americans this is true, but for the majority it is not. The current social security and welfare systems have given older people some independence. Most of them can now maintain their own homes rather than having to move in with their children or into government housing. Independence and continuity—remaining in familiar neighborhoods with past friends and associates—are desired by both older and younger people. Family sociologists have also found much more intergenerational family interaction—through telephone calling, frequent visiting, and vacations—than they expected. Irving Rosow (1967), in his study of older apartment-dwellers in Cleveland, and Bruce Lemon and his colleagues (1972), in their study of retirement communities, found considerable social interaction and involvement among older Americans. All these findings belie the stereotype that older Americans are isolated.

Sterotypic Views of Retirement. A third stereotype of older people is that retirement is a period of crisis and adjustment. Rosamonde Boyd and Charles Oakes (1973) observe that the majority of blue-collar workers not only look forward to retirement but also, if guaranteed an adequate income, will retire early. Herbert Parnes (1981) found that about half of the retirees he interviewed retired voluntarily, 7 out of 10 before age 65.[17] Even for white-collar workers who find some meaning in their work, there is no evidence that retirement precipitates a lengthy crisis.

Related to the view that retirement is a time of crisis is the common belief that society forces able-bodied older persons to retire. It is true that less than 5 percent of those over age 65 continue to work, but as we have just noted, many older workers choose to retire early if they are granted enough retirement income to live on comfortably. Although Congress raised the legal mandatory retirement age from 65 to 70 in 1978, and later removed all mandatory requirements, there is no evidence that any significant number of older people have chosen to work longer. James Schulz (1988) found that of every 1000 retirees, only 70 were forced to retire. Sometimes poor health is the reason for retiring. However, retirees in good health look forward to the freedom to do what they want.

Another myth about retirement is that it undermines the physical health of retirees and often leads to death. Many, upon observing an acquaintance, friend, or relative die shortly after retirement, presume that retirement shortens life. What they may be overlooking is that people can die at any age, whether working or not. Longitudinal studies have found that most retirees show a slight *improvement* in their overall health following retirement and that there is no difference in mortality rate between this group and those remaining in the labor force. *Retirement simply does not precipitate death.*

Still another mistaken view is that retirement is highly disruptive of family relations, since it supposedly alters the balance of power and division of labor between husbands and wives. Richard Kalish (1975) and others have observed that the retired male has time to dedicate to the rules of husband, father, grandfather—roles that in the past were often slighted in favor of occupational demands. In this sense, retirement may actually improve family relations. Many couples find they have more time to spend together—almost a second courtship period. Of course, retirement *can* be experienced as the alteration of a "power balance," with negative consequences for family relations. Even so, conflict is often managed within families and as such does not necessarily show up as an increase in divorce.

Contributing further to the view that retirement is a time of crisis is the common belief that retirement plunges people into poverty because it is often accompanied by a 50 percent decline in income. Gordon Streib and Clement Schneider (1971) and James Schulz (1988) found that while many retirees experienced a sharp drop in income, most said that they were getting along well enough. Research indicates that older people can apparently exist on less money and feel no decline in class status.

Another myth is that retirees are denied a normal role in the community and are forced into geriatric ghettos. Journalists often see older people as victims assigned by society to segregated communities. In reality, many middle-class older Americans have voluntarily moved to retirement communities. Irving Rosow's (1967) work indicates that social interaction increases among older persons in these segregated communities. A legitimate question is whether society provides desirable environments for its older population. A collateral question is whether society should provide older people with environments that shield them from loss of status. In any event, it is wrong to believe that all older persons are forced into geriatric ghettos. A few are pressured by their children to move to nursing homes, but this is the exception rather than the rule.

Misconceptions

Louis Harris and Associates (1975) were commissioned by the National Council on Aging to study attitudes toward older Americans. Their report, following 4250 interviews, reveals some interesting misconceptions among the younger population concerning the experiences of older Americans. Collectively, only 2 percent of a sample of Americans of all ages considered the years after 60 as the best of a person's life. Nearly one third of 18-to-64-year-olds—and a larger percentage of those over 65—saw those years as the least desirable.

Table 1–7 indicates that younger adults overestimate the problems of older people. For example, while only 23 percent of older subjects reported fear of crime as a serious concern of older Americans, fully 50 percent of the public believed that it was; only 12 percent of the older population reported loneliness as a serious problem, but 60 percent of the public perceived it as such. The pattern was the same for every one of a series of variables ranging from not feeling needed to living in poor housing.

This discrepancy may be explained in part by the fact that in a youth-oriented society most people are not conditioned to look forward to old age. Another explanation may be the mass media's tendency to focus on the less fortunate cases among the elderly. In addition, most people associate aging with death. Since medical science has conquered most of the communicable diseases of the younger population, it is principally older people who die in our society. The result is that Americans are often conditioned to view the older years as those of physical decline and death. They therefore tend to exaggerate the problems that

TABLE 1–7   Public Perceptions and Problems of Older Persons

	Very Serious Problems Actually Experienced by Older People	Very Serious Problems Public Expects Older People To Experience	Net Difference
Fear of crime	23%	50%	+27%
Poor health	21	51	+30
Not having enough money to live on	15	62	+47
Loneliness	12	60	+48
Not having enough medical care	10	44	+34
Not having enough education	8	20	+12
Not feeling needed	7	54	+47
Not having enough to do to keep busy	6	37	+31
Not having enough friends	5	28	+23
Not having enough job opportunities	5	45	+40
Poor housing	4	35	+31
Not having enough clothing	3	16	+13

Source: L. Harris and Associates, *The Myth and Reality of Aging in America* (Washington, D.C.: National Council on the Aging, 1975), p. 31.

accompany aging. Many look for examples to confirm their biases. Upon seeing four older persons, three of whom are well dressed and one poorly dressed, many, if not most, will remember the poorly dressed person.

We must constantly guard against too negative a view of the later phase of the life cycle. When Leslie Libow (1977) observes that 20 percent of persons 65 and over have trouble walking, we may fail to recognize that this means 80 percent of older people have no trouble getting around. Similarly, Libow's (1977) finding that from 5 to 15 percent of older people experience problems in thinking means that from 85 to 95 percent can think clearly. In the Cox and colleagues (1978) study of limitations on the daily activities of older persons (Table 1–6), less than half of the subjects experienced one or more of these limitations. Depending on the variable examined, from 60 to 90 percent of the sample had no limitation at all. Thus, while the problems confronted by older persons are real and must be dealt with, let us not be unduly pessimistic in our view of the lives of older Americans. The majority of older Americans believe they are in reasonably good health, think they have adequate incomes, and are convinced they are living their lives just about the way they would like.

Our discussion of ageism—the myths and stereotypes of aging—should not imply that older Americans do not have problems, but rather should show that their problems are often exaggerated by the public. The intent of government planners and service providers is realistically to identify the problems of aging and to work for their solution. And because there are so many myths surrounding the subject of aging, professionals in the field must examine unproved conceptions of aging with scientific objectivity. The gerontologist, trained in one of the behavioral sciences, is likely to perceive his or her role as that of a detached observer. The public-service worker in programs for older Americans, on the other hand, is likely to perceive himself or herself as an advocate.

Detached observers attempt to carefully describe how people think, feel, and act. Moreover, they periodically offer solutions to problems confronted by a particular group of people. Advocates are likely to be politically active and vocal in an effort to improve the situation of the people they serve, or whose cause they espouse. In the case of older Americans, advocacy often involves exaggerating their conditions, as well as propagandizing, lobbying, and moralizing for desired improvements in these conditions. Advocates may use, and even create, stereotypic views to further their cause. This text aims at filling the role of the unbiased observer attempting to present the reality of aging in America.

CONCLUSION

From the moment of conception to the moment of death, aging is experienced by the human organism. Throughout the early years of life, aging involves physiological growth and development; it is therefore generally viewed favorably by the individual and by significant others in his or her environment. Adult life and middle age tend to be periods of physiological stability and increasing social power and privilege, but parts, nevertheless, of the lifelong aging process. Old age may be seen as a period of physical decline as well as of declining social prestige. All of these are parts of one's life course, but it is not difficult to understand why older age is often negatively labeled by the general population and regarded with considerable aversion by those entering their later years. Research indicates, however, that the lives of older persons are not nearly as foreboding or as unhappy as the public believes. Most older persons lead reasonably healthy, happy, and fulfilling lives, just as do all other age groups. Moreover, older persons have the same opportunity for growth, development, learning, and new experiences that one finds at any age in life. As a result of having raised their families and retired from work, they are in all probability freer than any other age group to choose the new or old activities in which they will participate.

Joan Arehart Treichel (1980) distinguishes chronological aging, primary aging, and secondary aging. *Chronological aging* is the time that elapses from birth. It assumes importance in the human life cycle by providing others with some clue to the roles and patterns of behavior expected of us as members of a particular age group. The behavior of a 5-year-old is quite different from that of a 45-year-old. Since old age is negatively defined, many Americans invest a great deal of time and money in looking young. Jack Benny made a lifetime joke of always being 39 and thus avoiding the problems of old age.

Primary aging consists of the biochemical changes that accompany chronological aging. These include the daily loss of thousands of cells in the brain, a tendency for facial skin to dry out by age 30, and gradual deterioration of parts of the body, until finally death occurs. Primary aging is considered to be genetically determined to some extent.

Secondary aging is primary aging that has been accelerated as a result of a lifetime of stresses—emotional tension, physical trauma, disease, or other insults to the body.

We cannot slow down chronological aging. But scientific knowledge may allow us to better understand the processes of aging and, by suggesting changes in lifestyle, prevent various kinds of secondary aging and perhaps in the process slow down primary aging.

Many younger people feel that aging is simply not relevant to them, that older people have their best years behind them, that there is at most a hopeless gap in lifestyles and aspirations between younger and older people, and that the mere thought of getting old and dying is depressing. Thus, younger people often avoid studying problems of aging.

Richard Kalish (1975), however, argues that anyone concerned with the maintenance of human dignity must understand the *entire* life cycle, including the later years. He points out a number of reasons that the study of later life should be important to each of us, among them

1. To participate in providing resources for those who are old today and for those who will be old tomorrow (that's us, you and me) so that they—and we—can lead a more satisfactory life during the later years

2. To enable us to better understand the aging process so that we can lead a more satisfactory life ourselves today

3. To place the earlier years of the life span in proper perspective and to perceive individual development as a lifelong process[18]

The chapters that follow will examine some of the basic developments, opportunities, problems, and adjustments of aging. The lives of older Americans will be viewed from the context of the entire life cycle, and as much pertinent information will be presented as space allows. Gerontology, perhaps more than any other subject, utilizes an interdisciplinary approach. While the perspective of this text may be slightly biased in favor of the sociological view, findings from biological, psychological, economic, political, and anthropological studies will also be included. It is hoped that such a presentation will enhance the reader's understanding of the roles and lives, the lifestyles and behavior patterns of older Americans.

KEY TERMS

ageism	ethnocentric	primary aging
chronological aging	geriatrics	secondary aging
dependency ratio	gerontology	stereotype

REFERENCES

ALLEN, CAROLE, and HERMAN BROTMAN, *Charts on Aging in America*. Washington, D.C.: White House Conference on Aging, 1981.

ANDERSON, J. E., "Summary and Interpretation," in *Psychological Aspects of Aging*, ed. J. E. Anderson pp. 267–89. Washington, D.C.: American Psychological Association, 1966.

BENGTSON, VERN L., *The Social Psychology of Aging*. Indianapolis: Bobbs-Merrill, 1973.

BLACKMAN, ANNE, "Over 65 Set Growing 1,600 a Day in U.S.," in *Focus Aging* (2nd ed.), ed. Harold Cox, pp. 12–15. Guilford, Conn.: Dushkin Publishing Group, 1980.

BOTWINICK, J., and L. W. THOMPSON, "Individual Differences in Reaction Time in Relation to Age," *Journal of Genetic Psychology*, 112 (1968), 73–75.

BOYD, ROSAMONDE R., and CHARLES G. OAKES, *Foundations of Practical Gerontology*. Columbia: University of South Carolina Press, 1973.

BREEN, LEONARD, "The Discipline of Gerontology," in *The Daily Needs and Interests of Old People* by Adeline M. Hoffman. Springfield, Ill.: Chas. C Thomas, 1970.

CARLSON, A. J., and E. J. STIEGLITZ, "Physiological Changes in Aging," *American Academy of Political and Social Science*, 279 (1952), 18–31.

CHARATAN, FREDERICK, "Psychological and Psychiatric Aspects of Aging," in *What Do We Really Know About Aging*, ed. Antoinette Bosco and Jane Porcino. Stony Brook: State University of New York at Stony Brook, 1977, p. 22.

COX, HAROLD, GURMEET SEKHON, and CHARLES NORMAN, "Social Characteristics of the Elderly in Indiana," *Proceedings/Indiana Academy of the Social Sciences*, vol. XIII (1978), 186–97.

EISENSTADT, S. N., *From Generation to Generation: Age Groups and Social Structure*. New York: Free Press, 1956

HARRIS, CHARLES, *Fact Book on Aging: A Profile of America's Older Population*, pp. 1–30. Washington, D.C.: National Council on the Aging, 1978.

HARRIS, LOUIS, and ASSOCIATES, *The Myth and Reality of Aging in America*. Washington, D.C.: National Council on the Aging, 1975.

HEINZ, JOHN, CYRIL F. BRICKFIELD, ADELAIDE ATTARD, and CAROL FRASER FISK, *Aging America: Trends and Projections*, 1985–86 ed. Prepared by U.S. Senate Special Committee on Aging with American Association of Retired Persons, Washington, D.C.

HENDRICKS, JON, and C. DAVIS HENDRICKS, *Aging in Mass Society: Myths and Realities*. Cambridge, Mass.: Winthrop, 1981.

Issue Paper on the Minority Aging. Washington, D.C.: Urban Resources Consultants, 1978.

JANSEN, CLIFFORD, "Some Sociological Aspects of Migration," in *Migration*, ed. J. A. Jackson, pp. 60–73. New York: Cambridge University Press, 1969.

KALISH, RICHARD, *Late Adulthood: Perspectives on Human Development*. Monterey, Calif.: Brooks/Cole, 1975.

LARSON, REED, JIRI ZUZANEK, and ROGER MANNELL, "Being Alone Versus Being with People: Disengagement in the Daily Experience of Older Adults," *Journal of Gerontology*, 40, no. 3 (1985), 375–81.

LEMON, BRUCE W., VERN L. BENGTSON, and JAMES A. PETERSON, "Activity Types and Life Satisfaction in a Retirement Community," *Journal of Gerontology*, 4, no. 27 (1972), 511–23.

LIBOW, LESLIE, "Medical Problems of Older People," in *What Do We Really Know About Aging*, ed Antoninette Bosco and Jane Porcino, Stony Brook: State University of New York at Stony Brook, 1977, pp. 17–18.

MADDOX, GEORGE, Lecture, Indian State University, May 1982.

MILLER, SHEILA J., "Segregation of the Aged in American Cities," Unpublished paper, Wichita State University, 1967.

PARK, R. E., and E. BURGESS, *The City*. Chicago: University of Chicago Press, 1925.

PARK, ROBERT E., *Human Communities*. Glencoe, Ill.: Free Press, 1952.

PARNES, HERBERT S., *A Longitudinal Study of Men, Work, and Retirement*. Cambridge, Mass.: MIT Press, 1981.

POLLACK, O., *Social Adjustment in Old Age*. New York: Social Science Research Council, 1948.

ROSOW, IRVING, *The Social Integration of the Aged*. Glencoe, Ill.: Free Press, 1967.

SCHOCK, N. W., "Biology of Aging," in *Problems of America's Aging Population*, ed. T. L. Smith, pp. 37–46. Gainesville: University of Florida Press, 1951.

SCHULZ, JAMES, *The Economics of Aging*. (4th ed.). Belmont, Calif.: Wadsworth, 1988.

Social Security Administration, Office of the Actuary Personal Communication, June 1988.

SOLDO, BETH J., and EMILY M. AGREE, "America's Elderly," Population Bulletin, 43, no. 3 (September 1988).

SOLDO, BETH J., and KENNETH G. MORTON, "Changes in Health Status and Service Needs of the Oldest Old: Current Patterns and Future Trends," *Millbank Memorial Fund Quarterly*, 63, no. 2 (Spring 1988).

STREIB, GORDON F., and CLEMENT J. SCHNEIDER, *Retirement in American Society: Impact and Process*. Ithaca, N.Y.: Cornell University Press, 1971.

TREICHEL, JOAN AREHART, "It's Never Too Late to Start Living Longer," in *Focus: Aging* (2nd ed.), ed. Harold Cox, pp. 17–19. Guilford, Conn.: Dushkin Publishing Group, 1980.

YOUMANS, GRANT E., "Attitudes: Young Old and Old Old," *Gerontologist*, 17, no. 2 (April 1977), 175–86.

NOTES

1. Leonard Breen, "The Discipline of Gerontology," in *The Daily Needs and Interests of Old People* by Adeline M. Hoffman. Springfield, Ill.: Chas. C Thomas, 1970, p. 10.
2. For demographic trends, see L. A. Epstein and J. H. Murray, *The Aged Population of the United States*, Research Report No. 19, Office of Research and Statistics, Social Security Administration, U. S. Department of Health, Education and Welfare (Washington, D.C.: Government Printing Office, 1967), p. 967.
3. John Heinz, Cyril F. Brickfield, Adelaide Attard, and Carol Fraser Fisk, *Aging America: Trends and Projections*, 1985–86 ed., p. 13.
4. Ibid., p. 14.
5. Ibid., p. 22.
6. Social Security Administration, Office of the Actuary Personal Communication, June 1988.
7. Beth J. Soldo and Kenneth G. Morton, "Changes in Health Status and Service Needs of the Oldest Old: Current Patterns and Future Trends," *Milbank Memorial Fund Quarterly*, 63, no. 2 (Spring 1988).
8. Lecture, Indiana State University, May 1982.
9. Antoinette Bosco and Jane Porcino, eds., *What Do We Really Know About Aging* (Stony Brook: State University of New York at Stony Brook, 1977).
10. Beth J. Soldo and Emily M. Agree, *America's Elderly Population Bulletin*, 43, no. 3 (September 1988), 12–13.
11. Ibid, p. 13.
12. Ibid., p. 13.
13. Heinz et al., *Aging America*, p. 24.
14. J. Botwinick and L. W. Thompson, "Individual Differences in Reaction Time in Relation to Age," *Journal of Genetic Psychology*, 112 (1968), 73–75.
15. Leslie Libow, "Medical Problems of Older People," in *What Do We Really Know About Aging*, ed. Bosco and Porcino, pp. 14–20.
16. Reed Larson, Jiri Zuzanek, and Roger Mannell, "Being Alone Versus Being with People: Disengagement in the Daily Experience of Older Adults," *Journal of Gerontology*, 40, no. 3 (1985).
17. Herbert S. Parnes, *A Longitudinal Study of Men, Work, and Retirement* (Cambridge, Mass.: MIT Press, 1981), p. 27.
18. Richard Kalish, *Late Adulthood: Perspectives on Human Development* (Monterey, Calif.: Brooks/Cole, 1975), p. 2.

2

Theoretical Perspectives on Aging

THEORY AND RESEARCH

The goal of any scientific enterprise is to explain some aspect of the natural or social world in a logical and understandable manner. Science is often defined as the development of knowledge in an empirically validated and replicable manner. The three defining features of science are (1) the development of a general theory, (2) the testing and empirical validation of the theory, and (3) the replication of tests of the theory.

The scientific community has accepted a certain set of values concerning knowledge. These values include the beliefs that (1) there is order to social and physical phenomena, (2) we come to know the world through our senses, (3) knowledge is better than ignorance, and (4) skepticism is worthwhile because negative evidence contributes to knowledge.

All scientific explanations are grounded in theory: They attempt to account for a given set of phenomena with a theory that is predictive and empirically demonstrable. A *theory* is thus a set of logically interrelated propositions that account for some set of phenomena. Scientific theory differs from other forms of theory in that it must (1) generate propositions that are capable of being rejected, (2) explain why the propositions are related, and (3) be empirical and subject to testing.

Theory Development

The scientific method includes (1) establishing precise definitions of the variables the scientist is dealing with, (2) framing propositions that logically relate two or more phenomena, and (3) developing a theory. The sequence represented in Figure 2–1, is inductive: The scientist proceeds from definitions of variables to propositions relating two or more of the variables, and then from these variables to a theory.

Scientists never prove or disprove a theory. They merely develop a greater or lesser degree of confidence in it. This is because a theory does not rest on a single proposition but on a series of propositions, any one of which may be partly

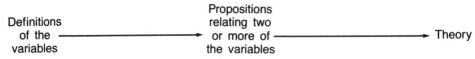

FIGURE 2–1 Theory Development

wrong. The empiricist derives hypotheses from a theory that states that if the theory is true, we should expect to find a predicted relationship between the variables. Sometimes the hypotheses are proved; sometimes they are disproved. Research findings always contribute to the theory by (1) supporting it if the hypothesized relations are proved valid, (2) reshaping it should some of the hypotheses be proved but others disproved, (3) refuting it should all the hypotheses be disproved, or (4) initiating a new theory should unanticipated findings lead the research in an entirely new direction.

Research Techniques

Since any scientific theory must be capable of being empirically tested, scientists have developed a variety of research techniques for this purpose. Cross-sectional studies, longitudinal studies, and cohort analysis are three techniques frequently used by gerontologists.

Cross-Sectional Studies. In this approach the researcher takes a sample of people at one point in time and attempts to identify their basic attitudes, beliefs, values, or behavior patterns. The most well-known cross-sectional studies are the public opinion polls of Gallup, Lubel, and others regarding national politicians and political issues. Thus on a certain date the pollsters might find that 51 percent of the population believes the President is doing a good job and 49 percent believes he is not. This does not indicate what the American public will believe about the President's performance a month or a year later. What it does say is that as of that date, this is what a cross section of the American public thinks about the President's performance.

Longitudinal Studies. Longitudinal studies, on the other hand, follow a sample of respondents over a period ranging from a few months to a lifetime. A sample of subjects first interviewed in 1985 could be interviewed again in 1990, 1995, and 2000, allowing researchers to see how their attitudes regarding the leading political figures or political issues change over time. Thus 60 percent of the sample may have favored unrestricted abortions for American women in 1985, but only 40 percent of the sample might favor them in 1990. The researchers would ask, "Why are the attitudes of the public on this issue changing over time?" Longitudinal studies establish trends and patterns of change among respondents.

Longitudinal studies that take a sample of cohorts (to be discussed shortly) and follow them over a long period have proved most fruitful in studies of the life cycle. Many previous errors made by scientists studying human behavior have arisen in cross-sectional studies of different age groups at a single point in time. A tacit assumption of these studies is that all other characteristics of the subjects are the same, when in fact they are not. A classic example of this is studies of the relationship between age and intelligence.

In one such study an intelligence test was given to all age groups in a very short period. The result was a cross-sectional analysis of the intelligence of different age groups at a single point in time; the analysis indicated a decline in IQ scores for the older age groups. Knowing that a higher level of education leads to higher scores on intelligence tests raised some questions, however. Since the older cohorts as a group were not as well educated as the younger ones, was the difference in the IQ scores of the different age groups a result of age or of education? Only longitudinal studies can answer this question.

Difference in education (a cohort effect) was found in later longitudinal studies to explain much of the decline in intelligence-test scores for the older age groups. In addition K. W. Schaie (1974) found that a bias built into intelligence tests favored motor performance and skills more easily exercised by the young, and that the test situation tends to intimidate those who have not recently experienced it. Future research will undoubtedly further clarify which kinds of performance measured by intelligence tests are most likely to improve or decline with the age of the respondent.

Cohort Analysis.   That younger people score higher on intelligence tests, at least in part because of their greater number of years of education, would be considered by gerontologists to be a cohort effect. Because these younger people were born and grew up at the same time, their experiences were unique to their age group and not shared by the previous generation. In terms of human development, time may be seen as a sequence of related biological, psychological, and sociological experiences. Gerontologists often use the term *cohort* or *generation* for a group of persons born at the same time and experiencing the same events.

Cohort analysis is utilized by gerontologists to compare groups of people born during specific periods (usually separated by five-to-ten-year intervals) as they move through the life cycle. These people usually experience particular historical events at approximately the same time in their biological, psychological, and sociological development, so they are affected by these events in a very similar fashion. Leonard Cain (1969) has found considerable differences between cohorts in such characteristics as attitudes toward labor-force participation, fertility rates, education, and sex.

Douglas Kimmel (1974) observes the effect of certain historical events on cohorts:

> Persons age 65 in 1975 were born in 1910 during a period in the United States of peace and isolation from world conflicts. They were at the forefront of industrial expansion and westward migration. Obviously a great deal has changed since then. Average length of education has increased by several years, and the task of living in society has become more and more complex. . . . If you are a college student today, your parents were probably born between the end of World War I and the years of the Great Depression. . . . They learned that economic security and material possessions may evaporate for reasons beyond their control. Your parents probably went to school during the Depression and their early socialization experiences, which influenced later attitudes and values, took place during this period of inadequate material resources.[1]

Such events can have prolonged effects on the attitudes, beliefs, and values of cohort members. Vern Bengtson (1969), moreover, holds that there is a complex interplay between the historical events that cohorts experience and their own stage of development. Thus the individual's life should be viewed as the product of a dynamic interaction between the social system and the personality system, each of which reflects both stability and change over time.

Biological events that a person commonly experiences over time include achievement and loss of reproductive capacity, growth and decline in physical vigor, and an increasing probability of organ disease. Psychologically an individual experiences the development of motor skills, perceptive and cognitive ability, and personality. Sociological events include the entrance and exit from major social institutions, marriage, work, social organizations, and a commensurate growth and decline in responsibility and power.

One's ability to cope with these biological, psychological, and sociological changes is related to several factors, not the least of which are such dramatic events as wars and depression. People approaching the end of their educational training and seeking employment can be set back by an economic recession over which they have no control. Similarly, persons who were considering a college education during the time of the Vietnam War may suddenly have found themselves drafted and as a result may have never completed their educational plans. Historical events, then, interact in complex ways with a person's development and *life chances* (the probability of a person of specified status achieving a specified goal or suffering a specified disadvantage). Cohort analysis is useful to gerontologists because it allows them to study the effects of these events on a broad group of individuals, all of whom experienced the same historical event at a similar stage of development. It can thus be a useful research tool for those interested in testing some of the assumptions of the various theories of human development.

DISENGAGEMENT THEORY

Theories in the social sciences can be more or less complex. What gerontologists have described as the earliest theories in their field seem to be less complex, and more philosophical than theoretical. The first two theories we shall consider, disengagement theory and activity theory, appear to be as much philosophical recommendations for later life as explanations of human behavior. One can, however, derive hypotheses from these perspectives and test them to determine their accuracy. In this sense the disengagement and activity perspectives can be classified as theories, though we recognize they are more narrow in focus and more prescriptive than many other theories in the behavioral sciences.

Disengagement is one of the earliest and most influential theories in gerontology. In its simplest form, and as originally described by Elaine Cumming and William Henry (1961), the theory states that aging involves an inevitable withdrawal, or disengagement, resulting in decreased interaction with those in the aging person's social milieu. The process may be initiated by the individual or by others in his or her social system. In either case, disengagement theory implies, it is a way in which society and the individual gradually prepare for the ultimate withdrawal of the individual, through an incurable, incapacitating disease and death.

A basic assumption of the theory is that both the individual and society are gratified by disengagement. For the individual, withdrawal brings a release from societal pressures for continued high-level productivity. For society, the withdrawal of older members presumably allows younger, more energetic, competent, and recently trained persons to assume the roles that must be filled.

The assertion that disengagement of the older members of society is necessary for the survival of the social system is an example of *sociological functionalism*, which views the elements and members of society as functionally interdependent. Specific behavior patterns within a social system can be regarded as either functional or dysfunctional. Functional patterns help to maintain the society and to integrate its elements; dysfunctional patterns promote social breakdown. Thus, many would argue that the disengagement of older Americans is functional, or useful, for society, since it allows a smooth transfer of power to younger people. However, there is no *proof* that the withdrawal of older persons from employment and other useful roles is necessarily good for society. It might just as well be argued that disengagement is bad, since it involves the removal, either voluntary or forced, of some of the most knowledgeable, capable, and experienced performers in society.

At the heart of disengagement is the forfeiting of the individual's major life role. For the female this has meant the parental role and for the male the occupational role. On the whole, men are seen as making an abrupt transition from engaged to disengaged while women are seen as making a smooth, gradual withdrawal from previous roles and patterns of activity.

Disengagement for men is seen as abrupt because their careers—the central focus of their lives—are suddenly terminated by retirement. Women, on the other hand, even when employed, are seen as concerned principally with family matters. Homemaking continues during employment and follows women into retirement. Substitute roles following retirement, which bring the respect of others and thereby self-esteem, are always readily available to women but not to men. This is not to say that men cannot assume alternative roles following retirement, but rather that such roles are not nearly as apparent and accessible as they are for women.

Role losses, both at the launching of offspring into the adult world and at retirement, are accompanied by diminished interaction—both qualitative and quantitative—between aging persons and others in their social system. Disengagement theory, if followed to its logical conclusion, would predict withdrawal from previous activities, followed by preoccupation with self and ultimately death.

The following brief work history of a steelworker perhaps best illustrates the rationale of disengagement theorists. Samuel Y was a manual laborer all his life; he had begun working at age 12 in a coal mine. Each subsequent job involved heavy labor only, whether it was pushing a wheelbarrow loaded with coal or stacking beams of steel weighing up to 100 pounds. Long before retirement at age 65, he began looking forward to the time when he would not have to strain his muscles during the daily grind. For Mr. Y, disengagement came sometime before mandatory retirement. He had been a foreman during his 40s and early 50s, but after he slipped one day and fell, breaking an ankle, his job as foreman was taken by a younger man who could move easily throughout the plant. He was then relegated to the paint rack, an assignment that required little walking but considerable strain on his shoulders and arms, for he had to wield a paint gun the whole day, spraying large sheets of steel.

Having gladly accepted mandatory retirement at age 65, Samuel Y now has time to enjoy his family, including children and grandchildren, whom he regularly visits. Although his eyesight is failing slightly, he can still do many of the things he enjoys, such as hunting, fishing, and gardening. Disengaging from the seven-to-four work routine seems to have considerably enriched his life.

Vern Bengtson (1973) argues that disengagement theory implies a dramatic shift from middle to older age marked by an entirely new balance of forces between the personality and the social systems of the individual. The manner in which the individual has organized the diverse roles that he or she is currently assuming into an organized and consistent view of self is called *personality. Social systems* are the variety of social groups the individual identifies as his or hers and with whose members he or she regularly interacts (family, fellow workers, members of the Lions Club, and so on). The extent to which social norms impinge on the individual is greatly reduced in older age, Bengtson argues, and the sources of psychological well-being in older age are considerably different from those in middle age. Whether this much of a shift in personality actually occurs is highly debatable.

Richard Kalish (1972) believes that the disengagement theory must be evaluated on three different levels, each of which should be carefully analyzed in terms of whether it applies to psychological disengagement or social disengagement. The levels of evaluation as he sees them are (1) disengagement as a process, (2) disengagement as inevitable, and (3) disengagement as adaptive.[2]

Disengagement is often viewed as a process, since for most people it does not occur all at once but over time. The last child may leave home when a couple are in their early 50s; parental responsibilities are thereby withdrawn. The wife may decide to give up her job after the expenses of putting children through college are no longer pressing. The husband may decide not to serve another term on the county council. Later he may decide to retire at age 62 rather than wait until 65. As a process, disengagement is always selective, in that the individual chooses to withdraw from some roles and not from others.

Disengagement is inevitable in the sense that almost everyone recognizes that at some point he or she will die. If increasing age brings with it an increasing probability of sickness and death, then disengagement is inevitable. People are considered ready to disengage upon recognizing that their life space is shrinking and their energy level declining. *Life space* refers to the area of the world, community, neighborhood, and home that the individual considers his or her environment. Older persons may give up driving, travel outside the neighborhood less frequently, and spend more time in their home or apartment. Their life space begins to shrink as they become less mobile and feel less capable of coping with broader and more diverse environments.

Disengagement is adaptive from both the individual and the societal points of view. Disengagement presumably allows the individual to withdraw from previous work roles and from competition with younger people as an adaptation to a presumed decline in energy. From the societal point of view, disengagement permits younger employees to assume critical positions as older employees become less efficient. It thereby allows for the smooth transition of power from one generation to the next.

The proponents of disengagement theory believe that disengagement is both inevitable and adaptive. Disengagement at a time of declining energy and health is believed by some gerontologists to allow the retention of meaningful family relationships at a relatively undiminished level as long as possible. This, in their opinion, requires the sacrifice of other kinds of engagement, such as work.

Proponents also believe that gradual withdrawal from the social system and declining involvement in activities constitute an inevitable part of the aging process. Howard Kaplan (1971) observes that people are too often evaluated not in terms of where in the life cycle they are, but rather in terms of where they are going or where they have been. To require older persons to be measured by the same criteria by which we measure younger persons is, in the view of disengagement theorists, unfair.

The critics of disengagement theory have been numerous, adamant, and persistent. They are quick to question the presumed inevitability of disengagement. Many gerontologists question whether the process is functional for either the individual or the social system. George Maddox (1965) points out that different personality factors might make an individual more or less amenable to disengagement. Since there is social pressure to disengage, gerontologists who focus on personality factors feel that those who throughout their lives have dealt with stress by turning inward and insulating themselves from the world will probably continue to manifest this pattern of withdrawal. On the other hand, those inclined to remain engaged have probably been so inclined over the course of their lives. This latter group might change some of their activities, but they will seek relationships allowing them to resist disengagement in general.

In responding to the critics, Elaine Cumming (1963) distinguishes between impingers and selectors. *Impingers*, being more anxious about disengagement, take an assertive stance in human interaction. *Selectors* are more passive in social relations. They primarily wait for others to confirm their own assumptions about themselves, and are sensitive only to cues tending to reinforce these views. Through this selective perception of social cues, selectors can insulate themselves from the negative connotations of disengagement. Developmental psychologists have argued that there is a gradual turning inward by individuals over the course of life. Thus one might expect people as they age to become less attentive to external events and more attuned to their own inner states. In Cumming's (1963) defense and restatement of disengagement theory, she argues that coping mechanisms derived from previous experiences will determine a person's level of engagement and disengagement during subsequent stages of the life cycle. Each individual develops defenses against negative or inconsistent communications from others regarding his or her self and personality. Some use selective perception in their communication with others, hearing only what they want to hear and ignoring what would be threatening. Others withdraw and thus avoid any communication that might be negative or critical. These are just two of a variety of mechanisms for protecting one's ego and view of one's self from contradictory information.

ACTIVITY THEORY

In direct opposition to disengagement theory is activity theory. Its proponents, such as Robert Havighurst (1963), maintain that normal aging involves maintaining as long as possible the activities and attitudes of middle age. This implies that substitutes should be found for those activities and roles that one is forced to give up at retirement.

Our understanding of disengagement can be only as great as our understanding of what *engagement* means to middle-class Americans. Middle-class values generally maintain that being active and productive is desirable for a successful life. Early in life the children of middle-class families are encouraged to become involved in as many activities as possible. Little League baseball, music lessons, Girl Scouts, the YMCA, and other activities can consume the spare time of these children. Adult life for this group is a continuation of the pattern, with career, the Elks, the country club, church, the ladies' auxiliary, and so on, consuming most of the hours of the day.

This group is likely to view retirement and disengagement with considerable ambivalence, since its members' lives have been centered in the so-called Protestant ethic, with its positive orientation toward work, activity, and social responsibilities. Activity theory reflects these common attitudes and is frequently expressed in the writings and philosophy of the "Golden Age" magazines. Many older Americans insist that they would "rather wear out than rust out." The assumptions of activity theory are thus in direct conflict with those of the disengagement theorists, according to Havighurst (1963).

Activity theory assumes that the relationship between the social system and personality remains fairly stable as an individual passes from middle age to old age. It holds that the norms for old age are the same as those for middle age, and that the older person should be judged in terms of middle-aged people's criteria of success.[3]

According to activity theorists, any behavior by older persons that would not be appropriate in middle-aged persons is considered maladjustment. Fred Cottrell and Robert Atchley (1969) found in their sample of retired women that very few described themselves as old, preferring "middle-aged" or "just past middle age."[4] This tendency was found even among women who had passed their seventieth birthday. Thus it would appear that older people themselves view middle-age people's patterns of behavior as desirable for themselves. In all likelihood this reflects their acceptance of the dominant values in American society and something of age discrimination as well.

The inability of Dr. Maura K, a former university professor, to adjust to retirement perhaps best illustrates the beliefs of the activity theorists. Dr. K retired from academic life after 25 years of a university-oriented existence. A philosophy professor throughout her career, she had been active in almost every departmental and campuswide committee and council. She was active in off-campus civic activities as well. Suddenly, after 25 years of days crammed with classes, committee meetings, and civic responsibilities, she found herself with the ample free time she had always complained about not having.

Instead of enjoying relief from responsibilities, however, she found that time lay heavily on her hands. No classes; no committee meetings—her colleagues weren't quite as eager to talk to her as before. She could not seem to adapt to spending her time puttering around her yard. She started haunting her old department, trying to keep up with developments there and at the university in general. She was confronted, however, with the usual questions directed at retirees—"What are you doing here?" "Why aren't you in Florida basking in the sun?" "Why don't you learn to enjoy life?" Dr. K's mandatory retirement was not pleasant because she could find few activities to substitute for work-related roles and none that gave her the same satisfaction.

Activity theory emphasizes the stability of personality orientations as an individual ages; it ignores the need for societal-structured alternatives to roles and activities the individual loses as part of the aging process. One obvious difficulty of the theory is that it does not seriously consider what happens to the person who cannot maintain the standards of middle age in the later years. Accepting the belief that one must remain active while experiencing physiological losses as part of aging can result in considerable frustration, anxiety, and guilt if one is unable to perform to the expected level.

Bruce Lemon, Vern Bengtson, and James Peterson (1972) have isolated what appear to be two fundamental propositions of activity theory: (1) There is a positive relation between social activity and life satisfaction in old age, and (2) role losses such as widowhood and retirement are inversely related to life satisfaction. Their findings from a study of people moving to a retirement community did not support these propositions. Only social activity with friends was in any way related to life satisfaction. Their study therefore raised questions about the validity of the basic propositions of activity theory and so cast doubts on the theory itself. On the other hand, studies by Jeffers and Nichols (1970), Havighurst and colleagues (1966), and others have repeatedly found positive associations among morale, personal adjustment, and activity levels.

HUMAN DEVELOPMENT THEORIES

Criticism of both the disengagement and activity theories has led to alternative ways of looking at the problems of aging. Some gerontologists have argued that to understand the experiences of older persons we must understand what has happened to them at earlier stages in the life cycle. Certainly few would disagree that it is the experiences of an entire life that shape an individual's perceptions, attitudes, and means of adjustment to his or her later years. Thus some gerontologists argue that human development theories may be fruitful in explaining the adjustments of old age.

Freud

Sigmund Freud (1949) emphasized the development of the sexual function in humans. Some of his basic premises were:

1. Sexual development manifests itself soon after birth.
2. Sexual life consists of obtaining pleasure from various zones of the body.
3. The development of the sexual function has two phases. The early phase increases steadily until the end of the fifth year and is followed by a lull (the latency period). The second phase begins at puberty.[5]

How the sexual function is developed in the early period is thought to have important consequences for adult life. Freud (1949) believed that personality development begins with the oral phase, soon after the birth of the child. The first organ to make libidinal demands upon the mind is the mouth. The mouth, as an erotogenic zone (a zone in which sexual feelings can be aroused), is the means through which nourishment is provided and the child's physiological needs thereby satisfied. However, the child's persistent sucking tendency is an indication of the need to obtain pleasure through the mouth, independent of nourishment. Freud (1949) labeled this need sexual.[6]

Freud (1949) characterized the stage following the oral as the sadistic-anal. Although sadistic impulses are said to occur during the oral phase, their extent increases greatly during the anal. Satisfaction is sought in aggression and in the excretory function. Mastery of bowel and bladder functions is achieved in this stage.

According to Freud (1949), the sadistic-anal phase is followed by the phallic phase. This is the period in which the Oedipus complex develops. The boy begins to manipulate his penis and desires sexual relations with his mother.[7] Realizing that he is competing with his father for the mother's attention, he fears he will be castrated by the father. Ultimately he represses his earlier sexual desires for the mother and begins to identify with the father. During the phallic phase he pursues pleasure derived from the sexual function.

The fourth of the Freudian phases of development is the period of latency. Freud (1949) argues that after the early developmental stages come a few years in which very little personal development takes place. This period lasts until the onset of puberty, which introduces the genital phase. In this fifth phase, normal heterosexual interests occur. The organization of the individual's drives around the sexual function is then completed.

Thus for Freud (1949) there is a close relationship between the adult personality and the sexual life of the child. Adjustment and personality formation are largely biological and the result of instinct.

Erikson

Charlotte Buhler (1968), Carl Jung (1971), and Erik Erikson (1964) have all attempted to trace human development through the entire life cycle rather than merely through the child and adolescent phases. Erikson's (1964) "eight stages of life" is perhaps the most complete of these theories. There is some similarity between the first five of these stages and the stages of the Freudian model. Erikson's theory is set in terms of paradoxical demands placed on the child at each stage of development.[8]

According to Erikson, the first of these stages centers in the infant's conflict between developing feelings of trust and a sense of distrust. Erikson believes that the infant's first social achievement is a willingness to let the mother out of sight without undue anxiety or rage, because she has become an "inner certainty" as well as an "outer predictability." This achievement of trust, furthermore, implies not only that one has learned to rely on the sameness and continuity of the outer providers but also that one may trust oneself and the capacity of one's own organs to cope with urges.

The second stage occurs in later infancy, when the anal musculature has matured and is focused on a growing sense of autonomy versus a sense of shame and doubt. Parental firmness must protect children at this stage against the potential anarchy of their as yet untrained sense of discrimination, their inability to know when to hold on and when to let go of parents' support and other support objects. While the child's home environment encourages independence, it must also offer protection against meaningless and arbitrary experiences of shame and doubt.

The third stage, the period of greatest locomotor development, focuses on a developing sense of initiative versus a sense of guilt. Erikson believes that the child's need for autonomy is concentrated on keeping out potential rivals and is to no small extent an expression of jealous rage most often directed against encroachments by younger siblings. Initiative brings the anticipation of rivalry with those who have preceded one in some area or endeavor and who presumably are better fitted for the thing to which one's initiative is directed. Infantile sexuality and the incest taboo unite here to bring about a specific developmental problem in which the child must turn from an exclusive attachment to parents to the slow process of becoming a parent, a carrier of tradition.

The fourth developmental stage, Erikson asserts, comes in the middle years of childhood, during which there is a struggle between children's sense of industry and their sense of inferiority. Children at this stage recognize once and for all that there is no workable future within the boundaries of their family. They are now ready to approach skills and tasks that go far beyond the pleasurable functioning of the limbs. The individual develops the trait of industry to bring productive situations to completion, an aim that gradually replaces the whims and wishes of the autonomous organism.

The fifth stage occurs in adolescence and involves a sense of ego identity (certainty of self and a sense of continuity and belonging regarding career, sex role, and value system) versus role confusion. The central developmental task is to find one's position in life as a productive and responsible adult having a consistent set of attitudes about oneself, including an integrated sexuality. This stage is resolved when one's education is completed, an occupation begun, and a marriage partner secured.

At the sixth stage, according to Erikson, one develops the capacity for sexual intimacy versus isolation. A youth does not become capable of a fully intimate relationship until his or her identity crisis is fairly well resolved. One prerequisite is a clear concept of self. Only then can one fuse that identity with another in full appreciation of the other's uniqueness. Many early attempts at intimacy, according to Erikson, are attempts to find one's identity through a romantic relationship with another.

Erikson's seventh stage involves a conflict between generativity and stagnation that occurs in one's productive years, which extend from young adulthood into old age. This stage is critical to the individual's sense of achievement and fulfillment in life. Failure to cope with this developmental stage is likely to result in stagnation, bitterness, and physiological and emotional decline.

Erikson describes the final stage as integrity versus despair. This stage is precipitated by the awareness of the finitude of life and of the closeness to death. A feeling of integrity is the ultimate fulfillment of the previous seven stages along with the recognition that one's offspring provide a continuity of life between oneself and the newborn generation. Failure to cope with this developmental stage results in states of meaninglessness, despair, and a feeling of the uselessness of one's life.

Evaluation

Most developmental theorists believe that each stage of life presents different developmental tasks that must be mastered before one can enter the next stage of life. Failure at any level implies inability to move on in the expected pattern.

The developmental theories, much like the disengagement and activity theories, offer a unique way of looking at the individual's adaptation to the later years of life. They encourage the gerontologist to connect any explanation of the individual's current behavior to his or her history and thereby perceive a developmental progression throughout the individual's life. They posit not a desired pattern of behavior in the later years, such as disengagement or activity, but rather a variety of different adjustment patterns based on the individual's personality and previous experiences.

One problem with the developmental theories, which tend to be general and abstract, is that they offer little hope for those people who have arrived at old age without having mastered the developmental tasks of the earlier phases of life. What happens to the individual who experiences stagnation instead of generativity in the later phase of the life cycle? Is bitterness inevitable, as Erikson (1964) suggests? Is there nothing people can do to put their lives in order after making mistakes at earlier stages? From this perspective, the developmental theories seem unduly pessimistic.

CONTINUITY THEORY

While gerontologists who are psychologically oriented have tended to turn to human-development theories because of their dissatisfaction with the disengagement and activity theories, those who are sociologically oriented have tended to turn to continuity theory. Building on the well-established sociological concept of the continuity of socialization and on the developmental psychologists' views on the stages of life, this theory is based on the continuity of behavior patterns through the different phases of life.

Sociologists have long argued that the experiences a person has at a given point in life often prepare that person for the role he or she must assume at the next stage of life. The little girl playing doctor, the boy building a model rocket ship, the young woman working as a camp counselor, and the apprentice imitating the master craftsman are all developing skills that they can use in a later stage of life. Formally, by advising, encouraging, and sending children to school to acquire desired skills, parents attempt to socialize them into adult roles. Informally, by the games they are taught to play, the gifts they receive, and the models of adult behavior provided them by parents, children learn the proper attitudes and values required for assuming adult responsibilities. Thus both formally and informally child-rearing practices contribute continuity to the socialization process by which the individual is prepared for the next stage of life. Similarly, there is considerable *anticipatory socialization*, by which a person imagines what it will be like to assume the roles and responsibilities of the next period of life.

Each successive grade in school is predicated on what is taught in a previous grade. Education builds knowledge and skills in increments, so that the high school graduate is presumed to be considerably more informed than a fourth-grader, who is herself superior in this respect to those in the grades below her. During the life course, movement into adult status in one's early twenties presumes successful handling of adjustment problems in the teen years. Life cycles thus have considerable continuity from one stage to the next, with each succeeding age built on the experiences and skills of the previous period. Atchley (1989) observes that adults in middle and later life use continuity as a primary adaptive strategy for dealing with changes associated with normal aging.

Having in mind this logical development of the individual life course and the different tasks and skills mastered at each stage in life, one can appreciate why retirement might be attended with problems, since nothing in the previous years in any way prepares one for it. Retirement poses considerable discontinuity from all of the previous stages of life: Career and occupational skills are no longer needed; work is not expected to be a vital part of one's life; leisure time is now ample; and the constant drive for achievement and success no longer dominates one's life.

Continuity theory holds that in the course of growing older, the individual is predisposed toward maintaining stability in the habits, associations, preferences, and lifestyle that he or she has developed over the years. The theory asserts that we can understand an individual's reaction to aging only by examining the complex interrelationships among the biological, psychological, and social changes in his or her life and previous behavior patterns. Exponents of the theory believe that people's habits, preferences, associations, state of health, and experiences will in large part determine their ability to maintain their lifestyle while retiring from full-time employment and perhaps having to adjust to the death of a loved one. A person's lifelong experience thus creates dispositions to a certain lifestyle that he or she will attempt to maintain if at all possible. Moreover, Atchley (1989) observes that the lack of the perception of continuity is likely to mean that an individual's life seems chaotic and unpredictable—a state that every person attempts to avoid. McCrae and Costa (1984) argue that stability of lifestyle from the continuity perspective becomes something more than the psychological need to retain one's identity: It becomes a desire to control resources and to maintain desired roles in the social system for as long as possible.

The disengagement and activity theories both posit a single direction that is supposedly the most appropriate for successful adaptation to the aging process. Continuity theory, on the other hand, starts with the single premise that the individual will try to maintain as long as possible his or her preferred lifestyle, and then holds that adaptation can go in any of several different directions depending on how the individual perceives his or her changing status and attempts to adjust to this change. Continuity theory does not assert that one must be disengaged or active in order to be well adjusted in the later years, but rather that the decision regarding which roles are to be discarded and which maintained will in large part be determined by the individual's history and preferred style of life. Atchley (1989) asserts that past experiences have taught most adults to recognize the things they can do well and avoid those they do poorly. The loss of the parental and work role often frees individuals to concentrate on the areas they define as their strengths and to avoid those they define as their weaknesses.

Warren Peterson (1976) seems to approach the perspective of continuity theory in arguing that when disengagement occurs, it is a very selective process. The individual, in Peterson's view, always maintains the roles that conferred the greatest status and relinquishes those that were less valuable. In other words, the individual maintains as long as possible his or her previous self-concept by continuing in those activities and roles most directly related to this ideal self and discarding those less directly related. Like the proponents of continuity theory, Peterson (1976) believes that we can predict retirement-adjustment patterns only by knowing the individual's history as well as by having some understanding of his or her ideal self and the relation of past roles to this ideal.

Two case histories may give some clue to the selective relinquishing of roles to which Peterson refers. Claudius S was a professor of political science at a well-known university. During his career he had written innumerable articles and several books in his field and was a nationally recognized scholar. Dr. S had never been extremely effective as a teacher since he was not a particularly good public speaker and did not enjoy this responsibility. Upon his retirement, he was given an office at the university and spent the next two years writing a book on social movements. Relinquishing the teaching role, which he never really enjoyed, in favor of total dedication to writing—which he enjoyed very much and which brought him considerable prestige—is easily understandable.

In contrast, Clarissa J, a professor of political science at a neighboring college, was recognized as an excellent teacher by both colleagues and students. During her academic career, however, she did very little writing and did not seem to enjoy this aspect of her work. Upon retiring, she spent the next several years lecturing at various universities and public gatherings throughout the Midwest. In these two case histories one can easily see Peterson's pattern of retirees giving up those roles that brought them the least status and maintaining those that conferred the greatest status.

Continuity theory has the advantage of offering a multiplicity of adjustment patterns—rather than just one—from which the older individual can choose. The "disadvantage" of continuity theory is the difficulty encountered in trying to test it empirically. Each individual's pattern of adjustment in retirement must become a case study in which the researcher attempts to determine to what degree that individual was able to continue in his or her previous pattern of living. Sociologically, some test of the theory could be developed based on what we know about the lifestyles of those occupying different social-class positions and how aging affects these patterns. Still, we could anticipate considerable individual variation.

AGE STRATIFICATION THEORY

This theory, introduced primarily by Matilda Riley (1972; 1988) and her colleagues, is particularly attractive to social gerontologists. A stratified society is one that is divided or arranged on the basis of classes, castes, or social strata. According to age stratification theory, age is the basis for this stratification. Thus children, teenagers, young adults, mature adults, and older persons can be identified as distinct status groups in any society. Age is almost universally a basis for acquiring different roles, status, and deference from others. Older people, for example, vary in status from industrial societies, where they are generally accorded low status and the less important roles, to traditional Asian societies, where they are often given high status and the more important roles.

Persons of different age categories are differentially viewed and treated in all societies. Age tends to qualify and disqualify people for desired roles and privileged positions. In the United States, one most often cannot obtain a driver's license until age 16; marry, without parents' consent, until age 18; become a senator until age 30. You are not likely to become the president of General Electric at 25. In the 1980 U.S. presidential election, one of the campaign issues was whether Ronald Reagan was too old to be President.

It is apparent that much can be inferred about a person's social position and status from his or her age. Moreover, members of a cohort having been born during a given time period and shared similar historical events and experiences, have much in common, whether they realize it or not. Family and social gatherings often find older persons drawn together in conversation about the "good old days."

Age stratification theory allows the social scientist to look at any age group in terms of its distinctive demographic characteristics (size, racial composition, sex ratio) and history as well as its relationship to other age groups in the same society. The theory also allows us to view a member of a particular age group as a member of a particular status group in a structured social system and as an active participant in a changing society. Considering generational differences in experiences, attitudes, and behavior helps us to understand and explain generational conflict. While this theory may have limited value in the explanation of any single individual's behavior, it does lend itself to historical and sociological explanations of the attitudes and behavior of age cohorts.

Age stratification theory has so far yielded few empirical studies. It remains to be seen whether it will become more widely accepted and lead to a variety of helpful research approaches to the behavior of older persons. Anne Foner (1984) and other exponents of the theory argue that not only age but also social class, sex, and ethnicity stratify people in social systems. Thus age is just one of a number of variables that create a stratified society. By considering all of these variables we can easily conclude that an older person has multiple advantages or disadvantages.

OLDER AMERICANS AS A MINORITY GROUP

Many would argue that the best way to study the problems of older Americans is to view this group as a minority faced with the same difficulties that other minority groups have confronted. Like blacks, Native Americans, and Asian Americans, older people are discriminated against because they share a common biological characteristic. As with racial discrimination, the discrimination against older people is promoted by the relative ease with which the undesirable characteristic is observed. Proponents of this view also argue that older people are like other minority groups in that they usually have low incomes, low status, and unequal opportunity and are generally viewed by others as inferior.

Arnold Rose (1964), while not going so far as to define older Americans as a minority group, does argue that they could be considered a subculture of American society. He believes that a subculture among age groups emerges when members of an age group interact with each other significantly more than they interact with persons in other age categories. This, he asserts, occurs when the members (1) have a positive affinity for each other because of such factors as long-standing friendship or common problems, interests, or concerns, and (2) are excluded from interaction with other groups in the population to some significant extent. Both sets of circumstances, according to Rose, could readily apply to older Americans, who are most often not actively involved in an occupation or career, are dependent on others for their income, and are generally excluded from the mainstream of American life.

The weaknesses of both the minority-group and subculture theories is that they do not apply to all situations or all older persons. In the United States Congress, for instance, the seniority system favors older representatives and senators, delegating considerable prestige and power to them. In reality, not all older Americans live on low incomes. Middle- and upper-class senior citizens may have considerable retirement incomes and lead quite comfortable lives. Studies by Donald Cowgill (1962) and Harold Cox and Albert Bhak (1980) do indicate that older people are found predominantly in certain sections of large cities. On the other hand, less than 5 percent are moving to the totally segregated sun cities of California, Arizona, and Florida. Moreover, by far the great majority live in age-integrated neighborhoods, and their social interactions are often with family members, cutting across generation lines. In short, the heterogeneity, variable lifestyles, diverse family ties, and social-interaction patterns of older Americans simply do not seem to support the subculture and minority-group theories suggested by Rose (1964). Gordon Streib (1968), in attacking what he believes is the minority-group myth, says;

> The aged do not share a distinct, and separate culture: membership in the group defined as "aged" is not exclusive and permanent, but awaits all members of our society who live long enough. As a result, age is a less distinguishing group characteristic than others such as sex, occupation, social class, and the like. . . . The aged are not organized to advance their own interests and are not particularly attracted to such organizations. Nor are they systematically deprived of power and privilege.[9]

Perhaps the most realistic way to view older people is to see them as a status group similar to other such groups in society. Leonard Cain (1969) has noted that every society has established means of grouping persons of approximately the same age into *age sets*. These means include (1) age status systems, whereby status is differentiated on the basis of age; (2) socialization, by which individuals are formally prepared for subsequent age statuses; (3) rites of passage, by which individuals formally transferred from one age status to another; (4) age grading, the identification of persons of comparable ages as distinct categories; and (5) the generational phenomenon, establishment of intergenerational patterns among those of different age sets.

That age does serve as a basis of grouping people in society seems in little doubt. S. N. Eisenstadt (1965) has observed that age differences are among the most basic and crucial aspects of human life and destiny. All societies are confronted with age-related role changes and the progression of power and capacities connected with age changes. Thus the transition from youth to older age is subject to social and cultural definitions. Age factors differentially integrate individuals into the community. Whether older age is viewed as a desirable or undesirable status in contemporary American society, it must be recognized that those 65 and older are a distinct group of individuals who have survived many of life's obstacles to reach this age stratum. Even if this age group is generally little valued by society, living to age 65 and beyond is considered by almost everyone to be more desirable than the alternative.

AGING AS AN EXCHANGE

James Dowd (1975), in criticizing the basic assumptions of both the disengagement and activity theories, states that

> neither theory, . . . while focusing for the most part on descriptive accounts of the peculiar relationship between the social psychological variables of social interaction and life satisfaction, attempts to offer anything but the most perfunctory of explanations for the decreased social interaction itself. Rather this phenomenon is given the status of a sociological "given," that is, it is treated as something requiring no additional explanation.[10]

Dowd believes that the methodological difficulty (the difficulty in finding the appropriate research technique to either prove or disprove a theory) of disengagement theory precludes answers to the question of why social interaction decreases in older age. That is, the theory produces untestable assumptions so effortlessly that it precludes any search for alternative answers. Thus, older persons are seen as suffering from lower income and poorer health than their younger counterparts and therefore are unable to remain as engaged in social life as they were when younger.[11] In Dowd's view, the overemphasis on the disengagement and activity perspectives has retarded the development of alternative theoretical perspectives.

Dowd believes that decreased social interaction in older age can perhaps best be explained in terms of an intricate process of exchange between society and its older population resulting from the older people's power-dependent relationship. The basic premises on which exchange theory rests are these:

1. Society is made up of social actors in pursuit of common goals.
2. Pursuing these goals, actors enter into social relations with other actors; these entail some costs in the form of time, energy, and wealth.
3. Actors expect to reap desired goals as their reward; for this they are willing to assume the necessary costs.
4. Whatever the exchange relationship, each actor will attempt to maximize rewards and minimize costs.
5. Exchange processes are more than an economic transaction, since they involve intrinsic psychological satisfaction and need gratification.
6. Only those activities that are economical will be repeated.

Power enters an exchange relationship when one of the participants values the rewards to be gained in the relationship more than the other participant does. The exchange theorist's view of power is that it is derived from imbalances in social exchanges. From Peter Blau's (1964) perspective, much of social life is an intricate exchange in which every participant approaches and withdraws in patterns that add to or subtract from his or her store of power and prestige.

Sue and Tim are college students who have been dating each other for the last two months. Their relationship could be used as an example of an exchange relationship. The question that an exchange theorist would immediately ask is what each party is getting out of the relationship. Sue, young and attractive, chooses to be seen dating Tim, the star of the university basketball team, in order to prove to others how desirable a date she is and thus to improve her fellow students' opinion of her. Tim, on the other hand, by dating the most attractive woman on campus, may be able to show how his popularity in athletics can become a valuable resource in other areas of life, such as attracting members of the opposite sex. Thus, we can see a balanced exchange relationship, one that each participant wants to continue because of the benefits derived.

Power would enter this relationship if Tim wanted to continue it and Sue wanted to terminate it. In this case, in any exchange between them Sue would be able to bargain more effectively than Tim because she is willing to terminate the relationship at any point. Tim, who wants to continue the relationship more than Sue, would have to make concessions to her in order to persuade her to continue to date him. Thus we would have an imbalanced exchange relationship, in which Sue can exercise more power and thereby more easily control Tim because she is not as committed to continuing the relationship.

In viewing aging as an exchange, James Dowd (1975) argues that decreased social interaction is the eventual result of a series of exchange relationships in which the power of older persons over their social environment is gradually diminished until all that remains is the humble capacity to comply. Where the worker was once able to exchange skill, knowledge, or expertise for needed wages, the final exchange becomes one of compliance with mandatory retirement in return for sustenance in the form of social security, retirement pensions, and Medicare. Table 2–1 sets forth Dowd's concept that the probability of continued engagement in social relationships is a function principally of the existing power relationships between the aging person and society. The skills of many aging workers may rapidly become outmoded, resulting in an unfavorable power imbalance. The danger for the less powerful party—the older person—is that this unbalanced exchange relationship becomes institutionalized and thereby provides a normative basis for future unbalanced exchanges.

Peter Blau (1964) notes that the resources of any complex work organization are limited. Therefore it is possible for management to balance one exchange relationship only by unbalancing others. As one group gains a relative advantage,

TABLE 2–1   Disengagement and Power Relationships

Individual Readiness to Disengage	Society	
	Positive	Negative
Positive	Power Balance (Mutually satisfying exchange)	Power Imbalance (The individual with critical expertise is forced to remain engaged.)
Negative	Power Imbalance (The individual with little critical expertise is forced to retire? Disengage?)	Power Balance (Continued role incumbency, e.g., of religious and political leaders, is institutionally sanctioned.)

another group is threatened. Younger workers exchange their labor for wages and the implicit promise of job security and promotion. The longer the older worker remains on the job, the more he or she blocks the career path of younger workers.

From the perspective of exchange theory, then, the primary problem facing aging workers is their decreasing power resources. As their particular skill or expertise becomes outmoded or its value reduced in any way, they have little to exchange that is of critical value. One answer, therefore, to the question of why older persons disengage is not that disengagement is mutually satisfying for the individual and society, but rather that in the exchange relationship between the two, society enjoys a distinct advantage. Dowd (1975) believes that one of the advantages of the exchange perspective is that it rejects the functionalist disengagement notion of reciprocity between the individual and the social system (in which both are seen as benefiting from disengagement) and requires an explicit analysis of both sides of each social transaction (exchange) so that we can determine who is benefiting more and why.

Exchange theory offers a new perspective from which to view the process of aging and the interaction between the individual and the social system. Research alone will be able to determine its value as an explanation of the aging process.

THE SYMBOLIC INTERACTION PERSPECTIVE

Symbolic interaction theory, as developed by George Mead (1934), Charles Cooley (1902), William Thomas (1937), and other social thinkers, is one of the basic theoretical perspectives of sociologists. The acquisition of language by human beings makes them distinctly different from any other form of life, according to the symbolic interactionists. Through language humans live in a symbolic environment as well as a physical environment and can be stimulated to act by symbols as well as by physical stimuli. Through language (symbols) humans have the capacity to stimulate others in ways other than those in which they themselves are stimulated. Thus the sergeant may tell his soldiers that it is their patriotic duty to fight and risk their lives saving a hill in order that he might be seen as an effective leader and thereby be promoted to lieutenant. The symbolic interactionists assume that the individual communicates to others in order to evoke meanings and values in others. In the previous example the sergeant believed that the soldiers' sense of patriotic duty would make them willing to risk their lives.

The exponents of symbolic interaction theory maintain that by communicating symbols, humans can learn myriad meanings and values, and hence ways of acting, from one another. Thus they assume that most adult behavior is learned specifically in symbolic communication rather than through trial-and-error conditioning.

Thinking is seen by the symbolic interactionists as a process by which possible solutions and other future courses of action are assessed for their relative advantages and disadvantages in terms of the values of the individual; one option is then chosen for action. Thinking is a symbolic process of deductive trial and error.

Sheldon Stryker (1959), outlined what he considers the basic assumptions of the theory:

1. Humankind must be studied at its own level. Valid principles of human social psychological behavior cannot be inferred from the study of nonhuman forms, since humans are qualitatively and quantitatively different from their predecessors in the evolutionary process. Thus, principles derived from other forms of life cannot completely account for human behavior.

2. The most fruitful approach to human social behavior is through the analysis of society. Interaction is the basic building block of society from which both individual and societal patterns of behavior are derived. Utilizing this block, sociology builds in the direction of collective behavior; social psychology builds in the direction of the behavior of individuals.

3. A baby is neither social nor antisocial but rather asocial, with potentialities for social development. A baby has impulses, but these impulses must be channeled in a given direction.

4. In the interaction process, the human being is an actor as well as a reactor, and does not simply respond to external stimuli. What constitutes a stimulus depends on the activity in which a human being is involved. A human's environment is a selected segment of the "real world," the selection having been made in the interest of behavior initiated by that human being. Thus, through the learning of a culture (including specialized cultures found in particular segments of society), we are able to predict each other's behavior most of the time and adjust our own behavior to the predicted behavior of others.

LABELING THEORY

Labeling theory, one of the current social psychological perspectives on human behavior, is derived from symbolic interaction theory. Its basic assertion is that one derives a concept of self from interaction with other people in one's social milieu. We tend to think of ourselves in terms of how others define us and react to us. The behavioral corollary of labeling theory is that once others have placed us in distinct categories, they react to us on the basis of these categories, and our self-concept and behavior change accordingly. As we observed in Chapter 1, most people behave the way others in their social world expect them to.

Thus from the labeling perspective, the behavior of older persons may depend largely on the reactions of significant others in their immediate social milieu. The reactions of these significant others depend on how they categorize older Americans. The behavior of older Americans therefore is determined in large measure by the norms of the social group to which they belong, according to labeling theory.

Building on the concepts of the labeling perspective, Jack Zusman (1966) has proposed a social breakdown syndrome. Also on the basis of labeling theory, Joseph Kuypers and Vern Bengtson (1973) have constructed a social reconstruction model that they believe offers considerable promise for explaining the behavior of older Americans and intervening in it in order to help them remain independent as long as possible. Let us briefly consider each of these constructs.

Zusman's (1966) multistage cycle of social breakdown is consistent with the pattern illustrated in Figure 2–2. Among the stages Zusman suggests are the following:

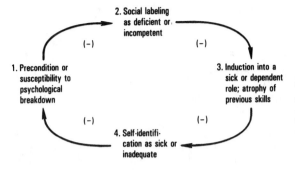

FIGURE 2–2
The Social Breakdown Syndrome (a vicious cycle of increasing incompetence)

Source: Vern L. Bengtson, *The Social Psychology of Aging* (Indianapolis: Bobbs-Merrill, 1973), p. 47. © 1973, The Bobbs-Merrill Company, Inc.

1. The individual is susceptible to psychological breakdown because of identity problems or inappropriate standards concerning social relationships.
2. The individual is labeled by others as incompetent or deficient in some respect.
3. The individual is induced into a role of sickness or dependence and learns the behavior associated with that role; his or her previous skills atrophy.
4. The individual identifies himself or herself as sick or inadequate. The malignant cycle begins again, for the individual is now even more susceptible to the stages of psychological breakdown.

Kuypers and Bengtson (1973), applying the Zusman model to older Americans, theorize as follows:

1. The elderly are likely to be susceptible to and dependent on social labeling because of the nature of social reorganization in later life. That is, role loss, vague and inappropriate normative information, and lack of reference groups all serve to deprive the individual of feedback concerning who he is.
2. Second, this feedback vacuum creates a vulnerability to, and dependence on, external sources of self-labeling, many of which communicate a stereotypic portrayal of the elderly as useless or obsolete.
3. Third, the individual who accepts such negative labeling is then inducted into the negative, dependent position—learning to act like old people are supposed to act—and previous skills of independence atrophy.
4. Fourth, he accepts the external labeling and identifies himself as inadequate, setting the stage for another vicious spiral.[12]

Thus the complex interplay between an older person and his or her social milieu can largely determine that person's self-concept and behavior.

Kuypers and Bengtson suggest that assistance to the aging individual who may be experiencing various stages of the social breakdown syndrome might result in an entirely different outcome for the individual. Indeed it can reverse the social breakdown syndrome, as Kuypers and Bengtson illustrate in their social reconstruction cycle. This construct (1) characterizes the dynamic interaction between the individual and the individual's social system over time, and (2) portrays three inputs that can help older people maintain their self-confidence and independence (Figure 2–3):

1. The individual is liberated from an age-inappropriate view of status. The functionalist work ethic, which suggests self-worth, is contingent on performance in economically "productive" social positions and is particularly inappropriate to old age. Consequently, a more humanitarian frame of self-judgment needs to be developed.

2. Social services to older persons are improved. Older people's capacity for adapting to their new circumstances can be enhanced by reduction or elimination of the debilitating environmental conditions that many older people face, such as poor housing, poor health, and poverty.

3. Older persons are assisted in developing greater confidence in their ability to manage their own lives. Those serving older people could delegate some of their power and control over service programs to the older people themselves, thereby allowing them some measure of self-determination in the areas of policy and program administration.

The symbolic interaction theory seems to offer a number of advantages over other theoretical perspectives on aging. First, it views aging as a dynamic process revolving around the interaction between the individual and his or her social world rather than a process governed by single deterministic or functionalist imperative. Second, it offers no philosophical mandate to disengage or remain active in the later years; it is value-free. Third, it suggests the social-psychological effect of negative labeling and the vague and often inappropriate behavioral expectations that older Americans find themselves confronted with. Finally, to counter the effect of negative labeling of older Americans, the social reconstruction model suggests realistic solutions that practitioners could easily implement in intervening on behalf of this group.

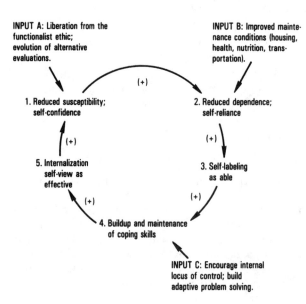

FIGURE 2–3
The Social Reconstruction Syndrome (a benign cycle of increasing competence through social-system inputs)

Source: Vern L. Bengtson, *The Social Psychology of Aging* (Indianapolis: Bobbs-Merrill, 1973), p. 48. © 1973, The Bobbs-Merrill Company, Inc.

CONCLUSION

Research in the field of gerontology has often been applied rather than theoretical. Older Americans daily experience so many problems demanding immediate solutions that researchers have invested much of their time in seeking these solutions, often leaving broader theoretical questions aside.

The 1950s and 1960s saw the emergence of the disengagement and activity theories. Empirical examination of these theories led researchers to conclude that neither adequately explained the life course of older Americans. Nor was neither theory found to be highly correlated with life satisfaction for older Americans.

The 1970s saw a proliferation of other theoretical perspectives on aging. Many of these were broader theories of human behavior that had been developed much earlier but could be easily utilized in explaining the behavior patterns of older Americans. Among these, human development, continuity, exchange, age stratification, and symbolic interaction seem to offer considerable promise for future research and testing.

Continuity theory, the most direct spin-off from the disengagement and activity theories, would seem to be the most difficult to support or refute. Hypotheses derived from this theory are often tied to the researcher's knowledge of the individual's previous lifestyle. Support for the theory based on a series of case histories may be exceedingly long in developing.

The age stratification, exchange, and symbolic interaction theories, on the other hand, offer innumerable hypotheses that can be easily tested by traditional research tools. These theories are therefore likely to appear more frequently in future research reports. Symbolic interaction seems somewhat broader, more sociologically grounded, and therefore more useful.

Whichever of these new theories eventually proves most valuable to gerontologists, there seems little doubt that all of them offer alternative explanations of aging as well as a more value-free approach and a multiplicity of new directions for future research in the field.

KEY TERMS

activity	disengagement	selectors
age sets	exchange	sociological functionalism
cohort	impingers	stratification
continuity	labeling	symbolic interaction
developmental	minority group	

REFERENCES

ATCHLEY, R., *Social Forces in Later Life*. Belmont, Calif.: Wadsworth, 1980.

ATCHLEY, ROBERT, "A Continuity Theory of Normal Aging," *The Gerontologist*, 29, no. 2 (April 1989), 183–90.

BARRON, M. L., "Minority Group Characteristics of the Aged in American Society," *Journal of Gerontology*, 8 (1953), 477–82.

BENGTSON, VERN L., "Adult Socialization and Personality Differentiation: The Social-Psychology of Aging," in *Contemporary Gerontology: Issues and Concepts*, ed. J. Barren. Los Angeles: Los Angeles Gerontology Center, 1969.

BENGTSON, VERN L., *The Social Psychology of Aging*. Indianapolis: Bobbs-Merrill, 1973.

BENGTSON, VERN L., and D. D. BLACK, "Intergenerational Relations and Continuities in Socialization," in *Life Span Developmental Psychology: Personality and Socialization*, ed. P. Baltes and W. Schaie. New York: Academic Press, 1973.

BLACK, D. W., and K. J. GERGEN, "Cognitive and Motivational Factors in Aging and Disengagement," in *Social Aspects of Aging*, ed. Ida H. Simpson and John C. McKinney, pp. 289–95. Durham, N.C.: Duke University Press, 1966.

BLAU, PETER M., *Exchange and Power in Social Life*. New York: John Wiley, 1964.

BLAU, ZENA, *Old Age in a Changing Society*. New York: New Viewpoints, 1973.

BLOOM, MARTIN, "Life span Analysis: A Theoretical Framework for Behavioral Science Research," *Journal of Human Relations*, 12 (1964), 538–54.

BUHLER, CHARLOTTE, "The Developmental Structure and Goal Setting in Group and Individual Studies," in *The Course of Human Life*, ed. Charlotte Buhler and Fred Massarick. New York: Springer, 1968.

BUHLER, CHARLOTTE, and FRED MASSARICK, *The Course of Human Life*. New York: Springer, 1968.

BULTENA, GORDON L., "Life Continuity and Morale in Old Age," *Gerontologist*, 9, no. 4, pt. 1 (1968), 251–53.

CAIN, LEONARD D., "Life Course and Social Structure," in *Handbook of Modern Sociology*, ed. R. E. L. Faris, pp. 272–309. Chicago: Rand McNally, 1964.

CAIN, LEONARD D., JR., "Age Status and Generations Phenomena: The New Old in Contemporary America," *Gerontologist*, 7, no. 2 (1969), 83–92.

CARP, FRANCES M., "Some Components of Disengagement," *Journal of Gerontology*, 23 (1968), 382–86.

CAVAN, RUTH S., R. J. HAVIGHURST, and H. GOLDHAMER, *Personal Adjustment in Old Age*. Chicago: Science Research Associates, 1949.

COOLEY, C. H., *The Nature of Human Nature*. New York: Scribner's, 1902.

COTTRELL, FRED, and ROBERT C. ATCHLEY, *Retired Women: A Preliminary Report*. Oxford, Ohio: Scripps Foundation, 1969.

COWGILL, DONALD J., "Segregation Scores for Metropolitan Areas," *American Sociological Review*, 27 (June 1962), 400–402.

COX, HAROLD, and ALBERT BHAK, "Determinants of Age Based Residential Segregation," *Sociological Symposium*, no. 29 (Winter 1980), 27–41.

CUMMING, ELAINE, "Further Thoughts on the Theory of Disengagement," *UNESCO International Social Science Bulletin 15* (1963), 377–93.

CUMMING, ELAINE, LORS DEAN, DAVID NEWELL, ISABEL McCAFFREY, "Disengagement: A Tentative Theory of Aging," *Sociometry*, 23 (1960), 23–35.

CUMMING, ELAINE, and WILLIAM H. HENRY, *Growing Old*. New York: Basic Books, 1961.

DEROCHES, H. F., and B. D. KAIMAN, "Disengagement Potential: Replication and Use as an Explanatory Variable," *Journal of Gerontology*, 23 (1971), 76–80.

DEROCHES, H. F., and B. D. KAIMAN, "Disengagement Theory in Sociocultural Perspective," *International Journal of Psychiatry*, 6, no. 1 (1968), 69–76.

DEROCHES, H. F., and B. D. KAIMAN, "Stability of Activity Participation in an Aged Population," *Journal of Gerontology*, 19 (1964), 211–14.

DOWD, JAMES J., "Aging as Exchange: A Preface to Theory," *Journal of Gerontology*, 30 (1975), 584–94.

EISENSTADT, S. N., *From Generation to Generation: Age Groups and Social Structure*. New York: Free Press, 1965.

ERIKSON, ERIK H., *Childhood and Society* (2nd ed.). New York: W. W. Norton, 1964.

FONER, ANNE, "Age Stratification as One Form of Social Stratification." Paper presented at the annual meeting of the American Sociological Association, San Antonio, 1984.

FREUD, SIGMUND, *An Outline of Psychoanalysis*. New York: W. W. Norton, 1949.

HAVIGHURST, ROBERT J., "Successful Aging," in *Processes of Aging: Social and Psychological Perspectives*, ed. Richard H. Williams, Clark Tibbitts, and Wilma Donahue, p. 299. New York: Atherton, 1963.

HAVIGHURST, ROBERT J., BERNICE L. NEUGARTEN, and VERN L. BENGTSON, "A Cross-National Study of Adjustment to Retirement," *Gerontologist*, 6 (1966), 137–38.

HENRY, WILLIAM E., "Engagement and Disengagement: Toward a Theory of Adult Development," in *Psychobiology of Aging*, ed. R. Kastenbaum, pp. 19–35. New York: Springer, 1965.

HENRY, WILLIAM E., "The Theory of Intrinsic Disengagement," in *Age with a Future*, ed. P. Form Hansen, pp. 415–18. Copenhagen: Munksgaard, 1964.

JEFFERS, FRANCES C., and CLAUDE R. NICHOLS, "The Effects of Aging on Activities and Attitudes to Physical Well-Being in Older People," in *Normal Aging*, ed. Erdman Palmore, pp. 301–10. Durham, N.C.: Duke University Press, 1970.

JUNG, CARL G., *The Stages of Life*, trans. R. F. C. Hull. Reprinted in *The Portable Jung*, ed. Joseph Campbell, pp. 3–22. New York: Viking, 1971.

KALISH, R. A., "Of Social Values and the Dying: A Defense of Disengagement," *Family Coordinator*, 21 (1972), 81–94.

KAPLAN, HOWARD B., "Age-Related Correlates of Self-Derogation: Contemporary Life Space Characteristics," *Aging and Human Development*, 2 (1971), 305–13.

KIMMEL, DOUGLAS C., *Adulthood and Aging*. New York: John Wiley, 1974.

KUTNER, B., "The Social Nature of Aging," *Gerontologist*, 2, no. 1 (1962), 5–9.

KUYPERS, JOSEPH A., and VERN L. BENGTSON, "Competence and Social Breakdown: A Social-Psychological View of Aging," *Human Development*, 16, no. 2 (1973), 37–49.

LEBO, D., "Some Factors Said to Make for Happiness in Old Age," *Journal of Clinical Psychology*, 9 (1953), 385–90.

LEMON, BRUCE, W., VERN L. BENGTSON, and JAMES A. PETERSON, "Activity Types and Life Satisfaction in a Retirement Community," *Journal of Gerontology*, 27, no. 4 (1972), 511–23.

LIPMAN, A., "Role Conceptions and Morale of Couples in Retirement," *Journal of Gerontology*, 16 (1961), 276–81.

LOETHER, H. J., *Problems of Aging*. Encino, Calif.: Dickenson, 1967.

MCCRAE, R. R., and P. T. COSTA, JR., *Emerging Lives, Enduring Dispositions*. Boston: Little Brown, 1984.

MADDOX, G., "Activity and Morale: A Longitudinal Study of Selected Elderly Subjects," *Social Forces*, 42 (1963), 517–21.

MADDOX, G., "Fact and Artifact: Evidence Bearing on Disengagement Theory," in *Normal Aging*, ed. Erdman Palmore, pp. 318–28. Durham, N.C.: Duke University Press, 1970.

MADDOX, G., "Themes and Issues in Sociological Theories of Human Aging," *Human Development*, 13 (1970), 17–27.

MANIS, JEROME G., and BERNARD N. MELTZER, *Symbolic Interaction: A Reader in Social Psychology*, Boston: Allyn & Bacon, 1972.

MARTIN, W. C., "Activity and Disengagement: Life Satisfaction of In-Movers into a Retirement Community," *Gerontologist*, 13, no. 2 (Summer 1973), 224–27.

MEAD, GEORGE G., ed. *Mind, Self and Society*. Chicago: University of Chicago Press, 1934.

NEUGARTEN, B. L., "New Thoughts on the Theory of Disengagement," in *New Thoughts on Old Age*, ed. R. Kastenbaum, pp. 3–18. New York: Springer, 1964.

NEUGARTEN, B. L., *Personality in Middle and Late Life*. New York: Lieber-Atherton, 1964.

NEUGARTEN, B. L., R. T. HAVIGHURST, AND S. TOBIN, "The Measurement of Life Satisfaction," *Journal of Gerontology*, 16 (1961), 134–43.

NEUGARTEN, B. L., and J. MOORE, "The Changing Status System," in *Middle Age and Aging*, ed. Bernice Neugarten. Chicago: University of Chicago Press, 1968.

NEUGARTEN, B. L., J. W. MOORE, and J. C. LOWE, "Age Norms, Age Constraints, and Adult Socialization," *American Journal of Sociology*, 70 (1965), 710–17.

PALMORE, ERDMAN B., "Differences in the Retirement Patterns of Men and Women," *Gerontologist*, 5 (1965), 4–8.

PECK, R., "Psychological Developments in the Second Half of Life," in *Psychological Aspects of Aging*, ed. J. E. Anderson, pp. 42–53. Washington, D.C.: American Psychological Association, 1956.

PETERSON, JAMES, VERN BENGTSON, and BRUCE LEMON, "An Exploration of the Activity Theory of Aging: Activity Types and Life Satisfaction Among In-Movers to a Retirement Community," *Journal of Gerontology*, 27 (1972), 511–23.

PETERSON, WARREN, Lecture given at a workshop on "Critical Problems of Aging," Indiana State University, 1976.

PHILLIPS, B. S., "A Role Theory Approach to Adjustment in Old Age," *American Sociological Review*, 22 (1957), 212–17.

PRASAD, S. B., "The Retirement Postulate of the Disengagement Theory," *Gerontologist*, 4 (1964), 20–23.

RILEY, M. W., "On the Significance of Age in Sociology," in *Social Structure and Personalities*, ed. Matilda White Riley in association with Bellina Huber and Beth Hess. Beverly Hills: Sage, 1988, pp. 24–42.

RILEY, M. W., M. JOHNSON, and A. FONER, "Aging and Society," in *A Sociology of Age Stratification*, vol. 3. New York: Russell Sage, 1972, pp. 397–456.

ROMAN, P., and P. TAIETZ, "Organizational Structure and Disengagement: The Professor Emeritus," *Gerontologist*, 7 no. 3 (1967), 147–52.

ROSE, A., "A Current Theoretical Issue in Social Gerontology," *Gerontologist*, 4 (1964), 25–29.

ROSE, ARNOLD M., and WARREN H. PETERSON, "The Impact of Aging on Voluntary Associations," in *Handbook of Social Gerontology*, ed. Clark Tibbitts. Chicago: University of Chicago Press, 1960.

ROSOW, I., *Social Integration of the Aged*. New York: Free Press, 1967.

SCHAIE, K. W., "Translations in Gerontology: From Lab to Life," *American Psychologist*, 29 (1974), 802–7.

SIMPSON, IDA, *Social Aspects of Aging* (2nd ed.). Durham, N.C.: Duke University Press, 1972.

STRACHEY, JAMES, and W. D. ROBSON, ed., trans., *Sigmund Freud: The Future of an Illusion*. Garden City, N.Y.: Doubleday, 1961.

STREIB, GORDON F., "Are the Aged a Minority Group?" in *Middle Age and Aging*, ed. Bernice Neugarten, pp. 35–46. Chicago: University of Chicago Press, 1968.

STRYKER, SHELDON, "Symbolic Interaction as an Approach to Family Research," *Marriage and Family Living*, 21 (1959), 111–19.

TALLMER, M., and B. KUTNER, "Disengagement and the Stress of Aging," *Journal of Gerontology*, 24 (1969), 70–75.

THOMAS, W. I., *Primitive Behavior: An Introduction to the Social Sciences*. New York: McGraw-Hill, 1937.

THOMPSON, W. E., and G. STREIB, "Personal and Social Adjustments in Retirement," in *The New Frontiers of Aging*, ed. W. Donahue and C. Tibbitts. Ann Arbor: University of Michigan Press, 1957.

TOBIN, S., and B. L. NEUGARTEN, "Life Satisfaction and Social Interaction in the Aging," *Journal of Gerontology*, 16 (1961), 344–46.

WILLIAMS, RICHARD H., CLARK TIBBITTS, and WILMA DONAHUE, eds., *Processes of Aging: Social and Psychological Perspectives*, vol. 2. New York: Atherton, 1963.

YARROW, M. R., and O. W. QUINN, "Social Psychological Aspects of Aging," Paper presented to the annual meeting of the Midwest Psychological Association, Chicago, 1957.

YOUMANS, E. G., "Some Perspectives of Disengagement Theory," *Gerontologist*, 9 (1969), 254–58.

ZUSMAN, JACK, "Some Explanations of the Changing Appearance of Psychotic Patients: Antecdents of the Social Breakdown Syndrome Concept," *Millbank Memorial Fund Quarterly*, 64, no. 1 (January 1966), 2.

NOTES

1. Douglas Kimmel, *Adulthood and Aging* (New York: John Wiley, 1974), p. 27.
2. R. A. Kalish, "Of Social Values and the Dying: A Defense of Disengagement," *Family Coordinator*, 21 (1972), 81–94.
3. Robert J. Havighurst, "Successful Aging," in *Processes of Aging: Social and Psychological Perspectives*, ed. Richard H. Williams, Clark Tibbitts, and Wilma Donahue (New York: Atherton, 1963), p. 299.
4. Fred Cottrell and Robert C. Atchley, *Retired Women: A Preliminary Report* (Oxford, Ohio: Scripps Foundation, 1969).
5. Sigmund Freud, *An Outline of Psychoanalysis* (New York: W. W. Norton, 1949), pp. 14–37.
6. Ibid., p. 17.
7. Ibid., p. 37.
8. Erik Erikson, *Childhood and Society*, 2nd ed. (New York: W. W. Norton, 1964), pp. 219–31.
9. Gordon F. Streib, "Are the Aged a Minority Group?" in *Middle Age and Aging*, ed. Bernice Neugarten (Chicago: University of Chicago Press, 1968).
10. James J. Dowd, "Aging as Exchange: A Preface to Theory," *Journal of Gerontology*, 30 (1975), 584–94.
11. Ibid.
12. Joseph A. Kuypers and Vern L. Bengtson, "Competence and Social Breakdown: A Social-Psychological View of Aging," *Human Development*, 16, no. 2 (1973), 37–49.

3

Historical
and Cross-Cultural
Comparisons of Aging

INTRODUCTION

Whereas sociologists are likely to examine in great detail the older person's roles, status, functional utility, and lifestyle in a particular culture at one point in time, anthropologists most often compare and contrast these variables and their interrelationships in a variety of cultures. Comparisons of the position and status of older persons in different cultures have yielded a number of patterns, which vary with the type of culture and the perceived role of older persons in it.

Every society has a group of persons who are defined as old. *Age grading* seems to be a universal phenomenon in all societies: Anthropologists maintain that without exception every society has divided its people into categories based on age. At different points in history, however, the age at which one was considered old has varied considerably. Forty-year-olds in many primitive societies would have been considered very old, having outlived the great majority of their cohorts.

According to Thomlinson (1965) the potential *life span* of humans is about 120 years, if deaths from all causes except degenerative diseases are eliminated.[1] However, *life expectancy*—the age to which the average person can expect to live—has varied considerably over time. Archaeologists have studied the age at death of our prehistoric ancestors and concluded that about 95 percent of them died before the age of 40. An estimated 75 percent did not reach the age of 30. (See Table 3–1.) The high mortality rates in the prehistoric period are presumed most often to be the result of periodic famine and frequent malnutrition, each a characteristic of unstable food supplies.

Shelburne Cook (1972) has estimated that less than half the Greek population in the Hellenistic and Roman eras reached what we would today consider young adulthood. Those who survived the precarious early years of life might have expected to live longer than average since many babies died during childbirth and early childhood.[2] Figure 3–1 indicates life expectancy at age 15 in various historical periods.

Cook has also observed that at birth the ancient Egyptian male could have expected to live approximately 22 years. Those who survived early childhood

TABLE 3–1 Percentages of Prehistoric Populations to Have Died by Ages 30, 40, and 50

	Age 30	Age 40	Age 50
Neanderthal	80.0%	95.0%	100.0%
Cro-Magnon	61.7	88.2	90.0
Mesolithic	86.3	95.5	97.0

Source: Shelburne Cook, "Aging of and in Populations," in *Developmental Physiology and Aging*, ed. P. S. Timiras (New York: Macmillan, 1972), p. 595.

could have expected to live to be 25, and those who reached age 25 could probably have expected to live to age 48.[3]

It is estimated that during the Middle Ages the average male at birth lived to be approximately 33.[4] David Fischer (1978) observes that the first census in the United States was taken in 1790, at which time less than 20 percent of the American population survived to the age of 70; today more than 80 percent can expect to do so.

In the early historical period the old were usually valued because their experience and knowledge were useful for the survival of the entire culture. The old held the culture's customs and traditions. Only the advent of senility could diminish the esteem in which they were held, and even then they were sometimes given special statuses.

Although the old were generally accorded a much higher status in primitive societies than they are in modern industrial nations, there was, of course, considerable disparity in how they were treated. According to Fischer (1978), statements by the Greek historian Herodotus indicate that at one extreme the Issedones gilded the heads of their aged parents and offered sacrifices before them. They seemed to worship their oldest tribal members. At the opposite extreme were the people of Bactria, who disposed of their old folk by feeding them to flesh-eating dogs. Similarly, the Sardinians hurled their elders from a high cliff and shouted with laughter as they fell on the rocks below.[5]

One difficulty anthropologists have in comparing the roles, status, and general position of older persons across cultures is that some form of stratification exists in every society, and not all older persons are treated alike. Simone de Beauvoir (1972) observes that the role of the aged in any historical study is described from the male point of view. She notes it is men who express themselves in laws, books, and legends, essentially because the struggle for power has in the past been considered the concern of the "stronger sex." Among the apes, young males wrest power from old males; they alone are killed, not the aged females.

Traditional China granted old men a privileged position. This was a value of the prevalent Confucian ideology. In politics and in the family aged men occupied the top positions in a hierarchical society that lasted for thousands of years. In the family, everyone deferred to the oldest man. The wife was expected to be obedient to her husband, the son obeyed the father, and the younger son was obedient to the older son. The father literally had the power of life or death over his children. He arranged their marriages and supervised both his children and their

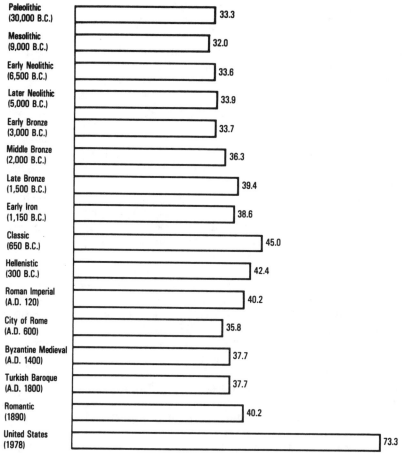

FIGURE 3–1   Life Expectancy at Age 15 for Different Historical Periods

Source: Adapted from J. Lawrence Angel, "Paleoecology, Paleodemography, and Health," in *Population, Ecology and Social Evolution,* ed. Steven Polgar (Chicago: Aldine, 1975), pp. 167–90.

children throughout his life. The oldest male's wife also occupied a role of respect over both the younger males and the younger females of the family. At 50 the man gained in importance; at approximately 70 he turned the household over to the oldest son and began to be worshiped as an ancestor.

Fischer (1978) mentions a stratification system among the aged: For slaves and servants old age was probably so cruel that an early death was a kind of blessing, but for the elite old age delivered the protection of power and property. Fischer also points out that old men were so important to the government of Rome that Cicero argued they were indispensable. Without old men, Cicero felt, there would be no civilized states at all.

DEMOGRAPHIC TRANSITION AND THE AGING
OF THE WORLD'S POPULATION

In discussing how population growth is related to culture and industrial development, contemporary demographers have developed a theory that a predictable pattern of population growth can be observed as the economic base of a culture changes from agricultural to industrial. This pattern, labeled *demographic transition,* is characterized by three distinct stages. In stage one we find a simple agricultural society in which there are high birthrates and simultaneously high death rates, resulting in a relatively stable population. Many children die in infancy and few people reach old age. A high birthrate is necessary to replace the dying and to guarantee the survival of the society. Social values emphasize large families with many children.

The second stage of demographic transition finds the underdeveloped agricultural country beginning to experience social change, adopt new technologies, and industrialize. Often new agricultural practices result in an increasing food supply, and more people can be fed. Simultaneously, new knowledge about health, sanitation, and medicine means that more lives are saved and people begin to live longer. These changes result in a high birthrate and a low death rate. The population of the society grows very rapidly. Demographers have long worried that as the underdeveloped countries in the world reach this stage of development the world and its resources will not be able to tolerate the resulting population explosion. Many countries, such as China and India, already had very large populations before experiencing stage two of the demographic transition. Government planners have tried to formulate policies that will enable their developing countries to avoid stage two. The current mainland Chinese government discourages large families, using instead the one-child family as the model for the society. The basic cause of the population explosion in stage two is that large families are no longer needed to offset premature deaths, but the people's values still endorse having large numbers of children.

By stage three of the demographic transition a nation is becoming industrialized and urbanized. Many young people leave the farm and move to the city to improve themselves economically. In urban areas children are no longer an economic asset, as they were on the farm, and families begin to have fewer of them. On the farm every child is a potential worker, but in the cities children contribute little to the economic well-being of the family until grown and are often considered a financial burden. Thus, the third stage of the demographic transition produces a shift in values such that small families are now emphasized. The birthrate is low and the death rate is low, and once again the population stabilizes. The Western European countries and the United States are examples of countries that have arrived at stage three: They are industrialized and have relatively stable populations.

An issue that the theorists of the demographic transition did not initially address is the changes that will occur in the age and sex composition of the population. In stage one we are likely to find a high proportion of young people and a small proportion of elderly in the population. The high birthrate results in the high proportion of young people in the population, and the high death rate results in a low proportion of old people since so few live to old age. There tend to be similar numbers of men and women in the population.

In stage two we still get a high proportion of young since people's values still endorse large families, but we simultaneously get a gradual increase in life expectancy since fewer die at any age in life. We still have a smaller proportion of old than young in the population.

In stage three, however, values have shifted and small families become the norm, resulting in fewer young people in the population. Moreover, medical technology has developed to the point that a large share of the population is living to old age. Whereas the old previously constituted 1 to 4 percent of the total population in agricultural societies, in the modern industrial nations they compose from 10 to 15 percent and demographers are predicting that these figures will go even higher. Furthermore, women tend to outlive men, resulting in an inbalanced sex ratio. As Donald Cowgill (1986) notes, "modern aging populations are more and more female and a greater proportion of them are widows."[6]

As was pointed out in Chapter 1, the family's responsibility for the care of its older members in times when the population is aging does not equal its sense of responsibility for younger members. And today the old are the fastest-growing segment of the world's population. Melvin Goldstein and Cynthia Beall (1982), citing 1980 United Nations data, observe that never have there been as many elderly as there are in the world today. By the end of the century the great majority of the world's elderly are expected to be found in the less developed countries (LDCs):

> The number of people aged 65 and over in the L.D.C.'s reached 129 million in 1980 and gained equivalency with the number of elderly in the D.C.'s [see Figure 3–2]. It is estimated that by the year 2000, 58% of the elderly (229 million) will reside in L.D.C.'s compared with only 42% (167 million) in D.C.'s. (United Nations 1980). Thus despite the low life expectancy and relatively small proportion of elderly typical in the L.C.D.'s (3.9% of the total population in 1980 vs. 11.4% in the D.C.'s) the actual number of the elderly living there is at an unprecedented high level and is increasing at a faster annual rate than in the D.C.'s. It is estimated that between 1980 and 2000 the number of elderly will increase by 29.5% in the D.C.'s and 77.5% in the L.D.C.'s (United Nations 1980).[7]

The response to the growing number and percentage of the population being elderly in developing nations has been quite diverse according to Linda Martin (1991). Cambodia, Laos, Malaysia, and Singapore have developed pronatalist policies. They are encouraging families to have larger numbers of children to offset the effects of an aging population. Prime Minister Lee Kuan Yew first suggested a pronatalist policy in Singapore in 1983 because the more educated women were not marrying and reproducing to the extent of those less educated. In 1987 the government introduced incentives for having three or more children. The birth of a third child resulted in a tax rebate of about $12,000 for working mothers, and an additional rebate of 15 percent of earned income.[8] As a rule government policies to encourage families to increase or decrease family size have not succeeded. The Singapore incentives are generous, however, and only time will tell if there is an increase in family size in that country.

A different reaction to an aging population in a developing country has come from Japan. The Japanese government is attempting to encourage older workers to remain working longer. Japan has given firms that retain workers beyond the age of 60 as much as $300 per worker per month.[9]

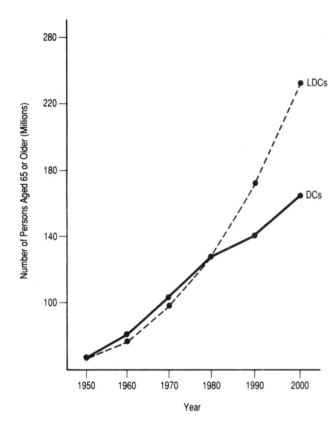

FIGURE 3–2
Increase in the Number of Persons Age 65 and Older in Developed Countries (DC) and Less Developed Countries (LDC) between 1950 and 2000

Source: Compiled from United Nations Population Division, Working Paper No. ESA/P/WP65 (1980), by Melvin C. Goldstein and Cynthia M. Beall, "Indirect Modernization and the Status of the Elderly in a Rural Third World Setting," *Journal of Gerontology*, 37, no. 6 (1982). Copyright © The Gerontological Society of America.

MODERNIZATION AND AGING

As a general rule, in nonindustrial, settled, agricultural societies the aged exercise considerable power and are granted high status. In industrial societies, on the other hand, the aged exercise relatively little power and are granted less status. Donald Cowgill and Lowell Holmes (1972), in their work on aging and modernization, found an inverse relationship between the degree of modernization in a culture and the status it accords older persons. In other words, the more industrialized the culture, the lower the status of the older person.

A closer look, however, reveals differential treatment of the elderly even in traditional societies. Tom Sheehan (1976), in a study of 47 traditional societies, found two different patterns of treatment of the aged. Approximately one fifth of these societies were geographically unstable, with semipermanent bands periodically relocating their villages, or, more rarely, being perpetually mobile. The lowest esteem for seniors was often found in these small and nomadic societies. Such societies have the fewest material resources, thus depriving seniors of an important means of gaining respect in the eyes of the young, and are usually located in harsh environments, which favor youth and vigor. Moreover, food is often in short supply and individual existence is precarious. The elderly may have to be sacrificed to insure the survival of the group. The majority of the societies

Sheehan studied consisted of tribes settled more or less permanently in fairly large villages and governed by a belief in their common ancestry or kinship. Another group of traditional societies were centered in agriculture or animal husbandry. The most highly developed social organizations were found in the societies with large landed peasantries; it was in these societies that older persons enjoyed the highest esteem.

It appears that once traditional societies become permanently located with stated residence and property rights, the old begin to exercise considerable power over the young by owning property and deciding who gets to inherit it. Where property is the only means of production, the aged can control the younger generations by controlling the property. The future occupations and chances for success of the younger generation are tied to the favor of their elders, who control all the resources. While one's parents are alive they are of critical importance because they provide employment and the means of survival in the form of resources. After they die, those who inherit their lands control these resources for themselves and their children. Therefore, in traditional societies that are permanently located, the individual is directly dependent upon the senior generation for the acquisition of the means of production. The anticipated transfer of property to the children at the death of the parent encourages the young to respect their older family members. It is easy to see why the young defer to their elders and seek their special favor. Similarly, it is easy to understand how the old, by developing stable institutions and controlling property, can maintain their power and privilege in the social system. This may also explain the higher value placed on the family in rural America, where the transmission of land to the next generation may secure that generation a livelihood and a secure position in the social structure.

Thus, rather than Cowgill and Holmes's (1972) prediction of an inverse relationship between the degree of modernization and the status accorded older persons, we find a curvilinear one: The old are accorded low status in simple nomadic societies, high status in settled agricultural communities, and low status in modern industrial nations. Moreover, a number of authors have argued that in the postindustrial period, which much of Western Europe and the United States appears to be entering, we are seeing a bottoming out of the low status accorded the elderly and a slight rise in their position (Palmore & Manton, 1974; Keith, 1980). Jennie Keith, for example, points out that

> in the present USSR and in the U.S. during the Depression . . . national pension funds have made older people quite literally valuable and sought after members of households. Such national support systems are one reason that the relationship between modernization and old people's status appears on closer examination to be curvilinear, i.e., the decline in status associated with modernization bottoms out and is reversed in most industrial societies.[10]

Thus our curvilinear relationship appears to be bimodal—starting at a low point in simple nomadic societies, reaching a high point in settled agricultural communities, dropping to a lower status during industrialization, and returning to a slightly higher status in the postindustrial period.

Tom Sheehan (1976) equates what happens to older persons in nomadic tribes with what happens to them in modern industrial societies. He believes that with the development of modern technology, social and geographic mobility become goals and individual autonomy reemerges as a primary value. The young forfeit the security of the village or family to work in factories and offices. They attain financial and social separation from many traditional restraints. Lifestyles turn away from extended family ties. There is now no special reason for younger family members to secure the favor of their parents and grandparents. The older family members lose the status, decision-making power, and security they had in earlier cultural settings. The result is that the old are considered much less valuable in the modern state. Thus in both nomadic and industrial cultural settings the old quickly become dependent on the young for their well-being and survival.

CRITICISM OF THE MODERNIZATION THEORY

The modernization theory advanced by Cowgill and Holmes (1972) is a generalization about the status of the elderly in a variety of cultures and over long periods. As with many other scientific generalizations, the critics have been able to point out many exceptions to the general principle. Bengtson et al. (1975:689) have observed that the theory suffers "from a romanticized and naive portrayal of eldership in pre-industrial society." They apparently feel that the aged might not even have had the universal high status predicted for them in the settled agricultural countries. Other critics have charged that there is considerable variation in the status of the elderly within any society and that social class and gender probably account for more of the variation than does the kind of culture (Dowd, 1980; Williamson, Evans & Powell, 1982).

Leo Simmons (1945) was one of the first to study the status of the elderly on a cross-cultural basis. He observed that in all societies we must specify which aged we are speaking of—the ill or the healthy, the chronologically ancient or only the generationally elderly, the male heads of households or the familyless widows, the wise leaders or the village failures. Corinne Nydegger asserts that anthropological studies have shown that generalizations about the "esteem of the aged" are generally as superficial and just plain wrong in other societies as in our own.

Others have charged that there is a considerable difference between the ideal—normative statements people make about how the elderly are treated—and the real—the conditions they actually live under (Williamson, Evans, & Powell, 1982:59). Thus anthropological accounts of what members of a society say about how the elderly are treated may reflect the idealized norms of the group rather than the actual treatment.

In every society the ability to function is crucial. The frail elderly will generally experience a loss of status (Glascock & Feinman, 1981). Feebleness is not valued in any society (Nydegger, 1985). It is easy to maintain high status for the elderly when they constitute a low percentage of the population and only the strong among them survive. It is another matter when they compose a high percentage of the population and many are frail.

Even in settled agricultural communities not all of the aged are large landowners able to exercise power and status. Nydegger (1985) observes that control of resources is incorrectly attributed to the aged as a group when in fact resources are differentially distributed among them. Where the elderly accumulate power they do command respect, but the respect is due to their power and not their age (Press & McKool, 1972). Moreover, the industrialization of Japan since World War II has produced the shift to a lower status for the Japanese elderly that Cowgill and Holmes (1972) predicted. David Plath (1983) points out the changing status of the elderly in Japan:

> These days when elders do live with married children, family power and authority almost always are in the younger hands, and from the junior's point of view, it is best for the elders to live separately—close by, perhaps, but nevertheless apart. The ideal husband, says the slogan, is one who comes re-Tsuki, Ka-tsuki, babanuki (without house, without car, without granny).[11]

It appears that the modernization theory predicted accurately the loss of status of elderly Japanese as the nation industrialized.

CRITICAL VARIABLES DETERMINING THE STATUS OF THE AGED

A number of variables, separately or more often in some combination, seem to affect the status accorded older persons in various cultures. These include family form, religion, knowledge base of the culture, harshness of the environment, means of production, speed of social change, and percentage of elderly in the population.

Family Form

The form of the family is often related to cultural type and to the structural relations among the institutions in a society. In traditional societies that are primarily agricultural, the extended family (most often comprising mother, father, their sons, and their sons' wives and children) is often the prevalent form. The extended family is most often *patriarchial*, which means that power and lineage are traced through the male side of the family. The wife, upon marriage, moves in with the husband's family, and when children are old enough to marry, the parents arrange for their marriages and expect the wives of their sons to move into their household and their daughters to move into the households of their husbands.

In this family arrangement the oldest male member of the family exercises the greatest power, privilege, and authority. Individualism is discouraged. The individual is always subserviant to the demands of the group. The concept of romantic love (strong, intense emotional attachment between members of the opposite sex) is nonexistent; marital success depends on the amount of family disruption caused by the entrance of the new bride. If she gets along well with her in-laws and does not cause problems in the family setting, the marriage is considered good. The son's happiness is secondary to the good of the group. The extended family works best in stable cultures that are primarily agricultural. As we have seen, it is also in such cultures that the older members exercise the greatest power and maintain the highest status.

Industrialization leads to the breakup of the extended family. One no longer depends upon land as the principal means of production. New jobs, careers, resources, and opportunities become available. Modern industry requires labor that can be moved from place to place as needed. Extended-family ties are broken in the process. If the labor force were not mobile, the industrial system would break down. The nuclear family—husband, wife, and children—becomes dominant. The influence of the father and mother over adult children is weakened. The size of the family declines as children become units of consumption rather than production and thereby become less desirable.

The difference between extended and nuclear families in terms of the status of the aged can perhaps best be seen in Israel. Hanna Weihl (1970) observes that the older people among the migrants from the Orient are given higher status than the older immigrants from the Western countries. The migrants from the Orient evidence considerable commitment to the concept of the extended family, in contrast to the commitment to the nuclear family evidenced by migrants from the West.

Religion

The ethical codes of the religions of the Far East have generally supported the extended family and the higher status of its elder members. Confucianism dictates that the aged are to be given tender loving care and are to be exempt from certain responsibilities. In pre–World War II families in China and Japan, children cared for their elders and older family members exercised the most authority. This meant also that the elders were the most respected members of the family.

Although Christianity clearly admonishes people to honor their fathers and mothers, this principle has probably had less impact in the Western world than one might expect. The pressure of industrialization results in the educational functions of family socialization being gradually replaced by formal training outside the home. Wealth changes from land to tangible property. The emphasis shifts to productivity. Degradation generally occurs for the older, and supposedly slower, workers.

Knowledge Base

In traditional agricultural societies, the old are the reservoirs of knowledge—of past problems and their solutions, of old customs and the appropriate religious rituals. In industrial societies, books, libraries, universities, and current research enterprises are bases for the generation and transmittal of knowledge. The freshly trained college student is often more valuable in the business and industrial world than the older and more experienced employee, whose knowledge and expertise may have become obsolete. American society has a sophisticated educational system that prepares young people to enter an occupation, but it is ill equipped to retrain older workers when this is required by new technologies. The inability to maintain control of critical knowledge in modern society has thus been another factor in the general loss of status of older persons.

Harshness of the Environment

The harshness of the environment and the amount of physical labor required for survival can reduce the usefulness and thereby the status of the older members of a culture. The Sirono of the Bolivian rain forest, for example, generally believe that

> the aged are quite a burden; they eat but are unable to hunt, fish, or collect food; they sometimes hoard a young spouse, but are unable to beget children; they move at a snail's pace and hinder the mobility of the group. When a person becomes too ill or infirm to follow the fortunes of the band, he is abandoned to shift for himself.[12]

Cowgill and Holmes (1972) note that there is some difficulty in adjusting to reduced activity in old age in a society dedicated to hard physical labor. Kibbutz society in Israel is one example; there, older persons may arrive at an ambiguous status because of their inability to keep up physically with younger people.

Speed of Social Change

Related to the changing knowledge base in modern society is the speed with which social change occurs in a culture. Cowgill and Holmes (1972) believe that rapid social change in modern societies tends to undermine the status of older persons. Change renders many of the skills of older Americans obsolete. They can no longer ply their trade, and so there is no reason for them to teach it to others. In a rapidly changing society the younger people are nearly always better educated, especially about recent technology, than their elders. Thus the latter lose their utility and the basis of their authority.

Referring to both the speed of social change in modern society and the location of the knowledge base in a society, Wilbur Watson and Robert Maxwell (1977) hypothesize that societies can be arranged along a continuum whose basis is the amount of useful information controlled by the aged. They believe that the more the elders control critical information, the greater their participation in community affairs will be. Their participation is in turn directly related to the degree of esteem in which they are held by other members of the community. Watson and Maxwell believe this control of information and consequent social participation decline with industrialization and its rapid sociocultural change.[13]

Watson and Maxwell (1977) argue that one of the most fruitful approaches to the investigation of human societies relies heavily on the information storage and exchange model known as *systems theory*.[14] Erving Goffman (1959) has demonstrated that groups that share secret information tend to be more unified than those that do not. All stored information, according to Goffman, involves a stated arrangement of elements in the sense that it is a record of past events.[15]

In traditional societies, one of the main functions of old people is to remember legends, myths, ethical principles, and the appropriate relations with the supernatural, and they are frequently asked about these matters. Elliott (1886) described this pattern among the Aleuts of northern Russia:

> Before the advent of Russian priests, every village had one or two old men at least, who considered it their special business to educate the children; thereupon, in the morning or evening when all were home these aged teachers would seat themselves in the center of one of the largest village courts or oolagumuh; the young folks surrounded them and listened attentively to what they said.[16]

Watson and Maxwell (1977) believe that the printing press ended this kind of arrangement. In industrialized societies the important information is written down, printed, and sold in bookstores.[17]

Some historians have argued that older people are economically, politically, and socially more conservative than younger people and tend to have a stabilizing effect on any social system. The young, being much more changeable, offer adaptability and in some ways may increase their chances for survival of the social system.

The adult members of a society tend to hold secure, comfortable, and often high-status roles. To them any rapid social change might undermine their current status and position. The young, on the other hand, are attempting to fit themselves into desirable roles in order to acquire status, privilege, and power. Rapid social change often offers them the possibility of a number of new roles they may well be qualified to fill. Thus the middle-aged and older members of society are likely to favor stability rather than change in the social order, while the young are more likely to favor social change.

Percentage of Elderly in the Population

In most of the traditional societies of Africa, Asia, and Latin America, the old constitute less than 3 percent of the population. It is easy to reserve a special status for such a small group. In most of the European countries, the United States, and Australia, the old comprise from 10 to 17 percent of the population. It may become increasingly difficult to preserve a privileged status for a group that comprises such a large percentage of the population. (See Table 3–2.)

THEORETICAL VIEWS ON THE CHANGING STATUS OF THE ELDERLY

Proponents of sociological *functionalism* (introduced in the discussion of disengagement theory in Chapter 2) have always maintained that a society is much like a human organism: In each of these systems, all the parts fit together in a cooperative, interdependent relationship. Sociologists generally believe that the family, religious, educational, economic, and political systems constitute five basic institutions existing in every society. The beliefs, behavior patterns, and normative expectations that emerge from these institutions are complementary and overlapping. The cooperative interdependence of these institutions is what makes the survival of a society possible. Much of the research by archaeologists, anthropologists, and sociologists on the power, privilege, and status obtained by older people in different societies has been conducted from a functionalist perspective.

The findings thus far indicate that premodern sociocultural systems come basically in two broad categories: nomadic tribes and permanently settled agrarian societies. Nomadic tribes frequently live in harsh environments in which the very survival of the group is often in doubt. Aged members cannot move as quickly as the tribe needs nor do they have the skill to provide for their own sustenance, let alone that of other members. At some point they become a detriment to the group and have to be discarded. In other words, if the tribe attempts to feed and transport some of its oldest members, the survival of the entire group might be in doubt. Under those conditions the old exercise little power and are accorded relatively low status.

TABLE 3–2 Percent of Population 65 and Over, 1980 (Countries with 5 Million or More)

Young Populations (Less than 4%)
2%—Ivory Coast, Afghanistan
3%—Morocco, Sudan, Ghana, Guinea, Mali, Niger, Nigeria, Senegal, Upper Volta, Kenya, Madagascar, Malawi, Mozambique, Rwanda, Tanzania, Uganda, Zambia, Zimbabwe, Angola, Zaire, Iraq, Saudi Arabia, Syria, Yemen, Bangladesh, India, Iran, Nepal, Pakistan, Sri Lanka, Kampuchea, Indonesia, Philippines, Thailand, Guatemala, Dominican Republic, Bolivia, Peru, Venezuela

Youthful Populations (4%–6%)
4%—Algeria, Egypt, Tunisia, Somalia, Cameroon, South Africa, Turkey, Burma, Malaysia, Vietnam, North Korea, South Korea, Mexico, Haiti, Brazil, Colombia, Ecuador
5%—Ethiopia, Taiwan
6%—China, Chile

Mature Aging Populations (7%–9%)
7%—Hong Kong
8%—Cuba
9%—Japan, Canada, Argentina, Yugoslavia

Aged Populations (10% and Over)
10%—Poland, Romania, Australia
11%—United States, Portugal, Spain
12%—Netherlands, Bulgaria, Czechoslovakia
13%—France, Hungary, Greece
14%—Belgium, West Germany, Switzerland, Italy
15%—Denmark, United Kingdom, Austria, East Germany
17%—Sweden

Source: Population Reference Bureau, *1983 World Population Data Sheet* (Washington, D.C.: Population Reference Bureau, April 1983). Data are centered on the year 1980.

In a settled agrarian society, agriculture is likely the main business and land the principle means of production. Stable institutions and the established right to own land considerably change the power, privilege, and status of older persons. By controlling the means of production in the form of land ownership, the aged maintain their status long after their physical dexterity begins to wane. Moreover, they occupy an advantaged position in the family, religion, and knowledge base of their society. They are the reservoirs of knowledge, customs, the past, and religious rituals. They become functionally important to their society's chance of survival and are therefore accorded a high status.

Industrialization changes the family structure, knowledge base, educational institutions, economy, religion, and governmental structure of a sociocultural system. The nuclear family becomes the norm and there is considerably less commitment to extended-family members. The industrial economy demands a mobile labor force, which in turn necessitates the breaking of extended-family ties. The knowledge base of the system shifts from its senior members to bookstores, libraries, colleges, and research enterprises. Productivity is of prime value, but the old are seen as less productive and are therefore generally devalued. Rapid social change makes much of the knowledge and many of the skills of old persons obsolete. Thus, modern industrial nations find their older members to be of less utility to the survival of the system, and they accord them low status and less wealth and resources.

The functionalist school of thought in the social sciences is often challenged by other theoretical perspectives. One such perspective, symbolic interactionism, can be utilized in analyzing the status of the elders in a society.

Symbolic interactionists have tended to rely heavily on the concept of social roles in explaining the behavior of individuals and their relationship in a group. Rather than asking about the functional importance of older persons' roles in the survival of the system, they want to know (1) what roles older persons are expected to assume and (2) what value is attached to these roles by others in society. It may well be that the role of religious leader, whether priest or Brahman, is not crucial to the survival of the system if the system could survive in the absence of the role. What is important is how valuable the role of religious leader is believed to be by others in the society. Thus, in the extended family we find that the role of grandparent is highly valued and respected. In the conjugal family, on the other hand, we find the role of grandparent reduced to baby-sitting. In terms of utility to the sociocultural system, the grandparent role is probably about equally important in different cultures, but it is accorded considerably more importance and thereby status in one culture than it is in others.

From the symbolic interaction perspective, anthropologists and sociologists should pay close attention to the following factors in examining the position of the aged in any sociocultural system:

1. The roles the aged assume in the society
2. The value attached to these roles by other persons in the society
3. Whether the roles performed by elders represent role continuity or role discontinuity (that is, whether or not the roles they occupy at one stage of life prepare them for the skills they will need at the next stage of life)

ROLES AND STATUS OF THE AGED IN THREE CULTURES

The Abkhasians: Role Continuity in Later Life

Sula Benet, in a 1971 issue of *The New York Times Magazine,* wrote an article entitled "Why They Live to Be 100, or Even Older, in Abkhasia." Whether the Abkhasians are as old as they claim, they provide an example of a group in which role continuity from one stage of life to the next is the expected and practiced pattern. In addition, the Abkhasians enjoy secure roles and statuses in extended families that are relatively constant throughout the life cycle. Whereas Americans lose status during their later years and people in many Oriental cultures gain status during their later years, older Abkhasians maintain virtually the same status in later life.

The Abkhasians live in a rough mountainous region northeast of the Black Sea in southern Russia. Members of this society are believed to regularly live to be 120 years or older. After visiting the region Benet wrote,

> In the village of Dzhgerda, . . . there were 71 men and 110 women between 81 and 90 and 19 people over 91—15 percent of the village population of 1,200. . . . In 1954, the last year for which overall figures are available, 2.58 percent of the Abkhasians were over 90. The roughly comparable figures for the entire Soviet Union and the United States were 0.1 and 0.4 percent, respectively.[18]

Abkhasia is described as a very hard land to scrape a living out of. Abkhasians, recognizing the harshness of their environment, say that it is one of God's afterthoughts, but a beautiful one. Many Abkhasians are between 80 and 120 and still go to work every day. A Russian scientist writes,

> After spending months with them, I still find it impossible to judge the age of older Abkhasians. Their general appearance does not provide a clue. You know they are old because of their gray hair and the lines on their faces but are they 70 or 107? There is no way to tell.[19]

At 100 years of age and older, according to the reports of the Russian scientists who have visited them, most work regularly, are still blessed with good eyesight, and have most of their own teeth. Most of them take walks of more than two miles a day and swim in the mountain streams.

For centuries the Abkhasians have been horsemen, and they believe it is very important to be lightweight. According to Benet, there is a saying among the Abkhasians that when one lies on his side he should be so small around the middle that a dog can pass beneath him.

Since 1932 the Soviet government has sent doctors, psychologists, sociologists, and other scientists to study the reasons for the Abkhasian longevity. The findings indicate that 40 percent of the elderly men and 30 percent of the elderly women can see well enough to thread a needle without wearing glasses. Forty percent had not experienced any loss in hearing. A nine-year study of Abkhasians over 100 reported no cases of either mental illness or cancer. According to the Soviet scientists, all showed clear and logical thinking, and most correctly estimated their physical and mental capacities. Abkhasians are hospitalized only rarely, for stomach disorders and childbirth. They apparently set their own broken bones and practice an elaborate system of folk medicine using more than 200 indigenous plants to cure a wide variety of ills. When all else fails they are taken to the hospital, but with the full expectation that they will get well.

The Abkhasians do not have a phrase for old people. Those over 100 are called "long-living" people. Benet described some of the explanations for their longevity that the Soviet scientists have considered. One possible explanation is genetic selection. In wars or other conflicts the Abkhasians have always been cavalrymen. Some scientists feel that repeated hand-to-hand combat during the centuries of Abkhasian existence may have eliminated those with poor eyesight, obesity, and other principal shortcomings, thus producing a healthier group of Abkhasians in each succeeding generation. There are no records with which to substantiate this, however.

Some scientists are inclined to believe that the Abkhasians live as long as they do because of their diet and the value they attach to remaining slim. Benet reports that overeating "is considered dangerous in Abkhasians and fat people are regarded as ill." Their diet consists of fruits, vegetables, and meat. Body fat and blood cholesterol are considerably lower in Abkhasians than in industrial workers, and heart attacks and circulatory problems much less common.

The Abkhasians themselves, according to Benet, believe that their longevity is due to their sex practices and work habits. Their values are strongly ingrained with self-discipline, in work and in sexual matters as well. Thus, an Abkhasian is expected to conserve his or her sexual energies rather than grasping at whatever sweetness is available at the moment. The norms of the culture call for sexual relations to be postponed until after 30—the traditional age of marriage. It was once even considered unmanly for a new husband to exercise his sexual rights on the wedding night. Abkhasian men have been known to father children at the age of 100. Sex, to the Abkhasians, is a pleasure to be regulated for the sake of one's health—like good wine it becomes better with age.

The Abkhasians also attach much importance to their work habits, according to Benet. From the beginning of life until its end, Abkhasians do what they are capable of doing because they and those around them consider work vital to their lives. They make demands on themselves that they can meet. During the growing years the demands are increased gradually; during the later years they are decreased gradually. Individuals over the age of 100 decrease their work loads to about four hours a day but lose no status by doing so. Both the Abkhasians and the doctors agree that these work habits have a great deal to do with Abkhasian longevity. Abkhasians candidly state that work helps vital organs to function optimally.

Sociologists and psychologists are likely to view the stability and consistency of the Abkhasians' status throughout the life cycle as well as the degree of social integration in their lives as important factors in their longevity. Abkhasians are born into a family in which their status is ascribed and secure. Their family group is a work group as well as a social group, and they are a part of it throughout their lives. Group identity gives each individual an unshakable feeling of security and continuity, according to those who have studied these people. Abkhasians seem to maintain or gain status throughout the life cycle, and there are no abrupt changes in their lives. A 99-year-old Abkhasian states:

> It isn't time to die yet. I am needed by my children and grandchildren, and it isn't bad in this world—except that I can't turn the earth over and it has become difficult to climb trees.[20]

Another possible explanation for Abkhasian longevity is that physical exercise and exertion are a regular part of their lives. They live in a mountainous region and walk daily. They maintain themselves by being herders and farmers. They work at physical labor daily. They tend to be what the gerontologist would refer to as activity theorists. The Abkhasians say that it is better to move without purpose than it is to sit still.

The Western Model: Role Discontinuity in Later Life

The Abkhasian culture structures work as a daily part of life while gradually increasing the assigned tasks and the amount of skill required to complete them. There is considerable preparation for the next task a person is expected to master. Thus, the Abkhasian way of life stresses a gradual transition from one stage of life to the next and much role continuity. Western industrial nations, by comparison, are typically characterized by considerable role discontinuity, by long periods in which not much is expected of the individual, and by periods, such as retirement, in which not only is the work role removed but simultaneously the individual experiences a loss of status.

In the United States, we find a disjointed pattern of work activities over the life cycle. From birth to somewhere between the ages of 18 and 22 (depending on whether the individual attends college), not much is expected of people in the way of work. They are encouraged to attend school and participate in social and recreational activities, and discouraged from assuming adult responsibilities. If they work at all, they usually do so part-time and primarily for the purpose of having a little spending money. Upon completing their education, Americans are expected to acquire jobs, be totally dedicated to careers and upward mobility, get married, settle down and raise families, and become responsible and respected members of the community. Sociologists are quick to observe that there is considerable role discontinuity in this pattern and considerable lack of preparation of youth for the responsibilities of adulthood. During the 40 to 50 years in which adults are expected to be dedicated to their careers, they have little or no energy left over for leisure pursuits and sometimes not even adequate time for family responsibilities.

Industrial nations usually require their employees to retire at a given age. In the United States the retirement age has been considered 65. Congress in the last few years first passed laws prohibiting mandatory retirement prior to age 70. As of 1992 the law bans mandatory retirement at any age. By law, then, business and industry are currently prohibited from forcing a person to retire at any age. The fact remains, however, that less than 5 percent of the population actually works beyond age 65. Thus, upon retirement people are expected to cease their ambitious striving for success and upward mobility, forget about the previous 40 or 50 years of overriding commitment to work, and sit back and relax during their remaining years. Simultaneously, they experience a considerable drop in status in the eyes of peers and community. Thus industrial nations are often characterized by sudden role shifts and inadequate preparation for the new positions that individuals assume.

Cowgill and Holmes (1972) believe that disengagement is to be expected in modern industrial nations such as the United States. The older people become in these societies, the more likely they are to experience a loss of status, prestige and power. In

> Austria, Norway, and the United States, where individualism is more pronounced, where the work role is largely divorced from the family, and where success is mainly through individual effort and failure is viewed as the individual's responsibility, the status of the aged appears to suffer most; it is here that people feel useless, dread feeling dependent, and play empty roles.[21]

Table 3–3 compares the culture of the long-lived Abkhasians with the culture of the United States, where life expectancy is shorter and an 80-year-old person is considered very old. First, as the Soviet scientists have argued, the Abkhasians may have experienced an evolutionary process in which wars and battles over the centuries tended to kill off their weaker members. The short history of the United States would not allow similar comparisons. The United States has not existed long enough for any long-range evolutionary process to have killed off the weaker. Historians tell us the early immigrants to this country included both the strong and the weak. On the one hand, some early immigrants were European nobles who had been deeded large tracts of land in the American colonies by the English or French king. Simultaneously, however, debtors, vagrants, and criminals were given free passage to the colonies to keep them from overcrowding European jails.

The diet of Abkhasians offers a marked contrast to that of Americans. As

TABLE 3–3 Comparison of the Abkhasian and U.S. Cultures

Category	Abkhasian	United States
Evolution	Hand-to-hand combat may have killed off the weak, creating a stronger group of people.	No long evolutionary process. Early ancestors include both the strong and the weak.
Diet	Believe it important to be slim. Diet is higher in protein.	Tend to overeat. Diet contains a lot of carbohydrates and fatty foods.
Work (roles)	Work throughout the entire life cycle.	Don't work until around 20. Don't work after 65.
Retirement (roles)	Never retire.	Most often forced to retire.
Social Integration	Are part of family and work group throughout life.	Are encouraged to break family ties early. Must be mobile. Move from place to place.
Feeling of Usefulness	Feel useful and needed throughout life.	Often feel a burden on their friends and relatives in old age.
Ascribed vs. Achieved Status	Status throughout life is ascribed.	Outside of sex and age, most status is achieved.
View of Old People	Have no negative feeling or word for the old. Speak of certain individuals being "long-living."	Old is considered bad. Use a variety of cosmetics and dyes to make themselves look young.
Power and Privileges in Old Age	Do not retire or lose status in the later years.	Lose power and privileges at retirement.
Economy	Agricultural.	Industrial.

Source: Adapted from Sula Benet, "Why They Live to Be 100, or Even Older, in Abkhasia," *The New York Times Magazine*, December 26, 1971. © 1971 by The New York Times Company. Reprinted by permission.

observed earlier, the Abkhasians believe it is very important to remain slim. Abkhasians who are even slightly overweight are questioned about their health. Companions will want to know if they have been sick lately. The caloric intake of Abkhasians is 23 percent lower than that of industrial workers. Americans tend to overeat, and their diet is rich in carbohydrates and fatty foods. Being overweight seems to be the norm rather than the exception, particularly for middle-aged and older Americans.

Abkhasians work every day of their lives at some task appropriate to their skill and ability. Thus, as Abkhasian children grow and develop they are given increasingly more complex tasks. Later in the life cycle the work responsibilities of those over 100 may be reduced to four hours a day, but they continue to work every day. The work history of Americans is quite different. Young people don't work at all or work only part-time for approximately the first 20 years of their lives. Then they are expected to work very hard for the next 45 years, in most cases at complex tasks requiring considerable skill. When they arrive at age 65 they are expected to retire, engage in leisure pursuits, and do very little or no productive work. Compared with the work histories of Abkhasians, in which smooth and gradual transitions are made from one stage of life to the next, the U.S. pattern is irregular and disjointed.

There is no way of estimating the effect of these disparate work patterns on longevity, but one cannot help but wonder if the Abkhasian pattern is considerably easier to adjust to. One additional difference in work life between the two cultures is that Abkhasians, having an agricultural economy, are always involved in work requiring considerable physical exertion. A large percentage of the U.S. population works at office tasks or other primarily sedentary jobs requiring little physical exertion. Most doctors believe that regular physical exercise contributes to health and longevity. Moreover, psychological strain often accompanies work in American society: One is expected to be upwardly mobile. Thus, whatever current success and job security one might have, he or she is expected to strive even harder for future promotions and new positions. A degree of psychological insecurity is thereby produced in the individual.

In terms of degree of social integration throughout the life cycle, the ledger clearly favors the Abkhasians. The Abkhasian family is a production unit that works together to produce needed foods and services. From birth to death one is tightly integrated into a close family that is also a work group. The family is both a consumption and a production unit. The American family, by comparison, is a nuclear unit consisting of husband, wife, and children. Though the American family is slightly patriarchal (the husband exercises greater authority), it is moving in the direction of shared responsibility between husband and wife. The family is *neolocal,* the young couple being expected upon marriage to establish a residence independent of either set of in-laws. Shortly after completing one's education or apprenticeship one is expected to break the tie with his or her family or origin, marry, and enter an occupation. Any strong emotional ties to one's parents or extended relatives would be seen as a threat to the industrial system, which requires a mobile labor force. Strong extended-family ties would discourage the individual from moving away from his or her home community. The family system is a small, fragile unit that is broken frequently by divorce. The parent was expected to break family ties early in life, and children 20 years later are expected to do likewise. There is considerably more insecurity, less certainty, and less of a tightly knit group of which one is a part throughout the life cycle.

The Abkhasians, working as part of a family unit throughout their lives, are likely to see their value to the production unit. They feel needed and useful throughout the life cycle. Americans, in contrast, are required to do nothing after retirement. This creates lingering doubts in many individuals of their usefulness during the later years. They are most likely to feel that their usefulness is over and that life has passed them by. Retired Americans frequently speak of themselves as being put out to pasture or placed on the shelf. Such slogans illustrate their self-doubt.

The Abkhasians have an ascribed status throughout their lives. This ascription is most often based on age and sex. That is, certain roles and the accompanying statuses are most often granted to them on these bases. Since desired roles and statuses are automatically granted, there is little pressure to compete for them. American society, on the other hand, has placed a high value on achieved status. Not all positions are granted on the basis of age and sex. Many roles and the statuses they entail go only to a privileged few. Not everyone can become a doctor, a senator, a movie star, or an astronaut. While these positions are highly valued, relatively few achieve them in our sociocultural system. By encouraging all to aspire to the more preferred roles when in fact only a few will achieve them, American culture creates considerable strain for the individual trying to prove his or her worth by achieving such positions. For the many individuals who will not be able to do so, regardless of their efforts, the feelings of guilt and lack of accomplishment are considerable. An ascribed-status system would seem to offer the individual a greater feeling of security.

The Abkhasians have no negative feelings or derogatory terms for old persons. They speak of certain individuals as being long-living, but this carries no negative connotation. In the United States, old is considered bad. Americans invest great amounts of money in a variety of cosmetics from hair dye to facial creams to keep themselves from appearing old. If being old is defined and labeled as undesirable, then one can escape this negative label by not appearing old.

In the Abkhasian culture the old, as senior members of the family, are granted certain privileges and rights that younger members do not have. In the United States older persons lose considerable power and privilege upon retirement. The older they become the more of their former rights they are likely to lose. Self-devaluation during the later years seems unlikely in the Abkhasian system but almost inevitable in the American system.

Many of these differences between the two cultures may be explained in part by the fact that the Abkhasians have an agricultural economy and the United States an industrial economy. The demands of these two productive systems are quite different and result in a considerably different arrangement of the basic social groupings, values, and institutions of the two cultures.

The Sidamo: Aging in a Gerontocratic Society

Cowgill and Holmes's *Aging and Modernization* (1972) contains a chapter by John Hamer on the Sidamo of southwest Ethiopia, who are described as a gerontocratic society. Although Sidamo society is patriarchal, with the males exercising ultimate power over the females, old age in both sexes is highly esteemed. For the males in this society Hamer lists a number of life-crisis periods that include birth, early childhood, initiation, marriage, promotion to elderhood, exalted old age, and death. These are generally viewed as progressive and bring greater status to the individual as he advances through them.

For the males, the father–son relationship stresses respect for the father rather than friendship. The sons, if punishment is necessary, are punished by their fathers. The harshness of the punishment is based on the father's desire to raise the son properly and to keep him from becoming soft and dependent.

According to Hamer, grandfathers rarely, if ever, punish grandsons. They are seen by the young as wise and knowledgeable persons to turn to for advice in times of trouble or difficult decisions. The grandfather–grandson relationship tends to be a warm one.

Most young Sidamo men marry between the ages of 18 and 20, and this may be the period of greatest tension between father and son.

> The reason is that the father is the one who provides ego with the land, animals, and bridewealth which enable him to marry and begin to accumulate wealth. Fathers allocate a share of land to each son at marriage, with a slightly larger share going to the eldest. In addition, fathers often pick favorites, and though they cannot show partiality in the distribution of land, they may indulge one son at the other's expense by providing him with a larger share of animals and money.[22]

This system of land distribution results in considerable rivalry among brothers and considerable resentment against the father by the sons.

Promotion to the status of elderhood is considered by many to be the most important event in the lives of men; it usually comes in middle age. Once promoted to this preferred status, the elder ceases to do manual labor and is no longer expected to take part in military activities. His primary roles will be directing the work of the younger generation and resolving any conflicts that may arise. Elders often have many rituals to perform, such as cutting the throat of an animal on ceremonial occasions, sprinkling blood over the gathering, and pronouncing his blessing.

Hamer describes *Woma* as the most exalted stage of old age for Sidamo men. *Woma* is granted to very old men (in this case, about 70) who are believed to personify the highest ideals of the culture, such as courage, truth, justice, and moral strength. Persons granted *Woma* are seen as having greater wisdom than other men and the ability to predict the future.

As Hamer views it, death is the most sacred of all events in the Sidamo culture. All the deceased's relatives, regardless of the distance separating them, are expected to attend the funeral rites. Among the survivors performing the rites, age continues to take precedence over other factors. Thus, the eldest son is seen as assuming the authority of the dead father and is the first to place earth on the grave. The youngest sons are called upon to build a fence around the grave.

> Style, as well as artistry of fence construction, is dependent on the age of the deceased. For young men a circle of board is considered sufficient but for old men an elaborate bamboo enclosure is constructed, which entails a trip to the mountains for bamboo and long hours of work.[23]

The rigid status system based on age is thus apparent even in death. The older members receive considerably more elaborate burials than the young.

While the female is always subordinate to the male, she does accrue certain privileges because of age. Both boys and girls are taught deference to their elders at mealtime, when food is presented first to the elders and then young men, young women, and children. Early in their training, however, a division of labor emerges. Girls are taught to assist their mothers in food preparation while boys are directed to work with their fathers in food production. Upon marriage the wife must be subordinate not only to her husband but also to the elder men and women in his family.

During her middle years the wife reaps the first rewards that go with age. She becomes entitled to deference from a son-in-law based on avoidance taboos, which are usually ended after her daughter's first child. Certain ceremonial rites eventually fall on elder women. For example, the eldest woman initiates gatherings of other women for housewarmings. One of the privileges that come to a very old woman is described by Hamer:

> She no longer keeps her eyes focused on the ground when approaching other men, and may speak casually with them without first obtaining permission from her husband. An old woman may be invited to eat and converse with old men.[24]

The Sidamo have established a male-dominated gerontocracy. The life cycle of both men and women emphasize old age and the prestige it brings to the individual. Whereas American culture and the culture of most industrial nations are youth-oriented, the Sidamo are oriented to the old. For older women the senior roles involve gradual increases in responsibility. Old age among the Sidamo is equated with prestigious positions, privileges, and power. Thus the Sidamo, like the Americans, experience role changes in old age. The role changes for the Sidamo, however, bring the older person greater status and prestige in later life; the role changes in America bring the older person a loss of status and prestige.

The Abkhasian, American, and Sidamo societies represent three distinctly different ways in which older persons are treated. Among the Abkhasians older persons continue to perform the roles of their middle years. While they are gradually relieved of the amount of time they invest in work, this involves no loss of status. The roles and status of Abkhasians remain relatively constant in old age. In industrial nations such as the United States, old age brings forced retirement and a loss of roles and status. Older people in such societies are seen as being beyond their most productive years. The United States tends to be a youth-oriented society. Aging among the Sidamo brings changing roles that involve greater responsibility, prestige, and status during the later years. The Sidamo society is oriented to old age: The aged exercise the greatest power.

From a symbolic interaction perspective, the critical differences in how the old are regarded and treated in these three cultures are the roles the aged assume and the values attached to these roles by others in the society. Aging can bring, then, a continuation of the same roles and status, as among the Abkhasians; a withdrawal of roles and status upon forced retirement, as in the United States and other industrial nations; and new roles and greater status, as among the Sidamo. The desirability of these different patterns of dealing with the older members of society depends on one's beliefs about what the roles of the aged ought to be. From the perspective of the older person, the pattern of the industrialized societies may be the most difficult to cope with.

CONCLUSION

Studies of aging in different cultural settings have revealed a number of characteristics. As a general rule, older people receive greater respect, status, and thereby more favorable treatment in societies that are agricultural, have extended families, have institutionalized land ownership (which allows the elderly to control the means of production), have a less harsh climate, have some form of ancestor worship as part of their religious beliefs, change very slowly, and reserve the more powerful and prestigious political and religious roles for the elderly.

Retirement, a modern invention of industrial nations, is perceived with ambivalence by older persons. On the one hand, it is considered a well-deserved rest from the strenuous competition of work and career. On the other hand, it is a disengagement from the mainstream of adult life and all the power, status, and privilege that stage brings to the individual. There seems little doubt that retirement roles are not highly valued, so retired persons lose status in their later years.

Since cross-cultural studies of aging are at times contradictory and inconclusive, a number of hypotheses regarding the roles and status of older persons would seem in order. Among these are the following:

1. Cultures that are mobile, either geographically or socially, tend to undermine the status of older persons.

2. The more older persons are socially integrated into the mainstream of the culture, the more highly they will be regarded.

3. Retirement, since it tends to disengage and isolate older persons, will usually involve a loss of status on their part.

4. Rapid social change will always tend to undermine the status of the old, regardless of the society or historical period.

5. The moral and ethical values of all religions tend to demand respect for one's elders.

6. Older persons in all societies attempt to maintain their independence as long as possible.

7. Extended-family ties or cultural values that stress family obligations will improve the status of the elderly.

8. Old persons will attempt as long as possible to maintain those roles that brought them the highest social esteem and will discard the less valuable roles.

Many of the industrialized nations in Western Europe and North America appear to be entering the postindustrial phase of their development. In this period it seems that the survival needs of the people will be guaranteed and that there will be much greater concern for the quality of life. It should follow that the humane aspects of life will receive greater attention than they have in the past. Whether the postindustrial period with its emphasis on the quality of life will mean an improvement in the lives of older members of these societies remains to be seen.

KEY TERMS

age grading

demographic transition

functionalism

life expectancy

life span

neolocal

patriarchal

REFERENCES

ANGEL, J. L., "Human Biology, Health and History in Greece from the First Settlement Until Now," *American Philosophical Society Yearbook* (1954), p. 171.

BEAUVOIR, SIMONE DE, *The Coming of Age.* New York: Putnam's, 1972.

BENET, SULA, "Why They Live to Be 100, or Even Older, in Abkhasia," *The New York Times Magazine*, December 26, 1971, pp. 3–34.

BENGTSON, V. L., J. J. DOWD, D. H. SMITH, and A. INKELS, "Modernization, Modernitis, and Percep-

tions of Aging: A Cross-Cultural Study," *Journal of Gerontology*, 30 (1975), 688–95.

COOK, S. F., "Survivorship in Aboriginal Populations," *Human Biology*, 19, no. 2 (1947), 83–89.

COOK, SHELBURNE, "Aging of and in Populations," in *Developmental Physiology and Aging*, ed. P. S. Timiras, p. 595. New York: Macmillan, 1972.

COWGILL, DONALD, *Aging Around the World*, Belmont Calif.: Wadsworth, 1986.

COWGILL, DONALD O., and LOWELL D. HOLMES, eds., *Aging and Modernization.* New York: Appleton-Century-Crofts, 1972.

DOWD, JAMES A., *Stratification Among the Aged.* Monterey, Calif.: Brooks/Cole, 1980.

ELLIOTT, H. W., *Our Arctic Province: Alaska and the Sea Islands.* New York: Scribner's, 1886.

FISCHER, DAVID H., *Growing Old in America.* New York: Oxford University Press, 1978.

GLASCOCK, ANTHONY P., and SUSAN L. FEINMAN, "Social Asset or Social Burden: Treatment of the Aged in Non-Industrial Societies," in *Dimensions: Age, Culture, and Health,* ed. C. L. Frey, pp. 13–31. New York: Praeger, 1981.

GOFFMAN, ERVING, *The Presentation of Self in Everyday Life.* Garden City, N.Y.: Doubleday, 1959.

GOLDSTEIN, MELVIN C., and CYNTHIA M. BEALL, "Indirect Modernization and the Status of the Elderly in a Rural Third World Setting," *Journal of Gerontology,* 37, no. 6 (1982), 743–48.

HAMER, JOHN H., "Aging in a Gerontocratic Society: The Sidamo of Southwest Ethiopia," in *Aging and Modernization,* ed. Donald O. Cowgill and Lowell D. Holmes, pp. 15–31. New York: Appleton-Century-Crofts, 1972.

HENDRICKS, JON, and C. DAVIS HENDRICKS, *Aging in Mass Society: Myths and Realities.* Cambridge, Mass.: Winthrop, 1977.

HOLMBERG, ALLAN R., *Nomads of the Long Bow: The Simono of Eastern Bolivia.* Garden City, N.Y.: Natural History Press, 1985, © 1969.

KEITH, JENNIE, "The Best Is Yet to Be: Toward an Anthropology of Age," in *Annual Review of Anthropology,* ed. B. J. Seigeli, A. R. Bealls, and S. A. Tyler, pp. 339–64. Palo Alto, Calif.: Annual Reviews, 1980.

LINTON, RALPH, *The Cultural Background of Personality.* New York: Appleton-Century-Crofts, 1945.

MALTHUS, T. R., *Essay on the Principle of Population.* Homewood, Ill.: Richard D. Irwin, 1963 (first published in 1798).

MARTIN, LINDA G. "Population Aging Policies in East Asia and the United States," *Science,* vol. 251 (February 1991), 527–30.

NYDEGGER, CORINNE N., "Family Ties of the Aged in Cross-Cultural Perspective," *Gerontologist,* 23, no. 1 (1985), 26–32.

PALMORE, ERDMAN, "What Can the USA Learn from Japan About Aging?" *Gerontologist,* 15 (February 1972), 64–88.

PALMORE, ERDMAN, and KENNETH MANTON, "Modernization and Status of the Aged: International Comparisons," *Journal of Gerontology,* 29 (1974), 205–10.

PLATH, DAVID, "Ecstasy Years: Old Age in Japan," in *Growing Old in Different Societies: Cross Cultural Perspectives* by Jay Sokolovsky, pp. 147–53. Belmont, Calif.: Wadsworth, 1983.

PRESS, I. and M. MCKOOL, JR., "Social Structure and Status of the Aged," *International Journal of Aging and Human Development,* 3 (1972), 297–306.

RILEY, M. W., ANNE FONER, BETH HESS, and MARICA TOBY, "Socialization for the Middle and Later Years," in *Handbook of Socialization Theory and Research,* ed. D. A. Goslin, pp. 951–82. Skokie, Ill.: Rand McNally, 1969.

RUSSELL, J. C., *British Medieval Population.* Albuquerque: University of New Mexico Press, 1948.

SHEEHAN, TOM, "Senior Esteem as a Factor of Socioeconomic Complexity," *Gerontologist,* 16, no. 5 (1976), 433–40.

SIMMONS, LEO, *The Role of the Aged in Primitive Society.* London: Oxford University Press, 1945.

THOMLINSON, R., *Population Dynamics: Causes and Consequences of World Demographic Change.* New York: Random House, 1965.

UNITED NATIONS POPULATION DIVISION, Working paper no. ESA/P/WP65. New York, 1980.

WALLACE, RICHARD CHEEVER, and WENDY DREW WALLACE, *Sociology.* Boston: Allyn & Bacon, 1985.

WATSON, WILBUR H., and ROBERT T. MAXWELL, eds., *Human Aging and Dying: A Study in Sociocultural Gerontology,* pp. 2–32. New York: St. Martin's Press, 1977.

WEIHL, HANNA, "Aging in Israel," in *Aging in Contemporary Society,* ed. Ethel Shanas, pp. 107–17. Beverly Hills, Calif.: Sage, 1970.

WILLIAMSON, JOHN B., LINDA EVANS, and LAWRENCE A. POWELL, *The Politics of Aging: Power and Policy.* Springfield, Ill.: Chas. C Thomas, 1982.

NOTES

1. R. Thomlinson, *Population Dynamics: Causes and Consequences of World Demographic Change* (New York: Random House, 1965), pp. 75–78.
2. Shelburne Cook, "Aging of and in Populations," in *Developmental Physiology and Aging,* ed. P. S. Timiras (New York: Macmillan, 1972), p. 595.

3. S. F. Cook, "Survivorship in Aboriginal Populations," *Human Biology,* 19, no. 2, (1947), 83–89.
4. J. C. Russell, *British Medieval Population* (Albuquerque: University of New Mexico Press, 1948), p. 24.
5. David H. Fischer, *Growing Old in America* (New

York: Oxford University Press, 1978), p. 6.

6. Donald Cowgill, *Aging Around the World* (Belmont, Calif.: Wadsworth, 1986).

7. Melvin C. Goldstein and Cynthia M. Beall, "Indirect Modernization and the Status of the Elderly in a Rural Third World Setting," *Journal of Gerontology,* 37, no. 6 (1982), 743–48.

8. Linda G. Martin, "Population Aging Policies in East Asia and the United States," *Science,* Vol. 251 (February 1991), 527.

9. Ibid., p. 529.

10. Jennie Keith, "The Best Is Yet to Be: Toward an Anthropology of Age," in *Annual Review of Anthropology,* ed. B. J. Seigeli, A. R. Bealls, and S. A. Tyler (Palo Alto, Calif.: Annual Reviews, 1980).

11. David Plath, "Ecstasy Years: Old Age in Japan," in *Growing Old in Different Societies: Cross Cultural Perspectives* by Jay Sokolovsky (Belmont, Calif.: Wadsworth, 1983), p. 152.

12. Allan R. Holmberg, *Nomads of the Long Bow: The Sirono of Eastern Bolivia* (Garden City, N.Y.: Natural History Press, 1985), p. 6. © 1969).

13. Wilbur H. Watson and Robert T. Maxwell, eds., *Human Aging and Dying: A Study in Sociocultural Gerontology* (New York: St. Martin's Press, 1977), pp. 26–29.

14. Ibid., p. 17.

15. Erving Goffman, *The Presentation of Self in Everyday Life* (Garden City, N.Y.: Doubleday, 1959), p. 70.

16. H. W. Elliott, *Our Arctic Province: Alaska and the Sea Islands* (New York: Scribner's, 1886), pp. 170–71.

17. Watson and Maxwell, *Human Aging and Dying,* p. 20.

18. Sula Benet, "Why They Live to Be 100, or Even Older, in Abkhasia," *The New York Times Magazine,* December 26, 1971, p. 28. © 1971 by the New York Times Company. Reprinted by permission. Some have questioned the authenticity of the ages given by the Abkhasians.

19. Quoted in ibid., p. 29.

20. Quoted in ibid., p. 31.

21. Donald O. Cowgill and Lowell D. Holmes, eds., *Aging and Modernization* (New York: Appleton-Century-Crofts, 1972), p. 320.

22. John H. Hamer, "Aging in a Gerontocratic Society: The Sidamo of Southwest Ethiopia," in *Aging and Modernization,* ed. Cowgill and Holmes, p. 17.

23. Ibid., p. 19.

24. Ibid., p. 23.

4

Biological and Health Correlates of Aging

INTRODUCTION

Although a person ages from the moment of conception to the moment of death, we do not normally speak of an aging child. Aging for most of us carries some connotation of deterioration of health and vitality. Marion Lamb (1977) believes that most biologists concerned with the problems of aging have accepted this assumption and focused on what happens to the individual after maturity is reached. Moreover, much of the biological and medical research on aging has focused on the latter part of the mature adult's life cycle.

Strehler (1977) has defined *senescence* as:

> the changes which occur generally in the post-reproductive period and which result in decreased survival capacity on the part of the individual organism.[1]

Lamb (1977) accepts this definition and delineates three characteristics of the deleterious changes that occur during aging. First, aging involves a decrease in the ability to cope with one's environment. Second, age-related changes are cumulative. Death is often sudden, but it is a result of the progressive increase in the probability of an aging individual dying. Third, the processes of aging are common to all members of a species and are inescapable.[2] Among the three characteristics proposed by Lamb, this one is perhaps the most difficult for biologists to prove.

This third characteristic implies that aging is universal—that it must happen to all individuals. But although all individuals eventually age and die, the causes of their death are quite different. For one individual *arteriosclerosis* (hardening of the arteries) may slow the flow of blood throughout the body to the point that the heart becomes overworked and a fatal heart attack or stroke follows. But not all individuals suffer from arteriosclerosis, and those who do may show considerable variation in the severity of the problem. Similarly, some aging individuals will

I wish to express my most heartfelt thanks to Dr. Joe Albright, Department of Life Science, Indiana State University, for reviewing and editing the material on biology in this chapter.

experience tumors because of lowered resistance to these growths. Some of these tumors will be malignant and fatal. As with arteriosclerosis, however, not all older persons will have tumors, and of those who do, not all of the tumors will be malignant. In short, neither biologists nor medical doctors can find any characteristic of aging that happens to all individuals.

The goal of the biologist who studies aging, according to Strehler (1977), is to identify the basic aging processes that will occur in all older individuals of a species, whether these processes result in death or not. It may be that all individuals experience a lowered resistance to tumors but that some do not come in contact with the specific environmental factor that precipitates their growth. In other words, the complex interplay between individuals and their environments makes the detection of common causes of aging exceedingly difficult.

John Rowe (1987) points out that one of the compounding factors biologists run into in describing what he terms "normal" aging is that of separating aging changes from changes that occur as a result of specific disease processes. Rowe (1987) believes that the changes that occur with normal aging in the absence of disease are quite variable and potentially modifiable.

Ultimately the search for the universal characteristics of aging may have to be abandoned. Biologists may have to be satisfied with describing the characteristics of aging, some of which will be experienced by all individuals at some point in their lives. Thus the speed of aging can be seen as varying from individual to individual, and some aspects of the process may never be experienced by some individuals.

Adrian Verwoerdt (1973) believes that the maintenance of a dynamic equilibrium between oneself and one's environment is the hallmark of good health. She argues that disease develops when the biological or psychological mechanisms for coping with one's environment are taxed beyond capacity.

Lamb (1977) uses Figure 4–1 to illustrate the loss of vitality (the ability to sustain life) by the aging individual. In the upper diagram, when vitality (Z) falls below the death threshold, death occurs. If environmental conditions are more severe, the death threshold will be higher and the life span shorter. In the lower diagram Lamb compares the life courses and points of death of four individuals (A, B, C, and D) in order to indicate that people start life with different degrees of vitality, age (lose vitality) at different rates, and thereby die at different points depending on when their vitality drops below the death threshold. Since there are genetic differences among people in the rate of aging, vitality, or both, in Lamb's opinion, we cannot expect all people to die at the same age. The wavy line at the bottom of the lower diagram indicates that the environment is never completely constant for individuals, and therefore the point at which they will die is never completely predictable.[3]

That there is variation in the age at which an individual begins to display one of the characteristics attributed to older persons can be seen in such characteristics as graying hair and declining strength of handgrip. Lamb (1977) refers to a study by Keogh and Walsh (1965) of the point at which one's hair turns gray. Keogh and Walsh analyzed hair graying in Australian men and women into three categories—complete graying, some graying, and no graying. Some people were completely gray prior to age 30 yet others were not entirely gray even beyond 60 (Figure 4–2).

The rise and decline of handgrip strength over the life cycle can be seen in Figure 4–3. The mid 30s appear to be the point at which handgrip is the

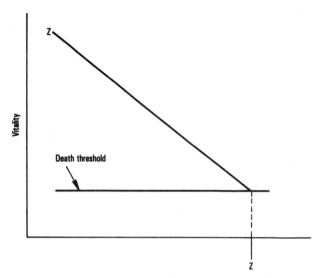

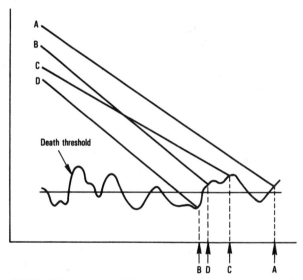

A,B,C,D, – Life course of four individuals
· · · · – Point at which individual would die

FIGURE 4–1
Diagrammatic Representations of Aging

Source: Marion J. Lamb, *The Biology of Aging* (New York: John Wiley, 1977), p. 4. Reprinted by permission of John Wiley and The Blackie Publishing Group.

strongest. There is then a gradual but regular decline in strength. These patterns of graying hair, handgrip strength, and other characteristics that are considered to be age-related seem very similar. There is considerable variation from individual to individual, but over time most individuals display some graying hair and some loss of handgrip strength. Eventually, all persons experience some of the following characteristics of aging: modest-to-complete graying of hair, some dryness and wrinkling of skin, some pigmentation and darker blotches on the skin, some loss of strength, a loss in height, and a stooped appearance (Figure 4–4).

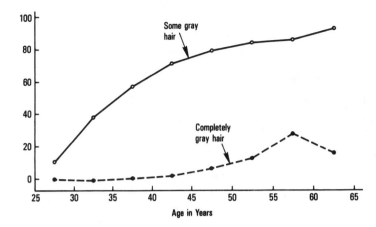

FIGURE 4–2
Hair Graying among 3872
Australian Men and Women

Source: Marion J. Lamb, *The Biology of Aging* (New York: John Wiley, 1977), p. 10. Reprinted by permission of John Wiley and The Blackie Publishing Group. Based on data from E. V. Keogh and R. J. Walsh, "Rate of Graying of Human Hair," *Nature*, 207 (1965), 877–78.

AGE-RELATED CHANGES IN HUMAN PHYSIOLOGY

Verwoerdt (1973) describes some of the most common and observable physiological characteristics of the elderly:

1. The skin changes in appearance, becoming darker, more pigmented, and more vulnerable to bruises and skin sores. It also loses elasticity.

2. The joints stiffen and the bone structure becomes less firm, which often results in a loss of height and stooped posture. There is also a loss of muscle strength. Thus the older person loses mobility and routine daily tasks become more difficult. Breathing, urination, and defecation can be impaired by these changes. Regular physical exercise and activity can reduce some of these deteriorating effects.

3. The heart muscle loses strength. Simultaneously, the hardening and shrinking of the arteries (arteriosclerosis) make it more difficult for blood to flow freely throughout the body. The body may compensate with an increase in

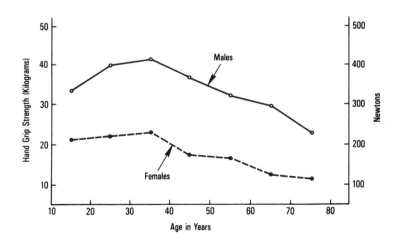

FIGURE 4–3
Changes in Handgrip
Strength with Age

Source: Marion J. Lamb, *The Biology of Aging* (New York: John Wiley, 1977), p. 11. Reprinted by permission of John Wiley and The Blackie Publishing Group.

VERY
YOUNG   YOUNG   YOUNGISH   STILL   FORMERLY   OLD
                                  YOUNG   YOUNG

FIGURE 4–4 Changes in Appearance over the Years

the systolic blood pressure. The increased workload placed on the heart and circulatory system can lead to strokes and heart attacks.

4. The exchange of oxygen and carbon dioxide in the lungs may become more difficult as the respiratory system of the older person becomes less efficient. This loss of efficiency may be a result of a weakening of the muscles and changes in the joints of the ribs and chest. The fibers of the lungs may lose their elasticity and the blood vessels may harden. The result is that it becomes more difficult for the older person to breathe.

5. The gastrointestinal system can change, leading to different dietary demands. Loss of control of bowel and bladder movements may fluctuate between constipation and incontinence. Older persons often decrease fluid intake and increase their liking for sweets. With the decline in metabolic rate, fewer calories are actually needed. Since eating is a social as well as a physiological event, in the absence of others old persons may not prepare and eat the right foods. The result can be loss of physical vigor and sometimes signs of malnutrition. Other older persons may compensate for their loneliness by overeating, which may be the only pleasure they derive from an otherwise dreary existence. The result may be an unhealthy accumulation of fat.

6. A common urinary problem of older Americans is frequent urination. Enlargement of the prostate gland can cause the problem in men while infection in the urethra or bladder is often the source of the problem in women. The removal of the prostate gland usually eases the problem for men. The belief that the removal of the prostate diminishes sexual performance is apparently inaccurate.[4]

Aging involves other physiological changes as well. The nervous system is altered, in part because of a loss in bulk of the brain. Brain weight in a 75-year-old is about 92 percent of that of a 30-year-old. Kidney filtration declines with age. The kidney-filtration rate of a person age 75 is 60 percent of the rate of a 30-

year-old. The sensations of touch and pain are reduced with age. Visual acuity diminishes. Less light reaches the retina in an aging eye, and the lens often acquires a yellow cast. Cataracts are increasingly found. Taste and smell become less sensitive. Reflexes and reaction time are slowed. The net effect is often that the individual feels less capable of mastering his or her environment, becomes increasingly defensive, and slowly begins to isolate himself or herself.

Aging often results in increased vulnerability to physiological, psychological, and sociological stress. The stresses of older persons may include disease, accidents, retirement, widowhood, economic insecurity, and loss of status. It may be that the people who live to a very old age are better able to deal with stress, because of genetic makeup or psychological and social skills.

That each of us at any age can see the stress placed on our older friends and relatives can make us anxious about what will happen to us when we get old. *Gerophobia* is a term coined by gerontologists for the abnormal fear of old age, disease, disability, and death that some individuals display at any age.

MAJOR CAUSES OF ILLNESS AND DEATH IN OLD AGE

Strehler (1977) has characterized human mortality rates according to three phases in the life span. First, the death rate rapidly decreases during the first few months and years of life. The longer the newborn survives, the better his or her life chances. Between the ages of 10 and 30 there is a low but slowly increasing mortality rate. From age 35 to age 100 mortality climbs very rapidly and at an ever-increasing rate (Figure 4–5). The following descriptions of acute and chronic health conditions will help explain the different causes of death in the younger and older populations.

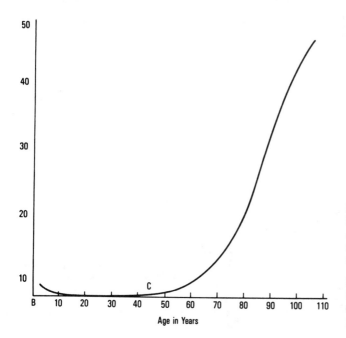

FIGURE 4–5
Percent Mortality Rate/Year versus Age (the fraction of those surviving to a given age dying during the next time interval)

Source: Adapted from Bernard Strehler, *Time, Cells, and Aging*, 2nd ed. (New York: Academic Press, 1977), p. 106.

Acute Conditions

As we saw in Chapter 1, the major reason for the advances in life expectancy at birth has been the success of medical science in dealing with the acute conditions that threaten the lives of young people. Acute conditions are those that are expected to be temporary. Thus, most of the diseases caused by viruses or germs tend to be acute. If an individual exposed to one of these diseases is not strong enough to resist the infection, illness occurs. In some of the less serious acute conditions, such as measles or chicken pox, illness usually lasts for a few days and recovery is rapid, most often within a week or two. The more serious illnesses, such as scarlet fever, bubonic plague, and smallpox, can easily result in death if the patient is weak and is not carefully nurtured back to good health.

Most acute conditions are passed from person to person. In attacking these diseases, medical scientists have often attempted to immunize people so that even if they come in contact with disease agents they will not become sick. Immunization in essence builds on the body's immune system, helping it develop immunities to these diseases.

Acute conditions are more likely to take young people's lives than older persons' lives (Figure 4–6). Older persons, having survived a variety of acute conditions during their younger years, have developed immunities to them and are affected much less often. Table 4–1 indicates the likelihood of contracting an acute condition by various age groups in the population.

Chronic Conditions

Chronic conditions are long-term disorders that either are permanent or can leave residual disability. Chronic conditions, unlike acute conditions, tend to come on slowly and often represent a gradual loss of body function. As the individual ages,

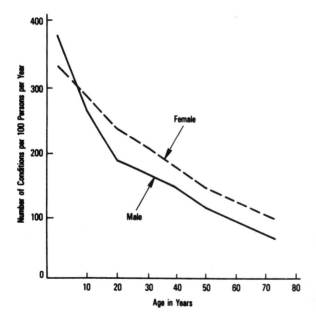

FIGURE 4–6
Incidence of Acute Conditions per 100 Persons per Year by Sex and Age, 1974–1975

Source: National Center for Health Statistics, Series 10, No. 114 (February 1977).

TABLE 4–1   Incidence of Selected Acute Conditions per 1000 Persons by Age, 1973

	All Acute Conditions	Infective and Parasitic	Respiratory	Injuries
17–44 years	172.8	15.7	89.2	33.8
45–64 years	102.3	7.3	55.1	20.0
65+ years	88.2	4.9	42.1	19.4

This table does not meet NCHS standards of reliability and precision.

Source: National Center for Health Statistics, *Health United States* (Washington, D.C.: Department of Health, Education and Welfare, 1975), pp. 479, 555. Based on health interview survey data.

acute conditions become less frequent and chronic conditions become more prevalent. Medical science has had considerably more success dealing with acute conditions than with chronic conditions, which doctors most often attempt to stabilize rather than cure.

As of 1982, the leading chronic conditions limiting the activities of the elderly were arthritis, hypertensive disease, hearing impairments, and heart conditions (Figure 4–7). Figure 4–7 indicates that the rate of chronic conditions is much greater for persons 65 and above than it is for persons 45 to 64. The likelihood of suffering from arthritis, for example, is 8 percent higher for those 65 and over. Similarly, the likelihood of hypertension is 59 percent higher for the 65-and-over age group.

The incidence of acute and chronic conditions experienced by the elderly varies by race and sex. Older men are more likely than older women to experience acute illnesses that are life-threatening, while elderly women are more likely to have chronic illnesses that cause physical limitations. Osteoporosis (a condition causing the bones to become porous and fragile), for example, is much more common among older women, while coronary heart disease is much more com-

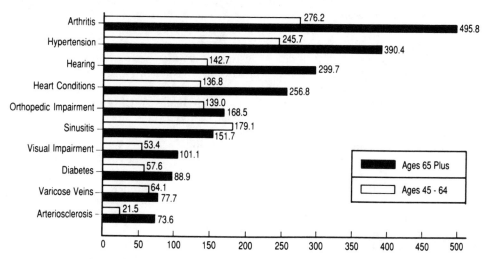

FIGURE 4–7 Top Ten Chronic Conditions for Elderly: Rates per 1000 Persons, 1982

Source: National Center for Health Statistics, 1982 HIS Survey.

mon among older men. Forty-five percent of the black population experiences hypertension versus only 33 percent of the white population.[5]

The older one becomes the more likely he or she is to experience one or more chronic conditions. Among 45-to-65-year-olds, about 72 percent have one or more chronic conditions. Among the population 65 and over, 86 percent have one or more chronic conditions. Multiple chronic conditions are a common problem among older Americans.[6]

Visual and auditory conditions sooner or later seem to afflict practically all older Americans. Within the 75-to-79 age group only 15 per 100 persons have 20/20 vision, even with correction.[7] Nineteen percent of those between 45 and 54 evidence some hearing loss. Beyond the age of 75, approximately 75 percent of the population has hearing impairments.[8]

There can be considerable variation in the seriousness of some of the chronic health conditions of older persons. The least severe health conditions are those the older person is aware of; they do not limit daily activities or at most restrict only a few minor activities. The more severe conditions are those that are serious enough to require medical care; they do disrupt older persons in their work and daily activities. The most severe health conditions are those that prevent older persons from caring for themselves; they require hospital or nursing-home care.

The most serious chronic conditions of the elderly in terms of their being able to remain independent are those that interfere with their mobility. Approximately 18 percent of the elderly report some limitation of mobility, in contrast with 1 percent of the 17-to-44 age group and 5 percent of the 45-to-65 age group. The major causes of mobility limitation among the elderly are arthritis and rheumatism, impairments of the lower extremities, heart conditions, and strokes.[9]

The three most common causes of death among older persons are heart disease, strokes, and cancer, accounting for 65 percent of all deaths. The leading cause of death for both sexes among those over 65 is heart trouble.

The acute conditions of the young are caused primarily by infectious organisms coming from outside the body. These illnesses tend to be short-lived, and recovery usually requires only a few days. The chronic conditions of older persons originate inside the body and are usually a result of a breakdown in body chemistry or a deterioration of some of the body's vital organs. Cancerous growths, which result from an abnormal division of cells, represent a breakdown in body chemistry. Heart trouble is an example of a deterioration of a vital organ. The diseases of old age often come on gradually and frequently result in permanent damage and limitation of activity. Undoubtedly doctors derive greater satisfaction from curing the acute conditions of the young than from controlling the chronic conditions of the old. Robert Butler (1975) has criticized the medical profession for not investing more research into the chronic diseases of older persons. These diseases may be less spectacular but they are more far-reaching than the diseases that have been the subject of intensive medical research.

BIOLOGICAL THEORIES OF AGING

Scientists have developed a wide variety of biological theories of aging, ranging from simple to complex. Many of these theories are intriguing, but none has yet convinced the scientific community of its validity.

Wear and tear is one of the oldest theories of aging, traceable to such thinkers as Aristotle and Descartes. This theory asserts that humans are like machines: After prolonged use the parts wear out. Thus while most people believe that vigorous activity helps the body's vital organs function efficiently, this theory suggests that it might wear them out. Realistically, reasonable amounts of exercise and activity do seem to keep the individual conditioned and healthy. In excess they could at some point begin to harm the person's health. Perhaps it is excessive strain on the body that the wear-and-tear theorists believe occurs over time.

Biologists see the aging body as having accumulated more and more damage due to minor diseases and injury. Most biologists do not agree, however, that senescence is caused by the accumulated effects of injury and infection. They are more likely to believe senescence is an innate process that occurs regardless of injury or disease.[10] Howard Curtis (1966), in attempting to discredit the wear-and-tear theory, repeatedly dosed mice with nitrogen mustard and tetanus toxin. After these stresses were removed, the animals were found to live as long as untreated mice. Scientists, therefore, doubt that senescence is entirely a result of wear and tear. Environment undoubtedly has something to do with aging and senescence, but how big a part it plays is highly debatable.

A popular but much too general theory of aging is that each individual has a *fixed amount of time* to live, and the faster he or she uses it the quicker it is gone. Thus those who lead vigorous lives would be expected to die young. The evidence indicates, however, that regular exercise prolongs life and that those who lead vigorous lives do not necessarily have shorter or longer lives than those who do not.

Very similar to the fixed-amount-of-time view is the *declining-energy theory*. The basic belief of this theory is that each individual has a fixed amount of energy or vitality (somewhat like a battery that cannot be recharged). Aging brings a decline in energy and vigor. Thus aging lessens one's resistance to and tolerance of environmental stress. This view is similar to the philosophy of vitalism popular in the Middle Ages. The "vital principle" espoused by the advocates of vitalism was thought to use the physical apparatus of the body, such as the nerves, muscles, and organs, to act on the natural world.[11] Supporters of the declining-energy theory believe that the gradual loss of energy over time and finally its disappearance are what bring about old age and death. Marcella Weiner and colleagues (1978) note, in discussing this theory, that a similar notion was implicit in Freud's theory of libido—an innate instinctual energy that conceivably dissipates with age.[12]

The belief in declining energy would be most amenable to the disengagement theorists, who assert that successful aging involves a gradual withdrawal from the mainstream of life. The aging individual should welcome this withdrawal as a result of his or her declining energy. This implies that the normal individual is at the mercy of social and environmental factors in later life. Neugarten, Havighurst, and Tobin (1968) argue, however, that people make choices that can alter both the biological and the social pressures they may be experiencing. People tend to select from the environment in accordance with long-established needs and in so doing to make a strong imprint on their future life course.[13] Regular exercise supplemented by a proper diet can revitalize older persons. People can choose the social roles they will occupy during their later years and direct considerable energy and vitality previously utilized in other activities to these roles. It would thus appear that neither energy nor vitality are given to the individual in fixed amounts.

The *collagen theory* relates the aging process to the connective tissues of the body. These tissues are made up of cells, fibers, collagen, and elastin. Collagen is found in most organs, tendons, skin, blood vessels, and other parts of the body. Some biologsts have argued that most of the aging changes seen in mammals can be related to changes in collagen. Aging connective tissues show increasing stiffness, at least in part as a result of these changes. Collagen stiffens with age and tissues containing collagen lose elasticity. Lamb (1977) reports that as animals get older the amount of readily soluble collagen in their bodies decreases. Change in amount and quality of the collagen in connective tissue apparently accompanies aging but is not believed to be a basic cause of senescence.

Frequently scientists have been led to believe that aging is related to the ability of cells to divide and reproduce themselves. This theory hinges on at least one crucial question—whether cells have a finite life span. Hayflick's (1979) research suggests that cells do have a life span. His studies indicate that cells grown in laboratory cultures die out after 50 doublings.[14]

Bierman and Hazzard (1973) also found that human cells grown in tissue culture do not divide indefinitely and show a decreasing capacity for division with age. They observed that cells from an embryo divide about 50 times in a culture; those taken from a 28-year-old duplicate about 30 times and those from older persons divide about 20 times. Table 4–2 illustrates the relationship between cell division and life span in humans compared with other animals. The Galapagos tortoise, interestingly, lives approximately 175 years and experiences 90 to 125 cell divisions. Unfortunately, there is no general age-associable loss in cells' ability to divide followed by the dying of cells. Nor can scientists be sure that cells in living organisms function the way they do in the laboratory cultures where these experiments were conducted.[15]

The proponents of this theory of *programmed aging* imply that a biological clock sets in motion the aging pattern after a certain amount of time has elapsed. The advantage of this theory is that it can explain the differential rate of cell division in different animals and the consistency with which cell populations double their numbers from sample to sample. Since these factors vary considerably from species to species, one would like to think that the clock is controlled by genetic material. This theoretical approach to aging is intriguing, but at present there is very little evidence to support it.

TABLE 4–2 Lifetimes of Cultured Normal Embryonic Human and Animal Fibroblasts*

Species	Range of Population Doublings	Mean Maximum Life Span in Years
Galapagos tortoise	90–125	175 (?)
Human	40–60	110
Mink	30–34	10
Chicken	15–35	30 (?)
Mouse	14–28	3.5

*A fibroblast is an undifferentiated cell giving rise to connective tissue.

Source: Adapted from L. Hayflick, "Why Grow Old?" *Stanford Magazine*, 3, no. 1 (1975), 36–43. Published by the Stanford Alumni Association.

Two other theories about the changes in cell division as one ages are the *error theory* and *mutation theory.* Their basic argument is that errors occur in the course of cell division. The errors that can occur are mutations, cross-linkages, and incorrect transcription in the formation of RNA from DNA synthesis in the cells. An error could produce two new faulty cells, which would then divide into four faulty cells, which would then produce eight faulty cells, and so on. The result could be a progressive loss of function and vitality in the part of the organism where the error occurred. Similarly any mutations occurring in cells over time or any pattern of numerous cell divisions could spread throughout the organ or body. It is generally believed that mutated cells are less efficient than the original cells. Scientists, however, cannot accept the argument that genetic mutations are necessarily directly linked to senescence. Genetic mutations can increase many times over with only a small reduction in life expectancy. Apparently some mediating factor minimizes the effects of genetic mutations in these cases. Thus the mutation and error theories remain highly speculative. Lamb (1977) argues that for the more general error theory to be accepted one must explain why different species have different characteristic life spans:

> It is necessary to postulate either (1) that the molecules in the cells and tissues of some species are less likely to suffer from damage than those of other species, or (2) that species differ in their abilities to repair damage or (3) that some species are more able to tolerate damage than others.[16]

Medvedev (1972), Sacher (1982), Cutler (1982), and others have argued that those people who live to sexual maturity have cells that contain great *reserve capacity.* Those with cells who lack reserve capacity, according to this perspective, probably did not live to sexual maturity and did not reproduce themselves.

These scientists point out that aging in its extreme manifestations occurs only in humans or in the domestic and zoo animals we choose to protect. Feral animals old enough to have decrements in physiological function comparable to that of middle-aged humans simply do not survive. As soon as they incur even slight decrements in, for example, running speed, jumping ability, or visual acuity, they are culled by predators. Similarly, as soon as vital organs or the immune system becomes less efficient the animal would either die of disease or be culled by predators. Aging, therefore, may be thought of as an aberration of civilization because it has permitted the expression of physiological decrements which otherwise would not have been revealed.

Hayflick (1988) perhaps best states the position of biologists who believe that aging relates to the cell's reserve capacity. He argues that natural selection has provided sexually mature animals with an extraordinary reserve capacity in all their organs. Reserve capacity has been achieved by natural selection processes in order to guarantee that animals will survive long enough to reach sexual maturity. The natural selection process favors animals with greater reserve capacity in vital systems. Redundancy, Hayflick (1988) believes, is the most effective means of ensuring that systems perform accurately for specific periods of time. Longevity-assurance mechanisms may be identical to the mechanisms that are hypothesized to produce redundancy, according to exponents of reserve capacity theory. Natural selection is directed toward favoring animals that survive long enough to reproduce. Survival to this point is best assured by animals with overcapacity or redundancy in vital systems. The greater the reserve capacity the greater the prospect of postdevelopmental longevity. Hayflick (1988) perhaps states the basic proposition of this perspective most succinctly:

> Thus the evolution of longevity assurance mechanisms that guarantee vigor in animals until sexual maturation may, indirectly, determine the post developmental longevity.[17]

Hayflick (1988) concludes that the question for biologists of "Why do we age?" may be the wrong question. The proper question to ask might be "Why do we live so long?"

To the general population, however, that believes extending life expectancy is the desired goal, the utility of the reserve capacity theory will ultimately be how can we use our knowledge of reserve capacity to extend the individual's life. Only time will tell whether this perspective on human aging is any more complete or useful than the others that have been developed by the biologists.

According to the *immune theory* of aging, advocated by some biologists, children gradually build up immunity to a variety of diseases, especially infectious ones. Control of these acute communicable diseases frequently is based on vaccinating people with small amounts of the potential disease-causing organism to allow the body time to build up resistance to it. As people grow they inevitably come in contact with an increasing number of potential disease-causing organisms, which stimulate the immune system and thus maintain the immunity initiated by vaccination. The development of the human immune system apparently peaks at about age 40. The system then begins to decline in effectiveness, and this decline speeds up with age.

Lamb (1977) observes that the immune response depends on a number of different cells and tissues and the complex interactions between them. Although it is difficult to explain aging in terms of this complex system, it is easy to imagine the opportunities for error and inefficiency in such a system. Immunities established during an earlier age may never entirely disappear; however, they may decline below some threshold level of effectiveness. Lamb points out that allergic reactions tend to be less common in the elderly and that old people are considerably less likely to be hypersensitive to antigens such as tuberculin that they probably encountered early in life.

An offshoot of the immune theory of aging is concerned with *autoimmunity*. This theory suggests that with age cell mutations or other changes may lead to proteins that the body does not recognize as part of itself; the body thus responds to them as if they were foreign substances. The immune reaction occurs when the body responds to foreign substances—those that are "not-self." When antibodies are produced in response to altered proteins (or certain other substances) no longer recognizable as self, the result is an autoimmune reaction: The body reacts against itself. The autoimmune reaction can explain some unexpected research findings. Studies have indicated that restricted food intake in youth extends the life span. Restricting food intake is known to delay the maturation of immune responses and therefore could delay the onset of autoimmune reactions. Experiments have also shown the life span of fish to be increased when they are kept at low temperatures, which slow the immune reaction and thus delay the appearance of autoimmune reactions. The autoimmune theory appears to be one of the more promising explanations of aging and mortality.

PSYCHOLOGICAL AND SOCIOLOGICAL ASPECTS OF ILLNESS

There is a complex interplay between the physical and psychosocial aspects of an individual's health that is difficult to untangle at any age, particularly among older persons. Many of the undesirable things that happen to older persons are partly physical and partly social. Thus some people are retired from their jobs (basically a social event), but an underlying assumption of this retirement may be that due to declining energy they are no longer able to compete with younger workers (a physical event). A man experiences the death of a spouse (a physical event) but finds that as a single person he no longer fits well in the group of friends he and his wife had shared (a social event). A woman may experience a heart attack and make an adequate recovery but withdraw from previous activities for fear of straining herself and causing another heart attack. She may stay home more, go out less, and begin to isolate herself from her spouse in the often mistaken belief that her heart cannot stand the excitement of sexual stimulation. The spouse then becomes concerned that he is no longer cared for.

Harold Cox, Gurmeet Sekhon, and Chuck Norman (1978) found that 40 percent of their sample of older Americans were somewhat isolated; they frankly stated that they often felt the need for companionship. Because of the complex interplay between the physical and social aspects of such problems, it is difficult to locate the primary source of the problem. A physical condition, such as a weakened heart or blocked arteries slowing the flow of blood to the brain, may result in behavior that a psychiatrist labels neurotic or psychotic. On the other hand, the irrational behavior may be caused by a social condition—the individual's inability to adjust to the variety of role changes and the loss of status that accompany aging. Or it may be caused by a combination of these factors. In any case, the result for the individual may be avoidance by friends and family and progressive isolation.

Marjorie Lowenthal (1964) tried to determine which among physical illness, mental illness, and social isolation were the independent and dependent variables. Physical illness might lead to social isolation, which then produces mental problems. On the other hand, mental problems could lead to social isolation, which is sometimes followed by physical decline. Or social isolation could be more of a cause than a consequence of mental illness. Lowenthal was never able to totally resolve the issue.[18] For older persons who experience physical and emotional problems simultaneously, it is often very difficult to identify the initial cause.

Moreover, the older persons themselves may be more or less objective in describing their state of health to the medical profession. Sid Stahl (1991) developed Figure 4–8 to indicate the degree of accuracy or inaccuracy that older persons may have in their perceptions of their own health.

Twenty-nine percent of Stahl's (1991) subjects believe they are not well and the doctors confirm their diagnosis (cell a). On the other hand, 24 percent of Stahl's subjects believe they are ill, but the doctors do not find evidence of a disease (cell b). Stahl labels these individuals as pessimists. They believe their health is worse than it is. In cell c of the chart we find that 20 percent of his subjects are what Stahl labels as optimists. They believe they are well when the doctors diagnose them as being ill. In cell d we find that 27 percent of the subjects believe they are well and their doctors agree with them. Thus it is

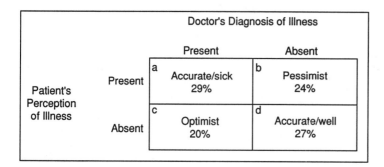

FIGURE 4–8
Accuracy of the Elderly's Perceptions of Their Health

Source: Sidney Stahl, "Health, Illness, and Disease Care for the Elderly." Paper presented at a 1991 workshop at Indiana State University on Problems and Opportunities in Later Life.

apparent from this data that the accuracy of the older persons' self-perceived state of health is frequently not believed to be correct by the diagnosis of the medical profession.

Related to the difficulty of distinguishing between the physical and psychosocial causes of illness and social isolation in later life is the older person's willingness to seek solutions to these problems. The evidence clearly indicates that older people tend to see doctors about physical illness more often and about mental problems less often. This seems unusual because many of the doctors who treat older people estimate that anywhere from 40 to 75 percent of their patients have psychological or psychosomatic problems rather than physical ones. Sainsbury (1968) found that 30 percent of his sample of older people could be classified as depressed. This study indicates that both psychosis and psychosomatic problems increase after age 65.[19] A study in New York City found that among persons with impaired mental health, 34 percent of those between the ages of 20 and 29 had seen a doctor, but only 21 percent of those between 50 and 54.[20]

In attempting to explain why older people seem to shy away from professional attention to their mental-health needs, David Cousert (1977) borrows from the symbolic interactionist perspective (discussed in Chapter 2). The advantage of these models is that they recognize the interaction among psychological, physiological, and sociological factors in the development of self-concept and patterns of behavior. Cousert finds a variety of reasons the older person might shy away from visiting a mental-health professional:

1. Family, friends, and physicians may be quick to label the older person mentally ill or senile long before the actual event. A visit to a psychiatrist would provide validation to the label.

2. Some more aggressive family members may be anxious to have a person committed to a nursing home or mental hospital. The psychiatric visit might then precipitate the very action that the older person is trying to avoid.

3. The psychiatrist or psychologist is likely to be able to find what would be considered a treatable emotional problem thus requiring further visits and further threats to the loss of independence on the part of the individual.

4. The individuals themselves might begin to have self-doubts and become further confused about their identity as a result of the visit to the psychiatrist.[21]

Cousert concludes that older persons avoid visiting mental-health professionals because it can lead to their being negatively labeled by family and friends, perhaps by the professionals, and ultimately by themselves. Being labeled mentally ill is difficult at any age, but it has particularly dire consequences for older persons, who at best will be treated as though they are senile and at worst could be institutionalized by their family. Moreover, such a label is likely to shake an already uncertain self-concept.

Cousert's (1977) basic argument is that the way people perceive the responses of others toward them will heavily influence their behavior. Thus treating people as though they are feeble and senile may encourage them to behave in this way even if they are perfectly healthy and rational. Research on reference groups and their effect on behavior indicates that when people identify with a group, such as the group of aged, they take on some of the significant characteristics of the group. Social psychologists generally agree that people seek maximum congruency among (1) their self-concept, (2) their perception of their own behavior toward others, and (3) their perception of the behavior of others toward themselves.

Older people may avoid seeing a mental-health professional partly because of the negative label (senile or mentally ill) they would receive from significant others following such a visit and partly because they themselves may hold a negative view of psychiatrists and mental-health treatment in general. In the latter case, a negative view of the mental-health professional might be based on what they have heard from significant others, or seen or heard through the media. Previous contact with a mental-health professional or a close friend who has visited a professional may reinforce the negative view. Finally the individual comes to accept the negative definition of the psychiatrist.

Figures 4–9 and 4–10 follow Zusman's (1966) social breakdown model and

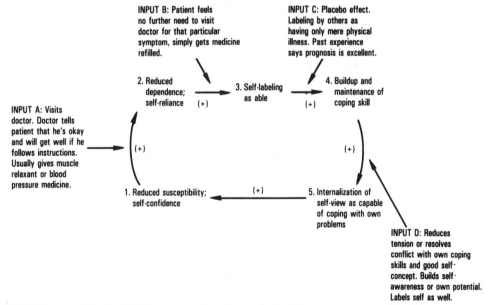

FIGURE 4–9 The Social Reconstruction Syndrome: Going to a Doctor

Source: Adapted from David Cousert, "Symbolic Interactionist Approach to Attitudes of Older People toward Psychiatrists versus Medical Doctors." Unpublished paper, Indiana State University, 1977.

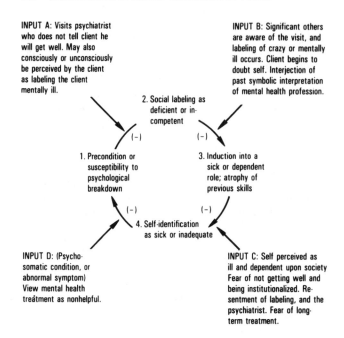

INPUT A: Visits psychiatrist who does not tell client he will get well. May also consciously or unconsciously be perceived by the client as labeling the client mentally ill.

INPUT B: Significant others are aware of the visit, and labeling of crazy or mentally ill occurs. Client begins to doubt self. Interjection of past symbolic interpretation of mental health profession.

2. Social labeling as deficient or incompetent

(−)   (−)

1. Precondition or susceptibility to psychological breakdown

3. Induction into a sick or dependent role; atrophy of previous skills

(−)   (−)

4. Self-identification as sick or inadequate

INPUT D: (Psychosomatic condition, or abnormal symptom) View mental health treatment as nonhelpful.

INPUT C: Self perceived as ill and dependent upon society Fear of not getting well and being institutionalized. Resentment of labeling, and the psychiatrist. Fear of long-term treatment.

**FIGURE 4–10
The Social Breakdown Syndrome: Going to a Psychiatrist**

Source: Adapted from David Cousert, "The Attitude of Older People toward Visiting a Psychiatrist." Unpublished paper, Indiana State University, 1977.

Kuypers and Bengtson's (1973) social reconstruction model in explaining the difference between the interaction of the medical doctor and the older person (which offers potential support to one's identity) and the interaction of the older person and the mental-health professional (which offers potential threats to one's identity). In Figure 4–9 an older person with shaken confidence and an uncertain identity visits a medical doctor with a health problem (step 1). The doctor, after examining the patient, tells him he is not seriously ill and will get well if he follows the doctor's instructions. The doctor often gives the patient a mild tranquilizer or something to lower his blood pressure (input A). The patient's uncertainty is eased and his confidence returns (step 2). The patient feels no further need to visit a doctor for that particular symptom and routinely gets more of the medicine as needed (input B). The individual gains confidence in his ability to handle his problem (step 3). Significant others, hearing the doctor's report, now define the older person as having only a minor physical illness. Prognosis for recovery is excellent. The individual is treated as normal by significant others (input C). This tends to bolster his confidence, thus building maintenance and coping skills (step 4). He can now internalize a view of himself as capable of dealing with his problems. If the need arises, he will return to the doctor who so capably helped him past the crisis.

Cousert (1977) sees negative rather than positive results when the older person visits a mental-health professional. Once again we begin with an individual whose confidence is shaken because he is experiencing some problem (step 1 in Figure 4–10). He visits a psychiatrist, who does not immediately assure him he will get well but tells him that his problem may require further diagnosis and office visits (input A). This may be perceived by the client as proof that he is mentally ill and has a serious problem (step 2). Friends and family come to know that he has visited a psychiatrist and must make other visits. They begin to define him as senile or losing his mind, thus labeling him as incompetent (input B). The person is in effect encouraged by those around him to act sick, and his interpersonal skills begin to deteriorate (step 3). He now becomes increasingly frightened. He is afraid of not getting well or of perhaps being institutionalized (input C). He begins to think of himself as sick and to act that way. Thus a further deterioration of confidence and further changes in behavior occur.

Cousert (1977) thus perceives a considerably different sequence of events for older persons who visit a psychiatrist than for older persons who visit a medical doctor. He believes the older person is likely to be reassured about his health by the medical doctor but may inadvertently receive information from the psychiatrist that leads to further anxiety and a loss of confidence. If Cousert is correct, this would in part explain why very few older persons seek out the services of mental-health professionals.

Talcott Parsons (1951) outlined what he considered to be the characteristics of the sick role at any age:

1. The patient is exempt from his normal role responsibilities such as working or supporting his family.

2. The person is exempt from any responsibility for himself. He is not expected to pull himself together nor is he blamed for acting sick because he is sick. Nurses or other family members will see that he is bathed, shaved, etc.

3. The patient is obliged to seek professional help.

4. The patient is obliged to want to and try to get well.[22]

The first two characteristics may be considered the privileges of the sick role. Not having to be responsible for one's job, family, and community is a privilege granted only to the sick, as is not having to be responsible for one's body and hygiene. Being obliged to seek professional help and get well can be seen as obligations of the sick role.

The problem for older Americans is that they are often granted the privileges of the sick role without the commensurate obligation to get well. Often their family and friends as well as doctors and nurses expect them to die. Thus they may be socially dead long before they are physically dead.

Older persons often fear being committed to a nursing home, because it represents a loss of independence for them. They are no longer masters of their own fate but are at the mercy of others—the nursing home staff. They also believe that a nursing home is a place where the aged are sent to die. Most would be correct in this assumption, unfortunately.

A nursing home is a place where a patient is expected to adopt the sick role. The nursing home staff expects the person to act sick, as do fellow patients, family, and friends. It takes a very strong-willed person not to act sick under these conditions.

Figure 4–11 indicates different patterns of response by the patient, his or her family, and the nursing home staff to the possibility of the patient's recovery from an illness. The person who is the least likely to recover, and who may be defined as socially dead, is the one who is subject to response pattern A—negative attitudes by all three parties. Recovery seems highly unlikely in this case.

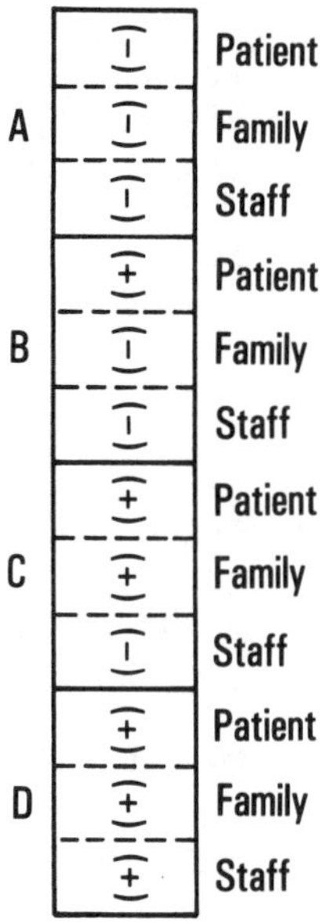

FIGURE 4–11
Patterns of Positive and Negative Attitudes about a Patient's Recovery

Patients who want to get well while their family and the nursing home staff do not expect them to get well (pattern B) are in a difficult situation. Significant others are pressuring them to behave in a way they do not believe is appropriate. If they act well, they are in essence deviating from the sick role that patients in a nursing home are supposed to adopt. Instead of remaining quiet and acting sick they are up and about, roaming throughout the nursing home. They may quickly be defined as an administrative problem and have limits imposed on their behavior by the staff. The staff may ask the family to pressure the patient to behave in the institutionally expected manner.

The patient and his or her family may expect recovery while the nursing home staff does not (pattern C). Patients in this case could be seen as being under less pressure to behave in a manner they do not prefer, since it is only the staff that opposes their future image of self and desire for recovery.

The patients with the best possible chance of recovery are the ones who want to get well, whose family wants and expects them to get well, and whose nursing home staff is working for their recovery. Unfortunately for older persons, this is only one of four possible patterns of response to their illnesses.

HOLISTIC HEALTH CARE

Recent decades have witnessed a growing and widespread desire by Americans to lead full, healthy lives and for each individual to promote that goal for himself or herself. Jogging, aerobics, yoga, diets, nutrition, vitamins, meditation, and a multitude of other health plans have all been touted as ways to improve our health and the quality of our lives. One underlying theme of all these plans is that people should be responsible for their own health and that there are a variety of ways they can promote and maintain their health. Dr. Bill Martz (1990) observes that nobody really knows what normal aging is, but of one thing we are sure and that is that aging processes are accelerated, not slowed, by physical inactivity. He believes that wellness at any age is enhanced by a reasonable program of exercise. Kevan Namayir, Marie Haug, and May Wykle (1985) observe that older adults are more likely to use self-help than to utilize medical services for many of the periodic ailments that confront them. Levin, Katy, and Holst (1979) view self-care as a social movement in this country. Certainly one of the outgrowths of the emphasis on health and self-care has been the emergence of *holistic health care.*

The exponents of holistic health argue that in order to understand the state of one's health we must understand all aspects of that person's life and the environments in which he or she lives. The holistic perspective views an individual's environments and his or her physical, mental, spiritual, and emotional states as totally interrelated. Health and disease are seen as ends of a continuum. There are dynamic balances or imbalances in a person's life that result in wellness at one end of the continuum or illness at the other. The holistic approach to medicine is contrasted with the traditional scientific view of medicine, which looks for causes of disease within a given human body. The medical view is essentially a reductionist one suggesting that humans are composed of ever reducible parts and that the essence of medicine is to find the cause of the malfunction of one of the parts of the body and to correct it. Willard Krabill (1986) explains that from the holistic perspective, however,

> the body is but one aspect of human beings who are really, all at once and in the same unit—a body, a mind, and a spirit. The physical, spiritual, and emotional/mental dimensions are but three windows looking in on the same entity.

Most of the world's people have accepted the unity of body, mind, and spirit. The separation of these components seems to have resulted from technological advances in the Western world (Ferguson, 1980). Increasingly health professionals are realizing that to treat and permanently cure any state of illness we need to understand all aspects of the afflicted person's life rather than just the part of the body that malfunctioned.

Geri Marr Burdman (1986:154) observes that

> wellness is a concept, a value, a lifestyle, and a process. The word wellness like the word health means different things to different people. A most commonly accepted definition encompasses feeling sufficiently good about oneself to take stock in one's own life and to intervene and nourish the self as necessary.

A goal of wellness is to live one's life in such a way that personal growth is continuous throughout the life cycle (Ardell 1985).

Krabill (1986) in a speech to nursing home personnel contrasted the different perspectives of the biomedical model and the wholistic (holistic) health model. His conclusions can be outlined as follows:

1. The body
   a. The biomedical model views the body as a machine made up of vari-

ous parts and subsystems that can be separated and viewed individually (reductionism).

b. The wholistic view is that the parts of the body are interrelated and inseparable.

2. Disease

    a. The biomedical model views disease as a malfunction in one specific organ or subsystem. It can be corrected or ameliorated with proper diagnosis or reparative technique—usually consisting of a chemical or biological agent specifically suited to render harmless the germ or biological malfunction that caused the disease.

    b. The wholistic model views disease as a disharmony between the individual and his or her internal or external environment. In disease, as in health, everything is interrelated. When the spiritual is sick, there are physical symptoms. When the physical is sick or injured, there are both emotional and spiritual spin-offs. Disease is caused by more factors than a simple pathogenic agent.

3. Health

    a. In the biomedical model health is viewed simply as the absence of disease. The preconditions for good health are maintaining sanitary living conditions and good personal health habits.

    b. In the wholistic model a sense of well-being is the essential feature of a healthy individual. The precondition for good health is the integration of the physiological, psychological, and spiritual dimensions of the individual.

4. Healing

    a. Exponents of the biomedical model believe that disease can be "conquered" either by self-limitation of the cause (pathogen) or by specific treatment. Prerequisites for cure are often presented to the patient in terms of drugs, operations, days in the hospital.

    b. Healing in wholistic medicine involves the reintegration of the three dimensions of one's personhood (body, mind, and spirit). The therapies may involve spiritual, psychological, or physical support from professionals in these three fields. The individual has a powerful predilection for self-healing, and most illnesses require no professional intervention.

5. Death

    a. In biomedical medicine dying is an illness to be treated, controlled, and cured if at all possible for as long as possible.

    b. In wholistic medicine death is viewed as a part of life—the next stage of growth. Death is a normal and natural phenomenon and is not to be resisted at all costs and by all means. There are fates worse than death. The physician should help people make decisions about the time and circumstances of their death. The gift of death is the ultimate wholeness, and the way we pass life on to those who follow us.

Whether the holistic health perspective will become more widely understood and utilized in health maintenance remains an unanswered question.

CONCLUSION

Today, more than ever before in the history of our country, a higher number and percentage of our population are living to the age of 65 and beyond. This is largely a result of the fact that medical science has succeeded in controlling the acute diseases of the very young, thus allowing more persons to live through the entire life cycle. The older population is more likely to suffer from and ultimately die of chronic conditions such as arthritis, diabetes, heart and circulatory problems, and emphysema—the diseases with which medical science has made the fewest advances. Despite having one or more chronic conditions, approximately 80 percent of older Americans lead full lives and pursue daily activities. Approximately 20 percent have chronic conditions that impair their mobility in their communities. On the other hand, 86 percent of older Americans have one or more chronic conditions, which make daily activities a little more difficult for them than they are for the average citizen. Despite these limitations a majority of older Americans, when asked to compare their health with that of others their age, believe they are in as good or better health than most of their friends and are not prevented from doing most of the things they want to do.

Physiological changes occur as people age. The skin tends to lose elasticity, to become darker and more pigmented, and to bruise more easily. Joints stiffen, the bone structure becomes less firm, and there is a loss of muscle strength. The respiratory system becomes less efficient. Changes in metabolism result in different dietary demands. It becomes more difficult to regulate bowel and bladder movements. Visual acuity diminishes, learning declines, and in general the body is less able to resist environmental stresses.

Scientists, in attempting to explain the aging process, have come up with a host of ingenious theories, none of which have been proved at this time. The major problem for biologists in determining the causes of aging is that whatever the characteristics of aging, the process eventually must happen to all individuals. Most, but not all, of the characteristics of aging will be experienced by any one person at some point in time. Moreover, there is considerable variation among individuals as to when any one characteristic will first be noticed. The only thing the biologist can say for sure is that ultimately all living organisms will die. But the causes and patterns of aging leading to an individual's death vary considerably.

Lamb (1977), in her book on the biology of aging, illustrates the changes in the body's cells over time that result in reduced vitality and ultimate death (Figure 4–12). In Lamb's view it is inevitable that in the process of cell division accidents will occur. These accidents include cross-linkages, errors in the DNA synthesis, and errors in the transcription and translation of genetic information. Once errors are made, further cell divisions perpetuate them. The result is less efficient cells and a loss of vitality. These errors may accumulate over time, creating changes in the body's tissues; for example, collagen may stiffen the joints. Any decline in cell efficiency, even a temporary one, can injure tissues, organs, and organ systems and ultimately result in death. Lamb recognizes (on the right side of Figure 4–12) all the corrective mechanisms that try to prevent the errors from becoming dangerous to the survival of the system. Over time, however, the errors overpower the body's ability to correct them, and the system's vitality deteriorates ultimately to the point of death.

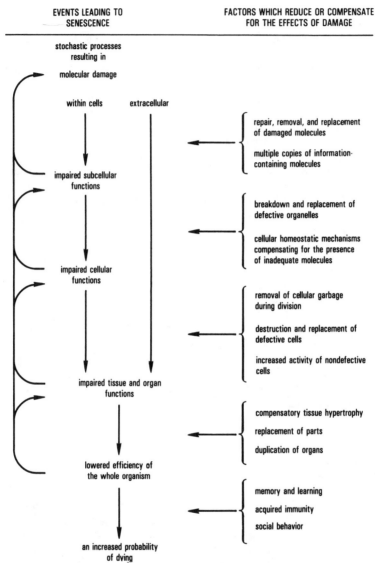

FIGURE 4–12 The Events Leading to Senescence and Death
Source: Marion J. Lamb, *The Biology of Aging* (New York: John Wiley, 1977), p. 164. Reprinted by permission of John Wiley and The Blackie Publishing Group.

One factor in aging that appears not to have been carefully examined thus far is the social psychology of sickness. The symbolic interactionists maintain that at any age much of people's behavior and self-concept is determined by the roles they assume and the expectations of others regarding how the occupants of a particular role are to behave. One problem for older Americans is that they are often expected to assume the role of a sick, senile, and feeble elder long before they have physiologically arrived at that stage. Similarly, in the case of illness in the later years, the family, medical personnel, and ultimately the individual himself or herself may not really expect recovery. The family may anticipate prolonged sickness and accelerating medical costs after the person recovers, medical personnel may equate prolongation of life with several chronic and debilitating conditions, and the individual may see that she or he is a burden to others. Thus people may be socially dead long before they are physically dead.

The effect of future medical discoveries on the prolongation of life is difficult to discern at this time. Some believe there is a limit to how far one can extend life expectancy beyond age 65, regardless of how many of the chronic conditions of older Americans are brought under control. Others see a considerable number of years added to each person's life. There is considerable evidence that preventive medicine, an ignored field, is now coming into its own. The degree to which some of the chronic health problems of older persons can be avoided or controlled by preventive medicine is highly speculative. There seems little doubt, however, that medical technology will improve, bringing some of the chronic conditions of old age under control and thus extending and improving the individual's life during the later years.

KEY TERMS

acute condition
arteriosclerosis
autoimmunity
biological theories of aging
chronic condition
collagen

declining energy
error or mutation
fixed amount of time
gerophobia
holistic health

immunity
programmed aging
reserve capacity
senescence
wear and tear

REFERENCES

ARDELL, DONALD B., *The History and Future of Wellness.* Dubuque, Ia.: Kendall/Hunt Publishing Co., 1985. © 1985 Kendall/Hunt.

ATCHLEY, ROBERT C., *The Social Forces in Later Life: An Introduction to Social Gerontology* (2nd ed.), pp. 33–38. Belmont, Calif.: Wadsworth, 1977.

BIERMAN, E. L., and W. R. HAZZARD, "Biology of Aging," in *The Biologic Ages of Man: From Conception through Old Age*, ed. D. W. Smith and E. L. Bierman. Philadelphia: Saunders, 1973.

BURDMAN, GERI MARR, *Healthful Aging.* Englewood Cliffs, N.J.: Prentice Hall, 1986.

BUTLER, ROBERT N., *Why Survive? Being Old in America*, pp. 174–224. New York: Harper & Row, 1975.

COUSERT, DAVID, "Symbolic Interactionist Approach to Attitudes of Older People toward Psychiatrists versus Medical Doctors." Unpublished paper, Indiana State University, 1977.

COX, HAROLD, GURMEET SEKHON, and CHUCK NORMAN, "Social Characteristics of the Elderly in Indiana," *Proceedings/Indiana Academy of the Social Sciences*, 8 (1978), 186.

CURTIS, HOWARD J., *Biological Mechanisms of Aging.* Springfield, Ill.: Chas. C Thomas, 1966.

CUTLER, R. G., "Longevity Is Determined by Specific Genes: Testing the Hypothesis," in *Testing the Theory of Aging*, by R. C. Adelman and G. S. Roth, pp. 25–114. Boca Raton, Fla.: CRC Press, 1982.

FERGUSON, MARILYN, *The Aquarian Conspiracy.* Los Angeles: J. P. Torcher, 1980.

HARRIS, CHARLES S., *Fact Book on Aging: A Profile of America's Older Population.* Washington, D.C.: National Council on the Aging, 1978.

HAYFLICK, L., "The Cell Biology of Aging," *Journal of Investigative Dermatology*, 73, no. 1 (July 1979), 8–14.

HAYFLICK, LEONARD, "Why Do We Live So Long," *Geriatrics*, 43, no. 10 (1988), 87.

KEOGH, E. V., and R. J. WALSH, "Rate of Graying of Human Hair," *Nature*, 207 (1965), 877–78.

KRABILL, WILLARD S., "The Contrast between the (Current) Biomedical Model and the (Future) Wholistic Health Model." Paper presented at the Indiana Conference for Nursing Home Personnel, Indianapolis, 1986.

KUYPERS, J. A., and V. L. BENGTSON, "Social Breakdown and Competence: A Model of Normal Aging," *Human Development*, 16, no. 2 (1973), 37–49.

LAMB, MARION J., *The Biology of Aging*. New York: John Wiley, 1977.

LANGER, S. K., *Mind: An Essay on Human Feelings*. Baltimore: Johns Hopkins, 1967.

LEVIN, L. S., A. H. KATY, and E. HOLST, *Self-Care: Lay Initiatives in Health*. New York: Prodist, 1979.

LOWENTHAL, MARJORIE F., "Social Isolation and Mental Illness in Old Age," *American Sociological Review*, 29 (1964), 54–70.

MARTZ, BILL, "Exercise for a Healthful Life," *Indiana University Center on Aging and Aged Newsletter*, Winter 1990.

MEDVEDEV, Z. H., "Repetition of Molecular Genetic Information as a Possible Factor in Evolutionary Changes of Life Span," *Experimental Gerontology*, 7 (1972), 227–38.

NAMAYIR, KEVAN, MARIE HAUG, and MAY L. WYKLE, Paper presented to the American Sociological Association Annual Meeting, Washington, D.C., 1985.

NEUGARTEN, B. L., R. J. HAVIGHURST, and S. S. TOBIN, "Personality and Patterns of Aging," in *Middle Age and Aging*, ed. B. L. Neugarten, pp. 173–77. Chicago: University of Chicago Press, 1968.

PARSONS, TALCOTT, *The Social System*, pp. 428–79. New York: Free Press, 1951.

RILEY, MATILDA, ANNE FONER, and ASSOCIATES, *Aging and Society, Vol. I: An Inventory of Research Findings*. New York: Russell Sage, 1968.

ROWE, JOHN W., "Toward Successful Aging: A Strategy for Health Promotion and Disease Prevention for Older Persons," Association for Gerontology in Higher Education, 1987.

SACHER, G. A., "Evolutionary Theory in Gerontology," *Perspective Biol Med*, 1982, pp. 25–339.

SAINSBURY, P., "Suicide and Depression," in *Recent Developments in Affective Disorders: A Symposium*, ed. A. Coppen and A. Walk. British Journal of Psychiatry Special Publication No. 2. London: Headley, 1968.

STAHL, SIDNEY, "Health, Illness and Disease Care for the Elderly," presented in 1991 at workshop, Problems and Opportunities in Later Life, Indiana State University.

STREHLER, B. L., *Time, Cells, and Aging*, (2nd ed.). New York: Academic Press, 1977.

VERWOERDT, ADRIAN, "Biological Characteristics of the Elderly," in *Foundations of Practical Gerontology*, ed. Rosamonde Ramsay Boyd and Charles G. Oakes (2nd ed.), pp. 51–67. Columbia: University of South Carolina Press, 1973.

WEINER, MARCELLA, ALBERT BROK, and ALVIN SNADOWSKY, *Working with the Aged: Practical Approaches in the Institution and Community*. Englewood Cliffs, N.J.: Prentice Hall, 1978.

ZUSMAN, J., "Some Explanations of the Changing Appearance of Psychotic Patients: Antecedents of the Social Breakdown Syndrome Concept," *Millbank Memorial Fund Quarterly*, 64 (January 1966), 1–2.

NOTES

1. B. L. Strehler, *Time, Cells, and Aging*, 2nd ed. (New York: Academic Press, 1977), p. 11.
2. Marion J. Lamb, *The Biology of Aging* (New York: John Wiley, 1977), p. 3.
3. Ibid., p. 4.
4. Adrian Verwoerdt, "Biological Characteristics of the Elderly," in *Foundations of Practical Gerontology*, 2nd ed., ed. Rosamonde Ramsay Boyd and Charles G. Oakes (Columbia: University of South Carolina Press, 1973), pp. 51–67. Copyright © 1969 and 1973 by the University of South Carolina Press. Paraphrased by permission of the University of South Carolina Press.
5. John Heinz, Cyril Brickfield, Adelaide Allard, and Carol Fraser Fisk, *Aging America: Trends and Projections* (Washington, D.C.: Department of Health and Human Services, 1986), p. 88.
6. Robert Butler, *Why Survive? Being Old in America* (New York: Harper & Row, 1975), pp. 174–224.
7. Ibid., p. 177.
8. Harris, *Fact Book on Aging*, p. 111.
9. Butler, *Why Survive?* p. 179.
10. Lamb, *The Biology of Aging*, p. 21.
11. Ibid., pp. 117–18.
12. Marcella Weiner, Albert Brok, and Alvin Snadowsky, *Working with the Aged: Practical Approaches in the Institution and Community* (Englewood Cliffs, N.J.: Prentice Hall, 1978), p. 13.
13. B. L. Neugarten, R. J. Havighurst, and S. S.

Tobin, "Personality and Patterns of Aging," in *Middle Age and Aging*, ed. B. L. Neugarten (Chicago: University of Chicago Press, 1968).

14. L. Hayflick, "Why Grow Old?" *Stanford Magazine*, 3, no. 1 (1975) 36–43.

15. E. L. Bierman and W. R. Hazzard, "Biology of Aging," in *The Biologic Ages of Man: From Conception Through Old Age*, ed. D. W. Smith and E. L. Bierman (Philadelphia: Saunders, 1973), p. 34.

16. Lamb, *The Biology of Aging*, p. 156.

17. Leonard Hayflick, "Why Do We Live So Long," *Geriatrics*, 43, no. 10 (1988), 87.

18. Marjorie F. Lowenthal, "Social Isolation and Mental Illness in Old Age," *American Sociological Review*, 29 (1964), 54–70.

19. P. Sainsbury, "Suicide and Depression," in *Recent Developments in Affective Disorders: A Symposium*, ed. A. Coppen and A. Walk, British Journal of Psychiatry Special Publication No. 2 (London: Headley, 1968), p. 8.

20. M. Riley, A. Foner, and associates, *Aging and Society, Vol. 1: An Inventory of Research Findings* (New York: Russell Sage, 1968), pp. 382–83.

21. David Cousert, "Symbolic Interactionist Approach to Attitudes of Older People Toward Psychiatrists Versus Medical Doctors" (unpublished paper, Indiana State University, 1977).

22. Talcott Parsons, *The Social System* (New York: Free Press, 1951), pp. 436–37.

5

Psychological Changes in Later Life

INTRODUCTION

The next two chapters deal either directly or indirectly with the changing personalities, roles, and lifestyles of older Americans. Since the early 1950s psychologists and sociologists have addressed the problems of personality development and changes from quite different perspectives. The early psychologists, following Freudian thinking, tended to see personality as almost permanently formed by adulthood and changing very little, if at all, during the adult and later years of the life cycle.

The sociologists, in contrast, were much more likely to see personality development as a lifelong process. Using the symbolic interaction frame of reference, the sociologists believed that personality resulted from the learning of new roles and the patterns of behavior expected of the people occupying those roles. Thus, one was not expected as a six-year-old to behave the way an older brother or sister did as a teenager. Similarly, one would not expect a father to behave the same way he had as a son, because his role had changed. Similarly, one would not expect a grandfather to behave in the same manner he had as a father; these two roles also call for different patterns of behavior.

The thinking of psychologists and sociologists on the subject of personality development seems to be converging somewhat. The psychologists are more frequently discussing the effect of assuming adult and later-life roles on personality change and adaption. Psychologists such as Daniel Levinson and his colleagues (1979) have attempted to very carefully document the stages and crises of adult life.[1] Similarly sociologists, such as Vern Bengtson (1973), are discussing personality changes over the life cycle and attempting to take into account biological, psychological, and sociological events that may alter the person's pattern of behavior.[2]

Both psychologists and sociologists now seem to be arguing that personality development should be viewed as a lifelong process. Neugarten (1968) believes that child psychologists and gerontologists may be segmenting personality development into just the years that their specialties focus on, ignoring what may have gone on before or what may happen later:

The effect has been, to speak metaphorically, that as psychologists seated under the same circus tent, some of us who are child psychologists remain seated too close to the entrance and are missing much of the action that is going on in the main ring. Others of us who are gerontologists remain seated too close to the exit. Both groups are missing a view of the whole show.[3]

While the individual's entire life history is important to understanding his or her behavior, shorter periods of time are easier for researchers to investigate. During any 10-year period in a person's life there occurs a variety of different events that leave a strong imprint on personality. Richard Kalish (1975) observes that a 10-year period for older Americans can bring changes in weight, hair color, stamina, sleep patterns, and health. As a gray-haired, overweight, 60-year-old with slightly high blood pressure, you may find you cannot work as long, as hard, or as efficiently as you did as a fit 50-year-old. This undoubtedly would have some effect on your personality.

In the social sphere you may be retired rather than employed, a widow or widower rather than married, no longer totally independent financially but living on retirement income along with some assistance from your children. Thus biologically, psychologically, and sociologically your life is quite different now than it was ten years ago.

The next two chapters—this one focusing on psychological changes in later life and the following one looking at changing roles, norms, and age constraints during the later years—will attempt to explain the changes in lifestyle that older Americans must make in order to adjust to the changes in self and the environment with which they are confronted.

PSYCHOLOGICAL AND PERFORMANCE CHANGES

In Chapter 4 we discussed the biological changes correlated with aging. In considering the changing abilities of older Americans we inevitably find some overlap between biological changes and losses in ability. While behavioral scientists and biologists may never completely agree on the primary causes of the changing abilities of older persons, ultimately biological, psychological, and social changes will have to be included in the explanations of the adaptations that older persons must make.

Data presented in Chapter 4 indicated that older persons generally experience a loss in handgrip and muscular strength and are slower in reacting to different stimuli. Moreover, older persons take longer in moving, and are generally less well coordinated and less capable of performing athletic movements such as running, swimming, and boxing. Birren (1964) indicates that all behavior mediated by the central nervous systems tends to be slow in the aging organism. This slowness results from a loss of cells and from age-related changes in nerve cells and fibers.

In Chapter 2 we discussed cross-sectional studies that indicated a gradual decline in intelligence with increasing age. Later longitudinal studies have indicated that if education is controlled there is no general drop in intelligence over the life cycle, except for a sharp decline in intelligence in the last few weeks before death.

The problem in attempting to establish the performance changes that accompany aging lies in determining which losses are a result of aging and which are caused by illness and deterioration of the body's vital organs—changes that are not common to all aging individuals. Stated simply, it is difficult to determine which performance changes are directly linked to aging and which result from the poor health of the older persons being studied. Illness will impair the performance of the individual at any age.

Birren (1963) attempted to determine the effect of illness on IQ by comparing two groups: (1) 31 institutionalized patients who had been diagnosed as psychotic with cerebral arteriosclerosis or senile psychosis, and (2) 50 persons who were considered to be well and in good health. Both groups were made up of individuals 60 to 70 years of age who had received no less than four years of formal schooling.[4] The IQ test scores of the two groups were significantly different, with the healthy group receiving the highest scores. Birren states,

> It is interesting to note that the Digit Symbol subtest which has been commonly found to decrease most with age, showed a smaller difference between the patient and control groups than did the information subtest which characteristically declines minimally with age. If deterioration in the senile psychosis were a process of accelerated aging the subtests such as the Digit Symbol, which show the largest difference with age, might also be expected to show the largest difference between the patient and control groups. This leads to the suspicion that the process of normal aging and senile decline are rather different.[5]

Birren (1963) also found a large difference between the two groups on verbal tests. This seems to follow the pattern of an earlier study, which found that a sample of healthy males over the age of 65 had higher verbal scores than a sample of younger respondents. This finding led Birren, Botwinick, Weiss, and Morrison (1963) to conclude that with age one tends to accumulate stored (particularly verbal) information. In a follow-up study of the elderly men in this sample, conducted five years later, some showed no change in intelligence while others showed a considerable decline. The researchers concluded that mental functioning is not something that declines gradually in the later years but seems rather to drop precipitously as the health of the individual declines.

Classical conditioning is the process by which two stimuli, only one of which has previously led to a particular response, are presented close together so that ultimately the subject will respond to the second stimulus in the same way she or he does to the first. Schonfield (1969) found that the conditioning of older persons takes considerably longer than that of younger persons.

In reviewing and summarizing the literature on mental functioning in later life, Botwinick (1970) concluded that good health and a high measured intelligence reduce age-related differences in verbal learning, whereas greater task difficulty increases the difference.

Canestrari (1967) offers the following explanations of the decline in problem solving with age:

1. Interference, perhaps based on earlier learning
2. Rigidity
3. Reduced ability to abstract
4. Greater difficulty in organizing complex materials

5. Loss of short-term memory capacity
6. Defects in ability to discriminate between stimuli
7. Inability to delay responses because of defects of inhibitory processes[6]

The results of all these studies seem to lead to the conclusion that aging differentially affects intelligence and that intelligence is fairly stable and predictable throughout adult life. Losses in intelligence during later life seem associated most often with ill health. There may be a tendency for the person's response patterns to slow down slightly with age due to changes in the central nervous system. There may also be a slight reduction of the older person's ability to solve complex problems. Vocabulary and verbal ability tend to accumulate with age, so that older subjects score better than younger ones. Kalish (1975) argues that the belief that older people diminish in capability with age may reflect

1. People's observations of the very old
2. The substantial number affected by terminal decline
3. Some modest decrements they may suffer
4. The prejudice and expectations of the perceiver[7]

Botwinick and Thompson (1968) conducted an interesting piece of research on the general tendency of younger people to respond more quickly than older people. They compared a group of younger persons from which athletes had been excluded with a group of older persons and found that the difference in response time was greatly reduced. They concluded that lack of exercise may be a significant factor in reducing the response time of older persons.

Another factor that mediates between differences in the response time of younger and older persons in crucial life situations is the more cautious approach to problem situations by older persons, which minimizes their need for quick responses. One would expect that due to a slower response time older drivers would have more accidents than younger drivers, but they don't. Case, Hulbert, and Beers (1970) compared drivers under 50, over 50, and over 65, and found that the younger drivers tended to drive faster, to brake less frequently, and to take more chances. The older drivers, by comparison, changed their rate of speed more frequently, pushed the brake pedal more often, and were generally more careful. Thus, even with a slower response time, they were involved in fewer accidents because of their more cautious approach to driving.

Furry and Baltes (1973) argue that the individual's energy level and the amount of time it takes him or her to become weary may contribute to age differences in learning ability. They found that older people become fatigued much more quickly in experimental settings and that differences in learning ability may result from the length of time the studies require.

Studies of simple and immediate memory have found only slight differences between young and old respondents. Bromley (1966) found, however, that if there is any interference with the simple act of memorizing, the younger respondents do better. He found, for example, that reciting numbers backwards or sorting them into classes resulted in a considerable decline in performance by the older respondents. Thomas Hess and Dominique Arnold (1986) found no age differences in memory for implied instruments, which suggests that aging has little effect on the processing and storage of such information. Young adults did remember more explicit information. Similarly, more complex tasks involving immediate memory clearly were carried out better by younger respondents. It may be that with more complex tasks, what is already known and stored in the minds of older respondents will interfere with the new materials to be memorized. More recently, Janet Cockburn and Philip Smith (1991), in a study of subjects aged 70 to 93, found that participation in social and domestic activities was a good predictor of verbal, visual, and spatial memory. Thus older persons who remain active with family and friends in their later years retain their memory much better than those who are less active. This suggests that memory loss among older subjects may be more a function of lack of use than of intellectual decline.

Lehman (1953), after studying several fields of scientific and artistic endeavor, concluded that the major new discoveries or techniques are made in the younger years of the person's work. For the innovation to become widespread it must be carefully developed; without such development its significance may be lost. When the life work of the scientist or artist is considered, the most productive years appear to be the 50s. Dennis (1966) found, moreover, that considerable productivity continues well into the 60s, 70s, and occasionally beyond.

Kalish (1975) has summarized what he believes to be the effects of losses in ability by older persons. He believes most older persons continue to perform fairly well, for the following reasons:

1. These decrements often occur very gradually, and the aging individuals can adapt to the slight changes almost without being aware that they are adapting.

2. Other people of their own age are also showing the same signs and this fact is communicable among them, sometimes openly but often more subtly.

3. Some evidence is available that older people (and, undoubtedly, younger people as well) can adjust to chronic problems and continue to enjoy life, even though the same problem might have appeared overwhelming when it was initially noticed.

4. These decrements and losses are only one aspect of life. If other aspects are satisfying, the importance of the deficits probably lessens.

5. A form of rehearsal for later age roles often occurs.[8]

In summary, the results of much of the work on performance losses of older persons seem to suggest older persons may experience slight losses in a number of areas, particularly where speed is required. Poor health is probably the single most important cause of these losses. Most older individuals adapt to these losses, perhaps without even realizing it. There is no gradual decline in mental ability. Unless there is a serious health problem, such as cerebral vascular disease or senile dementia, the great majority of older persons will experience no losses that would prevent them from continuing to lead normal and productive lives well into their 80s.

PERSONALITY

Douglas Kimmel (1974) believes that *personality* is an important variable in explaining behavior because it reveals differences in the ways people respond to situations and provides a system within which each person's behavior remains fairly constant over a variety of situations. Personality is the individual's adjustment to different environments. It is a result of heredity and biological factors, psychological conditioning, and social structuring (Figure 5–1).

Behavioral scientists often ignore heredity as a factor in human behavior, probably because there are no scientific tools for determining and measuring hereditary factors. The behavioral scientists must take them as a given. We know that people are born with certain biological needs, such as

1. Nourishment
2. Elimination of waste
3. Activity
4. Rest
5. Growth
6. Respiration
7. Sexual gratification

Beyond these factors, however, it does appear that individuals are born with certain programmed inclinations to behave in a certain manner. Selective breeding of animals has produced marked differences in temperament within a species. A thoroughbred horse, for example, tends to be high-strung and therefore can be easily trained to run for short distances at very high speeds. These are the horses that inhabit the racetracks of America. Quarter horses tend to be gentle, relaxed, and easygoing, at times to the point of being considered lazy. These horses make excellent riding horses and family pets. Animal husbandry suggests that in animals, at least, there is a certain temperamental disposition that is acquired at birth. Daniel Freedman (1958) found this to be the case with dogs, and Broadhurst and Erpenck (1965) with rats. Douglas Kimmel (1974) argues, moreover, that such internal processes as psychological functioning, hormone balance, and activation levels are probably closely related both with the way in which a situation is perceived and with the individual's predisposition to respond. If heredity is a factor, as research with animals tends to suggest, then individuals at birth may be predisposed to have more or less nervous energy, to be calm or high-strung, to be slim or heavy, or to have any of a variety of other characteristics that may affect their adjustment to the environment and ultimately their personality.

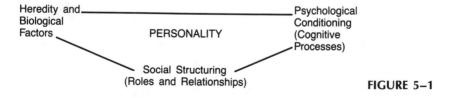

FIGURE 5–1

The psychological component of personality results from the cognitive processes that receive, interpret, and process information from the environment into a view of the world that allows one to adjust and react in a fairly stable and predictable manner over time. Kimmel (1974) speaks of the psychological aspect of personality as similar to an internal gyroscope, which, once set in motion, moves in a given direction and resists pressure to change. Thus the individual's experiences, cognitive processes, and current view of reality are fairly stable over time and tend to guide and direct his or her behavior in a variety of situations. Ultimately the individual develops a certain personality style that includes predispositions, traits, and fairly predictable patterns of behavior.

Examples of stability in patterns of behavior and personality can be found in studies of internally and externally oriented persons and field-dependent and field-independent persons. *Internally oriented persons* believe that they are in control of themselves and their environment and that they determine their own life chances, successes, and failures. *Externally oriented persons* believe that luck, chance, or fate determines what happens to them and that they are not in control of their own destiny. These patterns of response to the environment tend to become permanent and are carried by the individual from situation to situation. Over time individuals do tend to be internally or externally directed. Walter Mischel (1968) has argued that field-dependent and field-independent persons also tend to react to the environment fairly consistently over time. *Field-dependent persons* tend to be group-oriented and to want to go along as much as possible with what others in a particular social situation are doing—thus the term *field-dependent. Field-independent persons* feel no compulsion to go along with what everyone else is doing and may go their own way or just not become involved in the group activity. These patterns of response were found by Mischel to follow the individual through a variety of environments and circumstances.

Heredity and psychological traits do not allow one to explain how personality changes over time. It is here that *social structuring* comes into play, offering the best explanations of personality. A role is most often defined by sociologists as a set of norms and expectations placed on individuals who occupy a certain position in the social system. Thus one comes to expect that all doctors, for instance, will behave very similarly, and likewise with all ministers and all teachers. Walking down the corridors of a public school, one need not know the personality of a teacher to predict his or her behavior. All teachers will be standing in front of a class of students, leading a class discussion, or giving a lecture on some pertinent topic. Roles always carry expectations of reciprocity or patterns of behavior expected from others in the social situation. The students in the classroom will be expected to be attentive to the teacher's comments, to respond to questions, and to act interested even if they are bored. The social view of roles and their effect on personality leads one to expect changes in personality due to the fact that roles change over time. The role of husband is different from that of father. Similarly the role of grandfather is different from that of father. Over time roles change, resulting in changing expectations of one's behavior and ultimately changes in personality. Roles are learned through socialization, and over the life cycle new roles are constantly being prepared for and assumed by the individual as old roles are discarded.

Patricke Heine (1971) observes that the social model of personality more easily allows for and explains change. Moreover, consistency seems to vanish in this model into a collection of roles. Social roles are powerful explanations of personality change over time, as are other factors, such as age, sex, and occupation.

In summary, the three critical factors determining personality appear to be heredity, psychological conditioning, and social structuring. Heredity provides the individual with a range of biological drives (needs and urges that must be met) and certain predispositions to be energetic, nervous, relaxed, lethargic, or whatever. These predispositions may be altered or accentuated by environmental experiences. The psychological processes allow the individual to receive, interpret, and process experiences so that an appropriate adjustment or pattern of behavior can be adopted. Over time, personality traits and one's interpretation of environmental experiences allow a fairly stable and predictable behavior pattern to develop. These traits and behavior patterns that transcend situations become known as personality. Robert Carson (1979) maintains that individuals develop a personal style that, once established, tends to be maintained. Over long periods personality is altered by the social structure and the roles one assumes at different ages. The personal style of the individual will somehow have to be shaped to fit the occupational demands of being, say, a doctor, lawyer, or plumber.

STABILITY AND CHANGE IN PERSONALITY

In attempting to explain stability and change in personality, perhaps the symbolic interactionist view of the *I* and *me* concepts is most useful. The *I* is the individual's perception of himself or herself as a whole based on all of his or her past roles and experiences. The *I* is the response of the organism to the attitudes of others; the *me* is the organized set of attitudes of others that one assumes. In other words, the attitudes of others constitute the organized *me*; one then reacts toward these attitudes as an *I*. An individual may perceive his or her various *me*'s all at once or in a hierarchy according to the degree of positive attitudes he or she holds toward them. This perception constitutes the *I* or self-concept. It can constitute purely personal and idiosyncratic aspects of personality. It is assigned by the individual to himself or herself. The *me* is the definition of the person as a specific role player in a given relationship. The *me* is the organized set of attitudes of others that one assumes when entering a role. The *I* is the impulsive tendency of the individual to act. It is the initial unorganized aspect of human behavior—the undirected other. The act begins as an *I* and usually ends in the form of the *me*. The *me* brings the act under the control of societal expectation. The *self* mediates between the *I* and the *me*.

Kimmel (1974) attempts to integrate both the psychological and sociological perspectives on personality into a dynamic model that can explain both stability and change in personality (Figure 5–2). Remembering that personality is the fit between the individual's self and the environment, Kimmel represents what he believes to be the private aspects of personality, or the *I*, in the shaded portion of the diagram. These include memory, cognitive processes, physiological processes, and hereditary factors such as intelligence. The unshaded part of the diagram represents the public aspects of personality—the external environment of the individual. Social behavior and social roles are part of the external environment, and are determined largely by societal norms and expectations.

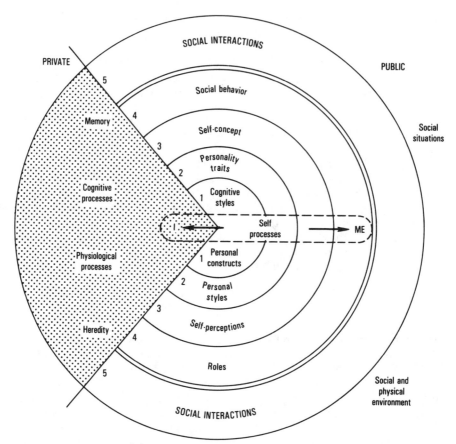

FIGURE 5–2 Conceptualization of Personality in Adulthood

Source: Douglas C. Kimmel, *Adulthood and Aging* (New York: John Wiley, 1974). © 1974 by John Wiley.

The diagram indicates that the individual's self-concept (level 3) and personality traits (level 2) are a mixture of public and private aspects of personality. The center of the model indicates the self as the interaction between the *I* and *me* aspects of personality. This model views personality as a dynamic system consisting of relatively unchanging content aspects of personality (levels 1–3) and relatively slowly changing process aspects of personality (levels 3–5).[9]

From birth to death one may see considerable shifts in the central focus of the personality system portrayed in Figure 5–2. During the developing years, individual, family, and societal pressures tend to propel the person outward into the social world. The person is expected to grow and develop, to assume new roles and responsibilities, and to move toward self-actualization. Adult life is characterized by the assumption of a wide variety of roles. With advancing age the individual is allowed to withdraw from some roles. The external social situation becomes less crucial, and the internal processes become more important. The individual's focus often shifts from the outer environment to thoughts and preoccupation with self. The disengagement theorists believe that this turning inward by older Americans ultimately results in their almost total concern for self and finally their death. Carl Jung (1971) best describes the process:

> Aging people should know that their lives are not mounting and expanding but that there are inexorable inner processes that enforce the contraction of life. For a young person it is almost a sin, or at least a danger to be too preoccupied with himself; but for the aging person it is a duty and a necessity to devote serious attention to himself. After having lavished its light upon the world, the sun withdraws its rays in order to illuminate itself.[10]

The young are seen by most behavioral scientists as in a period of maximum growth, development, and expansion. They are engaged in developing new *me's* as they learn new roles. In learning these new roles they must be considerably other-directed—sensitive to the cues given them by others as they learn the rules of the game. Adulthood brings growing confidence and a period of relative balance between internal orientation and external demands and increasing preoccupation with the self and internal processes. Buhler (1961) and Frenkel-Brunswik (1963) have come to similar conclusions about this pattern of lifelong development. They see the life course as a rising curve of growth and expansion culminating in the 40s, followed by a period of turning inward and finally an overall withdrawal from the community similar to the pattern described by disengagement theorists. Marjorie Lowenthal and her colleagues (1975) made a study of four groups of people, each occupying a different stage of life: high school seniors, newlyweds, parents of high school students, and older persons nearing retirement. They characterized the earlier stages of the life cycle as expansive, with high expectations for achievement. Middle-aged and older persons, they felt, were much more self-limited and apparently more concerned with minimizing frustrations by coping with life's problems and not setting their goals too high.

Studies that have attempted to determine the precise changes in personality that occur in old age have been somewhat inconclusive. Some of the findings indicate a considerable shift in personality in later years, but others have found no change.

Riley, Foner, and associates (1968) reviewed several studies of personality change in old age and concluded that old people were more rigid and less adaptive to changing stimuli than younger people. Attitudinally older people evidenced a high degree of dogmatism, a greater intolerance of ambiguity, and less concern about social pressure placed on them to conform. Moreover, they were found to be more passive, more conforming, and more preoccupied with their own emotions and inner selves.

In one of a series of studies of adult life done in Kansas City in the 1950s researchers repeatedly interviewed a sample of older Americans over a seven-year-period. The results, interpreted by Bernice Neugarten (1968), indicate three age-related personality changes:

1. A shift in sex-role perceptions
2. A personality shift toward increased interiority
3. A shift in coping styles of personality

Using the thematic apperception test, Bernice Neugarten and David Gutman (1958) asked respondents to describe an old man and an old woman in a picture. Whereas younger respondents saw the man and woman in traditional sex roles, older respondents saw the old man as increasingly submissive and the older woman as increasingly authoritarian and less submissive. The old man and old woman were increasingly seen as playing reverse roles by older respondents. Neugarten (1968) found that a shift away from the outer world toward interiority and concern for self is consistent with other studies. Bernice Neugarten, Robert Havighurst, and Sheldon Tobin (1968) found older subjects adopting a passive-mastery style of dealing with the environment rather than the actual-mastery style found in younger respondents. But although these studies indicate considerable change in personality, others indicate considerable consistency.

A number of typologies have been developed for patterns of adjustment to one's later years. Suzanne Reichard and her colleagues (1962) developed five different types—the mature, the rocking-chair people, the armored, the angry, and the self-haters. They found no clear age differences among these personality types, indicating consistency in the histories of the respondents in their sample. Kimmel (1974) believes that these findings indicate that the content aspects of personality in the form of personal styles and personal traits remain fairly consistent over time.

In summarizing the findings of the Kansas City Studies of Adult Life, Neugarten, Havighurst, and Tobin (1968) conclude that neither the activity theory nor the disengagement theory seems adequate. The findings indicated that older persons who are highly engaged in various social roles generally have greater life satisfaction than those with lower levels of engagement. The relationship was not a consistent one, however. Some older persons who ranked low in social-role activity had high life satisfaction while others were high in activity but low in satisfaction. This led the researchers to believe that personality is the critical determinant of adjustment to the later years. They assume that people having certain personality types disengage with great discomfort and show a drop in life satisfaction. Others, they believe, will have shown low levels of role activity accompanied by high satisfaction and will show relatively little change as they age. Therefore, personality becomes the focal point around which are organized the other variables in adjustment patterns.

Neugarten and her associates (1968) have developed a typology of adjustment patterns similar to the one developed by Reichard and colleagues (1962). It includes the following types:

1. Reorganizer
2. Focused
3. Disengaged
4. Holding on
5. Constricted
6. Succorance seeker
7. Apathetic
8. Disorganized

In terms of the activity model versus the disengagement model, the *reorganizers* substitute new activities for lost ones, pretty much as the activity theory would predict. The *focused* become selective in their activities, giving up some but being very choosy about any new activities. The *disengaged* voluntarily withdraw from former roles and responsibilities. All three of these patterns were found to be associated with high life satisfaction and secure personalities. The *holding-on* and *constricted* protect themselves from anxiety about aging by clinging to middle-age patterns (in the holding-on strategy) or increasingly closing out the world (in the constricted pattern). The *succorance seekers* are satisfied with their lives as long as they can find someone to depend on. They need someone to look after and care for them. The *apathetic* are disengaged and have been so throughout much of their lives. They gave up on life early and never altered their self-defeating beliefs about their inability to cope with their environment. The *disorganized* are low in activity and poor in psychological functioning. The last three patterns were associated with less satisfaction with life in general.

The conclusion would seem to be that the broad external and observable adjustment patterns of persons to their environments are fairly stable, consistent, and independent of age. In terms of the more specific traits and characteristics of personality, we find that aging, changes in health, and changing roles and statuses precipitate considerable change over time in people's coping mechanisms. Thus we find both consistency and change in personality over the life cycle.

SELF-ESTEEM

Several studies have noted fluctuations in self-esteem over the life cycle. Marguerite Kermis (1986) reports that men's sense of achievement and leadership ability peaks between the ages of 35 and 49 and declines thereafter. Women's sense of achievement and leadership, on the other hand, peaks during the childbearing and child-rearing years and then declines until age 65, when it again rises. Measures of personal adjustment for men are high in youth, relatively low until age 50, higher until retirement, and sharply lower thereafter. Fluctuations in self-esteem throughout the life cycle seem to reflect people's awareness of the life tasks before them and their perceived ability to deal with them. Fluctuations in self-concept, then, do not reflect changes in age but rather people's assessment of potential crises and their resources for dealing with them (Newman & Newman, 1980).

Behavioral scientists' assumption that a positive self-concept is crucial to a healthy personality frequently leads to the following question: What is the effect of an aging body and deteriorating physical appearance on the individual's self-concept? Some individuals even dislike being seen in a bathing suit because they feel they would be embarrassed by their appearance.

Matilda Riley and her associates (1968), in their review of gerontological research, found that older people compared with younger people were

1. Less likely to admit shortcomings
2. Less likely to consider themselves in good health
3. Less concerned about their weight
4. Among those still working, equally likely to view their job performance as adequate
5. Almost as likely to view their intelligence as being as good as others

6. More likely to consider themselves as having positive moral values
7. Somewhat more likely to feel adequate in their marriage or as parents[11]

Since looking in the mirror as an 80-year-old is quite different from looking in the mirror as a 20-year-old, one wonders how older persons are able to maintain high self-esteem. The answer probably lies in their reference groups. Most of the friends and associates of old people are other old persons. Other than family members, older people's significant others are likely to be persons near their own age. Thus, they may compare themselves favorably with others in their reference groups. Many older persons are proud that they have outlived many of their friends. This, then, becomes a source of self-esteem.

Kalish (1975) has found that economic status can also be a factor in the self-esteem of older Americans. Kalish (1975) reports that people living at, or higher than, the standard of living they had anticipated maintained high self-esteem after 60. For those whose standard of living was lower after age 60 than they had anticipated, self-esteem was considerably lower. Kalish found those having a childhood fear of being left alone had low self-esteem after age 60. Kalish concludes,

> If the older people have a reasonably stable recent history, an anticipated standard of living, and no strong fears of being left alone, their self-esteem rises with age.[12]

Therefore, the deterioration of physical appearance and body image in old age does not necessarily lead to a loss of self-esteem when other factors are considered. The fact that one's friends and relatives are aging simultaneously and the fact that one has outlived many of his or her cohorts tend to add to one's feeling of accomplishment. These factors, coupled with reasonably good health and a secure income, give considerable confidence to older persons.

ADJUSTMENT TO AGING

Successful adjustment to any age is difficult to define and even more difficult to measure. Neugarten, Havighurst, and Tobin (1961) tried to develop a measure of life satisfaction that could be used in studying the adjustment of older Americans. The variables they included in this measure were as follows:

1. Zest (enthusiasm and involvement in life's tasks) versus apathy (being listless or bored with life)
2. Resolution and fortitude—the willingness to accept responsibility for one's life rather than blaming oneself too much or constantly blaming others
3. Strong relationship between desired and achieved goals—the extent to which people accomplish the things in life that they set out to do
4. Self-concept—holding a positive view of oneself
5. Mood tone—happiness, optimism, and spontaneity versus sadness, loneliness, and bitterness[13]

Most often referred to as the Havighurst scale, this measure has become the most widely used scale in gerontological research. Many gerontologists, though, have questioned its validity. It is probably true that one of the major difficulties in research in the field of aging is developing a measure that actually measures the precise concept we are studying. Whether a better measurement of life satisfaction will be forthcoming remains to be seen.

Clark and Anderson (1967) have suggested that the following factors are correlated with successful adjustment to aging:

1. Sufficient autonomy to permit continued integrity of the self
2. Agreeable relationships with other people who are willing to provide help when needed without losing respect for the recipient of the help
3. A reasonable amount of personal comfort in body and mind and in one's physical environment
4. Stimulation of the mind and imagination in ways that do not overtax physical strength
5. Sufficient mobility to permit variety in one's surroundings
6. Some form of intense involvement with life, partly in order to escape preoccupation with death[14]

These, of course, represent ideal life circumstances for the elderly. They represent what the older person would like to have in terms of lifestyle and mastery of the environment. But the loss of a spouse, the loss of one's good health, or the loss of an adequate income due to inflation means that many—probably most—never achieve this state of affairs.

Clark and Anderson (1967) interviewed a sample of elderly people in San Francisco and attempted to identify the sources of high morale as well as the sources of low morale. Table 5–1 indicates the results of this study. "Entertainment and diversions" tops the list of high-morale factors while "dependency" tops the list of low-morale factors.

Since many older persons will not live in ideal circumstances, having a positive outlook on life and being masters of their own destinies, what are the patterns by which they might adjust to their inevitable losses? Buhler (1961) outlined what she considers to be four accommodations by the elderly to the aging process:

1. A desire to rest and relax now that they have completed their necessary life work
2. A desire to remain active and the ability to do so
3. The waning of strength or of the determination to continue their work even if they are not fully satisfied that they have accomplished everything they set out to do. This may involve considerable resignation and unhappiness.
4. Frustration, anxiety, and guilt as a result of leading lives they now find meaningless[15]

Kalish (1975) states that a fifth dimension should be added to this typology:

People may, regardless of the degree of previous satisfaction they experience, find in their later years some meaningful activities or relationships that compensate for whatever old age has required of them.[16]

TABLE 5–1   Sources of High and Low Morale among the Elderly

Sources of High Morale	Percentage Reporting This Factor
Entertainment and diversions	69
Socializing	57
Productive activity	54
Physical comfort (other than health)	52
Financial security	46
Mobility and movement	40
Health, stamina, survival	20

Sources of Low Morale	Percentage Reporting This Factor
Dependency (financial or physical)	60
Physical discomfort or sensory loss	57
Loneliness, bereavement, loss of nurturance	50
Boredom, inactivity, immobility, confinement	38
Mental discomfort or loss	18
Loss of prestige or respect	12
Fear of dying	10

Source: M. Clark and B. C. Anderson, *Culture and Aging* (Springfield, Ill.: Chas. C Thomas, 1967). Reprinted by permission.

Kalish uses the example of a retired economics professor who has spent the last 20 years developing new hybrids of chrysanthemums. Similarly, Mr. Jones, retired from his sales job for the past several years, has been breeding, training, and selling quarter horses. He seems to find as much satisfaction in this avocation as he did in his vocation. It is a mistake to assume that money is the only thing that pushes people to work hard at a given task. Once assured of a secure income, people can find a wide range of activities and interests in which to engulf themselves. Whether or not they are paid for the activity, if it brings a sense of accomplishment, a degree of status, self-respect, and some recognition from others with a similar interest, it can be fulfilling.

Most older Americans who feel good about their retirement will freely attest that the most enjoyable aspect of retired life is their freedom of choice. They can now choose what activities they do or don't want to get involved in, the amount of time they want to invest, and the point at which they want to withdraw. Freedom from the responsibilities of a job and child rearing can be seen as one of the major advances of later life. At no other time in the life cycle is one granted so many choices that are free of expectations or normative pressures to behave in a particular manner. Each age in life has its advantages and disadvantages. The freedom to choose in the later years would appear to be a major advantage of this age.

STRESS

Stress is most simply defined as bodily or mental tension. Stress always requires some adjustment. Excessive stress can overtax one's adaptive resources and result in a breakdown in functioning. Eisdorfer and Wilkie (1977) have found, however, that mild stress actually improves the performance and efficiency of the organism; extreme stress tends to impair effectiveness.

The human organism under stress musters biological, neural, and psychological defenses. Biological defenses are usually immunological processes. Sezle (1956) labeled the emotional response to stress the *defense alarm reaction.* In essence, this reaction puts the individual on a "war footing," prepared for "fight or flight."

Unfortunately, many social situations and work-related stresses in modern life do not allow one the option of "fight or flight." Being reprimanded by your boss in front of your coworkers at an office meeting is a good example. In this case, either of these courses would probably mean the loss of your job. Recalling such incidents later can reproduce stress-related bodily reaction over and over again. Ulcers, colitis, asthma and other psychosomatic disorders often result from unresolved stress.

Marguerite Kermis (1986) has identified several psychological defenses to stress. Task-oriented defenses involve the cognitive capacities and consist of direct attempts to solve the cause of the stress. Ego defenses are largely unconscious devices that protect the self from harm. Kermis observes that even defensive adaptation to stress may be very costly in terms of physical or mental fatigue. Persons under severe stress may respond inappropriately over and over, thus aggravating the situation. A person scolded by the boss may become aggressive, arguing frequently with the boss and belittling the boss to fellow employees. Another person scolded by the boss may proceed to avoid the boss at all costs, frequently calling in sick and even missing work deadlines. Such ego-defense reactions will guarantee these individuals what they fear the most—that they will be fired.

People placed under prolonged and unresolved stress find their resistance to other stresses greatly diminished. There is a growing body of literature suggesting that when a person experiences multiple stresses a serious illness will almost surely follow within a year. Eisdorfer and Wilkie (1977) argue that disease-causing stress often interacts with aging to accelerate degeneration. Fries and Crapo (1981) assert that people who feel hopeless and helpless are least able to deal with stress. They believe that those who feel helpless show an increase in mortality.

Holmes and Rahe (1967) have found the major causes of stress to be (in decreasing order of impact) (1) death of a spouse, (2) divorce, (3) marital separation, (4) jail term, and (5) death of a close family member. They found, moreover, that stress caused by these unfortunate circumstances or any significant life change, even ones viewed positively by the individual, can result in susceptibility to illness. Conversely, when the individual's life is relatively stable and he or she is experiencing few upheavals, little or no illness tends to be reported.

Life events that are anticipated and come at expected times are less stressful than those that are unanticipated. Kermis (1986) observes that the risk of coronary heart disease increases following the death of a spouse—but much more markedly for those in middle life than for those in later life. It would appear that the aged have anticipated and prepared for the loss and are less affected by it than are younger people not expecting it.

Stress, no matter how brief or slight, harms the individual's well-being. Those able to maintain an internal focus of control and a feeling of mastery of their environment are much more likely to be able to deal successfully with the stresses of old age.

Maladjustment

The point has been made in previous chapters that older persons are confronted with a series of losses. Older persons often find themselves trying to hang on to a lifestyle they found comfortable during their adult years but now find difficult to maintain.

Most gerontologists believe that maladjustment in later life is the result of psychological and social stresses placed on individuals as they attempt to adjust to various problems. The greatest stress seems to be placed on the disadvantaged. A review of 34 different studies of these problems found that 29 of them concluded that the lowest-status groups had the highest rates of psychosis and hospitalization.[17] Most researchers have found a negative relationship between socioeconomic status and severe mental illness. A study by Locke and associates (1960) found that the rates of hospital admission for mental disorders in old age were several times higher among those with elementary school educations or less than among those with high school educations, when controlled for sex and race.

Gerontologists and social scientists generally believe that mental illness is greater among the disadvantaged because these people are placed under greater stress than other social groups. They are often living on inadequate diets, in poor housing, and in deteriorating communities. Leighton's (1967) research indicates that community disintegration is a major factor in mental illness.

Erdman Palmore (1970) has proposed that five social stresses of old age are experienced by the advantaged as well as the disadvantaged:

1. Loss of income
2. Loss of role and status
3. Loss of a spouse (bereavement)
4. Isolation through disability
5. Loss of cognitive functioning

This list indicates some of the various social, psychological, and physical stresses to which older Americans are often subjected. Retirement usually reduces the income of older persons by about 50 percent. Without raising the question of the adequacy of retirement incomes, no one questions that a 50 percent reduction in income is an adjustment that may produce stress. The loss of the role and status of being an employed and responsible member of the community often brings a sense of meaninglessness and uselessness for older Americans. The loss of a lifelong spouse is perhaps most devastating. It represents a deterioration of the most intimate aspects of the individual's life. Isolation through disability and loss of cognitive functioning, while having social and psychological consequences, is a result of primarily physiological decline.

Older persons, then, are confronted with different kinds of stress. One source of stress is social and begins at retirement, which is often forced on the individual. It has the effect of removing the individual from his or her career and the mainstream of life and simultaneously reducing his or her income. The loss of a spouse seems to create the strongest psychological stress. Finally, stress can result from physiological decline, which simultaneously has the social effect of isolating the individual. Older persons, because of the losses they experience in later life, often feel threatened by their environment and unable to cope with their problems.

Incidence of Maladjustment

Robert Butler and Myrna Lewis (1982) believe that the best evidence available indicates that about 85 percent of the elderly, or approximately 19 million people, will adjust to the problems of aging without any serious emotional difficulties, even though some of them live in conditions known to be conducive to emotional problems. The remaining 15 percent are believed to suffer from some type of emotional problem. Considerably more than 15 percent of the older population lives under conditions known to be related to mental illness even though they may have experienced no problems. Twenty-five percent, approximately 5 million persons, live in poverty or near poverty, which is known to produce emotional strain. An additional million are estimated to have a serious physical illness, and still another million are social isolates. Thus it has been estimated that 7 million older persons live in conditions known to be conducive to maladjustment and mental illness.[18] Fortunately, the coping mechanisms adopted by many of the persons living under these conditions prevent them from having serious emotional and adjustment problems.

Carole Allen and Herman Brotman (1981) report that

> older people use mental health services at about half the rate of the general population. Five percent of patients admitted to psychiatric facilities (both inpatient and outpatient) are 65 and older. Among the elderly, admission rates are generally higher for women, for younger elderly aged 65 to 74 and those with no spouse.[19]

The remaining 10 percent of the older population believed to be suffering from emotional problems are admitted to local hospitals and mental health clinics, receive outpatient psychiatric care, or go untreated.

Butler and Lewis's (1982) classification of the most common emotional disorders among older people has been summarized by Charles Harris (1978):

1. Late-life schizophrenia (also called *paraphrence* or *senile schizophrenia*) (Generally, a newly developed schizophrenic disorder is rare in older persons.)
2. Affective psychoses—may include involutional melancholia and manic-depressive psychoses
3. Psychotic depressive reaction—severe depressions related to some definable life experience
4. Paranoid states—psychotic disorders presenting a delusion usually persecutory or grandiose as the main abnormality
5. Neuroses—may include anxiety neurosis, hysterical neurosis, depressive neurosis, and hypochondriacal neurosis
6. Personality disorders—lifelong defects in personality development[20]

Because these disorders can have physiological as well as psychosocial causes, it is often difficult for the psychiatrist to determine the precise cause of the problem.

Suicide, Drug Abuse, and Alcoholism

Other effects of stress experienced during aging include suicide, drug abuse, and alcoholism. One in 5 suicides in the United States is committed by a person over 65, though this age group represents approximately 1 in every 10 persons in the United States. Suicides are disproportionately higher among older persons. The pattern of suicide for men tends to increase with age. The suicide rate for women, on the other hand, peaks in the middle years (45 to 54) and declines thereafter. (See Table 5–2.) The reasons for the different ages at which the suicide rates peak for men and women are unknown at the current time.

Another almost totally uninvestigated area of stress in the older population is the relationship between physical health and mental health. For some older persons who are dying and who know that they are dying, suicide may represent a form of euthanasia. Those who are dying and in pain and are aware that the longer they live the worse the pain will be may find suicide the solution to their problems. The following case illustrates the circumstances leading to the suicides of some older persons. Dr. Bryan was a psychology teacher at a well-known university. After a number of X-rays and medical diagnoses he learned that the cause of his recurring headaches was an inoperable brain cancer. Moreover, he was told he would die sometime in the next six months and that the headaches would come more regularly and be more painful. Professor Bryan finished the spring semester, made out his final grades, cleaned off his desk, and went outside behind his office and shot himself. Who can say, given the circumstances, whether this was a rational or irrational decision?

Very few studies have been done on drug abuse by the elderly. Lawrence Krupka and Arthur Veneer (1979) found that 67 percent of their sample of elderly people used at least one over-the-counter drug and 98 percent consumed a social

TABLE 5–2 Suicides per 100,000 Population by Age and Sex, 1974

Age	Male	Female
5 to 14	1.4	0.4
15 to 19	11.0	3.2
20 to 24	24.1	6.2
25 to 29	23.8	8.1
30 to 34	22.6	8.7
35 to 39	23.1	9.8
40 to 44	22.5	12.4
45 to 49	25.8	13.2
50 to 54	27.3	12.8
55 to 59	30.7	11.2
60 to 64	29.7	9.3
65 to 69	30.5	8.3
70 to 74	36.4	7.6
75 to 79	42.5	7.7
80 to 84	45.2	5.7
85 and over	45.2	3.8
All ages	18.1	6.5

Source: U.S. Public Health Service.

drug daily. The older drug users in this study averaged 2.0 prescription, 1.8 over-the-counter, and 1.8 social drugs daily. This meant that 5.6 drugs were consumed per individual, with males averaging 7.5 and females 4.7.[21] One is led to suspect that these figures represent a different kind of abuse than what we read about among younger persons. The refilling and overuse of prescriptions, the saving of unused medicines for a later date, and the willingness of doctors to grant prescriptions to older persons are perhaps more likely to be their sources of drugs rather than the black market. One suspects that older persons are more likely to justify the misuse of drugs as good for their health rather than as a countercultural gesture, which we find among the young.

Overall, one might expect older persons to be the least likely group to be classified as alcoholic. Phyllis Snyder and Ann Way (1979) point out that older Americans are less likely to drink than younger Americans and that if they do drink they are more likely to be moderate rather than heavy drinkers. Leslie Drew (1968) observes that alcoholism is a self-limiting disease: Either it burns out as the alcoholic ages, or the alcoholic dies before reaching old age. Even so, it is estimated that there are more than 3 million alcoholics over the age of 60 in the United States.

Sheldon Zimberg (1974) has identified two types of older alcoholics: one for whom alcoholism has been a lifelong pattern and another for whom alcoholism appears to be a reaction to the stresses of growing old. Lawrence Schonfeld and Larry Dupree (1990) divide older drinkers into the "early onset" alcoholics who have demonstrated alcohol-related problems through most of their adult life and the "late life onset" alcoholics who began drinking after some traumatic occurrence in their later lives. Undoubtedly the latter form of alcoholism responds more readily to treatment. Older alcoholics are often overlooked in treatment programs and by society in general because they usually drink at home, create no public disturbance, and are seldom arrested. Therefore, they frequently escape public attention and awareness of their problem.

Snyder and Way (1979) have outlined some of the major causes of alcoholism among the elderly:

1. Loneliness—nearly 60 percent of admissions to a Chicago treatment facility were widowed, separated, or divorced.
2. Retirement, which sometimes brings a loss of self-worth
3. Increased leisure time, which can lead to involvement in a variety of recreational activities that encourage one to drink[22]

Margaret Bailey and her associates (1965) found the peak periods in the prevalence of alcoholism to be from 45 to 54 and from 65 to 74. Elderly widows showed the highest rate of alcoholism.[23] The period 45 to 54 would appear to be one of shifting roles from the young to the middle years. Often children leave home during this time and the individual begins to recognize the first signs of some of the inevitable physiological losses. No one has yet investigated whether role changes and altered lifestyle in the middle years create stresses that some attempt to resolve through alcohol. Similarly, one wonders if the 65-to-74-year-olds are adjusting to the role changes that accompany retirement and the onset of old age and if this does not create stress, which some will attempt to assuage through the use of alcohol. These unanswered questions should prove fruitful topics for researchers interested in the problems of alcoholism and aging.

Suicide, drug abuse, and alcoholism in later life have not been studied extensively by gerontologists or social scientists. Therefore, there is simply not enough evidence available at present to connect them with the social ills of later life.

CONCLUSION

In this chapter we view personality development as a lifelong process. The three principal components of personality are the physiological, the psychological, and the social. The individual at birth has a genetic composition that may predispose him or her to be nervous, relaxed, energetic, lethargic, or whatever. In addition, the individual has a variety of biological drives and urges that must ultimately be satisfied. Psychologically the individual receives, processes, and incorporates new information into a view of his or her environment and a strategy of coping with it. Over time the individual develops personal traits and habits as he or she learns to cope with a variety of social situations. These traits and habits become a fairly stable part of personality and guide the individual through diverse social situations. Over the life cycle one acquires new roles and responsibilities. While personal traits predispose an individual to behave in a well-established manner when confronted with a new role, the norms of society demand certain behavior, which is independent of personality, from all who occupy that role. Thus the social structure and normative role expectations force changes in personality throughout the life cycle.

This chapter also discussed later life and personality in terms of adjustment to a series of losses. As a result of aging, physiological decline, the loss of previous roles and status, and changing societal expectations, the individual often finds later life to be increasingly insecure and becomes increasingly unable to cope with his or her environment. While the majority of older Americans develop mechanisms for coping with the inevitable losses of old age, some do not. For the latter, emotional problems as well as alcoholism, drug abuse, and suicide have been seen to result from the stresses of later life.

KEY TERMS

apathetic	field-dependent personality	internally oriented persons
constricted	field-independent personality	personality
disengaged	focused	reorganizer
disorganized	holding-on	self
externally oriented persons	*I* and *me* concepts	social structuring
		succorance seeker

REFERENCES

ALLEN, CAROLE, and HERMAN BROTMAN, *Chartbook on Aging in America*. Washington, D.C.: White House Conference on Aging, 1981.

BAILEY, MARGARET, PAUL W. HABERMAN, and HAROLD ALKSNE, "The Epidemiology of Alcoholism in an Urban Residential Area," *Quarterly Journal of Studies on Alcohol*, 26 (1965).

BENGTSON, VERN L., *The Social Psychology of Aging.* Indianapolis: Bobbs-Merrill, 1973.

BIRREN, JAMES, *The Psychology of Aging.* Englewood Cliffs, N.J.: Prentice Hall, 1964.

BIRREN, JAMES, BOTWINICK, WEISS, and MORRISON, "Interrelations of Mental and Perceptual Tests Given to Healthy Elderly Men," in *Human Aging*, ed. James Birren, J. Botwinick, A. D. Weiss, and D. F. Morrison. Public Health Service Publication No. 986. Washington, D.C., 1963.

BOTWINICK, J., "Geropsychology," in *Annual Review of Psychology*, ed. P. H. Mussen and M. R. Rosenweig. Palo Alto, Calif.: Annual Reviews, 1970.

BOTWINICK, J., and L. W. THOMPSON, "Individual Differences in Reaction Time in Relation to Age," *Journal of Genetic Psychology*, 112 (1968), 73–75.

BROADHURST, P. L., and H. J. ERPENCK, "Emotionality in the Rat: A Problem of Response Specificity," in *Studies in Psychology*, ed. C. Banks and P. L. Broadhurst. Aylesbury Bucks, England: Hazell, Watson & Viney, 1965.

BROMLEY, D. B., *The Pyschology of Human Aging.* Baltimore: Penguin, 1966.

BUHLER, C., "Old Age and Fulfillment of Life with Considerations of the Use of Time in Old Age," *Acta Psychologica*, 19 (1961), 126–48.

BUTLER, ROBERT, and MYRNA LEWIS, *Aging and Mental Health: Positive Psychosocial Approaches.* St. Louis: C. V. Mosby, 1982.

CANESTRARI, R. F., "Research in Learning," *Gerontologist*, 7, no. 2, pt. 2 (1967), 61–66.

CARSON, ROBERT C., *Interaction Concepts of Personality.* Chicago: Aldine, 1969.

CARSON, ROBERT, *The Behavioral Approach to Therapy.* Morristown, N.J.: General Learning Press, 1979.

CASE, H. W., S. HULBERT, and J. BEERS, *Driving Ability as Affected by Age.* University of California at Los Angeles, Institute of Transportation and Traffic Engineering Report 70-18. Los Angeles, 1970.

CLARK, M., and B. C. ANDERSON, *Culture and Aging.* Springfield, Ill.: Chas. C Thomas, 1967.

COCKBURN, JANET, and PHILIP T. SMITH, "The Relative Influence of Intelligence and Age on Everyday Memory," *Journal of Gerontology*, 46, no. 1, (1991) 31–36.

DENNIS, W., "Creative Productivity between the Ages of 20 and 80 Years," *Journal of Gerontology*, 21 (1966), 1–8.

DREW, LESLIE, "Alcoholism as a Self-Limiting Disease," *Quarterly Journal of Studies on Alcohol* (1968), pp. 963–68.

EISDORFER, C. NEWLIN, and I. WILKIE, "Stress, Disease, Aging and Behavior," in *Handbook of the Psychology of Aging*, ed. J. E. Birren and K. W. Schaie, pp. 251–75. New York: Academic Press, 1977.

FREEDMAN, DANIEL G., "Constitutional and Environmental Interactions in Rearing Four Breeds of Dogs," *Science*, 127, no. 3298 (1958), 585–86.

FRENKEL-BRUNSWIK, ELSE, "Adjustments and Reorientation in the Course of the Life Span," in *Psychological Studies of Human Development*, ed. Raymond Kuhlen. New York: Appleton-Century-Crofts, 1963.

FREUD, SIGMUND, *An Outline of Psychoanalysis*, trans. James Strachey. New York: W. W. Norton, 1963.

FRIED, M., *Social Differences in Mental Health in Poverty and Health*, ed. J. Rosa, A. Antonovska, and K. Zola. Cambridge, Mass.: Harvard University Press, 1969.

FRIES, J. F., and L. M. CRAPO, *Vitality and Aging.* San Francisco: W. H. Freeman, 1981.

FURRY, C. A., and P. B. BALTES, "The Effect of Age Differences in Ability: Extraneous Performance Variables in Assessment of Intelligence in Children, Adults and the Elderly," *Journal of Gerontology*, 28 (1973), 73–80.

HARRIS, CHARLES, *Fact Book on Aging: A Profile of America's Older Population.* Washington, D.C.: National Council on the Aging, 1978.

HEINE, PATRICKE JOHNS, *Personality in Social Theory.* Chicago: Aldine, 1971.

HESS, THOMAS, and DOMINIQUE ARNOLD, "Adult Age Differences in Memory for Explicit and Implicit Sentence Information," *Journal of Gerontology*, 41, no. 2 (1986), 191–94.

HOLMES, T. H., and RAHE, R. H., "The Social Readjustment Rating Scale," *Journal of Psychosomatic Research*, 11 (1967), 213–18.

JUNG, CARL G., "The Stages of Life," trans. R. F. C. Hull, in *The Portable Jung*, ed. Joseph Campbell. New York: Viking, 1971.

KALISH, RICHARD A., *Late Adulthood: Perspectives on Human Development.* Monterey, Calif.: Brooks/Cole, 1975.

KERMIS, MARGUERITE D., *Mental Health in Late Life: The Adaptive Process.* Boston: Jones & Bartlett, 1986.

KIMMEL, DOUGLAS C., *Adulthood and Aging.* New York: John Wiley, 1974.

KRUPKA, LAWRENCE, and ARTHUR VENEER, "Hazards of Drug Use among the Elderly," *Gerontologist*, 19, no. 1 (1979), 90–95.

LEHMAN, H. C., *Age and Achievement.* Princeton, N.J.: Princeton University Press, 1953.

LEIGHTON, A., "Is Social Environment a Cause of Psychiatric Disorder?" in *Psychiatric Epidemiology and Mental Health Planning*, ed. R. E. Monroe, J. D. Klee, and E. B. Brody, pp. 337–45. Washington, D.C.: American Psychiatric Association, 1967.

LEVINSON, DANIEL J., and OTHERS, "Stages of Adulthood," in *Socialization and the Life Cycle*, ed. Peter I. Rose, pp. 279–93. New York: St. Martin's Press, 1979.

LOCKE, B. Z., M. KERAMER, and B. PASAMANICK, "Mental Diseases of the Senaim at Mid-Century," *American Journal of Public Health*, 50 (1960), 998–1012.

LOWENTHL, MARJORIE, MAJDA THURNHER, DAVID CHIRIBOGA, and ASSOCIATES, *Four Stages of Life*. San Francisco: Jossey-Bass, 1975.

MAUGHAM, W. SOMERSET, *The Summing Up*. New York: Doubleday, 1938.

MISCHEL, WALTER, "Continuity and Change in Personality," *American Psychologist*, 44, no. 11 (1969), 1012–18.

MISCHEL, WALTER, *Personality and Assessment*. New York: John Wiley, 1968.

NEUGARTEN, BERNICE, "Adult Personality: Toward a Psychology of the Life Cycle," in *Middle Age and Aging*, ed. Bernice Neugarten. Chicago: University of Chicago Press, 1968.

NEUGARTEN, BERNICE, L., "Summary and Implications," in *Personality in Middle and Later Life*, ed. Bernice Neugarten. New York: Atherton Press, 1964.

NEUGARTEN, BERNICE, L., and DAVID L. GUTMAN, "Age-Sex Roles and Personality in Middle Age: A Thematic Apperception Study," *Psychological Monographs*, 72, no. 17, whole no. 470 (1958).

NEUGARTEN, BERNICE, L., ROBERT J. HAVIGHURST, and

SHELDON S. TOBIN, "The Measurement of Life Satisfaction," *Journal of Gerontology*, 16 (1961), 168–74.

NEUGARTEN, BERNICE, ROBERT HAVIGHURST, and SHELDON TOBIN, "Personality and Patterns of Aging," in *Middle Age and Aging*, ed. Bernice Neugarten, pp. 173–78. Chicago: University of Chicago Press, 1968.

NEWMAN, B. M., and P. R. NEWMAN, *Personality Development through the Life Span*. Monterey, Calif.: Brooks/Cole, 1980.

PALMORE, ERDMAN, "The Effects of Aging on Activities and Attitudes," in *Normal Aging*, ed. Erdman Palmore. Durham, N.C.: Duke University Press, 1970.

REICHARD, SUZANNE, FLORINE LIVSON, and PAUL PETERSON, *Aging and Personality*. New York: John Wiley, 1962.

RILEY, M. W., A. FONER, and ASSOCIATES, *Aging and Society, Volume 1: An Inventory of Research Findings*. New York: Russell Sage, 1968.

SCHONFELD, LAWRENCE, and LARRY DUPREE, "What Triggers Their Drinking," *Aging*, 3611, (1990), 5–5.

SCHONFIELD, D., "Learning and Retention," in *Contemporary Gerontology: Concepts and Issues*, ed. J. E. Birren. Los Angeles: Andeurs Gerontology Center, 1969.

SEZLE, H., *The Stress of Life*. New York: McGraw-Hill, 1956.

SNYDER, PHYLLIS K., and ANN WAY, "Alcoholism and the Elderly," *Aging*, January–February 1979, pp. 8–11.

ZIMBERG, SHELDON, "The Elderly Alcoholic," *Gerontologist* (June 1974), pp. 222–25.

NOTES

1. Daniel J. Levinson and others, "Stages of Adulthood," in *Socialization and the Life Cycle*, ed. Peter I. Rose (New York: St. Martin's Press, 1979), pp. 279–93.
2. Vern L. Bengtson, *The Social Psychology of Aging* (Indianapolis: Bobbs-Merrill, 1973), pp. 9–10.
3. Bernice Neugarten, ed., *Middle Age and Aging* (Chicago: University of Chicago Press, 1968), p. 137.
4. James E. Birren, "Psychological Aspects of Aging: Intellectual Functioning," *Gerontologist* (1968) pp. 16–19.
5. Ibid., p. 17.
6. R. F., Canestrari, "Research in Learning," *Gerontologist*, 7, no. 2, pt. 2 (1967), 65.
7. Richard A. Kalish, *Late Adulthood: Perspectives on Human Development* (Monterey, Calif.: Brooks/Cole, 1975), p. 40.
8. Ibid., p. 46.

9. Douglas C. Kimmel, *Adulthood and Aging* (New York: John Wiley, 1974), pp. 300–305.
10. Carl G. Jung, "The Stages of Life," trans. R. F. C. Hull, in *The Portable Jung*, ed. Joseph Campbell (New York: Viking, 1971).
11. M. W. Riley, A. Foner, and associates, *Aging and Society, Volume 1: An Inventory of Research Findings* (New York: Russell Sage, 1968), p. 63.
12. Kalish, *Late Adulthood*, p. 57.
13. Bernice L. Neugarten, Robert J. Havighurst, and Sheldon S. Tobin, "The Measurement of Life Satisfaction," *Journal of Gerontology*, 16 (1961), 168–74.
14. M. Clark and B. C. Anderson, *Culture and Aging* (Springfield, Ill.: Chas. C Thomas, 1967), pp. 232–33.
15. C. Buhler, "Old Age and Fulfillment of Life with Considerations of the Use of Time in Old Age," *Acta Psychologica*, 19 (1961), 126–48.

16. Kalish, *Late Adulthood*, p. 65.
17. M. Fried, *Social Differences in Mental Health in Poverty and Wealth*, ed. S. J. Rosa, A. Antonovska, and K. Zola (Cambridge, Mass.: Harvard University Press, 1969).
18. Robert Butler and Myrna Lewis, *Aging and Mental Health: Positive Psychosocial Approaches* (St. Louis: C. V. Mosby, 1973), p. 115; and Herman B. Brotman, "Who Are the Aging?" in *Mental Illness in Later Life*, ed. Edward W. Busse and Eric Pfeiffer (Washington, D.C.: American Psychiatric Association, 1973), p. 36.
19. Carole Allen and Herman Brotman, *Chartbook on Aging in America* (Washington, D.C.: White House Conference on Aging, 1981), p. 90.
20. Charles Harris, *Fact Book on Aging: A Profile of America's Older Population* (Washington, D.C.: National Council on the Aging, 1978), p. 150.
21. Lawrence Krupka and Arthur Veneer, "Hazards of Drug Use Among the Elderly," *Gerontologist*, 19, no. 1 (1979), 90.
22. Phyllis K. Snyder and Ann Way, "Alcoholism and the Elderly," *Aging*, January–February 1979, p. 10.
23. Margaret Bailey, Paul W. Haberman, and Harold Alksne, "The Epidemiology of Alcoholism in an Urban Residential Area," *Quarterly Journal of Studies on Alcohol*, 26 (1965), 13.

6

Age Norms,
Age Constraints,
and Adult Socialization

In the previous chapter we discussed the physiological, psychological, and social changes that a person must adjust to in later life. Whereas the last chapter focused heavily on the psychological adjustment to these events, this chapter will look more closely at the social aspects of aging.

Observing ten-year periods throughout the life cycle, Richard Kalish (1975) notes,

> To grasp what has happened during the past decade, you must examine more than one dimension of your past existence. It is immediately obvious that you have had ten years of experiences—pleasant and unpleasant, exciting and boring, warming and embittering, ego building and ego destroying.[1]

Older persons often find their lives considerably changed during the later years. Their children have most often left home and gone to establish their own families. They are retired and find themselves spending considerably more time around their homes with their spouse. They usually have considerably less income on which to attempt to maintain their preferred lifestyle. Most have experienced some chronic health problem to which they must adjust. They have probably lost former friends due to death and frequently have lost touch with younger people in the community. Thus, the lives of older persons may be considerably altered during the later years.

David Goslin (1969) defines *socialization* as

> the process by which individuals acquire the knowledge, skills and dispositions that enable them to participate as more or less effective members of groups and society.[2]

Socialization is a process of learning how one is expected to behave in a given role or social situation. It is a lifelong process, since change is a constant part of one's life. We are always assuming new roles and positions in the social system. Some of the difficulties inherent in the changes of life are mitigated by the fact that they are often anticipated, desired, and prepared for. A young man or woman may spend considerable time anticipating and planning a marriage. Hope chests, bachelor parties, wedding plans, showers, and so on may all be part of the process. Sociologists have coined the term *anticipatory socialization* for this phenomenon. Thus the person imagines what it is going to be like to assume the new, and in this case, desired role. While the actual performance of the role may not be exactly what the person had expected, he or she will probably feel more comfortable in the new role as a result of his or her preparations.

One problem older Americans are confronted with as they plan for the next phase of their lives is that some of the roles they will be assuming are positive and desirable while others are not. Retirement after 40 years of striving to succeed in a career may be desirable. Being a widow or widower, or being sick, are usually roles that are not desired. Thus, older Americans must for the first time in their lives look forward to a variety of undesirable events in their future. This is the first time in one's life that future events are not viewed positively and anticipated with high expectations. The child looks forward to adulthood and can't wait to reach the age of 21. The junior executive looks forward to becoming the president of the company. Older persons, for the first time in their lives, look to their future with some degree of antipathy. Everything in their future is not necessarily going to be good.

Still, the evidence indicates that there is considerable planning and preparation for the future by middle-aged and older persons. Considerable anticipatory socialization does take place. A study by Harold Cox and Albert Bhak (1980) indicated that as early as age 55, some Americans sell their large homes in which they raised their families and move to smaller houses or apartments located nearer to desired services.[3] Thus many Americans prepare well in advance for the later years.

There are societal norms and expectations about how one is to act at any age in life. A mother may scold her 7-year-old son "to grow up and act his age," and a 70-year-old man may be referred to as a "dirty old man" because he shows an interest in the opposite sex at an age when society believes he should no longer be interested in sex. At any age there will be discrepancies between how one is expected to act and how one would like to act.

In a youth-oriented culture such as that of the United States, many people do not like to think of themselves as getting old. By thinking of oneself as old, the individual loses the privileges of the adult and middle years. Bernard Phillips (1957) reports a study done at Elmira and Kips Bay, New York, in which respondents were asked if they identified themselves as being old, middle-aged, or young. A measure of psychological adjustment and maladjustment was then given to the respondents. Psychological adjustment was defined as "the efforts of an individual to satisfy his personal needs as well as to live up to the expectations of others."[4] Maladjustment was defined as "behavior which does not completely satisfy the individual and social needs of the person, even though it may reduce his drive tension."[5] A significantly higher proportion of the maladjusted respondents were found among those who identified themselves as old (Table 6–1). This relationship held when controlled for employment status, marital status, and age.[6] Elizabeth Mutran and Peter Burke (1979), in a study of age identification found the same results as Phillips (1957). They reported that it is not the individual's chronological age that is important but rather his or her subjective identification with being "old" that leads to overall dissatisfaction. For men, retirement forced the individual to restructure his self-concept and begin developing an identity of

TABLE 6–1   Percentage of Maladjusted Respondents by Age Identification

Age Identification	Elmira		Kips Bay	
	Percent	N*	Percent	N*
Middle-aged	31	(343)	28	(287)
Old	58	(118)	49	(199)

*In this table and Table 6–2 N refers to the total number in each category.

Source: Bernard S. Phillips, "A Role Theory Approach to Adjustment in Old Age," *American Sociological Review*, 22 (1957), 216.

being old. Mutran and Burke (1979) found that retirement was also crucial to the development of an old-age identity for black women since historically they have shared the role of provider. For white women, chronological age and poor health were directly linked to the old-age identity; retirement was not, seemingly because a career was not their central life interest. In any event, identifying oneself as old in a youth-oriented society is apparently not a healthy thing to do.

LIFE SPACE

The changing social environment of older Americans is clearly illustrated by the concept of *life space*. One thinks of a newborn child's life space in terms of limited but expanding horizons. The child's life space may be a single room in a house or apartment. Much of the child's first years are spent in a single room where he or she sleeps, eats, and plays. The child of one to three begins to walk and move around, and his or her life space becomes the entire apartment or house. The child from three to six years begins to travel around the yard and perhaps one block of the neighborhood. Thus, his or her life space is increasing. Upon entering school he or she is allowed to move about in a school district or neighborhood of several blocks.

The mature adult's life space is the whole world. He or she is confronted with both national and international issues and is expected to be an active participant in the community, to regularly take part in local and national elections, and occasionally to go to war.

Older persons find their life space beginning to shrink. Upon retirement they find themselves not going to the office, not being involved in major business decisions, and tending to travel more frequently in their neighborhood rather than throughout the city. Eventually, declining health, poor vision, or related problems may force them to quit driving, and thus they are even more likely to stay in their own neighborhood. Ultimately they may find themselves staying in their own house or apartment most of the time. Health reasons may limit their leaving the house. Thus both the physical and social environment of older Americans usually shrink gradually. Socially one no longer sees his or her cronies at the office, lifelong friends die, and the opportunity to make new friends may be limited. Upon the death of a spouse, one no longer fits comfortably in a group of married couples.

ROLE

Roles are socially acceptable and expected ways of behaving associated with a particular job, function, or task. In simple terms, a role is a pattern of expected behavior associated with a position in society. The norms of expected behavior are very strong, and much pressure to conform is placed on people who occupy a certain role. Sociologists have maintained that one can better predict a person's behavior by knowing the position he or she holds than by knowing the idiosyncratic aspects of his or her personality. For example, all ministers behave somewhat alike regardless of their personalities.

One's role in a social setting is usually accompanied by another, reciprocal role. Thus if there is a mother, there is a child. If a teacher is expected to lead interesting lectures and discussions, students are expected to be responsive, attentive, and ask pertinent questions.

Since change is an integral part of life, the individual is often in the process of discarding old roles and learning new ones. Thus a girl may no longer be a teenager, but a bride; in a few years, she may no longer be solely a wife, but a wife and mother.

Some of the roles people assume throughout the life cycle are desired and sought by them while others are expected and forced on them by others. A young man may want to become a husband but not be anxious to be a father. Nevertheless, if children are born in the marriage he will be expected to assume the role of father.

Each role carries with it a given status. *Status* is the position of dominance or subordination associated with a role. The role of father in a family carries high status, privilege, and power. The role of son carries low status, privilege, and power. The father makes decisions and directs the son's early life. The son is expected to comply.

There are both advantages and disadvantages to the roles one assumes in later life. The major advantage that many older Americans express at retirement is that for the first time in their lives they are free to choose their roles and activities. Until retirement, many of the roles that adults assume are expected and carry heavy demands for their time and effort. For example, the endless work of rearing and nurturing children involves constant attention, diaper changing, and feeding during the child's early years followed by careful concern for the next several years. Most parents breathe a sigh of relief once their children are reared and successfully launched on their own. Parenthood, while it may be a desired role, carries heavy demands on the individual's time and energy. Moreover, the norms surrounding parenthood are so strong that no self-respecting individual seriously considers abandoning this role once it is assumed.

The retired couple usually have their children reared, no longer must go to work every morning, and can now choose what they want and don't want to do. There is probably greater freedom of choice for older Americans than for any other age group. One is free to volunteer at the local hospital or go to the golf course every day. One can remain in Chicago throughout the year, move to Florida during the winter months, or pick up and move permanently to Florida. There is probably a wider range of roles to assume for older Americans than for any other age group in our society. Even the roles that are forced on the elderly by the social system allow them considerable freedom. For example, one becomes a grandfather and grandmother through no choice of his or her own. The grandparent role, however, allows one to spoil the grandchildren, if he or she chooses, without being responsible for their discipline.

On the other hand, the roles available for the aged to choose among are not highly valued in our society and do not bring high status. Most of these roles, whether leisure, recreational, volunteer, or family, are valued less than the roles assumed by the adult and middle-aged groups in the population.

Phillips (1957), in examining a number of role changes among the elderly and correlating these with adjustment, found that the retired were more likely to be maladjusted than the employed; the widowed were more likely to be maladjusted than the married; and those over 70 were more likely to be maladjusted than those under that age (Table 6–2). It would appear that role changes in later life, just like those at an earlier age, involve some adjustment by the individual. Phillips's study does not indicate how long those individuals had been retired or widowed, and therefore there is no way to determine if they ultimately adjusted to the new role.

The information we have on the desirability of the retirement role is confusing at this time, however. Reichard, Livson, and Peterson (1962) found that people who were both older and retired had greater ego strength, indicated less projection of hostility, had fewer obsessional defenses, and were more open, freer from anxiety, and less depressed. They concluded that the period of greatest difficulty was from 64 to 69, when the transition to new roles and circumstances is still in process. Once the transition has taken place, the strength just cited appeared.[7]

Bill Bell (1976) found, in a study of retirement adjustment, that 12 percent of his sample had increased their community contact after retirement and experienced an increase in life satisfaction. This suggests that the more time the individual invests in community contact after retirement, the more positive is the change in life satisfaction. Bell concluded that community involvement gives the individual rewards similar to those he or she received from employment.

TABLE 6–2 Percentage of Maladjusted Respondents by Role

Role	Elmira		Kips Bay	
	Percent	N*	Percent	N*
Employed	22	(171)**	27	(161)**
Retired	42	(98)**	40	(200)**
Married	27	(173)**	30	(221)**
Widow or widower	40	(217)**	47	(180)**
Age 60–69	29	(277)**	31	(254)*
70 or over	52	(187)**	40	(233)*
Not treated differently	34	(366)**	32	(355)**
Treated differently	53	(87)**	48	(118)**

*Difference is significant at the .05 level.
**Difference is significant at the .01 level.

Source: Bernard S. Phillips, "A Role Theory Approach to Adjustment in Old Age," *American Sociological Review*, 22 (1957), 216.

Families of retired individuals were apparently not able to provide these precise satisfactions.[8]

Old people find less social pressure placed on them for role performance, and they can choose among a variety of roles. Simultaneously, they are better able to resist social pressure. They no longer have to worry about pleasing the boss or establishing business and political ties in the community. They are therefore freer to follow their own inclinations. Douglas Kimmel (1974) observes that

> women, as they age, seem to become more tolerant of their own aggressive egocentric impulses; while men, as they age, seem to become more tolerant of their own nurturant and affiliative impulses.[9]

The lack of concern for social pressure can be seen in the following letter thanking a friend who sent a radio as a gift. Her response to her roommate seems to illustrate total honesty and the total lack of social constraint that older persons experience.

> Dear Mr. Gary:
>
> Just a short note of thanks to you and your associates in the Adult Education Association for the more than generous donation which you gave to the Senior Citizen's Fun Fund (SCFF) recently. Your kind contribution meant a new clock radio for me. Thank you so much for the lovely gift. It is just wonderful that an absolute stranger like yourself would take time off from his own business to remember people like us. I am 82 years old and I have been here at the home for 16 long years. They treat us well, but the loneliness is sometimes hard to bear.
>
> My roommate, Mrs. Eisenblatt, is a very nice person but is very stingy. She has a radio but she never would let me use it and she turns it off when I come into the room. Now, because of your thoughtfulness, I have my very own radio.
>
> My son and daughter-in-law are very nice and they come to visit me once a month. I appreciate it, but also understand their sense of obligation. This makes your gift all the more wonderful because it was given not as a sense of duty, but from a feeling of compassion from a fellow human being.
>
> Today Mrs. Eisenblatt's radio went out of order and when she asked me if she could use mine, I told her to go f_____ herself.
>
> Yours truly,

Kimmel (1974), in reviewing studies of personality changes in later life, argues that the life cycle of an individual involves moving from an early period of expansion in young adulthood, in which one is rapidly learning and acquiring new roles and is very careful to note the observations of others about their behavior, to a period of balance between external and internal pressures in the middle years, to an increasing focus on internal processes in old age and much less concern for external pressures.

AGE SYNCHRONIZATION

Most people have an idea of what age in life is most appropriate for the accomplishment of the major life tasks. They consider age a factor in judging their peers' successes and failures as well as their own. One often hears people refer to themselves as marrying early or late, which implies that they have an idea of what the right age is to marry. While there are normative expectations about the ages at which certain life tasks are to be accomplished, Dennis Hogan (1985) argues that there are such widespread individual variations in the achievement of these tasks that the norms are meaningless. Uhlenberg (1980) asserts that a normal expected life pattern for females would involve marrying, bearing children, and surviving to age 50 with the first marriage intact. Hogan (1985) points out that of cohorts born in 1870 who lived to reach adulthood, only 44 percent experienced this normative pattern. Many of these cohorts never married and because of higher death rates many were widowed prior to age 50. The proportion of women born in 1930 who followed this pattern increased to 60 percent— still far from a universal pattern because of the widespread individual variation in the achievement or failure to achieve certain well-defined life tasks. Most of the members of a society, rightly or wrongly, believe that there is an orderly progression through the basic life transitions that everyone should follow within a limited age range.

There appear to be three major areas of accomplishment that require some coordination in a person's life—family, career, and age group. Jaber Gubrium (1976) speaks of these as spheres within and between which persons can be seen as late, early, or on time.

> For the most part, an individual in our society marries in his early twenties, completes the childbearing period in his late twenties, reaches a career and income peak in his late forties or early fifties, is widowed sometime thereafter and begins to consider himself old in his mid seventies.[10]

One may enter a career early but marry late. On the other hand, one may marry in the early 20s (about the right time), enter a career simultaneously (also about the expected time), but not achieve the career success he or she expected by the middle 40s. The lack of synchronization of the major events in one's life creates anxiety for the individual. People who are, say, divorced in their 30s, reach a career peak in their early 40s, and remarry in their late 40s would, according to Gubrium, experience considerable tension due to the lack of synchronization between the different spheres of their life.

Table 6–3 indicates the results of a study by Bernice Neugarten and colleagues (1965) on what people felt was the best age to achieve given critical life tasks. While these respondents represent a cross section of ages and opinions, there are sometimes differences in attitude based on age. The researchers reported that a 20-year-old felt it would be perfectly all right for a 17-year-old to marry as long as the boy had a job. A 45-year-old man, on the other hand, felt that it would be foolish to marry that young, and that both partners would suffer later.

Still, most people believe there is a desirable age for marrying, raising children, achieving career success, and retiring. Upon meeting someone for the first time, Americans quickly observe the age and sex of the individual and then draw some conclusions about his or her behavior. Age is a critical social category carrying certain societal norms and expectations.

Robert Merton (1957) developed a typology of deviant behavior based on the individual's conformity to culturally prescribed goals and the normative expectations regarding how one was to achieve these goals. Gubrium (1976) has modi-

TABLE 6–3 Consensus in a Middle-Class, Middle-Aged Sample Regarding Various Age-Related Characteristics

	Age Range Designated as Appropriate or Expected	Percent Who Concur	
		Men	Women
Best age for a man to marry	20–25	80	90
Best age for a woman to marry	19–24	85	90
When most people should become grandparents	45–50	84	79
Best age for most people to finish school and go to work	20–22	86	82
When most men should be settled on a career	24–26	74	64
When most men hold their "top" jobs	45–50	71	58
When most people should be ready to retire	60–65	83	86
A young man	18–22	84	83
A middle-aged man	40–50	86	75
An old man	65–75	75	57
A young woman	18–24	89	88
A middle-aged woman	40–50	87	77
An old woman	60–75	83	87
When a man has the most responsibilities	35–50	79	75
When a man accomplishes most	40–50	82	71
The prime of life for a man	35–50	86	80
When a woman has the most responsibilities	25–40	93	91
When a woman accomplishes most	30–45	94	92
A good-looking woman	20–35	92	82

Fifty middle-aged men and 43 middle-aged women were asked to indicate the age for which each of these statements is most descriptive.

Source: Reprinted from "Age Norms, Age Constraints, and Age Socialization," *American Journal of Sociology*, 70 (1965), 710–17, by B. L. Neugarten, J. W. Moore, and J. C. Lowe, by permission of The University of Chicago Press. © 1965 by The University of Chicago Press.

fied the table to explain individuals' conformity with or deviance from the timing of major life events. Gubrium identifies the sources of time-disoriented relationships as inconsistencies within social spheres, such as marrying early and having one's children late; inconsistencies between social spheres—for example, having children late, at about the time one's career is peaking; or inconsistencies both within and between spheres, such as being divorced and starting a second family in the late 40s and not achieving a career peak until the late 50s. Gubrium borrows the Merton typology to show all the possible arrangements of time-ordered events in one's work career (Table 6–4).

Conformity, according to Gubrium, consists of having socially acceptable career goals and arriving at these goals at expected times.

Innovation would be the case when the individual accepts and internalizes the career goals but is not able to follow their culturally prescribed timing. For instance, an individual may plan to be a doctor but be forced out of medical school to take a job because of poor finances. Five years later he or she may reenter the program and ultimately complete it, though several years after his or her cohorts. Professional women who drop out of school to have children and reenter after their children enter first grade would be another example.

TABLE 6–4 Responses to Time-Disoriented Relationships

	Career Goals	Goal Timing
1. Conformity	+	+
2. Innovation	+	−
3. Ritualism	−	+
4. Retreatism	−	−
5. Rebellion	+	+

Source: Jaber F. Gubrium, in *Time, Roles and Self in Old Age*, ed. Jaber F. Gubrium (New York: Human Sciences Press, 1976), p. 120. © 1976 by Human Sciences Press.

In the pattern called *ritualism*, people have given up on achieving the culturally prescribed goals, but they conquer any lingering guilt feelings by acting as though they still plan to achieve the goals. They may work very hard at a job from which they know they will never be promoted. Their behavior becomes ritualistic.

In *retreatism* people have given up on the prescribed goals and on the timing for achieving these goals. They are not the least bit concerned about goals or the timing of events in their lives. Gubrium describes their behavior as nonnormative. He believes they are most often lifelong isolates.

People in *rebellion* believe that the culturally prescribed goals and the timing of these events are wrong. They want to restructure the current social order, creating a new system they believe will be better. They may keep or reject some or all of the prescribed goals and the expected timetables, depending on their view of what the social system ought to be. The Gray Panthers, led by Maggie Kuhn, who want to bring greater privileges and status to older Americans, typify this pattern.

Gubrium believes that middle-aged and older people who view the schedule of events as under their control perceive themselves as younger and more internally in control of their lives than do those who view the scheduling as externally imposed.

Beyond the timing of such events as marriage and child rearing, gerontologists have been concerned with the individual's perception of broad values. In attempting to determine if there are any changes in life tasks subjectively experienced by people at different ages, most researchers have examined the models of human development. In Chapter 2, Freud, Jung, and Erickson were discussed. These theorists all predicted that each individual will experience an orderly progression of changes at different points in the life cycle. If one follows the Erickson model, a logical question to raise is: Do adults see themselves as most concerned with intimacy in young adulthood, generativity in middle age, and integrity in old age?

Neugarten (1973), in attempting to test some of the models that propose various stages of adult development, examined changes in orientation toward instrumental and terminal values over the life cycle. *Instrumental values* are desirable modes of conduct such as being ambitious, capable, courageous, and achievement-oriented. *Terminal values*, on the other hand, are desirable end states, such as a sense of accomplishment, a feeling of freedom to do as one chooses, a feeling of happiness. Neugarten found that middle-aged women had a comparatively higher preference for instrumental values in the present but antici-pated a decline in this preference in old age. The older women reported a lower preference for the instrumental values in the present, though they recalled such values had been more important when they were middle-aged. Ryff (1982) found basically the same orientation toward instrumental and terminal values that Neugarten did. Women again showed greater preference for instrumental values during middle age than in old age. Ryff and Heincke (1983) found that these patterns of value orientation for middle age and old age did not differ by sex. Such outcomes indicate that certain aspects of Erickson's theory may accurately characterize the subjective experience of both men and women.

NORMATIVE CONSTRAINTS

Society feels that it has a significant investment in people at every age; their footsteps must be guided carefully so that they are responsible, productive mem-bers of society. Socialization trains persons to assume the roles they are expected to occupy during the next years of their lives. Both formally and informally, most socialization is directed at children and young adults in order to teach them to fill the roles they must assume as adults if society is to run well. Informally, parents provide a role model that children may emulate in order to learn the expected pattern of behavior. Formally, individuals are lectured to by parents, sent to public schools and colleges, and frequently sent to specialized training programs by the companies that employ them.

While great expense, time, and effort go into socializing individuals to assume adult roles, practically no training goes on 40 years later to prepare them to leave the world of work and retire in a meaningful fashion. Government, higher education, and private business have not been willing to invest in socializ-ing individuals for the roles they will be assuming in later life.

In terms of age constraints, the older one becomes the more likely he or she is to believe that there is a proper way for people of a given age to behave, or a proper age to marry or experience other major life events. On the other hand, the older people become the less likely they are to perceive constraints being placed on their behavior by society or the generalized other.[11]

Thus, most of the constraints placed on the behavior of older people are their own constraints, acquired and internalized through a lifetime of experiences. (Society has generally been little concerned about what older Americans do or don't do.) The French sociologist Emile Durkheim (1951) coined the term *anomie* to refer to states of normlessness in which the rules of life change so rapidly that people do not know how to conduct themselves. Anomie, or states of normless-ness, were thought by Durkheim to be extremely confusing, disconcerting, and frightening to the individual. He believed that anomie was one of the causes of suicide. The fact that society places very few normative constraints on older persons, along with the knowledge that the incidence of suicide rises dramatically for men after the age of 65, suggests that Durkheim was correct. The suicide rate for women, however, is highest between 45 and 55 and declines in the later years. Research on suicide has neither explained the sex difference nor explored whether anomie is a useful concept for explaining the patterns of suicide among older persons.

Only the future will determine if society will be concerned enough about older individuals to take an interest in the appropriateness of their behavior. At present there appear to be relatively few social constraints on older Americans and a general lack of concern for their lives by society.

ATTITUDES TOWARD OLD AGE

The most negative attitudes about older Americans are often expressed by children. Serock and colleagues (1978), in a study of children's attitudes toward older persons, found many of the stereotypes about old people being expressed by children:

"They are wrinkled and short."

"They have gray hair."

"They don't go out much."

"They chew funny."

"Old people sit all day and watch T.V. in their rocking chairs."

"They have heart attacks and die."[12]

The children in this study also saw themselves as taking care of older people, getting them their slippers, and taking them to the doctor, and occasionally they even mentioned that they would have to bury them. In a similar study conducted by Judith Burke (1981–82), children identified older adults as sad, lonely, and not busy; older adults were bypassed on items like "knows a lot" and "I prefer to have this person as a teacher." In a study of knowledge of aging in an elderly population, Helen West and Walter Levy (1981) found old people shared many of the same stereotypes of old people that were held by younger age groups. Males were found to be more biased than females against the old, and the very old were the most biased of all.

While the children in the Serock study (1978) expressed all the traditional stereotypes of aging, a Harris study (1975) conducted for the National Council on the Aging was a little more optimistic. Harris found that 74 percent of the public saw the old as friendly and warm, 64 percent as wise from experience, 41 percent as physically active, 35 percent as effectual and proficient, 29 percent as adaptive, and only 5 percent as sexually active.[13]

SOCIAL CLASS AND ADJUSTMENT TO OLD AGE

The adjustment to old age has only superficially been viewed from the position of one's social class background. Somewhat like minority groups, old people are often viewed by the general public as being all alike when in fact they come from different class backgrounds, have spent much of their lives in different occupations, and have had quite disparate life experiences.

Thomas Tissue (1979) studied the retirement adjustment of middle- and lower-class Americans and found some unexpected differences between the two groups. Blue-collar workers have generally lived on smaller incomes and been less affluent throughout their lives. The low incomes accorded them by social security and other retirement programs often represent only a slight decrease from what they were previously used to. The middle class, on the other hand, is used to a secure income and a desirable style of life throughout their adult years. If they are forced to rely almost solely on social security, their income loss is heavy. Moreover, the lower status and near poverty that some older Americans are forced to accept is a considerably greater loss in status for the middle class than it is for the lower class.

It is specifically these issues that Tissue addressed in comparing retired middle- and lower-class Americans. Tissue compares middle-class retirees to "social skidders" in adult life. "Social skidders" are defined by sociologists as people who started in a higher social class or social status position and find themselves dropping to a less desirable position. This skidding can be intergenerational, as when a son must accept a lower position than his father, or intragenerational, as when a person is unsuccessful in his or her career and is demoted. Wilensky and Edwards (1959) found social skidders to be more rigidly conservative that non-skidders and to hold on to a more rigid middle-class value structure.[14] Tissue (1979) states,

> Like a man falling from a skyscraper, our skidder reaches not in the direction of his fall, but back up the structure.[15]

The working-class elderly, by comparison, more frequently maintain an intact family unit, are more likely to be living with a spouse, and regularly see children and other family members (Tables 6–5 and 6–6). Middle-class respondents, according to Tissue, are more likely to read, attend movies, pursue hobbies, and watch television. Many of these activities illustrate their capacity for solitary enjoyment. Twenty-nine percent of the middle-class respondents report being not too happy with their current life compared with 17 percent of the working class.

TABLE 6–5 Life Space and Perceived Life Space of the Elderly

	Middle Class	Working Class
Life space		
Low (0–49 contacts)	47%	32%
High (50 plus contacts)	53	68
	100%	100%
	(127)	(129)
Perceived life space*		
Severe loss (in at least 4 of 5 roles)	55%	40%
Moderate to no loss (in 3 or fewer roles)	45	60
	100%	100%
	(127)	(129)

*Significant at .02 level.

Source: Thomas Tissue, "Downward Mobility in Old Age," in Socialization and the Life Cycle, ed. Peter I. Rose (New York: St. Martin's Press, 1979), p. 356. Reprinted with permission of the Society for the Study of Social Problems.

TABLE 6–6 Family Characteristics of the Elderly

	Middle Class	Working Class
Currently lives with spouse*	23%	36%
	(127)	(129)
Lives in own home*	17%	28%
	(127)	(129)
Children living in California*		
(For those with living children)		
Has none	11%	26%
Has one	28	30
Has two	29	20
Has three or more	32	24
	100%	100%
	(104)	(105)
Sees at least one child daily	26%	38%
(For those with living children)	(103)	(105)

*Significant at .05 level.

Source: Thomas Tissue, "Downward Mobility in Old Age," in *Socialization and the Life Cycle*, ed. Peter I. Rose (New York: St. Martin's Press, 1979), p. 356. Reprinted with permission of the Society for the Study of Social Problems.

In other words, feeling that retirement was working out worse than anticipated and that freedom from responsibility and additional free time were not the major benefits of old age and missing at least some part of one's previous job was a response pattern more common to those with higher socioeconomic origins.[16]

Dissatisfied with their retirement life, the middle class gives strong verbal support to the ethic of hard work for its own sake and a belief that one's fate is the result of one's abilities rather than luck or chance. Middle-class retirees appear to be more committed and more conservative than the general population in clinging to middle-class values. Is this the result of their status loss and their reaching back to a more preferred time in their life and to the values they believed in then? Only future research can tell us. Wilensky and Edwards (1959) would suggest that social skidders profess exaggerated allegiance to the values of the system in which they perceive they have failed.

AGE, GENDER, AND LONGEVITY

Age and gender are two of the principal factors always examined by demographers differentiating members of a population. As was pointed out in Chapters 1 and 4, any consideration of longevity clearly indicates that in terms of survival women are the stronger sex. Today, females surviving to age 65 can now expect on the average to live at least another 18 years and males another 14 (Allen & Brotman, 1981). Moreover, two thirds of all deaths occur after the age of 65 and 30 percent after the age of 80 (Brody & Brock, 1985). Because gains in longevity at the oldest ages have accrued more rapidly to women than to men, women clearly are in the majority. Carole Allen and Herman Brotman (1981) have estimated that by the year 2000 there will be 150 women for every 100 men at age 65 and 254 women for every 100 men at age 85.

Women currently outlive men by approximately 7 years. In addition, women on the average marry men who are 2.5 years older than themselves. The result is that women who marry can expect to live approximately 9.5 years as a widow. Robert Butler, Myrna Lewis and Trey Sunderland (1991) point out that 50.5 percent of the older women are widows, 4.4 percent are divorced, and 5.2 percent of all women never marry. Thus 60 percent of the older female population are living alone and independently directing their own lives. This is an interesting fact in a society that socializes women to want to be married and dependent on men.

A most common pattern of later life for older women then is one of living alone, on a low income, often in substandard housing and with little or no chance to find employment in order to improve their lot in life.

Women for a variety of reasons are likely to be living on considerably less income than men during their later years. Butler, Lewis and Sunderland (1991) observe that only 20 percent of the women have retired with private pension benefits over the last five years, compared to 40 percent of the men. Moreover, in 1989 the average monthly social security benefit was $458 for women, compared to $627 for men. Social security benefits for women workers average 76 percent of the amount of men. This is partly a result of the fact that during the child-rearing years, women are often out of the work force and are making no contributions to the social security program, which results in lower benefits upon retirement. Another factor is that women when working earn less than men. Women workers of all ages earned 65 cents for every dollar earned by men in 1990.[17] Thus upon retirement they have accrued less benefits.

The U.S. Bureau of the Census (1988) reports that social security is the only source of income for 20 percent of all older women and 12 percent of older men.[18] If no improvements are made in social security, by the year 2020 it is projected that 38 percent of all older women living alone will be poor. One of the common paths to poverty in old age is to become a displaced homemaker in mid-life. Displaced homemakers comprised 10 million women over the age of 45 in 1989 who have lost their primary source of income due to separation, divorce, widowhood, prolonged unemployment of spouses, disability, or loss of eligibility for public assistance.[19]

The increasing longevity of both men and women has led to a lengthening of normal adult roles, the addition of new roles, and considerable role flexibility over the life course. A woman who had a child in her 20s may be a mother for 50 or 60 years. Although in the traditional view she carried out the duties of a mother only for the first 20 of those years, she is still considered a mother. Thus, her increasing longevity has considerably lengthened this role. Retirement, which did not formally exist in 1900, now accounts for over one fourth of adult life. Thus a new adult role has been created.

Matilda Riley (1985) observes that increased longevity gives individuals opportunities to change job, career, marriage, and educational plans. Riley believes that women in particular have greater role flexibility due to longer life expectancy. Now that women survive many years after the children leave home, she argues, they are more likely to combine family roles with varied work, leisure, and community roles.

Although the feminist movement has improved the opportunities for women in careers traditionally defined as men's, equal opportunity still does not exist for the sexes. Riley (1985) reports that

> at work though women seem more durable than men, their roles are still typically defined and rewarded as inferior. In family, few men spend much time if any time caring for home and children.[20]

The traditional roles and values of a society are not easily changed, and women's role changes are still evolving.

Beth Hess (1985) believes that women still represent a deprived class in American society. They are the first to suffer from any downturn in the economy and from the current cuts in government social services programs. After pointing out that federal cuts in the social service programs will fall the hardest on single-parent mothers and their children, she states,

> Nor are older women ignored in this budget. They are expected to make their disproportionate contribution to economic recovery by reducing dependency on supplemental security income, food stamps, low income, home energy assistance and section 202 housing benefits from the Older Americans Act, and any reliance on community service block grant programs or the Legal Services Corporation—all of which are targeted for reduced or zero funding. So let's hear it for the ladies—young and old—who so selflessly are giving so much to the upward distribution of wealth required for an economic recovery in a late capitalist system. Where would we be without their willingness to sacrifice for the good of others.[21]

Unless there are some dramatic changes in the longevity patterns of the sexes, women are going to continue to outlive men by a number of years. This means that the older population is going to be disproportionately composed of females. In the past, pension plans and retirement programs have always been reduced considerably once the husband dies, thereby placing a large percentage of older women below the poverty line. Changes in federal laws governing pension programs and the advent of the dual-career family, in which the wife as well as the husband will have a retirement income, seem to bode well for improvement in the financial position of older women. Despite the improved opportunities for women since the mid-1970s, whether women will receive absolutely equal roles and opportunity throughout the life cycle remains to be seen.

CONCLUSION

No individual is entirely free to do exactly what he or she would like. Rather, all are conditioned by a socialization process that teaches how one is to behave and respond in social situations. Sociologists refer to roles as expected patterns of behavior associated with certain jobs, functions, or tasks in society. Since life involves a gradual but constant process of change, one is often learning to assume new roles and relinquishing old roles. Moreover, there are social expectations about the desirable age to assume certain roles. Ideally one marries and enters a career in one's early 20s, has children in the middle 20s, achieves a career peak in the middle 40s, has the children launched by the late 40s, and retires in the early to middle 60s.

The problem for many adults is that they cannot always assume these roles at precisely the expected age, and sometimes family and career goals are not reached at the prescribed time. Time-disoriented life patterns cause the individual frustration and strain, according to Gubrium (1976).

There are both advantages and disadvantages to the assumption of retirement roles. The advantage is that society does not feel that it has a large stake in what the person does during the retirement years. Older persons are freer to choose among a variety of roles than perhaps any other age group. Simultaneously, although there are normative constraints on the behavior of people at any age, there seems to be less pressure on older persons to perform their roles in a prescribed manner. Old age involves considerable freedom from external social pressure. However, by this age most persons have internalized society's norms into a well-developed conscience that directs most of their behavior and does not require external controls. The major problem with the roles assumed by older persons is that they are perceived by others to be generally low in status, privilege, and power.

Thus while one is freer to choose among a variety of roles in later life, most of these roles are not highly valued in our society and they often involve a loss of status. This loss is perhaps greatest for middle-class Americans, who have most often maintained responsible positions in the community prior to retirement and who experience the greatest loss in income, privilege, and power at retirement.

KEY TERMS

anomie

anticipatory socialization

conformity

innovation

instrumental values

life space

rebellion

retreatism

ritualism

roles

socialization

status

terminal values

REFERENCES

ALLEN, CAROLE, and HERMAN BROTMAN, *Charts on Aging in America*. Washington, D.C.: White House Conference on Aging, 1981.

BELL, BILL D., "Role Set Orientations and Life Satisfaction: A New Look at an Old Theory," in *Time, Roles and Self in Old Age*, ed. Jaber F. Gubrium, pp. 148–64. New York: Human Sciences Press, 1976.

BRODY, J. A., and D. B. BROCK, "Epidemiological and Statistical Characteristics of the United States Elderly Population," in *Handbook of the Biology of Aging*, ed. C. Finch and E. Schneider. New York: Van Nostrand Reinhold, 1985.

BURKE, JUDITH LEE, "Young Children's Attitudes and Perceptions of Older Adults," *International Journal of Aging and Human Development*, 14, no. 3 (1981–82), 205–22.

BUTLER, ROBERT N., MYRNA LEWIS, and TREY SUNDERLAND, *Aging and Mental Health: Positive Psychological and Biomedical Approaches* (4th ed.). New York: Macmillan, 1991.

COX, HAROLD, and ALBERT BHAK, "Determinants of Age Based on Residential Segregation," *Sociological Symposium*, no. 29 (Winter 1980), 27–41.

CUMMING, E., and W. HENRY, *Growing Old: The Process of Disengagement*. New York: Basic Books, 1961.

DURKHEIM, EMILE, *Suicide*. New York: Free Press, 1951.

GOSLIN, DAVID H., ed., *Handbook of Socialization Theory and Research*. Skokie, Ill.: Rand McNally, 1969.

GUBRIUM, JABER F., *Time, Roles and Self in Old Age*, ed. Jaber F. Gubrium, p. 113. New York: Human Sciences Press, 1976.

HARRIS, LOUIS, and ASSOCIATES, *The Myth and Reality of Aging in America*. Washington, D.C.: National Council on the Aging, 1975.

HESS, BETH, "Antidiscrimination Policies Today and the Life Chances of Older Women Tomorrow," *Gerontologist*, 26, no. 2 (1985).

HOGAN, DENNIS, "The Demography of Life-Span Transitions: Temporal and Gender Comparisons," in *Gender and the Life Course*, ed. Alice S. Rossi, pp. 65–80. New York: Aldine, 1985.

KALISH, RICHARD A., *Late Adulthood: Perspectives on Human Development*. Monterey, Calif.: Brooks/Cole, 1975.

KIMMEL, DOUGLAS C., *Adulthood and Aging*. New York: John Wiley, 1974.

MERTON, ROBERT, *Social Theory and Social Structure*. New York: Free Press, 1957.

MUTRAN, ELIZABETH, and PETER J. BURKE, "Personalism as a Component of Old Age Identities," *Research on Aging*, 1, no. 1 (March 1979), 37–63.

NATIONAL COMMISSION ON WORKING WOMEN ON WIDER OPPORTUNITIES FOR WOMEN, "Women, Work and Age: An Overview" (1989). Available at 1325 G Street N.W., Lower Level, Washington, D.C. 20005.

NEUGARTEN, B. L., "Personality Change in Later Life: A Developmental Perspective," in *The Psychology of Adult Development and Aging*, ed. C. Eisdorfer and M. P. Lawton, pp. 311–35. Washington, D.C.: American Psychological Association, 1973.

NEUGARTEN, BERNICE L., JOAN W. MOORE, and JOHN C. LOWE, "Age Norms, Age Constraints, and Age Socialization," *American Journal of Sociology*, 70 (1965), 710–17.

PHILLIPS, BERNARD S., "A Role Theory Approach to Adjustments in Old Age," *American Sociological Review*, 22 (1957), 212–17.

REICHARD, S., F. LIVSON, and P. C. PETERSON, *Aging and Personality: A Study of 87 Older Men*. New York: John Wiley, 1962.

RILEY, MATILDA WHITE, "Women, Men and the Lengthening Life Course," in *Gender and the Life Course*, ed. Alice S. Rossi, pp. 333–47. New York: Aldine, 1985.

RYFF, C. D., "Self Perceived Personality Change in Adulthood and Aging," *Journal of Personality and Social Psychology*, 42 (1982), 108–15.

RYFF, C. D., and S. G. HEINCKE, "The Subjective Organization of Personality in Adulthood and Aging," *Journal of Personality and Social Psychology*, 44 (1983), 807–16.

SEROCK, KATHY, and OTHERS, "As Children See Old Folks," in *Focus: Aging*, ed. Harold Cox, pp. 356–67. Guilford, Conn.: Dushkin, 1978.

TISSUE, THOMAS, "Downward Mobility in Old Age," in *Socialization and the Life Cycle*, ed. Peter I. Rose, pp. 356–67. New York: St. Martin's Press, 1979.

UHLENBERG, P. R., "Death and the Family," *Journal of Family History*, 5 (1980), 313–20.

U.S. BUREAU OF THE CENSUS, *Poverty in the United States: Current Population Reports*, Series P-60 No. 160. Washington, D.C.: U.S. Government Printing Office, 1988.

WEST, HELEN L., and WALTER J. LEVY, "Knowledge of Aging in an Elderly Population," *Research on Aging*, 3, no. 2 (June 1981), 202–10.

WILENSKY, H. L., and H. EDWARDS, "The Skidder: Ideological Adjustments of Downward Mobile Workers," *American Sociological Review*, 24 (1959), 215–31.

NOTES

1. Richard A. Kalish, *Late Adulthood: Perspectives on Human Development* (Monterey, Calif.: Brooks/Cole, 1975), p. 47.
2. David A. Goslin, in *Handbook of Socialization Theory and Research*, ed. David A. Goslin (Skokie, Ill.: Rand McNally, 1969), p. 6.
3. Harold Cox and Albert Bhak, "Determinants of Age Based on Residential Segregation," *Sociological Symposium*, no. 29 (Winter 1980), 27–41.
4. Bernard S. Phillips, "A Role Theory Approach to Adjustment in Old Age," *American Sociological Review*, 22 (1957), 213.
5. Ibid., p. 215.
6. Ibid., p. 216.

7. S. Reichard, F. Livson, and P. G. Peterson, *Aging and Personality: A Study of 87 Older Men* (New York: John Wiley, 1962).
8. Bill D. Bell, "Role Set Orientations and Life Satisfaction: A New Look at an Old Theory," in *Time, Roles and Self in Old Age*, ed. Jaber F. Gubrium (New York: Human Sciences Press, 1976), pp. 148–64.
9. Douglas C. Kimmel, *Adulthood and Aging* (New York: John Wiley, 1974), p. 313.
10. Jaber F. Gubrium, in *Time, Roles and Self in Old Age*, ed. Gubrium, p. 113.
11. Bernice J. Neugarten, Joan W. Moore, and John C. Lowe, "Age Norms, Age Constraints, and Age

Socialization," *American Journal of Sociology,* 70 (1965), 710–17.

12. Kathy Serock and others, "As Children See Old Folks," in *Focus: Aging,* ed. Harold Cox (Guilford, Conn.: Dushkin, 1978), pp. 102–3.

13. Louis Harris and associates, *The Myth and Reality of Aging in America* (Washington, D.C.: National Council on the Aging, 1975).

14. H. L. Wilensky and H. Edwards, "The Skidder: Ideological Adjustments of Downward Mobile Workers," *American Sociological Review,* 24 (1959), 215–31.

15. Thomas Tissue, "Downward Mobility in Old Age," in *Socialization and the Life Cycle,* ed. Peter I. Rose (New York: St. Martin's Press, 1979), p. 356.

16. Ibid., p. 362.

17. National Commission on Working Women of Wider Opportunities for Women, "Women, Work and Age: An Overview" (1989), p. 2. (Available at 1325 G Street N.W., Lower Level, Washington, D.C. 20005.)

18. U.S. Bureau of the Census, *Poverty in the United States: Current Population Reports,* Series P-60 No. 160 (Washington, D.C.: U.S. Government Printing Office, 1988).

19. National Commission of Working Women of Wider Opportunities for Women, p. 1.

20. Matilda White Riley, "Women, Men and the Lengthening Life Course," in *Gender and the Life Course,* ed. Alice S. Rossi (New York: Aldine, 1985), p. 339.

21. Beth Hess, "Antidiscrimination Policies Today and the Life Chances of Older Women Tomorrow," *Gerontologist,* 26, no. 2 (1985), 134.

7

Aging Minority Group Members

Many social scientists believe that relations between dominant and minority groups can be identified and defined on the basis of power. Eitzen (1980) argues that from this perspective the most crucial aspect of a minority group is that it is dominated by a more powerful group. A second characteristic of a minority group is that it comprises people whose characteristics differ significantly from those of people in the dominant group. These characteristics must be easily visible to the casual observer; they must make a difference. A third characteristic of minority group members is that they are *stereotyped* (often negatively) and often condemned by the dominant group. These stereotypes provide the dominant group with a rationale for keeping the minority group down and are sometimes accepted by the minority group itself. The final characteristic of minority groups is that they are all singled out for different and unfair treatment. Whether the discrimination is subtle or blatant, the effect is always detrimental to the minority group and frequently detrimental to the dominant group. In sum, the criteria of a minority group from this perspective are relative powerlessness, visible differentiation from the majority, negative stereotyping, and discrimination.

Eitzen (1980) delineates some of the bases of minority-group status:

1. Race, which is based on genetic differences among individuals and often results in differential treatment
2. Ethnicity, which identifies one as a member of a distinct subculture, which is in one way or another different from the dominant culture
3. Religion, which also is used as the basis for placing people in inferior positions. Jews have been persecuted because of their religious identity. The Amish are merely looked down upon by the dominant groups.
4. The impoverished comprise a minority group in most societies.
5. Sex, which singles women out for different treatment than men. Women are often considered incapable of leadership and relegated to less important roles in the social system.

6. Homosexuals and other subgroups are often identified as deviant by the dominant group in the society and therefore treated in a discriminatory manner.

7. The aged are often relatively powerless and discriminated against by the dominant group.

8. The deformed, handicapped, and obese frequently experience discrimination because they are different.[1]

Jacquelyne Jackson (1980), in her work on minority aging, defines Anglo-American men as the dominant group. She then specifies what she believes to be the minority groups in the United States:

1. Black American women

2. Black American men

3. Native American women

4. Native American men

5. Asian American women

6. Asian American men

7. Hispanic American women

8. Hispanic American men

9. Anglo-American women[2]

Whether the aged are a minority group was discussed in Chapter 2. There are those, such as Rose and Peterson (1965), who believe that the physiological characteristics of being old are easily observable and can therefore be used as the basis for different treatment. Moreover, the aged are generally negatively defined by others in the social system and receive less income and share a lower status than other age groups. Recognizing their unequal treatment, Rose and Peterson believe they band together and identify themselves as being discriminated against and thereby form a subculture. Gordon Streib (1968) has argued against older persons being considered a minority group. He doubts the exclusiveness of the group since all persons who live long enough will eventually become members. Streib also believes old people are much too heterogeneous, coming from different social-class, racial, and ethnic groups to form a common identity at age 65.[3]

The aged in American society probably do not think of themselves as a minority group, do not share a group identity, and do not form a subculture. On the other hand, many people are required to retire at age 70, do lose occupational roles and status at that time, are forced to live on approximately half the income they previously received, and have limited resources as they attempt to solve their current problems. In these ways older persons, whether recognizing themselves as a minority group or not, are discriminated against and do receive differential treatment.

If older persons in American society do indeed face problems not experienced by other age groups, then it becomes relevant to ask what the consequences are of being a member of a minority group and also of being old. One often encounters the concepts of double jeopardy—being old and black—and triple jeopardy—being old, black, and female.

Vern Bengtson and Leslie Morgan (1983) attempted to determine which of the following hypotheses better described the quality of life of the minority elderly:

1. Double jeopardy: Persons who are both old and members of a minority group experience the cumulative effects of these two burdens—more severe problems and a lower quality of life.

2. Age as a leveler: Aging leads to a diminishing of the differences found at a younger age in the quality of life of majority and minority groups.

They were unable to conclude that either perspective was more accurate. If we look at differences between dominant and minority groups in terms of income and self-rated health, the disadvantages to the minority elderly are striking. On other issues, however, such as family contact and support, we find some areas where the differences between the dominant-group elderly and the minority elderly seem slight and frequently favor the minority group. In this chapter we look at some of the unique problems confronting aging members of minority groups.

DEMOGRAPHIC CHARACTERISTICS

There has been a tendency to lump all groups into two categories for statistical analysis and presentation of data. Thus, we often see tables headed by the columns *Nonwhite* and *White*. The lumping of all minorities into the nonwhite category blurs many of the distinctions among them.

Native Americans, for example, generally have a shorter life expectancy than blacks, but one will not be aware of this when these two groups are placed in the nonwhite category. Blacks have more households headed by females than the Japanese, but this also cannot be discerned if both groups are placed in the nonwhite category.

Population

In terms of the numbers of people who live beyond age 55 in the United States, we find whites to be the largest group, followed by blacks, Hispanics, Pacific Asians, and Native Americans (Table 7–1).

There have been quite disparate growth patterns among the various minor-

TABLE 7–1 Population of Noninstitutionalized Elderly Minority Group Members 55 and Over

Race	Number
White	41,204,000
Black	3,872,000
Hispanic	1,113,000
Pacific Asian	275,000
Native American	89,000

Source: Federal Council on the Aging, *Policy Issues Concerning the Elderly Minorities,* DHHS Publication No. (OHDS) 80–20670 (Washington, D.C., 1979), p. 20.

ity groups in the United States in the twentieth century. Ultimately this affects the numbers of old members in these groups. Jackson (1980) reports that between 1900 and 1970 the total Japanese population increased by 683 percent while blacks were increasing by 255 percent. In terms of both numbers and percentage increases, the growth rates of the aged were greatest for Asian Americans and least for Native Americans. In recent years, the elderly population has been growing faster among minorities than among whites, and we can expect this trend to continue. In 1980 over 2.5 million persons, or 10 percent of the population 65 and over, were nonwhite. By 2025, 15 percent of the elderly population are projected to be nonwhite, and by 2050, 20 percent.[4]

The black population has been moving out of rural areas and into large cities. In 1978 the U.S. Bureau of the Census found that 55 percent of all black aged lived in the central cities.[5]

In 1978, 84 percent of the Hispanic elderly population lived in metropolitan areas (Table 7–2).[6] The older Pacific Asians tend to be concentrated in Los Angeles, Honolulu, San Francisco, San Diego, Boston, New York, and Washington. The census information does not specify the exact numbers of Pacific Asians at present. U.S. Bureau of the Census data are even less complete regarding American Indians. The percentage of American Indians who lived on identified reservations ranged from 3 percent among the Catawba to 77 percent among the Pueblo. According to the final report on the first National Indian Conference on Aging, there is a growing shift of the elderly Indian population to urban areas.[7]

Life Expectancy

Life expectancy for all aging minorities follows a general trend of lagging far behind whites' life expectancy at birth, almost catching up to it by age 65, and exceeding it thereafter. The life expectancy in 1977 of whites at birth was about 5 years greater than that of nonwhites, but this gap is considerably reduced by age 65. Since 1900 the gains in life expectancy have been greater for blacks than for whites. The U.S. Department of Health, Education and Welfare reports that from 1900 to 1976 the average length of life for blacks and other nonwhite groups increased by 35.3 years compared with 25.9 years for whites. For women, life expectancy is almost identical at age 70 (14.4 for white females and 14.3 for black females and others) and at age 75 blacks live longer.[8] (See Table 7–3.)

Nearly 673,000 (about 5 percent) of the Hispanic population are 65 or over, and of those almost 45,000 (6.6 percent) are 85 or older.

In a report prepared for the National Advisory and Resource Committee (1978), Dr. Sharon Fujii observed that even though the proportion of elderly in the population of Pacific Asians is very small, those who reach 65 years of age live longer than their white counterparts.[9]

In 1978 the National Clearinghouse on Aging reported on the life expect-

TABLE 7–2 Minority Populations in Urban Areas

	White	Black	Hispanic
Number living in urban areas	10,700,000	2,080,000	924,000
Percent of total group	27	55	84

Source: Federal Council on the Aging, *Policy Issues Concerning the Elderly Minorities*, DHHS Publication No. (OHDS) 80–20670 (Washington, D.C., 1979), p. 27.

TABLE 7–3   Life Expectancy by Sex, Race, and Age, 1976

	White		Black	
Age	Male	Female	Male	Female
0	69.7	77.3	64.1	72.6
65	13.7	18.1	13.8	17.6
70	10.9	14.4	11.3	14.3
75	8.5	11.2	9.7	12.2
85	5.1	6.4	7.2	9.1

Source: National Center for Health Statistics, *Vital Statistics of the U.S. 1976*, Vol. II, Sec. 5 (Washington, D.C.: Department of Health, Education and Welfare, 1976).

ancy of Native Americans. Life expectancy at birth is lower for Native Americans than for whites. By age 45 the gap has diminished. In 1970, Native Americans 45 years old had a life expectancy of 29.1 years compared with 30.6 years for whites; at age 55 it was 22.0 years compared with 22.3 for whites; and at 65 it was 15.4 years compared with 15.2 for whites.

Family Structure

It is often assumed that the black family is more extended (including brothers, sisters, aunts, uncles, and cousins) than the white family and that it includes an informal support network of relatives providing day-care services, parental surrogates, and related services more commonly handled by other organized groups for the white family. The Federal Council on the Aging found that most older blacks own their own homes and in most cases are the heads of households. In 1978 elderly black women headed 32 percent of black families where the head of the household was 65 and over. Approximately 41 percent of these elderly households headed by black women included children under 18, compared with 9 percent of families headed by elderly white women.[10]

According to the Asociacion Nacional Pro Personas Majores's final report on the Second National Hispanic Conference on Aging, the widely held belief that Hispanic elders live in extended families simply is not true. In 1975 only 9.7 percent of the elderly of Spanish origin, the majority of whom were women, lived in extended families; 60 percent lived with a spouse; and the other 40 percent (most of whom were women) lived alone.[11] Census data indicate that only 18 percent of the Hispanic elderly age 55 and over live alone or with nonrelatives, in comparison with 24 percent of the total United States population 55 and older.[12] The Federal Council on the Aging data indicate that within Hispanic communities, neighbors, friends, and churches provide the elderly with some support services.

The family structure of some of the Pacific Asian groups has been affected by past U.S. immigration laws, which prevented Asian males from bringing their families to the United States. The Federal Council on the Aging reports that proportions of Pacific Asian households headed by men living alone were twice as high in 1970 as the comparable proportion for the total U.S. population. Thus, many Asian men are deprived of family support during their later years. For Asians who do live in a family setting, the information is at present confusing. Studies at San Diego State University indicate that families and neighbors serve both as a coping mechanism for older persons and as traditional support networks.[13] Other studies of Asian families have reported a slow disintegration of family structure.[14]

Studies have indicated that older Native Americans still play an important role in the extended family, particularly those on reservations.[15] The increasing movement of the Native Americans from reservations to urban areas has often resulted in the acculturation of young Native Americans. Thus, the extended Native American family appears to be rapidly eroding in the United States.

Education

As one might expect, the education levels attained by minority groups are often considerably lower than those attained by whites. The Federal Council on the Aging (1979) reported:

> . . . median levels of educational attainment in the U.S. in 1978 for whites 60–64 (12.2), 65–69 (11.6), 70–74 (10.1) and 75 and over (8.8), while for elderly blacks 60–64 (8.5), 65–69 (7.9), 70–74 (6.6) and 75 and over (5.9).[16]

The council indicated further that 38 percent of the 60+ Hispanic females and 43 percent of their male counterparts had been to school for less than five years. The median number of years of education for the entire Hispanic population was 6.6 for males and 5.9 for females.[17]

Like the elders of other minority groups, three fifths of older Native Americans have completed less than eight years of schooling and only 2 percent had completed four more years of college.[18]

In 1986, the American Association of Retired Persons (AARP) reported that 41 percent of the white elderly had completed high school compared to only 19 percent of the elderly Hispanics and 17 percent of the elderly blacks. The minority groups still lag far behind the white population in terms of years of education they have completed.

Income and Employment

Elderly minorities beyond age 55 generally show higher rates of unemployment and lower incomes (Figure 7–1) than the general population. The Federal Council on the Aging (1979) reports that older black men (55+) had an unemployment rate of 5.3 percent compared with 2.6 percent for whites in that age group. Older black women had an unemployment rate of 4.5 percent compared with 3.0 percent for their white counterparts.[19]

In 1980 the median income of black elderly was considerably less than that of their white counterparts. Black men's median income was $4113 while the median for white men was $7408. Black women's median income was $2825, compared with $3894 for white women. By any standard, the black elderly are the most economically disadvantaged of any minority group. Overall, 35 percent live below the poverty level, compared with 13 percent of the white elderly. The poorest groups are older women, those living in rural areas, and the "oldest old" (85 or older). Approximately 21 percent of rural white women live in poverty, in contrast with 68 percent of rural black women.[20]

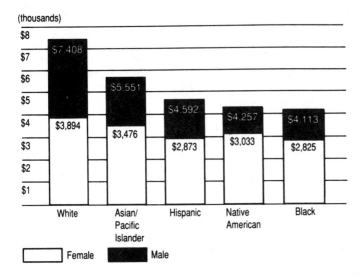

(thousands)

$8				
$7	$7,408			
$6		$5,551		
$5			$4,592	
$4	$3,894			$4,257	$4,113
$3		$3,476	$2,873	$3,033	$2,825
$2				
$1				

White Asian/ Hispanic Native Black
Pacific American
Islander

☐ Female ■ Male

FIGURE 7–1
Median Income for All Races
65+, 1980

Source: American Association of Retired Persons, *A Portrait of Older Minorities*, AARP Publication No. MA 3668 (1285) (Washington, D.C., 1986), p. 2.

In 1980 the median personal income of Hispanic men aged 65 and above was $4592. Elderly Hispanic women had a median income of $2873.[21]

The median income of Pacific Asian men in 1980 was $5551 and of women, $3476. The Pacific Asian minority group is somewhat better off financially than other minority groups.[22]

The incomes of Native Americans are low and approximate those of the black elderly. Because of limited education and lack of opportunity to develop their abilities, they are usually employed in low-paying, unskilled roles in mining, forestry, and manual labor. The median income for Native American males 65+ was $4257 and for females $3033. Moreover, fear of losing government support in the form of social security, supplemental security income, and food stamps prevents many Indians from selling their arts and crafts in order to supplement their income.[23]

While social security is the primary source of retirement income for both the dominant and minority elderly, there are significant differences in the social security benefits received by the various groups. Since social security benefits are based on past earnings as a general rule, all the minority groups receive smaller benefits than white males. Past discrimination in employment has kept most of minority-group members' earnings low throughout their working years, thus resulting in lower social security benefits during retirement. In 1970 black workers, both men and women, received social security pensions averaging $250 per year less than those for whites.

Home Ownership

We find disparate patterns of home ownership among the various minority elderly. The U.S Bureau of the Census estimates that 71 percent of all black families headed by elderly (60+) persons owned their homes in comparison with 84 percent of all white families. Since home ownership is relatively high among blacks, they are the least likely of all minorities to live in public housing or government-subsidized rental units.[24]

Fifty-four percent of elderly Hispanics own their own homes and 46 percent are renters. In terms of home ownership, Hispanics seem to be in poorer circumstances than the other minority groups and whites.

A study done by the San Diego Center on Aging found that 83 percent of older Japanese owned (or were buying) their own homes. Only 3 percent of this group were living with their adult children.[25] Japanese Americans appear to be as well off as whites in terms of home ownership. The study made no attempt to assess the quality or value of the homes owned by the different groups.

There were no available data on home ownership by Native Americans. The Federal Council on the Aging reports that elderly Native Americans were more likely to live in two- (or more) person households and in rural areas than elderly persons of all other races.

Sex Composition

Sex composition varies considerably among minority-group elderly. Jackson (1980) reports that there are more females than males among Koreans, whites, blacks, Japanese, Hispanics, and Native Americans (in descending order). There were more males than females among Filipinos and Chinese. Thus, there were 64 males per 100 females among the Koreans, but 431.4 males per 100 females among the Filipinos.[26]

Living Arrangements

Jackson (1980) identifies differences among the living arrangements of blacks, Hispanics, and whites (Table 7–4). The greater proportion of female-headed families among blacks and Hispanics in comparison with whites can be explained in part by the differences in longevity among the males in these three groups. Black and Hispanic men, who are more likely to have a shorter life expectancy than whites, leave more widows who become female heads of families.

Moving in with relatives is more common among women because they are more likely to be widowed and poor. The 1977 data in Table 7–4 indicate, however, that among blacks a slightly larger proportion of males than females 65 to 74 years of age were living with other relatives.

Jim Michel and Jasper Register (1984) found that elderly blacks were more likely than whites to take grandchildren, nieces, and nephews into their homes to live. Earlier Susan Schuller Friedman and Edgar Butler (1976) had found that Anglo aged persons were more likely to move into the households of younger family members, whereas in Chicano and black households it appeared that the opposite was the case.

Elizabeth Mutran (1985) found racial differences in assistance patterns. First, she found that blacks appear to be more involved in exchanges of help across generations, with the flow of assistance generally being downward. In white culture widowhood was found to be a strong predictor of an elderly person receiving help, but in black culture this is not the case. Blacks were more likely than whites to both give and receive help during difficult times.

The proportion of aged persons living with family members has been decreasing for both males and females of all ethnic and racial groups. The trend for all aged persons is to maintain their independence as long as possible and not to move in with relatives. The availability of age-segregated and government-

TABLE 7–4 Living Arrangements of Blacks, Hispanics, and Whites, by Sex, 65 to 74 and 75+ Years of Age, 1970 and 1977

Race/Ethnicity and Sex	Year and Age			
	1970		1977	
	65–74	75+	65–74	75+
Black females				
% primary indviduals	31.8	33.1	32.0**	41.0**
% family heads	17.8	17.1	19.0**	22.3**
% wives of family heads	31.9	15.2	35.7**	12.4
% with other relatives*	15.7	31.3	10.7	22.7
% secondary individuals	2.8	3.3	2.6	1.6
Black males				
% primary individuals	21.6	24.5	16.8	32.8**
% family heads	66.5	56.0	65.9	50.6
% with other relatives*	7.0	14.2	12.6**	14.0
% secondary individuals	4.9	5.3	4.7	2.6
Hispanic females				
% primary indviduals	21.4	25.0	27.1**	29.6**
% family heads	12.6	12.2	10.8	17.8**
% wives of family heads	38.8	18.4	37.8	15.1
% with other relatives*	25.6	42.8	23.1	35.2
% secondary individuals	1.6	1.6	1.2	2.3**
Hispanic males				
% primary individuals	13.9	16.2	14.8**	—
% family heads	74.4	59.1	71.3	—
% with other relatives*	10.1	22.4	13.4	—
% secondary individuals	1.6	2.3	0.5	—
White females				
% primary individuals	33.2	41.1	36.5**	49.3**
% family heads	7.8	9.8	7.4	8.5
% wives of family heads	45.4	21.0	47.9**	20.8
% with other relatives*	12.2	26.3	7.0	19.8
% secondary individuals	1.4	1.8	1.2	1.6
White males				
% primary individuals	13.0	20.3	12.1	20.1
% family heads	81.1	66.0	81.2**	71.9**
% with other relatives*	4.6	13.6	5.1**	6.8
% secondary individuals	1.3	0.1	1.6**	1.2**

*In 1977, "with other relatives" includes individuals in primary or secondary families or others not in subfamilies.

**Indicates percentage increase between 1970 and 1977.

Source: Jacquelyne J. Jackson, *Minorities and Aging* (Belmont, Calif.: Wadsworth, 1980), p. 134.
© 1980 by Wadsworth, Inc. Reprinted by permission of Wadsworth Publishing Company.

subsidized housing has made it less necessary for older persons to move in with family members. Most older persons apparently prefer to live near their children but not with them as long as they can maintain independent living arrangements.

The more economic conditions improve for older Americans, the less likely they will live in multigeneration families.

SOCIAL ASPECTS OF AGING

Sociologists, in viewing the effect of aging on minority-group members, are concerned about the changing role and status of these persons, the conditions that bring about these changes, and societal reactions to these changes.

Anyone's life course involves a series of role changes that accompany significant social events in one's life. One common pattern: The child begins school, graduates from elementary school and enters high school, graduates from high school and enters college, graduates from college and enters an occupation, marries, has children, watches the children leave home, becomes a grandparent, retires, experiences the death of a spouse, and ultimately dies. At each of life's junctures the individual assumes new roles and statuses that in turn bring new responsibilities requiring new skills. From the sociological perspective, one's life can be viewed as a series of adjustments to rather predictable and periodic changes in one's social position.

In discussing the adjustments of later life, Irving Rosow (1976) defines *roles* as the expected behavior considered appropriate for any set of rights and duties. He defines *status* as the representation of a formal office or social position that can be clearly identified by name—for example, president of the Chamber of Commerce. The person occupying this position can be classified and located within the social structure.[27]

Some of the major institutionalized roles that Rosow identifies are associated with occupation, social class, family, and age. He is not sure, however, that there is a consensus in society about what the age norms (expected patterns of behavior for persons of a given age) are.

Rosow argues that the greatest role and status changes among the elderly occur when the individual has lost the central institutionalized roles and statuses associated with family, occupation, and community. The major status losses, from this perspective, would result from retirement, widowhood, and inability to perform public roles because of failing health. The more important institutional roles grow steadily during adulthood, peaking in late middle age.[28]

Role emptying is a term used by Rosow to indicate the shrinking of responsibilities and duties within a role that often occurs during the later years. One is a parent but no longer has many parental responsibilities since the children have left home. As a result of their loss of responsibility and functions, the aged are often seen as socially expendable. A major problem of the later years is that individuals are not socialized for old age and that the roles of the elderly are not specific or structured.[29]

Formal institutionalized roles that center in occupation and community functions are performed most often by middle-aged adults. Rosow identifies informal roles as more prevalent among the very young and very old; these roles center in family, social groups, and neighborhoods. He believes the quality of life of older persons could be considerably improved by strengthening their informal roles.

Families, social groups, and neighborhoods tend to consist of individuals from the same race and social-class background. They are, therefore, most often homogeneous groups. As a result, Jackson (1980) argues, if Rosow's suggestions for strengthening the informal roles and social networks of older persons became public policy, they would perpetuate the segregation of society.[30] As we have seen, though, Rosow appears to have advocated these changes as means of improving the status of older persons in society. It is doubtful that he intended to perpetuate the segregation of social groups and neighborhoods, although this could be one of the results of such changes.

SERVICE NEEDS

Throughout history, the family has been the group responsible for its older members. The treatment of the elderly, whether favorable or unfavorable, was considered primarily a family matter. Modern industrial nations, with their ability to produce surpluses of goods and services, made retirement possible. Since the advent of social security and other federally funded programs there has been a tendency to shift the responsibility for aged family members away from the family and onto the government and other institutions. Many have felt that most of the government-funded social services provided for older persons have gone principally to whites and that considerably fewer services have been provided for minority group members.

The myth used to justify the fact that elderly members of minority groups have not received the quantity and quality of services they would seem to deserve is that the typical minority-group family is more extended than the white family and that it looks after its older members, thus rendering government services unnecessary. It is often observed that the family support systems for Native Americans, Asian Americans, blacks, and Hispanics are very strong. The extended family of aged whites is reputedly weaker than that of other ethnic groups, making government services to them more necessary.

In fact, the lack of services to older minority group members has meant that their families have had either to provide for them or to abandon them. Minority families might well have liked to shift the responsibility for their older members from themselves to the government, but they have not had the opportunity of doing so. The myth of the stronger family support system for minority elderly is believed by some to have been invented by public planners as a rationalization for not providing more services for the minority elderly.

Colleen Johnson and Barbara Barer (1990), in a study of family support networks among the inner city poor, concluded:

> The evidence on the whole suggests that these older blacks, like the inner-city whites in our sample, do not receive many supports from a spouse and children, because if present, these potential helpers may have too many distractions or competing commitments to assume a supportive role. Even with devoted family members, most blacks (as well as whites studied) who need help—men and women alike—still rely on formal supports: chore workers, special transportation services, meal programs and senior centers. At the same time, most older blacks, unlike the white sample, maintain extensive friendship and associational networks.[31]

The findings of the Federal Council on the Aging study (1979) indicate that the following special problems of the minority-group elderly should be considered by government planners:

1. Language and cultural barriers to services
2. Fewer median school years completed than those completed by the total elderly population
3. Low-paying, blue-collar jobs (many without social security or retirement benefits)
4. Inadequate benefits from federal income-supplement programs
5. Fewer opportunities for training and employment for those on income-maintenance programs
6. A struggle against skyrocketing inflation, high taxes, and increasing energy costs
7. Poor housing conditions, reflecting a federal housing policy unresponsive to minority needs
8. A fear of the increasing incidence of crime committed against their age group
9. Insufficient social and health care services, both mental and physical
10. An underrepresentation of members of their ethnic groups on federal, state, and local policy-making bodies
11. An emotional and mental attachment to their ethnic communities (i.e., natural support networks)
12. A fear of being removed from their cultural surroundings and placed in institutions such as nursing homes and other long-term care facilities
13. An underrepresentation of the number and socioeconomic characteristics of each of their ethnic groups by the census[32]

The council, after conducting a symposium, hearings, and meetings on the problems of providing services to the minority elderly, charged that current programs

1. Are designed without taking into account cultural diversities within the aging population
2. Overlook the traditional role of many older minorities in their extended families
3. Do not adequately involve the minority aging communities and their advocates in planning and implementation procedures
4. Suffer from a shortage of bilingual and bicultural staff on the federal, state, regional, and local levels
5. Underestimate the need of older minority subgroups for mental health services
6. Do not provide sufficient funds to minority colleges for the training of minority personnel, and for research in the field of minority aging
7. Use reporting and coding systems that do not accurately represent and

differentiate between the number of older minorities who are in need and those who are recipients of services

8. Lack coordination between federal policies and policies of state and local levels of government[33]

SUBCULTURAL AND VALUE DISPARITIES BETWEEN THE DOMINANT GROUP AND MINORITY GROUPS

Assimilation means to sociologists the fusion of often disparate groups into one homogeneous unit. America, at the outset, was made up of a variety of ethnic groups coming primarily from northwestern Europe and had a reputation for gradually assimilating these groups into one national culture. Later immigrants frequently came from southeastern Europe, Asia, and other parts of the world. Whereas the early immigrants were Caucasians, the later immigrants frequently represented different racial groups. While assimilation was the most common pattern in the early history of the country, it has not been the only pattern, and it has been selective. Assimilation has generally occurred more rapidly for Caucasians and more slowly for members of other racial groups. Americans whose racial features set them apart from Caucasians have not found assimilation so easy. The prevailing pattern in America has been the integration of Caucasian ethnic groups and the segregation of other groups.

Whereas *assimilation* refers to a blending of two cultures, *amalgamation* is the interbreeding of two peoples of distinct physical appearance until they become one stock. As with assimilation, amalgamation has more commonly taken place between different Caucasian ethnic groups than between Caucasians and other racial groups. That the study of aging minority-group members is considered a problem area in social gerontology indicates that members of several different ethnic and racial groups have not been fully assimilated into American society and in fact are sufficiently different to be identifiable as part of a subculture. Moreover, members of these subcultures are seen as having unique problems in later life that have resulted from their minority-group status.

The history of blacks from the slave period to the present is one of (1) assimilation from a variety of national and cultural backgrounds into American society and (2) indoctrination with the prevailing values of this society. If slavery did not destroy most of the cultural heritage of the slaves, it certainly limited blacks' communication with that culture as well as their opportunity to maintain its traditions, rituals, and practices. Blacks often adopted the values, somewhat modified by their slave status, of the white plantation community. Names, religious beliefs, and a variety of other values were frequently transmitted to the slaves through the white plantation owners and their families. While blacks were thus indoctrinated with certain white attitudes, the rigid system of segregation and discrimination prevented them from being totally assimilated into the white community. While amalgamation between blacks and whites during the slave period was usually the result of a relationship between white slave owners (or their sons) and black women, formal marriage was quite uncommon. Since the Civil War, amalgamation has been the exception rather than the rule in black–white relations.

That American blacks have generally lived in this country for several generations and been indoctrinated in public schools and the society at large with the prevailing values of the American culture raises a critical question: To what degree can we consider the problems of elderly blacks to be unique from those of elderly whites or the aged in other ethnic groups? Generally, black social gerontologists have argued that the problems of older blacks should be seen as unique. Gossie Harold Hudson (1976), chairman of the division of social services at Lincoln University, asserts:

> Regrettably most whites and many blacks do not label the problems of older blacks as Special, avoiding thereby careful or even superficial examination of their own prejudice.[34]

Duran Bell and associates (1976) argue that black problems result primarily from economic deprivation and that any difference found between older blacks and older whites as groups would disappear altogether if social-class differences were removed. They argue that if we compare lower-class blacks and lower-class whites, we will find few racial differences in health or income. Duran Bell and associates assert further that future research on the minority elderly should pose implicit interracial comparisons while recognizing the importance of social-class comparisons. André Hammonds (1991) believes, however, that even if the strength of the relationship in which elderly blacks and whites are compared is diminished by social-class comparisons, the relationship will have merely been interpreted and not explained away. In actuality both blackness and socioeconomic status must be understood by anyone attacking the problems of black elderly. Hammonds concludes that the problems of the black aged are unique and to some extent shared by all elderly blacks. The black elderly have experienced relative deprivation throughout their lives, being lower than whites in income; in opportunities for mobility, health, and housing; and in other respects. Being poor in old age is not a novel experience for blacks, since many of them have been

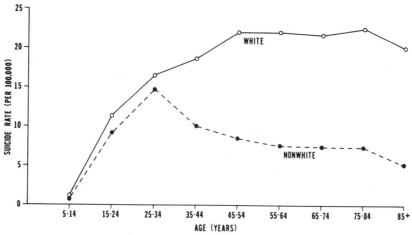

FIGURE 7–2 Suicide by Age and Race, United States, 1975

Source: National Center for Health Statistics

poor most of their lives. Many elderly whites, on the other hand, become poor for the first time in their lives when they retire. The problem of elderly blacks is unique according to Jackson (1980) because they have suffered from institutionalized racism throughout their lives and therefore confront the problems of aging from a social position different from that of others.

Richard Seiden (1981) examined white and nonwhite suicide rates throughout the life cycle. He found that both white and nonwhite suicide rates increase throughout the teen years and into early adulthood (to about age 30); then the black suicide rate begins to drop while the white suicide rate continues to rise (Figure 7–2). Seiden (1981), like Hammonds (1986) and Jackson (1980), argues that blacks experience economic and social deprivation early in life and develop coping mechanisms very early to deal with unfair situations. These coping mechanisms are carried into later life and help explain the lower suicide rate for blacks after age 30, according to Seiden. He asserts that because of racism the nonwhite elderly have been shut out of most positions of occupational power and authority. Therefore, retirement does not lead to the same loss of status for blacks that it does for whites.

THE ASIAN AMERICAN

Most of very elderly Chinese Americans today are first-generation Chinese Americans. F. L. K. Hsu (1971) argues that the values they brought with them to the United States were quite different from the prevailing values of American society. Hsu believes that Chinese society discourages financial independence from parents and the extended family, instead encouraging interdependence. American values of individual achievement, upward mobility, and competitiveness were alien to Chinese beliefs. Hsu asserts that for Chinese Americans reared to believe that children should not become financially independent of their parents, contemporary American values are most disconcerting. While in the homeland, the elderly maintain control over income, property, and jobs; no such control can be exercised in the United States. The only absolute claim for respect that elderly Chinese can attempt to place on their children is through community pressure. In China the upward mobility of an entire generation would have been impossible, according to Hsu, whereas in the United States it was possible. Thus the first-generation Chinese Americans have great difficulty maintaining the family form, lifestyle, and senior status that they had been taught to cherish in their homeland.[35]

Richard Kalish and Sharon Moriwaki (1973) point out that by law first-generation Japanese Americans could not own property. Instead it was often purchased in the name of a son or daughter, the naturalized child of the alien Japanese. What this meant was that first-generation Japanese could neither own property nor obtain citizenship until so late in their lives that financial security was difficult to achieve. In the homeland, ownership of property and the accumulation of financial resources would have allowed the older Japanese to maintain a position of leadership and respect in the eyes of younger family members and thereby to assure themselves that their children would look after them during their later years. Many of today's aged Japanese were even less likely to accumulate property because of their initial expectations of returning to their homeland after making their fortune. Unable to do so, they most often found it was too late in life to establish the rule of primogeniture, by which the eldest son would care for his parents in their later years.[36] Even the property bought in the name of the children was confiscated during World War II, though ultimately most of it was restored after the war. According to Kalish and Moriwaki,

> the Issei [first-generation Japanese American], the fruits of his most productive years often destroyed by the lengthy incarceration, and his dominant role having been effectively undermined, was forced to return to what he had been doing—often required to work with his sons or sons-in-law not as a respected patriarch but an equal or even subordinate.[37]

Kalish and Moriwaki observe that Americans who value autonomy and independence often become quite concerned when adult children turn from their elderly parents and fail to grant them a respected senior status. How much more upsetting this must be in a culture in which independence and autonomy are negatively valued in the first place!

Hsu (1971) observes that competition was not alien to traditional Chinese culture but that the purpose of the competition was to enhance the family rather than the individual. Elderly Chinese who are part of an extended family have a feeling of belonging, meaning, and pride through group identification that older Chinese Americans are often denied.

Some Japanese values are congruous with American values. Hard work, achievement, self-control, dependability, manners, and thrift seem to be values shared by both cultures. Elderly Chinese would appear, for a variety of reasons, to have more value conflicts as immigrant Americans. Elderly Chinese in traditional China were part of a network of primary relations stemming from the family. Usually all sons inherit the family wealth or land equally.[38]

Many of the early Chinese and Japanese immigrants to the United States intended to make their fortune and then return to a superior status in their homeland. For this reason, these early immigrants most often tried to indoctrinate their children with the traditional attitudes and values of their native land, according to Kalish and Moriwaki (1973). As with other ethnic groups, the second generations were more likely to adopt the standards of conduct of the country in which they were born rather than those of their parents' homeland. This contributed to considerable strain between the older family members and their children. Kalish and Moriwaki observe that the older Chinese and Japanese were often caught in an ideological dilemma:

> On the one hand, they recognized and at least to some extent accepted the values of their adopted homeland that being a burden to children is bad, that having the privacy and independence of one's own home is good, that the education of grandchildren should not be sacrificed for the care of grandparents. On the other hand, they recall their earlier learning that the older person is entitled not only to financial support, but to personal care and virtual devotion.[39]

NATIVE AMERICANS

The pattern of adjustment of Native Americans to the dominant American culture is different from that of any other minority group. Whereas others came to this country expecting to have to make adjustments and changes, Native Americans have been cultural islands resistant to the spread of the white population and culture. The tribes that settled in the Southwest have, to a considerable degree, been able to isolate themselves and maintain a separate culture. The intense settlement of the eastern half of the United States led to the rapid disintegration of many of the eastern tribes.

The percentage of the Native American population aged 65+ is also smaller. High birth and death rates have kept the Native American population young; half are less than 20 years of age. The percentage distribution by age resembles that of the total U.S. population in 1880.[40]

As a rule, the early tribes treated their older members fairly well and provided them with valued roles for their later years. Many tribes had developed a variety of ways to provide food for their older members, ranging from the sharing of food among hunting-and-gathering tribes such as the Shoshone and Plains Indians to the assumption of family responsibility for older members such as prevailed among the Pueblo.[41] The roles of bearer of tribal traditions and healer of the sick were often reserved to older tribal members. Ceremonial knowledge was paid for by younger members, who sought this information from their elders. Similarly, older tribal members were paid for treating illness, dispelling demons, and divining the whereabouts of lost articles. The old occasionally took on a religious aura in the eyes of the young, who felt that the older members of the tribe had extraordinary supernatural powers.[42]

The Hopi were one of the exceptions to this rule: They accorded respect to their elders only as long as the latter performed a useful function. After senility set in, old age was considered a burden and the old were often neglected.[43]

The murder of older tribal members was relatively rare among American Indians. John Ewers (1955) points out an exception:

> The Iroquois [would] allow an older man to give a large feast, during which a favorite son would administer the coup de grace from behind.[44]

Among the nomadic tribes the feeble were often abandoned.

Jerrod Levy (1967) maintains, however, that Native American tribes generally treated older members with deference and respect. Older members most often assumed the roles of leading, educating, and advising—roles usually associated with middle age in the American culture. Perhaps one other factor that contributed to the high status given older Native Americans was their paucity relative to the number of the younger generation, who therefore saw them as no threat.

The relocation and restriction of Native Americans to reservations and the destruction of wildlife brought an end to their cultures, according to Levy. The development of new economic activities has further destroyed their social organization and culture. The nomadic tribes have finally had to settle in one location and have been forced to do wage work, often provided by the federal government. The federal government's stock-reduction program forced the older stock owners to give their grazing rights to their heirs, thereby stripping them of managerial roles and the prestige that accompanies them.[45] Similarly, free medical services are competing with the healing rituals practiced by older tribal workers. Elderly tribal members have lost status in other ways as well:

> The domestic skills of the traditional aged are less important in a small household. Now almost all the children are either in government boarding school or public

school. Much of the domestic economy for the younger wage workers involves knowledge of English and arithmetic to cope with the cash stores that are springing up all over the reservations. Social change has resulted in the destruction of education and the advisory functions of the experienced older person.[46]

Thus, with Native Americans, as with most other cultures, rapid social changes tend to undermine the traditional roles and statuses assumed by older persons while creating new roles and opportunities for the young.

The Native American cultures are distinct from other minority groups in that they never wanted to be assimilated into the white American culture. While the ideal of a melting pot of persons of different cultures and ethnic groups tends to permeate the values of most Americans, Native Americans would appear to prefer cultural pluralism. They do not believe that the American culture is superior, and they prefer to maintain and perpetuate their own culture.

CONCLUSION

America—with its historic emphasis on the assimilation of different national, religious, and ethnic groups into a common culture—still contains a variety of minority groups that have not totally become a part of the American way of life. America has assimilated Caucasians of a variety of national, ethnic, and religious backgrounds much more rapidly than it has assimilated other racial groups. The American Indians did not want to be assimilated and thus tried to isolate themselves from the dominant culture. The Pacific Asians had the disadvantages of generally being late immigrants to the country, of being a different racial group, and of arriving in the country after it was relatively settled. They have therefore not been entirely assimilated into the American culture. The different Asian ethnic groups often share values and beliefs that are not consistent with the ideology of the American culture. This becomes a particular problem for the Asian American elderly, who find themselves unable to establish the kind of relationship with the younger generation they had come to expect as part of their cultural traditions. Their children have often begun to adopt at least some of the American values, and considerable generational strain is the result.

There are a number of themes running through all the research on minority groups. Members of minority groups generally receive lower incomes and have fewer job opportunities than do members of the dominant group. First-generation immigrants in particular are required to take the least-preferred jobs at the lowest salaries. Members of minority groups generally have a shorter life expectancy up to age 65 than do dominant group members, but at some point beyond that age they enjoy a longer life expectancy. Because of past discrimination, members of minority groups usually receive smaller retirement incomes, are more likely to live with extended relatives, are less likely to be able to maintain independent living in the later years, and are generally less well educated than the dominant group. They often receive fewer government services than the dominant group. The rationalization often heard is that the families of minority groups are very tightly integrated and that they consider it important to look after their older members. This rationalization begs the question since if the government provided needed services to older members of minority groups it would probably not be necessary for their families to assume this responsibility.

Research on the unique and unusual problems of the minority elderly has been limited so far. One would expect second- and third-generation members of ethnic minorities to become assimilated into the dominant culture. Assimilation, however, probably creates strain between first-generation immigrants and their children and solves none of the problems of the first generation, who are now in their later years. To what degree Native Americans will be able to remain in isolated enclaves where their culture can be maintained is debatable. The data tend to suggest a movement of younger men and women off the reservations and into urban areas.

Whatever the future trends may be, minority groups currently find themselves confronted with a variety of often unique and difficult problems. Many of these problems have been ignored by the federal planners of social services for older Americans.

KEY TERMS

amalgamation
assimilation
role

role emptying
status
stereotype

REFERENCES

AMERICAN ASSOCIATION OF RETIRED PERSONS, *A Portrait of Older Minorities*, AARP Publication No. MA 3668 (1285). Washington, D.C., 1986.

ATCHLEY, ROBERT C., *The Social Forces in Later Life.* Belmont, Calif.: Wadsworth, 1977.

BELL, DURAN, PATRICIA KASSCHAU, and GAIL ZELLMAN, *Delivering Services to Elderly Members of Minority Groups: A Critical Review of the Literature.* Santa Monica, Calif.: Rand McNally, 1976.

BENGSTON, VERN, and LESLIE MORGAN, "Ethnicity and Aging: A Comparison of Three Ethnic Groups," in *Growing Old in Different Societies: Cross-Cultural Perspectives*, ed. Jay Sokolovsky, pp. 157–67. Belmont, Calif.: Wadsworth, 1983.

EITZEN, D. STANLEY, *Social Problems.* Boston: Allyn & Bacon, 1980.

EWERS, JOHN C., "The Hole in Blackfoot Indian Culture," *Bureau of American Ethnology Bulletin*, 159 (1955).

FEDERAL COUNCIL ON THE AGING, *Policy Issues Concerning the Elderly Minorities*, DHHS Publication No. (OHDS) 80–20670. Washington, D.C., 1979.

FRIEDMAN, SUSAN SCHULLER, and EDGAR BUTLER, "Ethnicity, Alternative Family Patterns and Aging" (paper presented at the annual meeting of the Society for the Study of Social Problems, New York City, 1976).

HAMMONDS, ANDRÉ, "Poverty and Older Black Americans: A Demographic Portrait" (lecture at the Critical Problems of Aging Workshop, Indiana State University, 1991).

HSU, F. L. K., *The Challenge of the American Dream: The Chinese in the United States.* Belmont, Calif.: Wadsworth, 1971.

HUDSON, GOSSIE HAROLD, "Some Special Problems of Older Americans," *Crisis Magazine*, March 1976.

ISHIZUKE, KAREN C., and OTHERS, *The Elderly Japanese, Latino, Black, Chinese, Quamanian.* San Diego: Center on Aging, San Diego State University, 1978.

JACKSON, JACQUELYNE J., *Minorities and Aging.* Belmont, Calif.: Wadsworth, 1980.

JOHNSON, COLLEEN, and BARBARA BARER, "Families and Networks among Older Inner-City Blacks," *Gerontologist*, 30, no. 6, (December 1990), 726–33.

KALISH, RICHARD A., and SHARON MORIWAKI, "The World of the Elderly Asian American," *Journal of Social Issues*, 29, no. 2 (1973), 187–202.

KENNARD, E. A., "Hopi Reactions to Death," *American Anthropologist*, 39 (1937).

LEVY, JERROD, "The Older American Indian," in *Older Rural Americans: A Sociological Perspective*, ed. E. Grant Youmans, pp. 221–37. Louisville: University of Kentucky Press, 1967.

MICHEL, JIM, and JASPER REGISTER, "An Exploration of Family Interaction with the Elderly by Race, Socioeconomic Status, and Residence," *Gerontologist*, 24, no. 1 (1984), 48–54.

MUTRAN, ELIZABETH, "Intergenerational Family Support among Blacks and Whites: Response to Culture or Socioeconomic Differences?" *Journal of Gerontology*, 4, no. 3 (1985), 382–89.

NATIONAL ADVISORY AND RESOURCE COMMITTEE, *Pacific/Asian Elderly Research Project*. Special Services for Groups, Inc., 1978.

ROSE, A., and WARREN PETERSON, *Older People and Their Social Worlds*, pp. 3–16. Philadelphia: F. A. Davis, 1965.

ROSOW, IRVING, "Status and Role Change through the Life Span," in *Handbook on Aging and the Social Sciences*, ed. Robert H. Binstock and Ethel Shanas, pp. 62–91. New York: Van Nostrand Reinhold, 1976.

SEIDEN, RICHARD, "Mellowing with Age: Factors Influencing the Nonwhite Suicide Rate," *International Journal of Aging and Human Development*, 13 (1981), 265–83.

STREIB, GORDON F., "Are the Aged a Minority Group?," in *Middle Age and Aging*, ed. Bernice

Neugarten, p. 36. Chicago: University of Chicago Press, 1968.

U.S. BUREAU OF THE CENSUS, *Current Population Survey* (unpublished data, March 1978).

U.S. BUREAU OF THE CENSUS, "Household and Family Characteristics," *Current Population Reports*, no. 340 (March 1978), 20, Table 3.

U.S. DEPARTMENT OF HEALTH, EDUCATION AND WELFARE, ADMINISTRATION ON AGING, "The Older Black Population," *Statistical Reports on Older Americans*, no. 5 (1976).

U.S. DEPARTMENT OF HEALTH, EDUCATION AND WELFARE, PUBLIC HEALTH SERVICE, *Vital Statistics of the United States*, Vol. II, Section 5 (1976).

U.S. DEPARTMENT OF HEALTH, EDUCATION AND WELFARE, PUBLIC HEALTH SERVICE, OFFICE OF THE SURGEON GENERAL, DIVISION OF PUBLIC HEALTH METHODS, *Health Services for the American Indians*, Public Health Service Publication No. 531 (Washington, D.C., 1957).

YEE, DONCE, "The Older Chinese" (statement presented at the San Francisco Meeting on the Minority Elderly, 1979).

NOTES

1. D. Stanley Eitzen, *Social Problems* (Boston: Allyn & Bacon, 1980), pp. 123–24.
2. Jacquelyne Jackson, *Minorities and Aging* (Belmont, Calif.: Wadsworth, 1980), p. 4.
3. Gordon F. Streib, "Are the Aged a Minority Group?" in *Middle Age and Aging*, ed. Bernice Neugarten (Chicago: University of Chicago Press, 1968), pp. 35–36.
4. American Association of Retired Persons, *A Portrait of Older Minorities*, AARP Publication No. MA 3668 (1285) (Washington, D.C., 1986), p. 2.
5. U.S. Bureau of the Census, *Current Population Survey* (unpublished data, March 1978).
6. Ibid.
7. Federal Council on the Aging, *Policy Issues Concerning the Elderly Minorities*, DHHS Publication No. (OHDS) 80–20670 (Washington, D.C., 1979).
8. André Hammonds, "Poverty and Older Black Americans: A Demographic Portrait" (unpublished paper, Indiana State University, 1991).
9. National Advisory and Resource Committee, *Pacific/Asian Elderly Research Project* (Special Services for Group, Inc., 1978).
10. U.S. Bureau of the Census, "Household and Family Characteristics," *Current Population Reports*, no. 340 (March 1978), 20. Table 3.
11. Ibid.
12. U.S. Bureau of the Census, *Current Population Survey*.
13. Karen C. Ishizuke and others, *The Elderly Japa-

nese, Latino, Black, Chinese, Quamanian* (San Diego: Center on Aging, San Diego State University, 1978), p. 57.
14. Donce Yee, "The Older Chinese" (statement presented at the San Francisco Meeting on the Minority Elderly, 1979).
15. Federal Council on the Aging, *Policy Issues*, p. 32.
16. Ibid.
17. U.S. Bureau of the Census, *Current Population Survey*.
18. Federal Council on the Aging, *Policy Issues*, p. 32.
19. Ibid., p. 23.
20. American Association of Retired Persons, *A Portrait of Older Minorities*, p. 5.
21. Ibid., p. 6.
22. Ibid., p. 1.
23. Federal Council on the Aging, *Policy Issues*, p. 33.
24. U.S. Bureau of the Census, *Current Population Survey*.
25. National Advisory and Resource Committee, *Pacific/Asian Elderly Research Project*, p. 57.
26. Jackson, *Minorities and Aging*, p. 35.
27. Irving Rosow, "Status and Role Change Through the Life Span," in *Handbook on Aging and the Social Sciences*, ed. Robert H. Binstock and Ethel Shanas (New York: Van Nostrand Reinhold, 1976), p. 184.

28. Ibid., p. 465.
29. Ibid., p. 466.
30. Jackson, *Minorities and Aging*, pp. 121–22.
31. Colleen Johnson and Barbara Barer, "Families and Networks Among Older Inner-City Blacks," *Gerontologist*, 30, no. 6 (December 1990), 732.
32. Federal Council on the Aging, *Policy Issues*, pp. 39–40.
33. Ibid., p. 42.
34. Gossie Harold Hudson, "Some Special Problems of Older Americans," *Crisis Magazine*, March 1976.
35. F. L. K. Hsu, *The Challenge of the American Dream: The Chinese in the United States* (Belmont, Calif.: Wadsworth, 1971).
36. Richard A. Kalish and Sharon Moriwaki, "The World of the Elderly Asian American," *Journal of Social Issues*, 29, no. 2. (1973), 192–93.
37. Ibid., p. 193.
38. Ibid., p. 195.

39. Ibid., pp. 201–2.
40. U.S. Department of Health, Education and Welfare, Public Health Service, Office of the Surgeon General, Division of Public Health Methods, *Health Services for the American Indians*, U.S. Public Health Service Publication No. 531 (Washington, D.C., 1957), p. 10.
41. Jerrod Levy, "The Older American Indian," in *Older Rural Americans: A Sociological Perspective*, ed. E. Grant Youmans (Louisville: University of Kentucky Press, 1967), p. 224.
42. Ibid., p. 226.
43. E. A. Kennard, "Hopi Reactions to Death," *American Anthropologist*, 39 (1937), 494.
44. John C. Ewers, "The Hole in Blackfoot Indian Culture," *Bureau of American Ethnology Bulletin*, 159 (1955), 243.
45. Levy, "The Older American Indian," p. 231.
46. Ibid., pp. 231–32.

8

Family Patterns in Later Life

The typical couple of two generations ago had a life expectancy that enabled them to live together for approximately 31 years after marriage, 2 years short of the time when their fifth child was expected to marry. As a result of declining family size and the improved survival prospects of the American population since 1900, the typical husband and wife of today are likely to see all their children marry and in all probability have one fourth of their married life yet to live when the last child leaves home. Thus, by the time most married couples are approaching the age of retirement their children have already matured, married, and established independent households. Consequently, the typical older family today comprises simply the husband and wife. Approximately two thirds of all aged persons are husband–wife couples living alone, most of whom maintain their own households.

Whereas previous family sociologists concentrated heavily on the initial adjustment to marriage and the inevitable consequences of the first child on the husband–wife relationship, sociologists today are now becoming interested in the opposite end of the family life cycle. The earlier research had indicated that the birth of the first child was the biggest single adjustment problem faced by the young married couple, and now, paradoxically, family research indicates that the nature and quality of the husband–wife relationship may be just as much affected 25 years later when the last child leaves home. For many couples, after a quarter of a century of assuming the roles and responsibilities of mother and father to growing children, it may be quite a change in lifestyle to return exclusively to the roles of husband, wife, companion, and lover. Nadine Brozan (1980) points out that while many middle-age couples are adjusting to the "empty nest" and the transition from parent to companion, they may be simultaneously confronted with the responsibility of caring for aging parents. Charles Depner and Berit Ingersoll-Dayton (1985) point out that women are most often the care givers for aging parents and that the older the parents become the more support they are likely to require. Dayton observes, moreover, that as a result of the growth of three- or four-generation families, the family structure has experienced a dependence squeeze. The delayed childbearing of many women and the longevity of aging parents has meant that a higher proportion of women today are simultaneously having parents and children in the dependent age groups (under 18 and over 65). The responsibility for aging parents quickly replaces the responsibility for aging children, and the notion of the "empty nest" as a time of considerable freedom for women is rapidly becoming a myth.

At any age in life, changes in roles, expectations, and patterns of behavior result in the need for both individual and social adjustments. The adjustments and family patterns that emerge following such events as the last child leaving home, the growing dependence of aging parents, the retirement of the husband, and the withdrawal of the family from previous levels of social involvement will be the principal focus of this chapter. From the perspective of the symbolic interactionist, the critical factors in the successful adjustment of older couples are their ability to successfully perform new roles and the value placed on these roles by significant others in their social milieu.

CHANGING ROLES AND THE AGING FAMILY

Early in the retirement years older couples must make a number of important decisions about their lives, including whether to

1. Remain in their current home with its history and memories, or move to a new home or apartment
2. Remain in the same community or move to a different one, perhaps a retirement community
3. Remain active in current organizations, join new ones, or simply not be bothered with organizational affiliations
4. Try to locate near children and close friends or move to a different section of the country
5. Seek activities satisfying to both husband and wife or participate independently

All of these choices are in one way or another related to the style of life one desires. This preferred style of life will ultimately dictate the roles one becomes actively involved in and the roles one will give up during the later years.

The ability to make these choices is based on the assumption that the older person is in good health and able to live independently. Financial dependence, poor health, or related problems may create role reversals in the family in which the children make these decisions for aging parents. Since it is the middle class that strives the most for mobility, one might expect the upper class (those who no longer strive for mobility) and the lower class (those who have given up) to be more concerned about their aged parents. The findings of a study by Paul and Lois Glasser (1962) did not show this to be the case.[1] They found no significant relationship between social class and support of parents. What they did find is that the more mobile the children, the more likely they were to help their parents.

Evidence from the Glassers' (1962) work and other studies indicates that caring for aging parents is often a concern of families in the middle years. The problems require a decision by the aged or their children. Should the children take the parent(s) in their home? Should the aged be given financial support by their children? Should the adult children contribute time and energy to help care for their sick parent(s)?

Many of these critical decisions, whether made by the older person or his or her children, are accompanied by role loss and result in decreased interaction between the aging persons and others in their social system. These changes in social interaction are both qualitative and quantitative. This would be the pattern expected by the disengagement theorists.

Most middle-class Americans adhere to the value of leading an active life and thus believe that substitutes should be found for those activities and roles the individual is forced to give up at retirement. According to this view, the aging person should not alter either the pace or the style of life during the retirement years.

From a symbolic interaction perspective, retired family members, rather than trying to disengage from previous roles or vigorously seek new ones, are most likely to maintain those roles they enjoy and choose new ones available to them because of their increased leisure time.

Bert Adams (1975) proposes three categories of retirement roles assumed by older families:[2]

1. The positively oriented disengaged, who are glad to give up work roles. They frequently have a working-class background.
2. The negatively oriented disengaged, who hate to give up work roles. They are more frequently middle-class in background and likely to believe that they have given up a highly valued part of their lives.
3. The self-employed, who have never given up the major life roles and probably never intend to.

To this typology should be added a fourth category—the actively reengaged, who are finding new and useful roles and activities that previous work-related responsibilities would not have allowed time for.

The symbolic interactionists maintain that what is defined as useful and meaningful activity at any age in life is determined in part by significant others in one's social milieu. When one's friends and close associates of the same age are retiring and when numerous new roles and opportunities are available to the aging individual, then disengagement need not follow, or, if it does occur, it need not be negatively labeled. Life can have newfound meaning, and excitement can be created by the very knowledge that one is free to choose among a variety of roles, that one's lifelong friends and associates are making similar choices, and that new activities may prove to be just as satisfying as previous work-related activities. Participation in such programs as the Retired Senior Volunteer Program, which involves retired Americans in a variety of charitable and humanitarian causes, may be just as important to the confidence of older Americans as their previous work roles. Self-esteem can easily be maintained when one sees that one's activities are useful, needed, and defined as important by significant others, even if they are done voluntarily for little or no remuneration. Thus it would seem that the aging family need not be a disengaged or totally active family but rather a selectively engaged one.

HUSBAND–WIFE RELATIONS

Blood and Wolfe (1960), Pineo (1961), and Rollins and Feldman (1970) have all examined family patterns over the *life cycle*. Blood and Wolfe as well as Pineo report a decrease in shared activity of husbands and wives from the beginning of the marriage to the end. Pineo speaks of marital *disenchantment*—a decline in marital satisfaction and a decrease in intimacy. While disenchantment occurs for both husbands and wives, it apparently occurs earlier for husbands. The reason seems to be that men tend to romanticize their wives more than wives do their husbands, with the result that the wives may fall faster and further from their husbands' idealization. Pineo has concluded that marriage over time is a process of gradual disenchantment with the marriage in general and the partner in particular.[3]

A careful examination of husbands' and wives' marital satisfaction by Rollins and Feldman (1970) indicates different patterns over the family life cycle in the subjective-affective state of each individual:

1. Husbands seem to be much less affected by the state of the family life cycle in their subjective evaluation of marital satisfaction. Their satisfaction varies only slightly from the beginning of marriage through the childbearing phase.

2. Wives experience a general decrease in marital satisfaction during the childbearing and child-rearing phase of the marriage until the children leave home. After the last child leaves home both husband and wife are similar in marital satisfaction.

3. For men there is an apparent setback in marital satisfaction just before they retire.

In short, childbearing and child rearing seem to have a rather profound and negative effect on marital satisfaction for wives. The most difficult time for husbands seems to be when they are anticipating retirement. Thus, marital satisfaction for husbands appears to be influenced more by their occupational experiences; wives are influenced more often by the birth and development of the children.

There has been very little research on the exclusive adjustment patterns experienced by older Americans. The adjustments of husbands and wives to the retirement years is less well documented than the earlier years of the marriage. Felix Berardo (1968) observes that researchers have long concentrated generally on the early phases of the life cycle to the neglect of the later stages.

In terms of the opportunity for husband and wife to have time together, to share common interests, and to have the opportunity to develop greater mutual respect and understanding, the pattern over the family life cycle would seem to be curvilinear. The early phase of marriage, prior to the arrival of the first child, seems to offer the husband and wife maximum opportunity for personal involvement and marital cohesion. The birth of the first child and the increasing time demands of the husband's career substantially reduce the time the husband and wife have to spend together in the middle years. The departure of the last child from home and the approaching retirement of the husband once again return the opportunity for greater involvement, shared activity, and marital cohesion.

This is consistent with the findings of Rollins and Feldman (1970) and Rollins and Cannon (1974), who report a curvilinear trend with a decline in marital satisfaction following the initial years, a leveling off, and then an increase during the postretirement years. Gordon Streib (1965) observes that the loss of the work role for husbands often results in expanded activity in other ongoing roles (husband, grandfather, and so on) that had remained latent. It would appear, then, that a part of the retirement process for men is the shifting of emphasis from occupational to family activity. Richard Kalish (1975) suggests that retirement and a general disengagement from previous career and social responsibilities for the husband in particular allow older men to maintain family activities as long as possible. This does not mean that men during their working years necessarily ignore family roles and responsibilities. It does mean that they will now have more time to dedicate to exclusive family roles. Morris Medley (1976) found that family life and standard of living were significant determinants of life satisfaction for both sexes at each stage of adulthood.

Family sociologists have not resolved the inconsistency between the earlier studies of the family life cycle reporting a decline over time in marital satisfaction and the later studies indicating a curvilinear relationship. Rollins and Cannon (1974) believe that the reported decreases in marital satisfaction in midlife are not due to aging, since if that were the case satisfaction would continue to decline. Rather, they believe the strains of career and parenting are what causes marital satisfaction to drop during the middle years. Jane Traupman and Elaine Hatfield (1983) found similar results when asking married couples when they felt over- and underbenefited in their marriage. Older women reported feeling overbenefited early in the marriage, underbenefited from their 30s to their 70s, and equally benefited with their husbands in their 70s and 80s. Future research will undoubtedly clarify this issue.

For many reasons, conjugal relationships and adjustment patterns in the postretirement years are probably a continuation of adjustments made earlier in the life cycle. Edrita Fried and Karl Stern (1948), for example, found that nearly all of the older couples whom they interviewed and who rated their marriage as satisfactory had a previous history of good marital relations. Moreover, almost half of these marriages had become even more satisfactory as the partners aged. On the other hand, most of the older couples who rated their marriage as unsatisfactory stated it "had been unsatisfactory more or less from the beginning," and approximately half the marriages deteriorated further as the partners advanced in years. For many older couples, then, marital adjustment in the later years is simply a reflection of adjustments worked out earlier.

Ideal types are used by sociologists to describe those cases taken to a logical extreme in order to illustrate a particular relationship or pattern of behavior. Perhaps no person or group exemplifies an ideal type, but there may be those who are very similar to it in their pattern of behavior.

Medley (1976) has identified what he believes to be three ideal types of marital relationships among older couples:

1. Husband–wife
2. Parent–child
3. Associates

Medley describes the *husband–wife* relationship as one in which the couple stress the intimacy and sharing in their relationship. These persons focus their marriage around husband and wife roles, although not necessarily to the exclusion of other roles. Couples characterized by the husband-wife relationship are likely to feel that interaction with one's spouse is the most rewarding aspect of marital life.

In the *parent–child* marriage one partner assumes the role of parent and the other the role of child. The spouse assuming the parent role behaves in a nurturing, protective, and dominant fashion toward the other partner. Concomitantly, the spouse assuming the child role behaves in a submissive and dependent manner. Failing health of one of the partners may quickly lead to this type of relationship.

The *associates* are couples who most often act as friends, and although they appreciate each other's company, they find their most rewarding moments outside of the intimacy of their relationships. The associates are apt to be efficient in the business of managing marital and family life. The friendship experienced by the pair, coupled with satisfaction derived from their parental and extrafamily roles, is likely to perpetuate their relationship.

Thus there is no single marital pattern that necessarily leads to good marital adjustment in later life. What we find are a variety of marital relationships, which various couples find satisfying depending on their individual needs and preferences. Beth Soldo and Emily Agree (1988) report that at any age in life married couples who are living together are likely to be the least dissatisfied with their lives. Apparently married life with all the commensurate adjustment problems is still found to be more satisfying than any other living arrangement.

Sexual Adjustment

One problem Americans confront in achieving an adequate sexual adjustment in their later years is the generally negative view held by society on this subject. Society considers a young man's interest in the opposite sex to be normal and expected, even to the point of slight worry when there appears to be a lack of interest. At a later age, however, this same interest is negatively labeled and we hear jokes about "dirty old men." The result is that a young man not interested in the opposite sex is a cause for concern, but an older man continuing to show an interest in sex is also a cause for concern. It is difficult to understand why society would come to expect all other biological systems to function throughout life except the sexual one.

Lobsenz (1974) observes that many Americans apparently feel that sexual interest declines with age, that sexual exertion may be dangerous to one's health in old age, and that therefore most older people tend to give up sex more or less completely. Research by Alfred Kinsey and his associates (1953), William Masters and Virginia Johnson (1970), and Eric Pfeiffer (1978) of the Duke University Center for the Study of the Aging finds these beliefs to be wrong. The findings of all these studies indicate that men and women in general good health are physiologically able to have a satisfying sex life well into their 70s, 80s, and beyond. Kinsey (1953) found that four out of five men over the age of 60 were capable of intercourse and that there was no evidence of sexual decline in women beyond the age of 60. Interestingly enough, in a research project at Duke University that followed a sample of respondents for 20 years (Pfeiffer, 1978), 15 percent of the men and women studied showed a steady rise in sexual interest and activity as they got older. The Duke findings indicate that two out of three men are sexually active past 65, and one of five is still active in his 80s.

The Masters and Johnson (1970) data indicate a slowdown in sexual activity with aging but not a cessation. Masters and Johnson found that males' capacity for erection and climax and women's capacity for orgasm were slowed but not terminated by aging.

The slowing of sexual activity during the later years was explored most carefully during the Duke longitudinal study. The pattern was found to be quite different for men than for women. Approximately 80 percent of the healthy and socially active males reported sexual interest at the beginning of the study. Ten years later no significant drop in this proportion was found. On the other hand, the proportion who were sexually active dropped from 70 percent at the beginning of the study to 25 percent ten years later. Thus interest remained high in the males, but sexual activity decreased considerably.

Of the healthy and socially active females only about one third reported sexual interest at the beginning of the study. This proportion did not change significantly over the next ten years: approximately one fifth of the women had sexual intercourse regularly over the next ten years. Fewer women than men, therefore, were still sexually interested and active, but of those who were active, aging did not seem to diminish the activity.

Busse and Pfeiffer (1969) believe the lower level of sexual interest and activity among aging females may be explained in part by the lower level of sexual interest expressed by women than men throughout the life cycle. Kinsey and colleagues (1953) reported a lower number of sexual outlets for women than for men at all ages. Ewald Busse and Eric Pfeiffer assert, furthermore, that declining sexual interest and activity for women may have occurred before their entry into the study (before age 60). Their data indicate that the median age of cessation of intercourse was nearly ten years earlier in women than in men.

The principal explanation for the cessation in sexual activity in women, however, appears to be a decline in interest by the husbands. Nearly all of the women attributed responsibility for the cessation of sexual intercourse to their husbands, and the men in general agreed.

The Kinsey (1953) studies indicate that married and nonmarried men do not differ appreciably in sexual interest and activity. Married women, by comparison, differed substantially from nonmarried women, with very few of the nonmarried women reporting any sexual activity and less than 20 percent reporting any sexual interest.

Like other areas of the older person's life, sexual adjustment tends to follow patterns set in the middle years, and these are likely to continue well into the 70s and 80s. Couples who have not remained sexually active during the middle years are likely to find that the older years bring decreased interest and responsiveness to sexual stimulation. As Masters and Johnson (1970) report,

> the most important factor in the maintenance of effective sexuality for the aging male is consistency of active sexual expression. When the male is stimulated to high sexual output during his formative years and a similar tenor of activity is established for the 31 to 40 year age range, his middle-aged and involutional years are marked by constantly recurring physiologic evidence of maintained sexuality. Certainly it is true for the male geriatric sample that those men currently interested in relatively

high levels of sexual expression report similar activity levels from their formative years.[4]

There appears to be a similar continuity from the middle years among women:

> Significant sexual capacity and effective sexual performance are not confined to the human female's premenopausal years. Generally, the intensity of physiologic reaction and duration of anatomic response to effective stimulation are reduced . . . with the advancing years. Regardless of involutional changes in the reproductive organs, the aging human female is fully capable of sexual performance at orgasmic response levels, particularly if she is exposed to regularity of effective stimulation.[5]

Masters and Johnson (1970) indicate that sexual ability does appear to deteriorate in old age, particularly among men, when the opportunity for sexual fulfillment is not present. They believe the problem of sexual adjustment in later life is psychological rather than physical. Factors that they believe can contribute to sexual impotence at any age are (1) boredom with one's partner, (2) preoccupation with career and economic pursuits, (3) mental and physical fatigue, (4) overindulgence in food and drink, (5) physical and mental infirmities, and (6) poor performance.[6] It is apparent that with the aging male the most critical factor is fear of failure and the emotional threat to identity and masculinity that this brings. Older wives are likely to lack insight into the fear-of-failure problem, take their husbands' lack of interest as a personal rejection, and respond in such a way as to compound the problem. Counseling the female, in this case, could probably readily eliminate the problem.

The Masters and Johnson (1970) data indicate that several major factors limit sexual responsiveness among older females, including (1) steroid starvation, which makes coitus painful, (2) lack of a regular sexual outlet, (3) the Victorian concept that women should not have an interest in sex, (4) physical infirmities, and (5) the fact that some women never learn to respond to sexual desire and use menopause as an excuse for abstinence.[7] Hormone therapy has been found to eliminate the pain associated with coitus experienced by some older women. It has been concluded from this that there is no time limit to female sexuality.

Mary Ann Sviland (1978) reports very positive results for older persons who participated in a sexual liberation and growth program:

> One husband aged 62 in a new sexual atmosphere of playful unhurriedness now consistently has two orgasms per sexual session when his prior lifelong pattern involved only one orgasm per session. . . . a few other couples in their midsixties now average four to six orgasms per week while one male aged 64, over a six month time span, twice exhibited only a 10-minute refractory period between orgasms.[8]

Robert Butler, Myra Lewis and Trey Sunderland (1991) report that many aging patients with health problems avoid sexual relations out of a fear of death. The older persons' fear that any kind of sexual stimulation may lead to heart attacks and strokes has led couples to acquire twin beds, separate bedrooms, and a habit of abstinence. This is unfortunate since most of these fears are unfounded and could easily be eliminated by understanding doctors who took the time to advise patients on these matters.

Thus, older couples can experience problems of sexual adjustment not confronted by younger couples. The evidence strongly indicates, however, that any difficulties can be overcome, and that human sexuality is not terminated with advancing years. The most crucial factor in sexual adjustment in the later years seems to be the opportunity for regular sexual stimulation and involvement. Stellye Weinstein and Efren Rosen (1988) found that seniors residing in age-segregated communities were significantly more sexually active than those residing in age-integrated communities. This suggests that the availability of members of the opposite sex who are similar in age results in greater sexual activity among seniors. Thus, according to Douglas Kimmel (1974), the principal limit on sexual activity for the aging person is male attrition, which leaves the female without a sexual partner and with little opportunity to find another.

Marital Adjustment to Retirement

Among the physical, economic, and emotional factors in adjustment to retirement by older Americans, the accommodation of the husband to the retirement role appears to be crucial. Aaron Lipman (1962) has observed that the husband's concept of self is acquired from his occupational role as a worker and from his familial role as a husband, father, and provider. The two roles are clearly demarcated, both geographically and temporally. Life on the job involves a different location with different actors, goals, and status. There is obviously some interpenetration of the roles: The male's success in family roles is determined in part by his success in the occupational role. That is, through the occupational role the husband manages to develop and sustain a satisfactory self-image and status in the home.

The wife's self-concept has, in the past, been tied to her management of the household. Of all the marital roles, the wife's homemaker role is the most stable. According to Ruth Cavan (1962), it seems the most basic, transcending all others. The mother role rises to a crest, declines, and disappears. Paid employment comes and goes. But homemaking as a role continues from the day after the wedding to the end of the marriage. Thus by virtue of her significance in the household and the attendant social roles of wife, homemaker, and companion, the woman manages to develop and sustain an acceptable self-image and status throughout her adult life.

Retirement, in the past, has altered the husband's roles while leaving the wife's relatively unchanged. While many wives in retired families are able to continue satisfactorily their traditional role as homemaker, a similar pattern of role continuity is denied the husband. The role of wage earner, formerly his primary role, is suddenly withdrawn. He is isolated from the occupational system, which can lead to adjustment problems. If the married male is to adjust to retirement, he must redefine his social function and his familial roles.

Some insights into this problem are provided by Lipman's (1962) study of a group of primarily upper-class retired couples in metropolitan Miami. Lipman found, among other things, that successful marital adjustment following retirement depends on the extent to which the husband replaces a self-conception functionally related to employment and the associated instrumental role of provider by developing an expressive role in the home:

> In retirement since men can no longer attain the work and achievement goals, striving for them and adherence to them is associated with poor adjustment. A feeling of usefulness and purposefulness is achieved by the male increasingly

through the assistance with household activities, and emphasizing expressive qualities such as giving love, affection, and companionship to his wife. A new and meaningful functional role is thus created that aids in individual adjustment.[9]

Aaron Lipman (1962) was also led to question the rather widespread assumption that women experience little or no role discontinuity following their husband's retirement, but simply retain their traditional role of housewife. He found that the husband's increased involvement in household activities and his emergent expressive orientation necessitates a reciprocal shift in the wife's domestic role and self-image. The wife can no longer view her major role as being that of a good homemaker. She and her husband must move from the previously defined sex-differentiated instrumental roles toward a common area of identity and role activities, which includes sharing and cooperation. Here, expressive qualities such as love, understanding, companionship, and compatibility become the most important things they can give in marriage.

The next generation of retirees may find the division of labor between husband and wife at the time of retirement much easier to negotiate. Families today are much more likely to have both the husband and wife working outside of the home. Thus, throughout their careers housework has in all probability been shared. This can make retirement less problematic. A new problem may emerge for the next generation, however. If both husband and wife are not the same age, one may be under pressure to retire early in order that the couple may initiate their retirement plans. One partner retiring considerably earlier than the other may feel somewhat deprived by the fact that travel and other activities must be postponed until the spouse's retirement.

Finally, it should be emphasized that retirement need not harm conjugal relations in old age. Streib (1965) asked a sample of adult children to assess their family situation and their relationship with their father after his retirement. Over 70 percent said their father's retirement had not created any serious difficulties; 30 percent felt retirement had brought their father closer to his immediate family, and 68 percent reported no change at all in this respect; and 93 percent felt their father had as much to say about family matters as he had before retirement. These responses indicate that there is considerable stability and harmony in family roles and relationships in retirement.

In comparing older persons who did and did not have children, Judith Rempel (1985) found the childless to be more financially secure and in better health while the parents tended to have more friends and were more satisfied with life. As with most choices one makes in life, there are positive and negative outcomes. Apparently the decision on whether or not to have children is no different.

INTERGENERATIONAL RELATIONS

Marvin Koller (1974), in discussing multigenerational families, defines a *generation* as the

thousands of persons who will share similar, but not identical experiences because they are born, live, and die within a common historical period.[10]

The thread that links multiple generations with a system of shared beliefs, norms, values, and cultural traditions is the family. Family units often transcend more than one generation and inculcate their members with a system of shared beliefs. The longevity of the current population means that family members may span three or four generations.

Ethel Shanas (1980) refers to four-generation families as "the new pioneers." She observes that these families are becoming more common and are creating a complex system of family interrelationships. What to call each family member of each generation, the differences between the first and last generations, and who is the head of the four-generation family are just a few of the problems she identifies.

The argument heard most often regarding multigenerational family interaction is that meaningful reciprocal relations between the generations have deteriorated. Many family sociologists have argued that modern urban mass society has created isolated nuclear families in which extended-family ties are either minimized or nonexistent. Upon completing educational training, young people are expected to establish themselves in a career, marry, and move to a household away from the influence of either set of parents. Industrial organizations prefer and often demand a mobile labor force that can be periodically moved as production and employee development demand. This system of values often results in younger family members being geographically separated from immediate and extended relatives on both sides. Family sociologists have thus felt that the isolated nuclear family is likely to be the most common one in modern industrial nations. Multigenerational or extended-family ties were expected to be a thing of the past.

But research into changing family forms and functions since the late 1950s simply has not found this to be the case. Eugene Litwak (1959–60), for example, in a study of extended-family ties, tested two hypotheses:

1. Occupational mobility is antithetical to extended-family relations.
2. Extended-family relations are impossible because of geographic mobility.

Litwak found that the extended-family form exists in modern urban society among middle-class families, that extended-family relations are possible in an urban society, that geographical propinquity is an unnecessary condition of these relationships, and that occupational mobility is unhindered by the activities of the extended family. Extended-family activities include advice, financial assistance, temporary housing, and similar assistance given during occupational movement.[11]

Lillian Troll, Sheila Miller, and Robert Atchley (1979) discuss the stereotypes of the modern family. They believe the most common stereotype is that the young couple are expected to establish a neolocal residence (a home independent of both sets of parents), raise their children with the advice of child psychologists rather than the wisdom of the grandparents, and be economically independent by virtue of the young husband's success. But

> in actual fact, most young couples seem to live reasonably close to both sets of parents, receive either help in the form of services (such as babysitting) or money (more in the middle class) and visit frequently.[12]

The evidence indicates, then, that the isolated nuclear family that was expected to emerge in modern industrial nations simply has not come to pass. Three- and four-generation families whose generations interact with and assist each other frequently in a variety of circumstances seem the most common pattern.

Marvin Sussman and Lee Burchinal (1968) found a variety of help patterns among family members, including the exchange of services, gifts, advice, and financial assistance. Moreover, this exchange of aid flows in a variety of directions, including inward from more distant relatives. Financial assistance, apparently, flows more often from parents to children.

Family social activities are also a source of emotional support for family members. Many family sociologists believe that the difficulty of developing satisfactory primary relationships outside the family in urban areas makes the extended family even more important to the individual.

The extended-family interaction and assistance pattern found in this country carries with it a system of satisfaction with and support for older family members. Ethel Shanas and Gordon Streib (1965) found that married children were willing to assume responsibility for aged parents, including giving them financial aid, providing a home for them, and locating close to them.[13]

What research findings indicate, then, is that there is a two-direction flow of assistance in multigenerational families. Adult working members of the family contribute both financially and socially to the children during the early years of their marriage. Simultaneously, adult members contribute financial aid, social support, and sometimes a home for older members. This protective function of the family is still one of its more useful and integrating activities. While some of the support for older members of the society has been shifted off of the family and onto government (as with retirement income), the family still provides many and often the most crucial services for its older members. Marvin Sussman and Morris Stroud (1959–64), in a series of studies, found that the illness of an older family member resulted in an almost instantaneous response from all other family members. The ill person is most often the recipient of large amounts of aid, service, and attention during hospitalization or after returning to the community.[14]

Victor Cicirelli (1983) did find that children with intact marriages were likely to give more support to aging parents than were children with disrupted marriages. His findings indicate that women with intact marriages often go so far as to stop working when aging parents are seriously in need of help.

The provision of support for older family members seems to depend on two factors—the need for support and the resources of the younger family members. Elizabeth Mutran (1985), controlling for age and sex, found that elderly black parents both give and receive more help than elderly white parents. This difference, however, may be related largely to greater need, since many blacks, because of past discrimination, find themselves in the lower socioeconomic groups that experience greater need. As to the second factor, Cicirelli (1983) found that employment among those with marital disruptions (divorced, death of spouse, remarriage), particularly divorced women, was quite high in comparison with adult children with intact marriages. A higher proportion of the maritally disrupted felt they could not continue to help their parents if their job was threatened by doing so. Horowitz (1982) found that women in intact marriages have the option of stopping work to care for aging parents, and there are indications that many do so when stresses become too great.

There are also sex differences in support patterns, with women most commonly being the care givers for the elderly (Depner & Ingersoll-Dayton, 1985). What we often find today is middle-aged and old women caring for the very old. Brody (1978) has observed

> that it is ironic that a new role has emerged for the "empty nest" cohort—women between 50–60 years of age; that of caregiver to the very old. Thus the "empty nest" is being refilled with grandparents.[15]

The family still provides a very personal, primary, and immediate response to the needs of its elder members. While government services are important to America's elders, it is doubtful that they could ever replace vital family support functions.

GRANDPARENTHOOD

A cross-national study of older persons in 1962 found that 40 percent of those over 65 in the United States had great-grandchildren; 23 percent in Denmark and 22 percent in Britain were also at the top of four-generation families. Peter Townsend (1966) found that in Britain the average woman becomes a grandmother at 54 and a great-grandmother at 72; men averaged three years later.[16] In Britain and the United States 75 percent of old people with children live no longer than 30 minutes away from them.

Increased life expectancy coupled with earlier marriages, a shorter child-rearing period, and fewer children have exposed more middle-aged and older couples to the role of grandparenthood than in any other period in history. Interestingly enough, though, the phenomenon of grandparenthood has been relatively ignored by researchers in both psychology and sociology.

An anthropological study by Dorian Apple (1956) provides us with one of the best clues to the critical determinants of the quality of the relationship between grandparents and grandchildren. Using ethnographic data from 75 cultures, Apple found that in societies where grandparents retain considerable household authority, either because of economic power or because of the traditionally high status granted them, the relationship between grandparents and grandchildren is most often formal and unfriendly. On the other hand, in societies in which the grandparents' generation retains little control or authority over the grandchildren, grandparents and grandchildren typically have warm, egalitarian relationships. Apple concluded that friendly relationships between grandparents and grandchildren will occur where the family structure does not allow grandparents to exercise family authority.

Sarah Matthews and Jetse Sprey (1985) found that grandchildren were most likely to describe their relationship with their maternal grandmother as close and least likely to describe their bonds with their paternal grandparents in this way. Since mothers are still the primary care givers for children, apparently the children interact more frequently with their maternal grandmother and in a more relaxed atmosphere—thus their more positive attitude toward maternal grandmothers.

Sue Updegraff (1968) found that American grandparents most often engage in companionable and indulgent relationships with their grandchildren and usually do not assume any direct responsibility or control over their behavior. It seems that only in the case of their grandchildren's being orphaned do grandparents give direct aid to or take full responsibility for them. The majority of grandparents do exhibit considerable pride and pleasure from involvement with their grandchildren.

Bernice Neugarten and Karol Weinstein (1964) have identified five major styles of grandparenthood:

1. The *formal* style is regarded by those who follow it as the proper and prescribed role of grandparents. Although these grandparents may give presents and babysit with grandchildren, they maintain clearly drawn lines between parenting and grandparenting and leave the parenting exclusively to the parents.

2. The *fun seekers* are informal and playful with grandchildren. They join them in a variety of activities specifically to have fun, almost as playmates. The emphasis is on mutual gratification.

3. The *distant figure* is the grandparent who emerges from the shadows on holidays and special occasions. Contact with the grandchildren is fleeting but benevolent.

4. The *surrogate parent* is most often the grandmother who cares for the grandchildren while the mother works.

5. The *reservoir of family wisdom* is a pattern centering in the grandfather and is distinctly authoritarian. The grandfather is the dispenser of special skills and resources.

The pattern found to be the most frequent by Neugarten and Weinstein (1964) was the formal style, followed by 33 percent of all grandparents; 26 percent were fun-seeking, 24 percent adopted the distant-figure style, 7 percent the parental-surrogate pattern, and 4 percent the reservoir-of-family-wisdom style. Neugarten and Weinstein found that fun seeking was followed more often by younger grandparents and the formal style more often by older grandparents.

Nye and Berardo (1973) point out that women are much more likely than men to look forward to assuming the grandparent role and to undergo considerable anticipatory socialization. They often visualize themselves as grandparents well ahead of the birth of the first grandchild.

The image of grandmother in most women's minds is a positive one that they are most likely to desire. According to F. Ivan Nye and Felix Berardo (1973), however, the role presents some anxiety for young grandmothers who still view themselves as attractive, since it is a threat to a youthful self-image.[17]

Nye and Berardo further observe that most men become grandfathers when they are reaching the apex of their careers. Their primary identity is still attached to the work role, and consequently they postpone much involvement in the grandparent role until after retirement.

The grandparent role can be onesided in either direction if not carefully guarded by the individuals assuming the role. On the one hand, to be able to play with, pamper, and spoil children while not being responsible for their behavior or discipline seems a bit unfair. In this situation the parents become responsible for all negative sanctions on behavior while the grandparents become the distributors of rewards. At the other extreme, the parents may expect the grandparents to always be available for baby-sitting on a minute's notice, may leave the children with them for extended periods while they vacation, or may even turn over total responsibility to them for rearing the children.

Richard Kalish (1975) observes that the closeness between grandparents and grandchildren might be due in part to the circumstances in life that they share. Neither group has much power to influence decision makers. Both are constantly reminded of their nonproductive roles, both are seen as leading a life of leisure, both are living with their time unstructured, both are thought to be inadequately educated, and both are seen as poor and weak. One wonders, however, if they are this aware of the similarity of their circumstance, and indeed if they perceive their positions in this manner. After all, their ages place them at quite diverse points in the life cycle.

Most grandparents, whether initially enamored with the grandparent role or not, come to enjoy the role because it involves a minimum of obligations and responsibilities while allowing much personal fulfillment and need gratification.

WIDOWHOOD

Sooner or later all older married persons must face the possibility of their partner's death or, conversely, the fact that they will die and their spouse will be removed from intimate family relationships during the later years. Since husbands generally die at a younger age than their wives, the widowed status is more common to women than to men.

The last half-century has seen the widowed female consistently outnumbering her male counterpart, and the margin is ever-widening. In 1940 there were twice as many widows as widowers. By 1950 widows had increased by 25 percent but widowers by only 3 percent. In 1960 widows outnumbered widowers by 3.5 to 1, and by 1980 this discrepancy had increased to more than 4 to 1.

The individual making the transition from the married to the widowed status is confronted with a variety of personal and familial problems. That the transition is not always successful is reflected in statistics indicating that widowed persons rather consistently show higher rates of mortality, mental disorders, and suicide. The death of a spouse is particularly devastating to older persons because they have become so accustomed to a style of life that is heavily involved with, and dependent upon, their marital partner.

Helena Lopata (1972) has studied role transitions in widowhood, and how these transitions may be affected by a particular society's structure, composition, and culture. In her view, changes in an individual's social relations and role involvements usually involve a series of stages:

1. Official recognition of the event
2. Temporary "disengagement" or withdrawal from established lines of communication
3. Limbo, which may involve ritualized action of an unusual or emergency nature that is not considered part of the individual's normal pattern
4. Reengagement

Lopata (1972) has pointed out the role changes and altered lifestyles of women in four different societies. The chosen lifestyle often depends upon the woman's involvement in her former role of wife and the way in which this role is connected with her other sets of social relations. In some groups, for instance, a wife may have obligations to her in-laws that extend until long after the husband's death.

Levirate is practiced among the Kgatlo in Africa as a means of caring for widows: A brother of the deceased husband takes his place in providing for the widow and her children, and sometimes fathers more children with her. In this tribe, all the males in the family will cooperate to obtain a *bogadi*, or bride price. The man who marries the woman has exclusive rights to her while he is living, but after death other males in the family may also claim rights to her. Any children who are born of the widow and "substitute" husbands are called "children of the rafters" and are considered to belong to the original husband, becoming his rightful heirs.

In traditional India around A.D. 200, laws were developed that greatly restricted the social life space of women. The ideal age for marriage was about nine or ten, and remarriage by widows was outlawed. The wife was expected to "revere her husband as a god," and the death of a husband was usually viewed as the result of some sin his wife had committed. The ideal act for the widow became *suttee*—being burned to death on the funeral pyre of her husband. Although the British outlawed this custom in 1829, it continued to be practiced in some areas of the country for some time.

In traditional China, the husband's family usually acquired extensive rights over the wife as the result of a very high bride price. On the other hand, remarriage among the working class was often discouraged because a woman's labor was highly valued and she was the only adult who could support her aged in-laws and her young children.

American widows, according to Lopata (1972), seemingly have more alternatives than widows in most other societies. In theory they may stay single or remarry at any time they choose; select a mate from any but a small group of close relatives; continue relations with their own family, their husband's family, or both; and fill their time with a career or with voluntary associations.

There seems to be much confusion among family sociologists regarding who experiences greater difficulty at the death of a spouse, the husband or the wife. Felix Berardo's (1968) evidence indicates that for a variety of reasons survivorship adaptation may be more difficult for the older husband, since the role of the wife remains relatively unchanged upon the death of her spouse. She continues to perform household tasks such as cleaning and cooking, in much the same manner as when her husband was alive. Indeed the ability to maintain certain standards of good housekeeping often represents a test of the degree to which the older woman is avoiding "getting old."

Consequently, a large proportion of aged widows can maintain separate quarters and are capable of taking care of themselves. Moreover, the older widow is more likely than the widower to be welcomed into the home of her married children and to find a useful place there.

In the case of the aged widower, however, the loss of the wife produces marked changes in his pattern of living. If the wife was the homemaker, all the responsibilities for maintenance of the household now fall on him. The husband must now prepare his meals, do the cleaning, maintain the budget, and provide himself with other types of general care. In addition, the widower must find an adequate substitute for the intimacy of that primary relationship once provided by his wife.

The widower's problems of adjustment may be compounded by the loss of his occupational role. For most of a man's adult life, his work has been a principal source of identity and self-concept. Retirement severs that identity and often removes the husband from contact with friends and coworkers. The combined retiree–widower status often places the man in a position of social isolation leading to reduced communication and interaction with significant others. Berardo (1968) has noted that widowers are least likely to

1. Be living with children
2. Have a high degree of kin interaction or be satisfied with extended-family relationships
3. Receive from or give to children various forms of assistance
4. Have friends either inside or outside the community or be satisfied with their opportunities to be with close friends

Bell (1963), on the other hand, has argued that the role of widow may be socially and psychologically more difficult than that of the widower, for a variety of reasons. He argues that in American society,

1. Marriage is generally more important for the woman than the man and that the loss of the role of wife is more basic to the woman.
2. The widow is more apt to be forced to "go it alone" because in comparison with the widower she receives less encouragement from family and friends to remarry.
3. The widow faces much more difficulty in providing and caring for herself and her children because her financial resources are usually considerably less than those of the widower.
4. There are far greater numbers of widows than widowers, and the majority of them are widowed at advanced ages; therefore, it is much more difficult for the surviving wife than for the surviving husband to change her status through remarriage.

Raymond Carey's (1979–80) empirical study of the difficulty of adjusting to widowhood concluded that adjustment was more difficult for widows than widowers, that anticipatory grief was an important factor in the adjustment of widows, and that follow-up visits by physicians and the local clergy were helpful to the widowed, 25 percent of whom were still depressed a year later.

This last point may be the crucial one with regard to the contrasting adjustment patterns of widows and widowers. There is such a surplus of women over the age of 65 that the widower who wants to remarry can no doubt do so, while the widow may want to remarry but simply not have the option to do so. In every decade since the turn of the century the remarriage rate for widowers has been more than double that of widows; with each successive increment in age the disparity widens, so that for persons 55 or older the remarriage rate for widowers is approximately five times as great. A woman who has been widowed at age 25 may find some small comfort in the knowledge that she has a more than 90 percent chance for remarriage. At age 45, however, this probability is reduced to 1 in 3 and at age 65 it drops to 1 in 32.

Widows and widowers both face adjustment problems at the death of a spouse. The widower may have a more readily available solution to his problem since a second marriage is most often possible. That women so outnumber men during the later years makes a second marriage much more likely for a man than for a woman. Moreover, it is not unusual for an older man, especially one who has a substantial income, to find a woman approximately his own age or several years younger who will be willing to marry him. The aged woman, on the other hand, has much less opportunity for a second marriage.

One critical aspect of successful adjustment by widows or widowers is their degree of dependence on the marital partner. In the parent–child relationship, in which one partner assumes a maternalistic or paternalistic concern in the care and supervision of the other partner, the death of a spouse may prove devastating. Over the years, the overly dependent spouse may have lost the necessary inclination, capability, and skill to be self-sufficient.

Knud Helsing, Moses Szklo, and Georg Comstock (1981) found that mortality rates were about the same for widowed and married females but were significantly higher for widowed males than for married males. The reason for this difference is unclear at present. These researchers found that remarriage reduces the mortality rate for both men and women. They found, further, that living alone was associated with significantly higher mortality rates than living with someone (whether a marital partner or not). It seems that a social support network is effective in softening a stressful life event such as bereavement. Living with someone, remarrying, and having a support network of friends have all been found to reduce the rate of mortality following widowhood.

One should not dwell too long on the negative aspects of widowhood. Thomas et al. (1988) argue that the loss of a spouse is not a barrier to positive psychological growth for the older person. Most women survive the death of a spouse without psychological damage, and it appears that a majority see themselves as stronger for having undergone the experience. Thomas et al. (1988) maintain that we do widows a disservice if we insist on focusing upon potential pathology associated with the transition period.

ALTERNATIVE LIFESTYLES

An alternative family pattern that has emerged among a segment of older Americans is that of living together without being formally married. There are a variety of social, legal, and financial pressures on older people that encourage this arrangement. First, many retirement programs that pay the surviving spouse a monthly income become void if he or she remarries. Many widows in particular feel that remarriage will bring an economic penalty in the form of lost financial security. Thus, living with a partner without a formal marriage is a way of maintaining economic independence while filling the various needs that the sharing of one's life with another person brings.

A second factor is that the property a couple may have accumulated during their marriage is now under the control of the surviving spouse. Children may discourage the marriage of an aging mother or father for fear that upon the death of their parent, his or her assets will be in the hands of the second marital partner, who is related to them only by marriage. Thus an older couple who choose to live together without marrying will reduce pressures from their children not to marry for fear of losing the parent's inheritance. The major danger for an aging couple who decide on this course of action is the feeling of guilt which may accompany the arrangement. Norms regarding heterosexual relations that have been acquired over a long life are not easily changed.

Due to the greater longevity of women and perhaps to differences in the age of the partners at the time of marriage, the average wife outlives her husband by 5 to 15 years. The result is an imbalanced sex ratio and a surplus of women during the later years. Awareness of this situation and the problems it creates led Kassel (1966) to suggest that polygyny after 60 ought to become an established American family pattern. Kassel believes that allowing one man to have several wives after 60 would offer the following advantages to older Americans:

1. Older women would have the opportunity to reestablish a meaningful family group.
2. Mealtime would regain a social atmosphere and the elderly would eat a more balanced diet.
3. The opportunity to pool funds would insure a more adequate income for older families.
4. In case of illness there would be others around to care for the sick person and less of a need for a nursing home.
5. Household duties could be shared and would therefore be lighter.
6. The problem of insufficient numbers of sex partners for older women would be solved.
7. Loneliness and social isolation would be curbed.
8. Group insurance would become less expensive and more feasible for older persons.

While the idea of polygyny is intriguing, the practice does not seem to be occurring readily in the United States. Since Kassel first suggested it, in 1966, neither medical doctors, psychiatrists, nor social gerontologists have seen fit to recommend it to older Americans. While feasible, polygyny would seem to clash with attitudes and values acquired over a lifetime. Older Americans as a group seem less prone than other age groups to experiment with alternative styles of life. One wonders, therefore, if Kassel seriously expected polygyny after 60 to become an established family pattern or was merely putting the reader on.

There are four different paths to living alone for the elderly other than widowhood. Brubaker (1985) categorizes older persons living alone as the never married, the career divorced, the newly divorced, and the serial divorced.

Brubaker (1985) argues that approximately 8 percent of the older population have never been married at any time in their life. Their family lives have never been restricted to the nuclear units but instead revolve around parents, siblings, nieces, nephews, and sometimes, fictive kin. Fictive kin are generally considered to be persons who are not blood related to the older person but are treated as family members. The elderly never married have adjusted to their single status throughout their adult life and are not likely to feel isolated or depressed about their status in later life. Extended relatives and fictive kin provide social networks and support in later life for those who never married.

Women who were divorced in their early or middle years and never remarried were classified by Brubaker as the "career divorced." These women enter later life with a long history of being divorced and most often like the never married have a social and support network of extended relatives and fictive kin. Moreover, many of these women raised their children on their own, and have the support of their own children in later life.

The newly divorced are described by Brubaker (1985) as men and women who seek a divorce after being married for many years and after their children have left home. Often these couples have been dissatisfied with their marriage for many years but did not divorce for the sake of their children. After the last child leaves home, however, the conflict between partners often intensifies to the point where there is no alternative except to divorce. Unlike the career divorced, these individuals are suddenly thrust into a new role in later life as unmarried persons with little time to adjust to being single. They often lack a network of friends or extended relatives who are able to provide the type of support and assistance in times of hardship that they previously relied on their spouses to provide. Of the three categories of the divorced, these women have the greatest adjustments to make because they face being alone in their later years when they had not planned to do so. In this way their situation is comparable to the suddenly widowed.

Older men and women who have been divorced and remarried several times during their lifetime have been classified by Brubaker (1985) as the "serial divorced." They either enter later life as divorced persons or become divorced again. Most have complex family relationships because they have been married more than once. The serial divorced, like the career divorced, have been unmarried before and are better able to handle the stresses of being divorced in later life than the newly divorced.

Elderly persons who have divorced, at any age in life, and who have children and grandchildren are considerably less likely to be isolated and much more likely to receive family assistance if they become physically dependent.

SECOND MARRIAGES

Remarriage of older persons who have lost a spouse through death seems to be a more common and accepted pattern among older persons. As Jessie Bernard (1956) remarks,

> the high proportion of successful remarriages, especially among the widowed, suggests that the loneliness of the later years might well be assuaged if older men and women were encouraged to remarry. Popular attitudes cannot be changed at will, of course; but if it is at all possible to create an attitude sympathetic to love and romance in the later years such an attitude might help.[18]

Remarriage seems to be the most realistic solution for single older persons who hope to maintain the approval of relatives and friends of their lifestyle. As previously stated, the biggest single deterrent to this pattern is the shortage of available men in the later years.

A century ago the extended family was considerably more common in the United States than it is today. The result was that older widowed persons often moved in with their children, were given a place in the family, and found many family roles that they were capable of performing.

But modern industry, as we have noted, requires a mobile labor force that can be moved from place to place. Hence, one does not always live in the same community as extended-family members. While Litwak's (1959–60) work indicated that families do provide support for their members even if they are geographically widely separated, this does not usually include providing them a permanent place of residence. Aging parents prefer to maintain their independence and are not anxious to move in with their children. Their children often have their own children to raise and are not anxious to have their aging parents move in with them. Figure 8–1 indicates that the practices of elderly men and elderly women living with children and other relatives both became less common between 1960 and 1979. Currently less than 5 percent of elderly men and less than 15 percent of elderly women are living with children and other relatives. Older persons who find themselves without an immediate family due to the death of a spouse now have only a few choices available to them. They may live alone, move into a home or apartment with another widowed person, or remarry if a suitable partner is available.

The story of Amy indicates the reluctance of older persons to give up their independence and move in with their children. Amy was just one year younger than her husband Bill, who was 67 when he died in 1978. She remained living in the house that she and her husband had built a number of years before. She had known for two years that her husband was dying, so she had more time than many widows to decide about remaining in her home. Amy had no intention of selling her home until two years later, when the upkeep became too much for her and she felt compelled to do so. After selling her house she moved into a small apartment complex not far from her son. Amy has always been independent. The only circumstance that has slowed her down is a continuing problem with her eyes—first glaucoma, then cataracts, and then a detached retina. The following

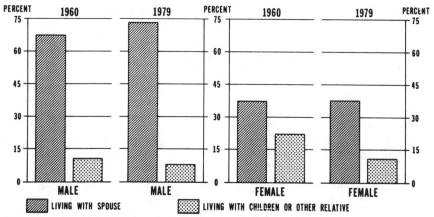

FIGURE 8–1 Living Arrangements, Persons Aged 65 and Older, by Sex, 1960 and 1979

Source: U.S. Bureau of the Census

year Amy, who was by now going blind, was forced to give up her apartment and move in with her son. She proclaims this was the most difficult decision of her life, since she did not want to give up her independence and did not at all like the idea of imposing on her children. Her failing eyesight, however, left her no other choice.

Second marriages in later life have been carefully examined by Walter McKain (1969). McKain argues that disengagement from employment and other social activities related to the work role makes the family the single most important factor in the life satisfaction of older Americans. He further believes that marriage is a positive force in health maintenance and that older men and women who remarry are probably adding years to their lives.[19]

McKain (1969) found that although children may not prefer to have their aging parents live with them, their support in the case of a second marriage is most helpful:

> One of the most important ingredients in a successful retirement marriage is a wholesome relation between the old couple and their children. Especially fortunate were those parents whose children lived nearby, visited their parents occasionally and stood ready to help the elderly couple in an emergency.[20]

In a later study McKain (1972) concluded that the success of second marriages was aided by the partners' having been well acquainted before marriage (many had known each other during their previous marriage), the approval of relatives and friends, living in a home that had not previously belonged to either partner, and having an adequate income.

It seems highly likely that second marriages in later life will become more common in the future. Only the unavailability of an acceptable partner would seem to prevent them from becoming even more common.

CONCLUSION

Families over a lifetime find themselves adjusting to and being shaped by a variety of circumstances and forces. Koller (1974) in his work on the multigenerational family used the power variable to illustrate the change in one's position in society over a lifetime (Figure 8–2). The young, in Koller's view, are low in power and generally depend on the parent generation for their support and survival. The parent generation in their middle years are at the peak of their power and occupy the positions of greatest trust and responsibility in society. The old are in a period of declining power. Intertwined with the power variable are such factors as changing roles, status, and privilege, which also shift over the life cycle.

Older families, because they are in a position of declining power and privilege, must adjust to new roles and statuses and altered styles of life. Over time, older couples see their children marry and leave home, the husband or wife or both retire from full-time employment, and the family may move to a smaller home or apartment.

Many changes in family life during the later years are seen as desirable. The husband and wife, free of occupational and child-rearing demands, are now able to spend time in other desired ways. Neglected family roles can now be reassumed. The husband and wife find that they have more time for each other as

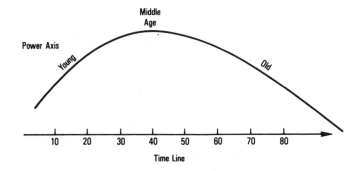

FIGURE 8–2
Changing Positions in Society over a Lifetime

Source: Adapted from Marvin R. Koller, *Families: A Multigenerational Approach* (New York: McGraw-Hill, 1974), p. 216.

well as time to dedicate to grandchildren and other family matters. They are now free to choose among a variety of social activities, volunteer chores, and recreational and social pursuits. Older persons frequently point out that the advantage of retirement is that it allows them to do what they want with their time. During most of their adult years, on the other hand, they found themselves doing what was expected of them.

On the other hand, the older couple often must adjust to some undesirable changes in their lifestyle. The retirement of one or both married partners means a reduced income, and often a loss in status in the eyes of former associates and friends. The later years may be accompanied by chronic health problems, declining energy, and the death of a spouse. One ultimately may have to give up one's independence and move in with children or to government housing or a nursing home. Dependence on one's children involves a role reversal. Formerly counselors to their children, older persons now find themselves being counseled.

In a study by Harold Cox, Albert Bhak, and Arthur Kline (1978) on the life satisfaction and marital adjustment of older Americans, two distinct personality types were identified, and representatives of these types were found to be quite different in their adjustment to the problems of older families. *Internally oriented* individuals believed the rewards they received followed from or were contingent upon their own behavior. *Externally oriented* people felt that the rewards they received were controlled by forces outside themselves and over which they had no control. The internally oriented believed there was a direct causal chain between their behavior and the reward or punishment. The externally oriented believed that reinforcement was not contingent upon their own actions but was the result of luck or fate and was therefore unpredictable. The internally oriented tend to be self-directed; the externally oriented are inclined to be fatalistic. Older married couples who were internally oriented were found to experience greater marital cohesion, to have a better marital adjustment in the later years, to be more satisfied with their lives, and to perceive greater difficulties for themselves following the death of a spouse.

KEY TERMS

disenchantment
external orientation
generation

ideal type
internal orientation
life cycle

REFERENCES

ADAMS, BERT N., *The Family: A Sociological Interpretation*. Skokie, Ill.: Rand McNally, 1975.

APPLE, DORIAN, "The Social Structure of Grandparenthood," *American Anthropologist*, 58 (August 1956), 656–63.

BALLWEG, JOHN A., "Resolution of Conjugal Role Adjustment after Retirement." *Journal of Marriage and the Family*, 29 (May 1967), 277–81.

BELL, ROBERT R., *Marriage and Family Interaction*, pp. 412–16. Homewood, Ill.: Dorsey, 1963.

BENGTSON, VERN L., and JOSEPH A. KUYPERS, "Generational Difference and the Developmental Stake," *Aging and Human Development*, 2 (1971), 249–60.

BERARDO, FELIX M., "Social Adaptation to Widowhood among a Rural-Urban Aged Population," *Washington Agricultural Experiment Station Bulletin*, 689 (December 1969), 28–29.

BERARDO, FELIX M., "Widowhood Status in the United States: Perspectives on a Neglected Aspect of the Family Life Cycle," *Family Coordinator*, 17 (July 1968), 191–203.

BERNARD, JESSIE, *Remarriage*. New York: Dryden, 1956.

BLOOD, R. J., and D. M. WOLFE, *Husbands and Wives: The Dynamics of Married Living*. New York: Free Press, 1960.

BRODY, E., "The Aging of the Family," *Annuals of the American Academy of Political and Social Science*, 438 (July 1978), 13–27.

BROZAN, NADINE, "The Sandwich Generation," *Aging*, ed. Eleanor Goldstein. Social Issues Series (1980), article 52.

BRUBAKER, T. H., *Later Life Families*. Beverly Hills, Calif.: Sage, 1985.

BURGESS, ERNEST W., "Family Living in the Later Decades," *Annals of the American Academy of Political and Social Science*, 279 (January 1952), 111–12.

BUSSE, EWALD W., and ERIC PFEIFFER, in *Behavior and Adaptation in Late Life*, ed. Ewald W. Busse and Eric Pfeiffer. Boston: Little, Brown, 1969.

BUTLER, ROBERT N., MYRA LEWIS, and TREY SUNDERLAND, *Aging and Mental Health*. New York: Macmillan, 1991.

CAREY, RAYMOND G., "Weathering Widowhood: Problems and Adjustments of the Widowed during the First Year," *Omega*, 10, no. 2 (1979–80), 163–76.

CAVAN, RUTH S., "Self and Role Adjustment in Old Age," in *Human Behavior and Social Processes*, ed. Arnold M. Rose, pp. 526–35. Boston: Houghton Mifflin, 1962.

CICIRELLI, VICTOR, "A Comparison of Helping Behavior to Elderly Parents of Adult Children with Intact Marriages," *Gerontologist*, 23, no. 6 (1983), 619–25.

COX, HAROLD, ALBERT BHAK, and ARTHUR KLINE, "The Motivation and Marital Adjustment Patterns of Older Americans," *Family Perspective*, 12, no. 1 (Winter 1978), 41–51.

COX, HAROLD, GURMEET SEKHON, and CHARLES NORMAN, "Social Characteristics of the Elderly in Indiana," *Proceedings/Indiana Academy of the Social Sciences* (1978), 186–98.

CUMMING, ELAINE, "Further Thoughts on the Theory of Disengagement," *International Social Science Journal*, 15 (1963), 377–93.

CUMMING, ELAINE, and WILLIAM HENRY, *Growing Old: The Process of Disengagement*. New York: Basic Books, 1961.

DAVIDSON, MARIA, "Social and Economic Characteristics of Aged Persons (65 Years Old and Older) in the United States in 1960," *Eugenics Quarterly*, 14 (1967), 27–44.

DAY, ALICE T., "Who Cares? Demographic Trends Challenge Family Care for the Elderly," *Population Trends and Public Policy*, no. 9 (September 1985), 1–16.

DEPNER, CHARLES E., and BERIT INGERSOLL-DAYTON, "Conjugal Social Support and Patterns in Later Life," *Journal of Gerontology*, 40, no. 6 (1985), 761–66.

DEUTSCHER, IRWIN, "Socialization for Postparental Life," in *Human Behavior and Social Processes*, ed. Arnold M. Rose, pp. 507–18. Boston: Houghton Mifflin, 1962.

FARBER, BERNARD, *Family Organization and Interaction*. San Francisco: Chandler, 1964.

FRIED, EDRITA G., and KARL STERN, "The Situation of the Aged within the Family," *American Journal of Orthopsychiatry*, 18 (January 1948), 31–54.

GLASSER, PAUL H., and LOIS N. GLASSER, "Role Reversal and Conflict between Aged Parents and Their Children," *Marriage and Family Living*, 24 (1962), 46–51.

HELSING, KNUD, MOSES SZKLO, and GEORG COMSTOCK, "Factors Associated with Mortality after Widowhood," *American Journal of Public Health*, (1981), 802–9.

HOROWITZ, A., "Predictors of Caregiving Involvement among Adult Children of the Frail Elderly." Paper presented at the 34th Annual Scientific Meeting of the Gerontological Society of America, Boston, 1982.

JACOBSEN, PAUL H., "The Changing Role of Mortality in American Family Life," *Lex et Scientia*, 3 (April–June 1966), 117–24.

KALISH, RICHARD A., *Late Adulthood: Perspectives on Human Development*. Monterey, Calif.: Brooks/Cole, 1975.

KASSEL, V., "Polygyny after 60," *Geriatrics*, 21 (1966), 214–18.

KERCKHOFF, ALAN C., "Husband–Wife Expectations and Reactions in Retirement," *Journal of Gerontology*, 19 (January 1964), 510–16.

KIMMEL, DOUGLAS C., *Adulthood and Aging*. New York: John Wiley, 1974.

KINSEY, ALFRED C., and ASSOCIATES, *Sexual Behavior in the Human Female*, Philadelphia: Saunders, 1953.

KOLLER, MARVIN R., *Families: A Multigenerational Approach*. New York: McGraw-Hill, 1974.

LIPMAN, AARON, "Role Conceptions of Couples in Retirement," in *Social and Psychological Aspects of Aging*, ed. Clark Tibbitts and Wilma Donahue, pp. 475–85. New York: Columbia University Press, 1962.

LITWAK, EUGENE, "The Use of Extended Family Groups in the Achievement of Social Goals: Some Policy Implications," *Social Problems*, 6 (Winter 1959–60), 177–87.

LOBSENZ, N. M., "Sex and the Senior Citizen," *The New York Times Magazine*, January 20, 1974.

LOPATA, HELENA Z., "Role Changes in Widowhood: A World Perspective," in *Aging and Modernization*, ed. Donald O. Cowgill, L. D. Holmes, and D. Lowell, pp. 299–308. New York: Meredith, 1972.

MCKAIN, WALTER C., "A New Look at Older Marriages," *Family Coordinator*, 21 (January 1972), 61–69.

MCKAIN, WALTER C., *Retirement Marriage*. Storrs: University of Connecticut, 1969.

MARIAS, JULIAN, *Generations: A Historical Method*, trans. Harold C. Raley. University of Alabama Press, 1970.

MASTERS, WILLIAM H., and VIRGINIA E. JOHNSON, *Human Sexual Inadequacy*. Boston: Little, Brown, 1970.

MATTHEWS, SARAH, and JETSE SPREY, "Adolescents' Relationships with Grandparents: An Empirical Contribution to Conceptual Clarifications," *Journal of Gerontology*, 40, no. 5 (1985), 621–26.

MEDLEY, MORRIS, "Life Satisfaction across Four Stages of Adult Life," *International Journal of Aging and Human Development*, 11 (1980), 193–209.

MEDLEY, MORRIS, "Marital Adjustment in the Post Retirement Years," *Family Coordinator*, January 1976, pp. 5–11.

METROPOLITAN LIFE INSURANCE COMPANY, "Widows and Widowhood," *Statistical Bulletin*, 47 (May 1966), 3–6.

MUTRAN, ELIZABETH, "Intergenerational Family Support among Blacks and Whites: Response to Culture or to Socioeconomic Differences," *Journal of Gerontology*, 40, no. 3 (1985), 382–89.

NEUGARTEN, BERNICE L., and KAROL K. WEINSTEIN, "The Changing American Grandparents," *Journal of Marriage and the Family*, 26 (May 1964), 199–204.

NIMKOFF, M. F., "Changing Family Relationships of Older People in the United States during the Last Fifty Years," *Gerontologist*, 1 (1961), 96.

NYE, F. IVAN, and FELIX M. BERARDO, *The Family: Its Structure and Interaction*. New York: Macmillan, 1973.

PFEIFFER, ERIC, "Sexuality in the Aging Individual," in *Sexuality and Aging*, ed. Robert L. Solnick, pp. 26–32. Los Angeles: University of Southern California Press, 1978.

PINEO, PETER C., "Disenchantment in the Later Years of Marriage," *Marriage and Family Living*, 23 (1961), 9–10.

REMPEL, JUDITH, "Childless Elderly: What Are They Missing?" *Journal of Marriage and the Family* (May 1985), 343–48.

ROLLINS, B. C., and K. L. CANNON, "Marital Satisfaction over the Family Life Cycle: A Reevaluation," *Journal of Marriage and the Family*, 36 (1974), 271–83.

ROLLINS, B. C., and H. FELDMAN, "Marital Satisfaction over the Family Life Cycle," *Journal of Marriage and the Family*, February (1970), pp. 20–28.

ROSE, ARNOLD M., and WARREN A. PETERSON, *Older People and Their Social World*. Philadelphia: David, 1965.

SHANAS, ETHEL, "Older People and Their Families: The New Pioneers," *Journal of Marriage and the Family*, 42, no. 1 (February 1980, 9–15.

SHANAS, ETHEL, and GORDON STREIB, *Social Structure and the Family: Generational Relations*. Englewood Cliffs, N.J.: Prentice Hall, 1965.

SOLDO, BETH J., and EMILY M. AGREE, *Population Bulletin*, 43, no. 3 (September 1988).

STREIB GORDON F., "Intergenerational Relations: Perspectives of the Two Generations of the Older Person," *Journal of Marriage and the Family*, 27 (November 1965), 469–74.

SUSSMAN, MARVIN B., and LEE BURCHINAL, "Kin Family Network: Unheralded Structure in Current Conceptualizations of Family Functioning," in *Middle Age and Aging*, ed. Bernice Neugarten, pp. 247–54. Chicago: University of Chicago Press, 1968.

SUSSMAN, MARVIN B., and MORRIS W. STROUD, "Studies in Chronic Illness and the Family." Unpublished paper, Western Reserve University and Highland View Hospital, 1959–64.

SVILAND, MARY ANN P., "A Program of Sexual Liberation and Growth in the Elderly," in *Sexuality and Aging*, ed. Robert L. Solnick, pp. 96–114. Los Angeles: University of Southern California Press, 1978.

THOMAS, L. EUGENE, ROBERT C. DIGUILO, and NANCY W. SHEEHAN, "Identity Loss and Psychological Crisis in Widowhood: A Reevaluation,' *International Journal of Aging and Human Development*, 26(3), 1988, 225–39.

THOMPSON, WAYNE, E., and GORDON F. STREIB, "Meaningful Activity in a Family Context," in *Aging and Leisure: A Research Perspective into the Meaningful Use of Leisure Time*, ed. Robert W. Kleemeier, pp. 177–211. New York: Oxford University Press, 1967.

TIBBITTS, CLARK, "Origins, Scope and Fields of Social Gerontology," in *Handbook of Social Gerontology*, ed. C. Tibbitts, pp. 3–26. Chicago: University of Chicago Press, 1960.

TOWNSEND, PETER, "The Emergence of the Four-Generation Family in Industrial Society," *Proceedings of the 7th International Congress of Gerontology, Vienna*, 8 (1966), 555–58.

TRAUPMAN, JANE, and ELAINE HATFIELD, "How Important Is Marital Fairness over the Lifespan," *International Journal of Aging and Human Development*, 17, no. 2 (1983), 89–101.

TROLL, LILLIAN E., SHEILA J. MILLER, and ROBERT C. ATCHLEY, *Families in Later Life*. Belmont, Calif.: Wadsworth, 1979.

UPDEGRAFF, SUE G., "Changing Role of the Grandmother," *Journal of Home Economics*, March 1968, pp. 177–86.

WEINSTEIN, STELLYE, and EFREN ROSEN, "Senior Adult Sexuality in Age Integrated Communities," *International Journal of Aging and Human Development*, 27(4), 1988.

NOTES

1. Paul H. Glasser and Lois N. Glasser, "Role Reversal and Conflict Between Aged Parents and Their Children," *Marriage and Family Living*, 24 (1962), 46–51.

2. Bert N. Adams, *The Family: A Sociological Interpretation* (Skokie, Ill: Rand McNally, 1975), p. 301.

3. Peter C. Pineo, "Disenchantment in the Later Years of Marriage," *Marriage and Family Living*, 23 (1961), 9–10.

4. William Masters and Virginia E. Johnson, *Human Sexual Inadequacy* (Boston: Little, Brown, 1970), p. 264.

5. Ibid., p. 247.

6. Ibid., p. 269.

7. Ibid., p. 264.

8. Mary Ann Sviland, "A Program of Sexual Liberation and Growth in the Elderly," in *Sexuality and Aging*, ed. Robert L. Solnick (Los Angeles: University of Southern California Press, 1978), pp. 111–12.

9. Aaron Lipman, "Role Conceptions of Couples in Retirement," in *Social and Psychological Aspects of Aging*, ed. Clark Tibbitts and Wilma Donahue (New York: Columbia University Press, 1962), pp. 475–85.

10. Marvin R. Koller, *Families: A Multigenerational Approach* (New York: McGraw-Hill, 1974), p. 5.

11. Eugene Litwak, "The Use of Extended Family Groups in the Achievement of Social Goals: Some Policy Implications," *Social Problems*, 6 (Winter 1959–60), 177–87.

12. Lillian E. Troll, Sheila J. Miller, and Robert C. Atchley, *Families in Later Life* (Belmont, Calif.: Wadsworth, 1979), p. 104.

13. Ethel Shanas and Gordon Streib, *Social Structure and the Family: Generational Relations* (Englewood Cliffs, N.J.: Prentice-Hall, 1965), p. 80.

14. Marvin B. Sussman and Morris W. Stroud, "Studies in Chronic Illness and the Family" (unpublished paper, Western Reserve University and Highland View Hospital, 1959–64), pp. 1–25.

15. E. Brody, "The Aging of the Family," *Annals of the American Academy of Political and Social Science*, 438 (July 1978), 13–27.

16. Peter Townsend, "The Emergence of the Four-Generation Family in Industrial Society," *Proceedings of the 7th International Congress of Gerontology, Vienna*, 8 (1966), 555–58.

17. F. Ivan Nye and Felix Berardo, *The Family: Its Structure and Interaction* (New York: Macmillan, 1973), pp. 533–63.

18. Jessie Bernard, *Remarriage* (New York: Dryden, 1956), p. 345.

19. Walter C. McKain, *Retirement Marriage* (Storrs: University of Connecticut, 1969), pp. 132–34.

20. Ibid.

9

Work, Leisure, and Retirement Patterns

INTRODUCTION

Work, free time, and leisure are differentially distributed to individuals over the life cycle. During the formative stages of life—childhood, adolescence, and early adulthood—ample free time and leisure are available to the individual. Furthermore, during these stages free time and leisure carry none of the negative connotations of frivolity, idleness, or sinfulness that they often do during the adult years. Children and young adults are presumed to need considerable free time to grow, develop, and mature.

During the adult years (early 20s to 65), however, American values dictate that commitment to work is to be the central interest of the individual; too much indulgence in free time and leisure pursuits is considered an indication of laziness and self-indulgence. One's identity, self-respect, and status are generally tied to involvement and success in the career world.

Upon retirement the amount of free time and leisure expands dramatically, but this is often difficult for the individual to accept. The difficulty of this adjustment is related in part to habit and inertia and in part to the long years of commitment to the work world and its values. The lifestyle one develops during a work history of 40 to 50 years, in which one's life is entirely structured around the nine-to-five workday and much of one's remaining social life is directly or indirectly connected with colleagues and work-related acquaintances, is not easily altered upon retirement. Similarly, the commitment to productivity, goal attainment, upward mobility, and other basic work-related values is not easily forgotten upon retirement. Thus, it is easy to understand the difficulty older Americans face in embracing free time and leisure during retirement. Dolores Melching and Merle Broberg (1974) have gone so far as to suggest a national sabbatical system that would give the individual one year off for every seven years of employment as a means of preparing the individual for retirement.

The adjustment problem Americans are often confronted with as they pass through different phases of the life cycle is that the transition from one phase to another is often not gradual and smooth but rather abrupt and disjointed. This problem is evident in the case of retirement.

The term *role continuity* has been used by sociologists for a process whereby people's activities and roles at one stage of life are adequate preparation for what will be expected of them at the next stage. What we often find in American society is a pattern of *role discontinuity* rather than continuity. Thus it is not clear that the large block of free time and leisure granted to youth is in any way an adequate preparation for the family responsibilities and work demands of early adulthood. Similarly, the work demands and numerous incentives for the individual to be productive during adult life seem not to be an adequate preparation for the free time and leisure activities of the retirement years. Thus, passing from one phase of the life cycle to the next in American society is often a somewhat difficult transition.

In this chapter we will discuss the meaning, relevance, and effect of changing opportunities and demands for work, free time, and leisure that the individual is confronted with during the adult and later phases of the life cycle.

WORK

The meanings of such diverse activities as work, leisure, and retirement to a member of a social system are often quite complex. Paradoxically the relevance of work and leisure activities for an individual is often intertwined in his or her thinking. Consequently, the concept of work or occupation has been difficult for sociologists to precisely define.

Robert Dubin (1956), for example, defined work as continuous employment in the production of goods and services for remuneration.[1] This definition ignores the fact that there are necessary tasks in society carried out by persons who receive no immediate pay. Mothers, fathers, housewives, and students do not receive pay for their valued activities.

Everett Hughes (1958) sees the meaning of an occupation in broad terms:

> An occupation, in essence, is not some particular set of activities; it is the part an individual plays in an ongoing set of activities.[2]

This definition is concerned less with the economic or remunerative aspects of work and more with its social and relational aspects.

Richard Hall (1975) attempts to incorporate both the economic and social aspects of work in his definition:

> An occupation is the social role performed by adult members of society that directly and/or indirectly yields social and financial consequences and that constitutes a major focus in the life of an adult.[3]

Similarly Clifton Bryant (1972) tries to include both the economic and social aspects of work life in his definition of labor: "Labor is any socially integrating activity which is connected with human subsistence."[4] By *integrating activity* Bryant means sanctioned activity that presupposes, creates, and recreates social relationships. The last two definitions seem to take a broader and more complete view of work in the individual's total life. Moreover, they could include the work done by mothers, fathers, housewives, and students.

One of the limitations of many of these definitions, Hall (1975) observes, is that they ignore the school and occupational experiences prior to full employment that are essential preparations for any occupational roles that one may assume. Delbert Miller and William Form (1969) have delineated four parts of work life: initial, trial, stable, and retirement periods.[5] The initial phase includes part-time jobs a person may have during adolescence. While these jobs may be important in developing work habits and attitudes, they are not truly occupations since they are recognized as temporary. At the other end of the life cycle, during the retirement period, the individual is not involved in an occupation, but his or her personality and behavior patterns have been strongly imprinted by the occupational identity acquired over a long career. Viewing the individual's work life as progressing through these stages has the effect of minimizing the financial reward and maximizing the social and psychological meaning attached to work by the individual and those who constitute his or her social world.

The advantage of definitions that attach strong importance to the meaning and social aspects of an occupational role is that they recognize the importance of work roles for which there is no, or very little, economic reward. The homemaker, while not receiving pay, may contribute considerably to a spouse's career and success. The college student in the period of anticipatory socialization and preparation for an occupational role may not be receiving any economic benefits. The retired salesclerk living on a social security check is receiving no money as an immediate result of involvement in an occupation.

The most appropriate definitions of work, therefore, seem to be those that emphasize the social and role aspects of an occupation, which an individual reacts to and is shaped by, whether or not he or she is financially rewarded for assuming these roles. From the perspective of the symbolic interactionists, one's work life and the roles one assumes during the workday will, in time, shape one's self-concept, identity, and feelings about oneself, and therefore strongly affect one's personality and behavior. Moreover, from this perspective, the individual's choice of occupations is probably strongly affected by the desire to establish, maintain, and display a desired identity.

Of critical concern to gerontologists is the link between work and retirement. If the individual uses his or her occupation to establish, maintain, and display a desired identity during the working years, how can this identity be supported during retirement? This question will be addressed later in this chapter when the concept of leisure is discussed.

Historical Perspectives on the Meaning of Work

One of the distinguishing features of contemporary urban society is the expectation that one should derive meaning from one's work. Historically, though, work has often been thought of as the province of slaves or the deprived classes; the elite supposedly had more important things to do with their time.

The single best analysis of the meaning of work in different historical periods is that of Adriano Tilgher (1930).[6] In the Greek era a clear distinction was made between manual and intellectual labor, the former being looked upon as a curse and nothing else. Generally, Greeks grudgingly accepted agriculture as not unworthy of a citizen because it brings a livelihood and independence. Greek landowners, however, delegated all manual work to slaves. Gentlemen were expected to develop the arts. Because of these attitudes toward work, the Greeks made significant contributions to art and literature but very few technological discoveries. Greeks felt that the mechanical arts were brutalizing to the mind and that their pursuit would make one unfit for thinking and truth. Free artisans were scorned as hardly better than slaves.

The Roman view was very similar to that of the Greeks. Cicero accepted agriculture and business as honorable if they were to lead to early retirement and the life of a country gentleman. The Romans also delegated most physical labor to slaves.

Current beliefs about the relevance of work seem to have emerged from the early Hebrew-Christian traditions. The early Hebrew tribes believed that people worked because they were obligated to expiate the original sin committed by their ancestors. If humans did not find their food like animals and birds, but had to earn it, this was because of their sinful nature. Early Christian belief followed this tradition, regarding work as punishment placed on humans by God because of original sin. It was the duty of every Christian to give work to the unemployed. Idleness was akin to original sin. Thus, work was never exalted as anything of value in itself, but only as an instrument of purification. Note that this concept of work was distinctly negative, emphasizing its penal nature.

The first hint of any positive meaning attached to work emerged from the early Christian belief that the fruits of one's labor could legitimately be shared with the less fortunate. With this view, work could be seen to serve useful social and humanistic functions. The result was that work very gradually began to assume positive connotations. This view of work was apparently maintained through the Middle Ages. Work was appropriate for all people and not just as a means of spiritual purification. Consistent with this view, early Catholic leaders insisted that every member of the clergy earn his living by the work of his own hands. The effect of the Church requiring the clergy to work was to raise the value of labor in people's minds. If the priests—the religious leaders of the community—worked, then work was not the providence merely of the less fortunate.

St. Thomas Aquinas drew a hierarchy of professions and trades according to their value to society. Agriculture was first, handicrafts second, and commerce last. He considered moneylenders and usurers outcasts, since interest is not earned by work, and since the only righteous sources of property and profit are work and inheritance.

Martin Luther added further dimensions to Christian beliefs about work. To the premise that work is the redeemer of fallen humanity he added the idea that work has both penal and educational characteristics, and that everyone should work. Work, he thought, is the universal base of society, the real cause of differentiation of social classes. Luther was unsympathetic toward commerce and asserted that the purpose of work should be maintenance and not profit. He discouraged any idea of upward mobility, arguing that to seek by means of work to pass from one class to another went against God's laws. Thus, according to Luther, God assigns to everyone his or her place, and one best serves God who stays in one's place.

Luther may be credited, then, with attaching positive value to all forms of work, since he believed that work is a form of serving God and there is just one best way to serve God: to do most perfectly the work of one's occupation. Thus Luther swept away all distinctions regarding the superiority of one kind of work to another. Every variety of work has equal spiritual dignity. All occupations are useful in the common life of humankind.

The contributions of John Calvin and other early Protestant thinkers to the subject of work, as Max Weber (1935) so ably pointed out, were to lead to the justification of commerce and banking and lay the groundwork of modern capitalism.[7] Calvin believed that at birth everyone was predestined to go to heaven or hell. People could determine which they were destined for by observing whether or not God favored them while they were living. Thus, Calvin followed the earlier Christian concept that work is the will of God, but added that profits and the accumulation of wealth are an indication of God's favor. The results of work (profit) should be used to finance ventures that bring greater profits, and thus further indications of God's pleasure. This represents a dramatic shift in earlier religious values regarding work, since people now had an obligation to God to attempt to achieve the highest and most lucrative occupation. Thus, striving for upward mobility is morally justified, if not mandated. Luther's concept that upward mobility is bad and that all callings are equal in the sight of God was swept away.

Tilgher (1930) and others have observed that the "religion of work," so fundamental in modern industrial society, is beginning to falter in the twentieth century as a new orientation toward recreation and leisure develops. The evidence to date, though, does not support this position. Morse and Weiss (1955), in a study of American workers, found that the vast majority would continue working even if they were given the opportunity to maintain their lifestyle without working.[8] Weber's (1935) observations of the positive consequences of the "Protestant ethic" on the attitudes and behavior of the workers in Western industrial nations apparently still carry considerable relevance.[9]

Some would argue that the cohorts currently entering the work force, being socialized in a different historical period, may be less committed to the work ethic than their parents and grandparents. This does not seem likely. The young people just entering the economic marketplace may indeed hold different attitudes than their parents toward work, but these attitudes will probably change as the young workers are socialized into an occupation and the work world. Nancy Vanlue (1974) asked a sample of social workers whether they derived more pleasure from their work life or their nonwork life.[10] She found that most respondents under age 40 considered their nonwork life more pleasurable. From age 40 on, however, respondents rather consistently indicated that their greatest satisfaction came from their work life. One wonders, then, if the purported discrepancy between younger and older workers' commitment to work is more a function of age and location in the life cycle than fundamental change in attitudes toward work held by the generation currently entering the labor market. Deriving greater satisfaction from work after age 40 might be a result of the fact that workers after this age are likely to be assuming the most powerful and prestigious positions in their organizations. Further, the high status accruing to the individuals who occupy these valued positions contributes to a positive self-concept and much more positive attitudes toward work and work-related roles. Martin Hanlon's (1986) study of age and commitment to work tends to support this contention. He found that age had little independent effect on work commitment. The greater the job satisfaction and the higher the prestige of the job, the more committed the individual was to his or her work. If this is indeed the case, it might contribute to our understanding of why some older workers are reluctant to retire.

Individual Motivation to Work

The subject of what has motivated people to work has often been investigated, but relatively few conclusions have been reached. The source of the difficulty seems to be the broad and diverse range of satisfactions that individuals can derive from their work lives.

The increasing complexity of modern society has led to the belief that many people work merely to earn a living. Indeed, Dubin's (1956) study of the "central life interests" of industrial workers concludes that work and the work place are generally not important concerns for this group. Louis Orzack (1959), in a study of professional nurses, found that 79 percent listed work as their central life interest, compared with only 24 percent of the industrial workers Dubin (1956) studied. This seems consistent with the oft-repeated phrase that white-collar workers live to work and blue-collar workers work to live.

There is a danger, however, in concluding that work is only a means to an end for most American workers. Studies have indicated otherwise. Morse and Weiss (1955), for instance, found in their national sample of employed men that work gives a feeling of being tied into the larger society, of having something to do, of having a purpose in life—functions that would not likely be found in nonwork situations. The conclusions drawn from this study seemed to be (1) that working is more than a means to an end; (2) that a man does not have to be at the age of retirement to be threatened by unemployment; and (3) that working serves functions other than an economic one for both middle- and working-class workers.

Morse and Weiss (1955) asked industrial workers why they would continue to work even if they had enough money to live without working. The workers listed the following positive reasons: (1) They enjoyed their work; (2) they wanted to be associated with people; (3) they wanted to keep occupied; (4) their work justified their existence; (5) their work gave them a feeling of self-respect; and (6) their work kept them healthy and was therefore good for them. A number of negative responses, however, resulted from the same question: (1) They would feel lost or go crazy; (2) they would feel useless; (3) they would feel bored; (4) they would not know what to do with their time; (5) they would work out of habit; and (6) they would work in order to keep out of trouble.

Morse and Weiss (1955) believe that not working requires considerable readjustment. Employed people do not often have alternative ways of directing their energy or of gaining a sense of identity and relationship to their society that are sufficiendy important to take the place of work.

Victor Vroom (1964) has attempted to delineate the components of work motivation.[11] The first component is wages and all the economic rewards associated with the fringe benefits of the job. People desire these rewards, which therefore serve as a strong incentive to work. Howard M. Iams (1985), in a study of the postretirement work patterns of women, found that unmarried women were very likely to work at least part-time after retirement if their monthly income was below $500. The economic inducement to work is apparently a strong one even for retired persons.

A second inducement to work is the expenditure of physical and mental energy. People seem to need to expend energy in some meaningful way, and work provides this opportunity. Vroom notes that animals will often engage in activity as a consequence of activity deprivation.

A third motivation, according to Vroom (1964), is the production of goods and services. This inducement is directly related to the intrinsic satisfaction the individual derives from successful manipulation of the environment.

A fourth motivation is social interaction. Most work roles involve interaction with customers, clients, or members of identifiable work groups as part of the expected behavior of their occupants.

The final motivation Vroom mentions is social status. An individual's occupation is perhaps the best single determinant of his or her status in the community.

These various motivations for work undoubtedly assume different configurations for different people and occupational groups. Social interaction may be most important for some while economic considerations may be most important for others. For still others the intrinsic satisfaction derived from the production of goods and services may be all-important. Thus the research by industrial sociologists has not yet produced a single adequate explanation of worker motivation.

The critical question for gerontologists is whether the same psychological and social factors that thrust people into work patterns for the major part of their adult life can channel them into leisure activities during their retirement years. Can people find the same satisfaction, feeling of worth, and identity in leisure activities that they did in work-related activities? Gordon Streib and Clement Schneider (1971) think they can. They argue that the husband, wife, grandmother, and grandfather roles may expand and become more salient in the retirement years. Simultaneously, public service and community roles become possible because of the flexibility of the retiree's time. Changing activities and roles, in their opinion, need not lead to a loss of self-respect or active involvement in the mainstream of American life.

FREE TIME

If we think of nonwork time as free time or leisure, it is apparent that the technological revolution in industry that has occurred during the last 150 years is making possible an ever-increasing amount of free time. Kaplan (1979) estimates that free time increased from about 2.18 hours per day in 1850 to about 7.48 hours per day in 1960. Similarly the amount of vacation time has been constantly increasing. In 1970, 40 percent of men and women in the labor force had accumulated vacation time of four weeks or more. Juanita Kreps (1963) estimates that men born in 1960 will have nine more years of nonworking time than men born in 1900.

Harold Wilensky (1963) observes, however, that most of the gains in free time have occurred in the manufacturing and mining industries and, since the 1940s, in agriculture. Professionals, executives, officials, civil servants, and self-employed persons have apparently not gained much leisure time. The increases are therefore not universal, but selective. Don Mankin (1978) believes, though, that eventually they will extend to all occupations. As hours of work decrease, vacation periods become longer, and retirement is allowed at younger ages, the free time available to the individual steadily grows, according to Mankin.

Sebastian DeGrazia (1962) points out, however, that more time away from the job does not necessarily imply more free time or leisure. DeGrazia maintains that the amount of free time and leisure available to Americans has not increased appreciably since 1850. His argument is that American society, and indeed each community, weaves its work and nonwork time together. Nonwork time is usually quickly absorbed by family, social, and community obligations, so that the individual actually gains nothing in free time. Our free time, according to DeGrazia,

is greater when compared with the days of Manchesterism or of the sweatshops of New York. Put alongside modern rural Greece or ancient Greece, though, or Medieval Europe and Ancient Rome, free time today suffers by comparison, and leisure even more.[12]

LEISURE

While never totally resolving the problem of what the distinction is between work and leisure, a number of social thinkers have attempted to clearly define the dimensions of each. The layman has the general view that work is something we do for pay and leisure is time spent away from work. While considerably more sophisticated, Ronald Pavalko's (1971) definition follows similar lines:

Clearly work and leisure are interrelated. While no universally agreed-upon definition of leisure exists, the most satisfactory way of thinking about leisure is as "free time." In this sense leisure is the reciprocal of work.[13]

Haworth and Smith (1975) assert that this distinction is not entirely accurate; they believe that one can have free time but not necessarily have leisure. DeGrazia (1962) follows this line of reasoning when he states,

Work is the antonym of free time but not of leisure. Leisure and free time live in two different worlds . . . anybody can have free time. Free time is a realizable idea of a democracy. Leisure is not fully realizable, and hence an ideal not alone an idea. Free time refers to a special way of calculating a special kind of time. Leisure refers to a state of being, a condition of man, which few desire and fewer achieve.[14]

Stanley Parker (1971) has rejected the notion of free versus nonfree time and attempted to position various aspects of both work and nonwork activity on a continuum (see Table 9–1). Parker defines work as the activity involved in earning a living, plus necessary subsidiary activities such as traveling to and from work. Work obligations involve doing things outside of normal working hours, such as voluntary overtime, grading papers, and working on one's expense ac-

TABLE 9–1   A Continuum of Work and Nonwork Activity

WORK TIME		NONWORK TIME		
Work	Work Obligations	Physiological Needs	Nonwork Obligations	Leisure

Source: Stanley Parker, *The Future of Work and Leisure* (St. Albans, England: Granada Publishing, 1971).

TABLE 9–2 Work and Leisure in Relation to Time and Activity

		ACTIVITY	
		CONSTRAINT -- FREEDOM	
Work Time	Work Employment	Work Obligations (connected with employment)	Leisure in Work
Non-work time	Physiological Needs	Nonwork Obligations	Leisure

Source: Stanley Parker, *The Future of Work and Leisure* (St. Albans, England: Granada Publishing, 1971).

count. Parker follows the traditional definitions of physiological needs: sleeping, eating, and related activities. Nonwork obligations might include parental responsibilities, redecorating the house, and other routine responsibilities almost everyone is forced to meet. These are what some authors define as *semileisure*. Leisure in Parker's (1971) scheme is time free from obligations either to self or to others—time in which to do as one chooses.

Parker attempts to refute the tendency to refer to work in terms of time and to leisure in terms of activity. He argues that both time and activity are dimensions of work and of leisure. Table 9–2 indicates that there is no reason to conceive of either work or leisure as being unidimensional, as has often been done. Leisure does take up time, and we do engage in activity in work.

John Kelly (1972) conceptualizes leisure along two dimensions: (1) the amount of choice the individual has in undertaking the activity and (2) the relation of the activity to work. Unconditional leisure, as Table 9–3 indicates, is chosen freely and is unrelated to one's work. Examples might be hunting, fishing, or traveling, if they were totally unrelated to one's work. Coordinated leisure is freely chosen but related to one's occupation in some way. The machinist working in a home workshop or the professor reading a work-related journal would be examples. Complementary leisure reflects the role expectations associated with one's occupation. Voluntary organizations, such as unions and professional associations, in which persons in given occupations are expected to participate, would be an example. Preparation and recuperation are activities related to the occupation and not freely chosen. The person who is too exhausted from work to do anything

TABLE 9–3 Time Dimensions of Leisure

		DISCRETION	
		Chosen	Determined
Work Relation	Independent	1. Unconditional Leisure	3. Complementary Leisure
	Dependent	2. Coordinated Leisure	4. Preparation and Recuperation

Source: John Kelly, "Work and Leisure: A Simplified Paradigm," *Journal of Leisure Research*, 4, no. 1 (1972), 50–62.

except watch TV, or the teacher who is preparing for tomorrow's class, would be an example.

Robert Atchley (1976) defines leisure as activities pursued as ends in themselves; they are unplanned and unrequired. Leisure in his view is action directed primarily toward self-satisfaction.

One problem confronted by Americans as they face the reality of increasing free time, and hence the potential for leisure, is an appropriate belief system and value structure with which to incorporate free time. As we have observed, Luther, Calvin, and other religious leaders of the Protestant Reformation extolled hard work, self-denial, and thrift as the means of salvation. Thus, work had spiritual value while leisure became identified with idleness, frivolity, sinfulness, and unproductive activities. Consequently, increased leisure often represents a crisis of values for many Americans. Bennett Berger (1963), moreover, has pointed out that the use of leisure by youth and the unemployed is often a concern of public officials, social workers, and the clergy, who are convinced that leisure activities ought to be wholesome and morally acceptable.

A related concern is the overemphasis on passive leisure activities of many persons who do not appear to desire challenge in their leisure activities. Don Mankin (1978) is concerned that as leisure time increases, our society will develop more expensive versions of amusement parks, nightclubs, recreational vehicles, adult games, and travel clubs. He believes that these activities emphasize passive consumption by a consumer-oriented public and are not conducive to the individual's growth and development.

Pavalko (1971) points out patterns of leisure activities by different occupational groups. These patterns were delineated by Alfred Clark (1956) in his study of 574 men in Columbus, Ohio. Respondents at the highest occupational prestige level were most likely to attend plays, concerts, lectures, conventions, and meetings of fraternal organizations; play bridge; visit art galleries; study; and entertain at home. The second group of respondents, in terms of occupational status, mentioned such things as out-of-town weekend visiting, football games, and parties. Level 3 respondents mentioned golf more often, and men at level 4 were more likely to mention working on automobiles. Respondents at the lowest prestige level were most likely to mention fishing, hunting, raising a garden, playing poker, spending time in a tavern, and pleasure driving.

Although no single pattern is apparent in these diverse activities, a more careful examination might reveal some trends. If we were to analyze the leisure pursuits of the different occupational groups in terms of whether the activity is physical or intellectual, it would seem that the upper-status groups, whose jobs tax primarily their mental capacities (often involving the manipulation of symbols or ideas), pursue primarily intellectual activities. Respondents at the two lowest levels were most likely to engage in physical activities. Since the work activities of these latter respondents are also for the most part physical, there seems to be some continuity between their work and nonwork lives. Thus, workers employing mental skills on the job pursue intellectual activities in their leisure, and workers with physical jobs pursue physical activities in their spare time.

Both Wilensky (1964)[15] and Dumazediers (1967; 1972)[16] suggest that future researchers think of leisure in three ways: (1) as an extension of work and a continuation of one's development, (2) as neutral and entertainment, and (3) as opposition and recuperation. What needs to be added to this typology is a fourth category—leisure that is independent of work life and strongly related to the individual's identity and self-concept. From a symbolic interaction perspective, leisure, in the true sense of the word, will be meaningful as a phenomenon different from work only when people attach their identities, their opinions of themselves, to some of the activities they pursue in their leisure time. Thus some of their collective self-concepts would be determined by the roles they assume in leisure activities and some by roles they assume in work activities. Only in this way can leisure be truly meaningful to the individual, and only in this way can a self-concept begin to emerge that is not totally dependent on work and career. This would involve changing attitudes and values regarding work and leisure, and the legitimization of leisure activities. Postindustrial society would seem to demand these changes.

Symbolic interactionists would argue that a person's choice of leisure activities is fundamentally related to his or her concept of self. Glasser (1967), in a study of shopping habits and human motivation, concluded that the purpose of a shopping expedition was to reaffirm the person's perception of his or her identity and to compare this with an ideal identity. Making purchases was a secondary goal. Numerous studies have concluded that the overwhelming compulsion governing all of an individual's actions and attitudes is the pursuit of a desired identity. This desired identity is a composite of ideas that one holds about behavior, ethical standards, physical appearance, and lifestyle. As Haworth and Smith (1975) comment,

> each person is engaged, unconsciously, in a continued quest, firstly to perceive clearly what this desirable identity is, secondly to achieve it within himself, and thirdly, to display it.[17]

Undoubtedly the leisure activities one pursues are related to this ideal self, consciously or unconsciously, and are a reflection of the identity the individual would most like to establish.

RETIREMENT

Demographic and economic trends in American society have resulted in an ever-increasing number of retired Americans. Streib and Schneider (1971) observed that for retirement to become an institutionalized social pattern in any society, certain conditions must be met. There must be a large group of people who live long enough to retire, the economy must be sufficiently productive to support segments of the population that are not included in the work force, and there must be some well-established forms of pension or insurance programs to support people during their retirement years.

The rapid growth in both the number and percentage of the American population 65 and above since 1900 was observed in Chapter 1. Currently, approximately 25 million Americans are in this age category. While the number and proportion of the population over 65 have been increasing steadily, the proportion of those who remain in the work force has decreased steadily. In 1900 nearly two thirds of those over 65 worked. Frank Sammartino (1979) reports that by 1947 this figure had declined to 47.8 percent. By 1987 only 16.5 percent of those 65 and older were still in the work force. There appears to be a somewhat greater convergence in the work and retirement patterns of men and women when comparing 1900 with 1970. The earlier pattern of work histories seemed to be for men to enter the work force earlier and retire later; women tended to enter later and retire earlier. Douglas Kimmel (1974) concludes that the current trends indicate that women are entering the work force earlier and working longer. Men, on the other hand, enter the work force later and retire earlier. Thus, the work histories of men and women are becoming very similar although the men, as a group, still have longer work histories than women. Not only are more women remaining in the labor force throughout their adult lives, but more women are entering the labor force. Carole Allen and Herman Brotman (1981) point out that in 1950 three out of ten U.S. workers were women; in 1980 four out of ten were. During this same period women in the workforce over 45 years of age grew from 25 to 40 percent.

The trend for both men and women for the past 30 years has been for larger numbers to choose to retire early. Allen and Brotman (1981) point out that in 1968, 48 percent of all new social security payment awards to men were to claimants under 65; by 1978 this figure had increased to 61 percent. In 1968, 65 percent of all new social security awards to women were to claimants under 65; in 1978, the figure was 72 percent. According to Allen and Brotman,

> the early retirement rate for male and female workers was 66 percent in 1978. The most recent figures available from the Social Security Administration indicate that since 1977, the number of people retiring early has declined slightly (to 64 percent in 1980). It is too early to tell whether or not this is a reversal of the early retirement trend.[18]

Simultaneously, fewer persons are choosing to remain in the labor force beyond the age of 65. Beth Soldo and Emily Agree (1988) report that 62 percent of the men and 72 percent of the women in 1986 who received social security benefits had retired prior to age 65 and therefore were receiving reduced benefits. The General Accounting Office reports that almost two thirds of those receiving private retirement benefits in 1985 stopped working prior to age 65. Of those who do remain in the labor force after age 65, Soldo and Agree (1988) report that 47 percent of the men and 59 percent of the women held part-time positions.

In an earlier chapter we observed the multiplicity of problems confronting the individual at retirement—the lowering of income; the loss of status, privilege, and power associated with one's position in the occupational hierarchy; a major reorganization of life activities, since the nine-to-five workday becomes meaningless; a changing definition of self, since most individuals over time shape their identity and personality in line with the demands of their major occupational roles; considerable social isolation if new activities are not found to replace work-related activities; and a search for a new identity, new meaning, and new values in one's life. Obviously, the major reorganization of one's life that must take place at retirement is a potential source of adjustment problems. Critical to the adjustment is the degree to which one's identity and personality structure were attached to the work role. For those individuals whose work identity is central to their self-concept and gives them the greatest satisfaction, retirement will represent somewhat of a crisis. For others, retirement should not represent much of a problem.

The Institutionalization of Retirement

People often hold paradoxical views on the meaning of retirement. On the one hand, they are likely to view retirement as a well-deserved right earned by long years of hard work. On the other hand, they tacitly feel they are being forced out of a chosen career and the opportunity for gainful employment.

The institutionalization of retirement seems a result in part of the declining crude birthrate. With fewer young dependents to support, one can support older dependents. Simultaneously, the rapid increase in mass production means that not as large a labor force is needed to produce the nation's goods and services; older workers are freed of the need to work until they die. Atchley (1976) asserts that the growth of the federal bureaucracy has further facilitated the retirement of older workers. A large government bureaucracy, in his opinion, has become the political counterpart of an economic corporation, facilitating the pooling of the nation's resources and thus allowing a segment of society to be supported in retirement.

Robert Kleemeier (1961) believes that six key factors explain the decline of the elderly in the labor force:

1. The tendency for certain types of expanding job openings to be filled by women rather than by elderly men, because of the better training of the women

2. The decline in self-employment, which has always been a leading type of gainful activity for elderly men

3. The rising general-income level, which has made it possible for an increasing proportion of older persons to live in retirement

4. The growth of old age assistance payments, old age insurance benefits, and private pension plans in the last 40 years

5. Increasing mechanization of agriculture and consolidation of farms (explaining the increase in retirement in rural areas)

6. The rise in the relative importance of large firms (There is clear evidence that both age discrimination in hiring and compulsory retirement policies are more likely to be found in these firms.)

Undoubtedly, all of these factors have resulted in the institutionalization of retirement in American society. Whether inflation and the strain on social security funds resulting from the increased number of persons arriving at retirement age will reverse the trend toward early retirement remains to be seen. Mark Hayward and Melissa Hardy (1985) have found that occupations characterized by complexity and high levels of social skill usually grant the employee tenure after a trial period. Tenure brings job stability and early pension eligibility. Persons in these occupations often choose to retire early. If the current trend toward early retirement continues, Americans will have to begin to alter some of their basic attitudes and values regarding the importance of work and leisure in their lives. Retirement would seem inevitably to involve some alterations in one's priorities regarding work and leisure. A successful adjustment to retirement seems to demand that the individual be able to establish and maintain a desired identity while pursuing leisure activities.

Social Factors in Adjustment

Retirement has often been viewed as a stressful event for the retirees. Raymond Bosse et al. (1991) point out that many believe that the stress of adjusting to the retirement role has lead to higher mortality and suicide rates for those over 65. Retirement is seen as particularly stressful for those forced to retire unexpectedly because of plant closings or poor health. Bosse et al. (1991) report that when retirees were asked what their most frequent problems were they were likely to state finances and boredom. Regardless of the stress of retirement—which is accompanied by changing roles and lifestyle for some—most older persons make a successful retirement adjustment and report that they enjoy the retirement years.

Among a variety of indicators of retirement adjustment, most studies have focused on two variables—the kind of work the individual was involved in, with its concomitant style of life, and the individual's preretirement attitude. Ida Simpson, Kurt Back, and John McKinney (1966) view the former variable as the critical one. They speak of the disjunctive effects of retirement, asserting that work is one of the most important avenues for integrating individuals into the social system because it gives them their identity, style of life, and social-participation patterns. Beginning with the assumption that work places the individual and his or her family in the social structure, they argue that retirement undercuts the individual's major social support by removing him or her from the work world in which these supports are rooted. They conclude it is not retirement per se that is responsible for lack of anchorage and adjustment in retirement, but rather individuals' work histories, which do not allow them to develop other social ties. Their findings indicate that orientation toward work is the main influence on preretirement attitudes and consequently postretirement adjustment among upper white-collar workers, that income deprivation in retirement is the main influence on retirement adjustment for semiskilled workers, and that none of the explanations accounted for much variability within the middle stratum.

Streib and Schneider (1971) focus on willingness or reluctance to retire as the critical factor in retirement adjustment. Their findings indicate that those who are favorably disposed toward retirement are much more likely to retire than those who are reluctant to do so, and the former are more likely to make a favorable retirement adjustment. This is true whether they chose to retire or were forced to retire.

Streib and Schneider, though they view retirement as a major role disjuncture due to the loss of the work role, are led to some conclusions differing from previous research on the effects of this loss. Viewing role sets and role change as a dynamic process, they found that the loss of the work role does not inevitably lead to either adjustment problems or disengagement. Many retirees, after losing their work role, expanded their activity in ongoing roles (that is, as husband, wife, grandmother, grandfather, friend, and so on) that had often remained latent and assumed new roles such as citizenship and service. Streib and Schneider's findings suggest that many retirees successfully cope with the role realignment precipitated by retirement.

Streib and Schneider suggest that an alternate approach, using the symbolic interaction perspective, would be to view the problems of retirement adjustment in terms of the reference groups that are significant for work and retirement, such as families, friends, and cliques at work. Following up on this suggestion,

Cox and Bhak (1978–79) studied the effect of reference groups on both preretirement attitudes and postretirement adjustment. Their work indicated that family, close friends, and work-group cliques were critical determinants of how the individual viewed retirement both prior to and after the event. They concluded that it was these critical reference groups that shaped individuals' preretirement attitudes and hence their postretirement adjustment.

Psychological Factors in Adjustment

Atchley (1976) perceives a number of phases the individual will go through in attempting to make an adequate retirement adjustment:

1. In the preretirement phase people are concerned about whether they will have an adequate income and about what leisure interests to pursue.
2. In the honeymoon phase people wallow in their newfound freedom.
3. In the disenchantment phase there is a letdown as the retiree adjusts to the slower pace of life.
4. In the reorientation phase the depressed person attempts to pull himself or herself together.

Ekerdt, Bosse, and Lenkoff's (1985) study did indicate that the first year of retirement was often one of enthusiasm and involvement in numerous physical activities. The second year of retirement often begins with a letdown followed by a period of reassessment of one's life and ultimately a return to higher levels of life satisfaction.

Reichard, Livson, and Peterson (1962) conducted a study of personality types associated with good and bad retirement adjustment. The personalities they identified as making good adjustments to retirement were the "mature," the "rocking-chair men," and the "activity-oriented." The mature were relatively free of neurotic conflict; they were able to accept themselves realistically and to find genuine satisfaction in activities and personal relationships. Feeling that their lives had been rewarding, they were able to grow old without regret. The rocking-chair men, because of their general passivity, welcomed the opportunity to be free of responsibility and to indulge in their passive needs in old age. The activity-oriented were unable to face passivity or helplessness in old age; they warded off their dread of physical decline by keeping active.

The poorly adjusted men consisted of the "angry men" and the "self-haters." The angry men were unable to reconcile themselves to growing old and became very bitter. The self-haters looked back on their lives with a sense of disappointment and failure, but unlike the angry men, they turned their resentment inward, blaming themselves for their misfortunes.

More recently Atchley (1976), in his book on the sociology of retirement, has argued that the individual's ability to adjust to retirement is directly related to which goals are most important in his or her life. Maintaining that everyone has goals, Atchley believes that achievement of these goals is the fundamental means by which one develops a strong sense of personal worth. The individual's goals might include such personal qualities as honesty, ambition, cheerfulness, and kindness. Material goals might include ownership of land, house, farm, and so on. Still other goals, according to Atchley, might involve successful role performance, such as being a good parent, lawyer, or artist. How the individual ranks his or her goals, Atchley (1976) feels, will directly affect the ease or difficulty with which he or she adjusts to retirement. Thus, people whose highest-priority goal is their career might find retirement more difficult than people who place a lower priority on their career. People who stress the importance of personal qualities might place their job far down the list, and thus retirement would not be much of a problem. Those with a strong emphasis on materialistic goals would find retirement difficult to adjust to in direct proportion to the degree that it interferes with the achievement of those goals. In any case, Atchley states,

> the crucial question . . . is whether retirement is a consequential change, a change that is important enough to necessitate a reorganization in the upper level of the individual's hierarchy of personal goals. If not, then retirement produces no actual change in the criteria the individual uses to select from among the behavioral alternatives available to him.[19]

Critical Aspects of Retirement

The disparate goals of different retirees and their relevance to retirement adjustment was noted in a study by Carol Cutler Riddick (1985). She found that leisure activity emerged as an important predictor of life satisfaction for homemakers and retirees, but not for those still working. The principal focus on many of the studies of retirement adjustment has been whether retirees can find meaningful activities in which they can maintain a positive self-concept. Kurt Back and Carleton Guptill (1966) find in their study of retirement that

> the overriding point of interest has been that retirement leads to a feeling of loss of involvement for males. . . . Without the job around which their lives had been built for some forty or fifty years, these retired men were unable to avoid feeling less useful, less effective and less busy than the men who were still employed. Different conditions of life in retirement did little to alter these feelings.[20]

Other than the void left by the loss of one's job and the loss of the value and meaning it had in one's feelings of usefulness and involvement, most of the consequences of retirement are positive. The data indicate that the negative orientation toward the self tends to decrease with age as the personality approaches closure.

Contrary to the popular belief that people get sick and die at retirement, the data indicate that the health of retired persons is as good as or better than it was when they were working, and that there is no significant difference in preretirement and postretirement mortality rates if age is controlled.

Fred Cottrell and Robert Atchley (1969) have found that retirement as such has little influence on such variables as depression, anxiety, anomie, or stability.[21] They argue that there is little or no evidence that retirement is in any way related to the common problems of older Americans. They believe that the most common problem of retirement is the limit it places on income.

One further effect of retirement is to reduce the set of individuals one interacts with. Family and close friends come to compose the social world of older Americans. Sheldon Stryker (1959) states that the concept of *significant others* represents the recognition that, in a fragmented and differentiated world, not all persons with whom one interacts have identical or even compatible perspectives and that, therefore, in order for action to proceed, the individual must give greater weight or priority to the perspectives of certain others. To speak then of significant others is to say that given others occupy a high rank in importance for a given individual.[22]

While not referring specifically to the concept of significant others, numerous studies have observed the importance of maintaining close friendships for the successful adjustment of older Americans. Erik Erikson (1959) postulates that the capacity for intimacy is one of the major developmental tasks of life. Zena Blau's (1961) study of the structural constraints of friendship among the aged documents the importance of the prevailing age–sex–marital status patterns in the establishment of friendships. Arth (1962), in his study of friendship in an aging population, is concerned with the importance of close friends in the social world of older Americans but does not define closeness. Irving Rosow's (1967) study of friendship patterns under varying age-density conditions credits the successful adjustment of older Americans to close friends.

Marjorie Lowenthal and Clayton Haven (1968) were the first to carefully consider the quality of the social relationships of older Americans. Using the concept of a *confidant*, they observed that the healthiest and happiest older Americans often seem to be those who are involved in one or more close personal friendships. They concluded that the maintenance of a stable intimate relationship is more closely associated with good mental health and high morale than are high social interaction, high role status, or stability of interaction and role. All of these studies suggest that significant others are of major importance to the successful adjustment of older Americans.

The composition of any individual's social world can be seen in terms of concentric spheres of social involvement, as illustrated in Figure 9–1. The first circle is the primary group of husband, wife, children, and a few very close friends. The second circle includes a wider range of associates, such as well-known friends in the individual's work, social-club, fraternal, and religious organizations. The third circle is a much larger group of casual acquaintances in the work and social worlds of the individual. These acquaintances are usually consid-

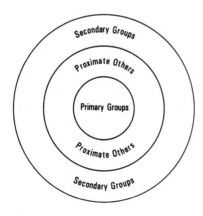

FIGURE 9–1
The Spheres of an Individual's Social Involvement

ered by sociologists to represent the individual's secondary-group associations.

It is the secondary associations that tend to be reduced after retirement. Therefore the importance of family and close friends (the two inner circles in the diagram) is magnified, and these people can appropriately be labeled the significant others of older Americans. These significant others will have the greatest impact on the individual's retirement adjustment.

Compulsory Retirement

Over the long course of civilization's development, work demands have been persistent for those who hoped to survive. Providing the necessary food and shelter in preindustrial society required the constant effort of as many hands as possible. Children started doing the simpler tasks early in their lives, and for the most part old people, while reducing their work loads gradually, still worked until the day they died. The level of productivity of most preindustrial societies was such that free time and leisure were scarce and work was most highly valued.

Industrialization initially brought little change in the demand for and value placed on labor. But it did begin to produce surpluses, and gradually physical survival was no longer problematic. The ever-increasing productivity of the industrializing nations ultimately led to the reduction both of work time in terms of hours per week and of work life in terms of years on the job. Early in the twentieth century child-labor laws were passed reducing considerably the involvement of children in factory and other work. These laws were seen as desirable by labor groups, who felt that their workers would be paid better if they did not have to compete with child labor. The 1930s brought social security and mandatory retirement as companies attempted to force older workers out in order to make room for younger employees. Although Congress passed a law in 1978 making mandatory retirement prior to age 70 illegal, most companies still do everything possible to encourage their employees to retire prior to age 65.

The United States, as well as other industrialized nations, now seems to be approaching a postindustrial period in which jobs have become scarce. In the past, women and blacks were frequently discriminated against in employment and found themselves being the last hired and the first fired during fluctuations of the business cycle. The civil rights and women's liberation movements have resulted in federal regulations that prevent blatant discrimination against these groups. Women in particular were often not regularly employed in the past but are demanding full employment today. There are those who believe that these changes in employment practices, coupled with modern technology and increasing productivity, have made our economic system incapable of providing enough jobs for all eligible citizens desiring work.

The result of these trends is increasing pressure to force the older worker to retire earlier to make room for younger workers and those members of minority groups demanding equal opportunity for employment. As we have observed, all the evidence indicates that as one grows older, jobs become increasingly hard to find and that the ones older workers are able to find often pay poorly. In periods of high unemployment the older worker who is not protected by considerable seniority is most likely to be unemployed. Similarly, older workers are the least likely to move with their company to a new location because of all the family and social ties they have built in their community.

Older workers' commitment to their work, while generally highly valued by the company, is also inflationary to some degree. From the perspective of management, older workers must be paid higher salaries, receive greater fringe benefits, and be granted greater vacation time. Thus older workers cost the company more. One can easily see why mandatory retirement policies are often considered to be good for business. From the individual's point of view, forced retirement is often negative: Income is reduced, the opportunity to work is removed, and there seems to be little or no cash value for a lifetime of commitment to the organization.

Alton Johnson and his associates (1979) have listed the arguments in favor of mandatory retirement:

1. Employment and promotion opportunities for younger workers are thereby created.
2. Older workers are less desirable than younger workers, since they generally have declining mental and physical capacities, are more difficult to retrain, are less educated, and are more inflexible with regard to work rules and scheduling.
3. All workers are treated alike and thus less productive older workers are not humiliated by being singled out for dismissal.
4. Social Security and pension benefits provide income opportunities for older workers that younger workers do not have.
5. An older work force is more costly for employers due to related fringe benefits such as health and insurance plans.
6. Mandatory retirement may be the only practical way of dismissing older workers who are insulated by existing seniority systems.
7. A mandatory age of retirement makes planning easier for both employers and employees.[23]

These researchers offer equally persuasive arguments against mandatory retirement:

1. Such policies discriminate against older workers.
2. Chronological age is a poor indicator of ability to perform work.
3. Mandatory retirement results in the loss of income, health, and identity of older workers.
4. Mandatory retirement reduces Social Security benefits for some workers who are at the highest earning years. This is especially true for late entrants in the labor force such as married women.
5. Older workers have skills and experience that younger workers do not; thus mandatory retirement reduces the total output of the economy.
6. Mandatory retirement increases the number of retirees, raising Social Security expenses and burdening the remaining members of the work force.[24]

Historically, most people have retired voluntarily because of poor health. However, the emergence of less physically demanding jobs and improved medical technology may result in other factors leading to the retirement decision. William Pollman (1971), in a study of Chrysler Corporation employees who had retired early, found that adequate retirement income was the most common reason given for retirement. Federal law now prohibits mandatory retirement policies by businesses, but many employers still put pressure on older employees to retire.

Preretirement programs undoubtedly would do much to ease the fears of many older workers and to facilitate a smooth transition to retirement. Unfortunately, most of the large companies that currently have preretirement programs offer their workers at most only discussions of what the workers can expect to make in retirement.

The business community and educational institutions have been willing to invest large amounts of money, time, and effort socializing the individual for a particular occupation or career. This socialization includes training in practical skills as well as in proper attitudes and values. During the later phase of the life cycle, however, there seems to be little interest in, or effort invested in, preparing the individual to withdraw from an occupation. In this respect business and education seem to be following a general societal pattern.

To remedy the inadequacies of current retirement counseling programs and in terms of retirement decisions and planning, the following suggestions would seem most desirable:

1. Adequate preretirement programs to prepare the worker for retirement should be provided by employers.
2. Pressure by employers to push older employees to retire early should be restricted.
3. Maximum freedom should be given individuals to choose and plan for the point at which they will retire.

CONCLUSION

Work, leisure, and retirement are different dimensions of human life. All three must be incorporated into the individual's style of life and defined in such a way as to give meaning to the individual's existence.

The "Protestant ethic," so aptly described by Weber, maintained that work was the redeemer of fallen humanity and leisure an indication of frivolity and sinful human nature. This belief has made it somewhat difficult for Americans to easily embrace leisure activities.

The industrial and technological revolutions, on the other hand, have resulted in a shorter workday and a shorter career for most Americans. The result is that a growing number of citizens have increasing free time in their daily lives and more years in retirement, but without a value structure to make these additional opportunities for leisure activities a meaningful part of their lives.

Ultimately one's identity and self-concept will be shaped as much by leisure pursuits as by work roles. This shift in emphasis from all-inclusiveness of work roles to one's sense of worth has not been entirely negotiated by most Americans. The work of Morse and Weiss (1955) indicates the pervasiveness of the "work ethic." The effect of changing values and the increasing acceptance of leisure activities in industry and other institutions in American society is difficult to gauge. One can only surmise that shifts in the American way of life are inevitable as the balance between work and leisure activities swings further in the direction of leisure.

KEY TERMS

free time
integrating activity
leisure
role continuity

role discontinuity
semileisure
significant others
work

REFERENCES

ALLEN, CAROLE, and HERMAN BROTMAN, *Chartbook on Aging in America*. Washington, D.C.: Administration on Aging, 1981.

ARTH, M., "American Culture and the Phenomenon of Friendship in the Aged," in *Social and Psychological Aspects of Aging*, ed. C. Tibbitts and W. Donahue, pp. 522–34. New York: Columbia University Press, 1962.

ATCHLEY, ROBERT, *The Sociology of Retirement*. Cambridge, Mass.: Schenkman, 1976.

BACK, KURT W., and CARLETON S. GUPTILL, "Retirement and Self Rating," in *Social Aspects of Aging*, ed. Ida Harper Simpson and John C. McKinney, pp. 120–32. Durham, N.C.: Duke University Press, 1966.

BERGER, BENNETT, "The Sociology of Lesiure: Some Suggestions," in *Work and Leisure*, ed. O. Erwin Smigel, pp. 21–40. New Haven: College and University Press, 1963.

BIER, WILLIAM C., ed., *Aging: Its Challenge to the Individual and to Society*. Bronx, N.Y.: Fordham University Press, 1974.

BLAU, ZENA SMITH, "Structural Constraints on Friendship in Old Age," *American Sociological Review*, 26 (1961), 429–40.

BOSSE, RAYMOND, CAROLYN ALDWIN, MICHAEL LEVINSON, and KATHRYN DANIELS, "How Stressful Is Retirement? Findings from the Normative Age Study," *Journal of Gerontology*, 46(1), 1991, 9–14.

BRYANT, CLIFTON, *The Social Dimensions of Work*. Englewood Cliffs, N.J.: Prentice Hall, 1972.

CAPLOW, THEODORE, *The Sociology of Work*. Minneapolis: University of Minnesota Press, 1954.

CLARK, ALFRED C., "The Use of Leisure and Its Relation to Levels of Occupational Prestige," *American Sociological Review*, 21 (June 1956), 301–7.

COTTRELL, FRED, and ROBERT ATCHLEY, *Women in Retirement: A Preliminary Report*. Oxford, Ohio: Scripps Foundation, 1969.

COX, HAROLD, and ALBERT BHAK, "Symbolic Interaction and Retirement Adjustment: An Empirical Assessment," *International Journal of Aging and Human Development*, 9 no. 3 (1978–79), 279–86.

DEGRAZIA, SEBASTIAN, *Of Time, Work and Leisure*. New York: Twentieth Century Fund, 1962.

DRAKE, JOSEPH T., *The Aged in American Society*. New York: Ronald Press, 1958.

DUBIN, ROBERT, "Industrial Workers' World: A Study of the 'Central Life Interests' of Industrial Workers," *Social Problems*, 3 (January 1956), 131–42.

DUMAZEDIERS, J., *Lo Spettacalo*. London: Collier-Macmillan, 1972.

DUMAZEDIERS, J., *Towards a Society of Lesiure*. London: Collier-Macmillan, 1967.

DURKHEIM, EMILE, *The Division of Labor in Society*, trans. George Simpson. New York: Free Press, 1947.

EKERDT, D. J., R. BOSSE, and S. LENKOFF, "An Empirical Test for Phases of Retirement: Findings from the Normative Age Study," *Journal of Gerontology*, Vol. 40 (1985), 95–101.

ERIKSON, ERIK H., *Identity and the Life Cycle*. Psychological Issues, Monograph 1. New York: International University Press, 1959.

FOX, ALAN, *A Sociology of Work in Industry*. New York: Macmillan, 1971.

GLASSER, R., *The New High Priesthood: The Social and Political Implications of a Marketing Oriented Society*. London: Macmillan, 1967.

GREENE, MARK R., *Preretirement Counseling, Retirement Adjustment, and the Older Employee*. Eugene: Graduate School of Management and Business, University of Oregon, 1969.

HALL, RICHARD, *Occupations and the Social Structure*. Englewood Cliffs, N.J.: Prentice Hall, 1975.

HANLON, MARTIN, "Age and Commitment to Work: A Literature Review and Multivariate Analysis," *Research on Aging*, 8, no. 2 (June 1986), 289–316.

HAVIGHURST, R. J., and OTHERS, eds., *Adjustment to Retirement*. The Netherlands: Koninklijke Van Gorcum and Corp. N.V., 1969.

HAWORTH, J. T., and M. A. SMITH, *Work and Leisure*. Princeton, N.J.: Princeton Book Company, 1975.

HAYWARD, MARK, and MELISSA HARDY, "Occupational Differences in Early Retirement Processes among Older Men," *Research on Aging*, 7, no. 4 (December 1985), 491–516.

HOFFMAN, ADELINE M., *The Daily Needs and Interests of Older People*. Springfield, Ill.: Chas. C Thomas, 1970.

HUGHES, EVERETT C., *Men and Their Work*. New York: Free Press, 1958.

IAMS, HOWARD M., "New Social Security Beneficiary Women: Correlates of Work." Paper read at the 1985 meeting of the American Sociological Association.

JOHNSON, ALTON, CHRISTOPHER FORREST, and FRANK SAMMARTINO, "Mandatory Retirement," in *Monographs on Aging*, no. 1, pp. 18–19. Madison: Faye McBeath Institute on Aging and Adult Life, University of Wisconsin, 1979.

KAPLAN, M., *Leisure: Lifestyle and Lifespan*. Philadelphia: Saunders, 1979.

KELLY, JOHN, "Work and Leisure: A Simplified Paradigm," *Journal of Leisure Research*, 4, no. 1 (1972), 50–62.

KIMMEL, DOUGLAS, *Adulthood and Aging*. New York: John Wiley, 1974.

KLEEMEIER, ROBERT W., ed., *Aging and Leisure*. Fair Lawn, N.J.: Oxford University Press, 1961.

KRAUSE, ELLIOT A., *The Sociology of Occupations*. Boston: Little, Brown, 1971.

KREPS, JUANITA M., *Employment, Income and Retirement Problems of the Aged*. Durham, N.C.: Duke University Press, 1963.

LOWENTHAL, MARJORIE FISKE, and CLAYTON HAVEN, "Interaction and Adoption: Intimacy as a Critical Variable," *American Sociological Review*, 33 (1968), 20–30.

MANIS, JEROME, and BERNARD MELTZER, *Symbolic Interaction: A Reader in Social Psychology*. Boston: Allyn & Bacon, 1972.

MANKIN, DON, *Toward a Post-Industrial Psychology*. New York: John Wiley, 1978.

MELCHING, DOLORES, and MERLE BROBERG, "A National Sabatical System: Implications for the Aged," *Gerontologist*, 14 (April 1974), 175–81.

MERTON, R. K., L. BROOM, and L. S. COTTRELL, "The Study of Occupation," in *Sociology Today*. New York: Harper & Row, 1965.

MILLER, DELBERT, and WILLIAM FORM, *Industrial Sociology*. New York: Harper & Row, 1969.

MORSE, NANCY, and R. S. WEISS, "The Function and Meaning of Work and the Job," *American Sociological Review*, 20, no. 2 (April 1955), 191–98.

NOSOW, SIGMUND, and WILLIAM FORM, *Man, Work and Society*. New York: Basic Books, 1962.

ORZACK, LOUIS, "Work as a Central Life Interest of Professionals," *Social Problems*, VII, 2 (Fall 1959), 125–32.

OWEN, JOHN D., *The Price of Leisure*. Montreal: McGill–Queen's University Press, 1970.

PARKER, STANLEY, *The Future of Work and Leisure*. St. Albans, Eng.: Granada Publishing Ltd., 1971.

PARNES, HERBERT S., *Work and Retirement: A Longitudinal Study of Men*. Cambridge: Massachusetts Institute of Technology, 1981.

PAVALKO, RONALD W., *Sociology of Occupations and Professions*. Itasca, Ill.: F. E. Peacock Publishers, 1971.

POLLACK, OTTO, *The Social Aspects of Retirement*. Homewood, Ill.: Richard D. Irwin, 1956.

POLLMAN, A. WILLIAM, "Early Retirement: Relationship to Variation in Life Satisfaction," *Gerontologist*, 11, no. 1, pt. 1 (1971), 43–49.

REICHARD, S., R. LIVSON, and P. C. PETERSON, *Aging and Personalities*. New York: John Wiley, 1962.

RHEE, H. A., *Human Aging and Retirement*. Geneva: General Secretariat, International Social Security Association, 1974.

RIDDICK, CAROL CUTLER, "Life Satisfaction for Older Female Homemakers, Retirees and Workers," *Research on Aging*, 7, no. 3 (September 1985), 383–93.

RILEY, MATILDA, ANNE FONER, and ASSOCIATES, *Aging and Society*. New York: Russell Sage, 1972.

ROBERTS, KENNETH, *Leisure*. London: Longman, 1970.

ROSENBURG, GEORGE S., *The Worker Grows Old*. San Francisco: Jossey-Bass, 1970.

ROSOW, IRVING, *Social Integration of the Aged*. New York: Free Press, 1967.

SAMMARTINO, FRANK, "Early Retirement," in *Monographs on Aging*, no. 1. Madison: Faye MacBeath Institute on Aging and Adult Life, University of Wisconsin, 1979.

SIMPSON, IDA HARPER, KURT W. BACK, and JOHN C. MCKINNEY, "Work and Retirement," in *Social Aspects of Aging*, ed. Ida Harper Simpson and John C. McKinney, pp. 35–44. Durham, N.C.: Duke University Press, 1966.

SOLDO, BETH J., and EMILY M. AGREE, *Population Bulletin*, 43, no. 3 (September 1988), Population Reference Bureau.

STREIB, GORDON F., and CLEMENT J. SCHNEIDER, *Retirement in American Society*. Ithaca, N.Y.: Cornell University Press, 1971.

STRYKER, SHELDON, "Symbolic Interaction as an Approach to Family Research," *Marriage and Family Living*, 21 (1959), 111–19.

TILGHER, ADRIANO, *Work: What It Has Meant to Men Through the Ages*, trans. Dorothy Fisher. New York: Harcourt, 1930.

VANLUE, NANCY, "The Sex Differential as It Relates to Public Welfare Personnel's Job Satisfaction." Master's thesis, Indiana State University, 1974.

VOLLMER, HOWARD M., and DONALD L. MILLS, eds., *Professionalization*. Englewood Cliffs, N.J.: Prentice Hall, 1966.

VROOM, VICTOR, *Work and Motivation*. New York: John Wiley, 1964.

WEBER, MAX, *The Protestant Ethic and the Spirit of Capitalism*, trans. Talcott Parsons. London: George Allen & Unwin, 1935.

WILENSKY, HAROLD L., "Professionalization of Everyone," *American Sociological Review*, 70 (April 1964), 137–38.

WILENSKY, HAROLD L., "The Uneven Distribution of Leisure: The Impact of Economic Growth on Free Time," in *Work and Leisure*, ed. Erwin O. Smigel, pp. 21–40. New Haven: College and University Press, 1963.

WILLIAMS, RICHARD H., CLARK TIBBITTS, and WILMA DONAHUE, eds., *Processes of Aging*. New York: Atherton, 1963.

NOTES

1. Robert Dubin, "Industrial Workers' Worlds: A Study of the 'Central Life Interests' of Industrial Workers," *Social Problems*, 3 (January 1956), 131–42.
2. Everett Hughes, "The Study of Occupation," in *Sociology Today*, ed. R. K. Merton, L. Broom, and L. S. Cottrell (New York: Harper & Row, 1965), p. 445.
3. Richard Hall, *Occupations and the Social Structure* (Englewood Cliffs, N.J.: Prentice Hall, 1975), p. 6.
4. Clifton Bryant, *The Social Dimensions of Work* (Englewood Cliffs, N.J.: Prentice Hall, 1972), p. 33.
5. Delbert Miller and William Form, *Industrial Sociology* (New York: Harper & Row, 1969), pp. 541–45.
6. Adriano Tilgher, *Work: What It Has Meant to Men Through the Ages*, trans. Dorothy Fisher (New York: Harcourt, 1930).
7. Ibid.
8. Nancy Morse and R. S. Weiss, "The Function and Meaning of Work and the Job," *American Sociological Review*, 20, no. 2 (April 1955), 192.
9. For a further discussion, see Max Weber, *The Protestant Ethic and the Spirit of Capitalism*, trans. Talcott Parsons (London: George Allen & Unwin, 1935), pp. 35–198.
10. Nancy Vanlue, "The Sex Differential as It Relates to Public Welfare Personnel's Job Satisfaction" (master's thesis, Indiana State University, 1974).
11. Victor Vroom, *Work and Motivation* (New York: John Wiley, 1964), p. 32.
12. Sebastian DeGrazia, *Of Time, Work and Leisure* (New York: Twentieth Century Fund, 1962), p. 90.

13. Ronald M. Pavalko, *Sociology of Occupations and Professions* (Itasca, Ill.: F. E. Peacock Publishers, 1971).
14. DeGrazia, *Of Time, Work and Leisure*.
15. Harold L. Wilensky, "Professionalization of Everyone," *American Sociological Review*, 70 (April 1964), 137–38.
16. J. Dumazediers, *Towards a Society of Leisure* (London: Collier-Macmillan, 1967), and *Lo Spettacolo* (London: Collier-Macmillan, 1972).
17. J. T. Haworth and M. A. Smith, *Work and Leisure* (Princeton, N.J.: Princeton Book Company, 1975).
18. Carole Allen and Herman Brotman, *Chartbook on Aging in America* (Washington, D.C.: Administration on Aging, 1981), p. 40.
19. Robert Atchley, *The Sociology of Retirement* (Cambridge, Mass.: Schenkman, 1976).
20. Kurt W. Back and Carleton S. Guptill, "Retirement and Self Rating," in *Social Aspects of Aging*, ed. Ida Harper Simpson and John C. McKinney (Durham, N.C.: Duke University Press, 1966), p. 129.
21. Fred Cottrell and Robert C. Atchley, *Women in Retirement: A Preliminary Report* (Oxford, Oh.: Scripps Foundation, 1969).
22. Sheldon Stryker, "Symbolic Interaction as an Approach to Family Research," *Marriage and Family Living*, 21 (1959), 111–19.
23. Alton Johnson, Christopher Forrest, and Frank Sammartino, "Mandatory Retirement," in *Monographs on Aging*, no. 1 (Madison: Faye McBeath Institute on Aging and Adult Life, University of Wisconsin, 1979), pp. 18–19.
24. Ibid., p. 19.

10

Living Environments in Later Life

Old age, as described earlier, is often a period of shrinking life space. This concept is crucial to our understanding of the housing problems and choices of older Americans. As older persons lose strength, experience health losses, and begin generally to feel less in control of their environment, they are likely to restrict their mobility to the areas where they feel most secure. For most older persons this means that they spend much of their time in their immediate neighborhood and increasing amounts of time inside their own house or apartment. The older one becomes the more likely he or she is to spend every moment at home. Hansen (1971) has estimated that persons over 65 spend 80 to 90 percent of their lives in the domestic (home) environment.[1] In comparing older persons with other groups, only small children and those living in institutions are so bound to house and neighborhood.

Charles Berresi, Kenneth Ferraro, and Linda Hobey (1983–84) found that perceived health and housing satisfaction were the two most powerful predictors of well-being among the elderly. While much attention has been given to the perceived health of the elderly and their life satisfaction, their satisfaction with their housing and living environments has received much less attention.

The house, neighborhood, and community environment is, therefore, more crucial to older persons than it is to other age groups. The contact that older persons have with the home and neighborhood can be very stimulating, or it can be very dangerous and threatening. Across the country older Americans' living circumstances range from some of the most desirable to some of the most undesirable neighborhoods, from the most exclusive homes to the most modest. Fifty percent of the elderly are housed in structures built before 1939.[2]

Charles Berresi and his colleagues (1983–84) found that home ownership per se does not positively affect well-being among older persons. Rather it is their satisfaction with the unit that is crucial.

Older persons are often in the position of trying to hold on to a house and a neighborhood in which they have lived most of their lives. Their current location often has for them a long history and much sentimental value. Charles Harris (1978) found that although almost 75 percent of the respondents could find some undesirable conditions in their neighborhoods, over 95 percent did not wish to move as a result of those conditions. Harris also found that the elderly were less likely to move than the general population; those who do move tend to stay in the same county to about the same degree as the general population.[3]

Montgomery (1965) made a study of older persons who lived in a small community in Pennsylvania and found that 76 percent of those interviewed were born in or near the community; 81 percent had lived in their current dwelling for ten or more years. Seventy-eight percent of this sample liked their neighborhood very well and 76 percent liked their house very well.[4]

Erich Fromm (1963) has argued that people need a sense of place, a feeling that they belong in their environment.[5] Perhaps a house and a neighborhood provide this sense of place for older persons.

The fact that a high proportion of older Americans own their own homes and a majority of them do not want to move does not mean that the elderly have no problems with their current housing, however. As Richard Kalish (1975) points out,

> first, a high proportion of their homes are extremely old and often rundown, second, many are located in high-crime areas, where older people are especially likely to be victims, third, rising property taxes often take a substantial portion of the older person's income, leaving no money for repairs, and finally, the elderly often remain in their homes because they have no adequate alternative.[6]

Older couples who give serious thought to their housing problems may conclude that with their children grown, a large house is a drain on their physical energy and economic resources. They may rationally decide, then, to move to a smaller house or an apartment. It is quite possible that the proceeds of the sale of the house may be inadequate for the purchase of a newer, smaller dwelling.

In this chapter, we discuss the housing needs of older Americans and the choices available to them.

RESIDENTIAL SEGREGATION OF THE AGED

Residential segregation is a settlement pattern whereby high proportions of identifiably different kinds of people are located in distinct zones and neighborhoods of a community. Thus, young people may be disproportionately found in given neighborhoods while older people may be found in other neighborhoods. Similarly, some areas of a city are known for their high concentrations of certain ethnic groups.

Where a person lives in the community indicates a great deal about the person's social status. Social ecologists such as McKenzie (1927), Park (1952), and Laumann (1966) have all argued that there is a direct link between territorial organization and culture and that a city's spatial order is a reflection of its social order.[7]

Many sociological studies have used income, occupation, and education as indicators of one's social status and made predictions regarding one's residential location. The researchers expected and found that persons of similar social class lived in similar sections of the city. Otis and Beverly Duncan (1955) used occupation as an indicator of residential segregation and found that persons whose occupations approach the extremes of the occupational-status scale were more residentially segregated than persons whose occupational status was nearer the center of the scale. Sociologists would expect the most unique status group to be the most segregated since its status position is most distinct.[8] Feldman and Tilly (1960), in a study of the association between social status and residential segregation, concluded that education used as a measure of lifestyle accounts for a substantially larger part of the variation in the association than does income used as a measure of resources.[9] Richard Coleman and Bernice Neugarten (1971), in their study of Kansas City, found that their respondents invariably referred to the resident's geographic location in terms indicating that it was a complex stratification system. The subjects ranked neighborhoods not only in terms of the individual's present social or financial status but also in terms of the person's status goals.[10]

Later studies began to use age as a critical variable for determining one's location in the urban community. Eisenstadt (1956), for example, observed that age differences are among the most basic and crucial aspects of human life and destiny. All societies are confronted with age-related role changes and the progression of power and capacities connected with age changes. Thus the transition from youth to old age is subject to social and cultural definitions.[11]

To the degree that age groups are differentially located among family, career, and status positions in society, we should expect to find them differentially located in the urban community. While not much work has been done on identifying concentrations of young and middle-age persons in the urban community, Donald Cowgill (1962) identified concentrations of older people in the 56 large cities he studied. Using the *Spencerian principle*—that increasing mass results in increasing differentiation of parts, including spatial segregation of heterogeneous elements—Cowgill suggests that community size may be a critical determinant of age segregation. Sheila Miller (1967) found that this trend had increased in the 1960s. In the seven cities she studied there was a marked increase in the segregation of the aged.

Some would argue that the residential segregation of older persons in the urban community is a result of the social-class and status position of this group. Others would argue that it is a result of changing family needs. Nelson Foote and his associates (1960) had earlier traced in some detail the changing housing needs resulting from the changing size of the family and the changing stages of the life cycle, including the shrinking stage in later life.

Stephen Golant (1972) notes, however, that changing needs do not automatically lead to an adjustment and that, particularly in old age, there is much inertia that retards such adjustments. He contends that concentrations of the elderly in urban communities are more likely to result from immobility than from mobility. Calvin Goldscheider's work (1971) on the mobility patterns of the older population does not seem to totally support these explanations. He found that 30 percent of the 50 + population move at least once over a five-year period and that 10 percent move annually. It seems unlikely that inertia alone would account for the age concentrations of the older population. What must be remembered is that not all older persons are residentially stable. Nor, for that matter, are all younger persons mobile.

Harold Cox and Albert Bhak (1980) conducted a study of age segregation in an average-size Midwestern city to determine if the age-segregation patterns that Cowgill (1962) and Miller (1967) found in the large urban community were true for smaller cities. They predicted that the young (20 to 24) and the old (65 +) could be considered distinct status groups, sharing some very similar and other very dissimilar problems in relation to the general population. They argued that these two age categories comprise people who are generally not totally involved in occupation and career, who depend on others for their income and security, and who are often excluded from the mainstream of American life. The young are not totally involved in the occupational status hierarchy because they are either in their education years or their apprentice years. Neither of these groups is well established in their careers. The college students have not entered an occupation; the noncollege students in the apprentice programs often experience frequent job changes as they attempt to acquire the necessary occupational skills. The old, because they have arrived at the age of retirement, are similarly not actively involved in occupational and career activities. The age groups in between 25 and 65, on the other hand, are likely to be involved in occupations and careers, greatly concerned with status and upward mobility, and inextricably enmeshed in the political, economic, and social structure of the culture. Cox and Bhak's (1980) predictions were as follows:

1. The "dependent groups" (20 to 24 and 65+) would be more residentially segregated than the "active groups" (25 to 64).
2. Within the dependent groups the young (20 to 24) and the old (65+) will be located in distinctly different zones of the city.

The general pattern of the findings in Table 10–1 conformed to the direction predicted by Cox and Bhak. The residential-segregation scores form a distinct U-shaped curve in which the young and old age groups were found to be more residentially segregated than the group in between. The 20-to-24 age group

TABLE 10–1 Differences in Residential-Segregation Scores by Age Groups*

Age Groups	Residential-Segregation Score**
20–24	26.5
25–34	10.5
35–44	12.0
45–54	8.0
55–64	10.0
65–74	13.5
75+	21.0

*High scores indicate greater residential segregation.

**Determination of the residential-segregation scores for these age groups was done in the same manner as Duncan and Duncan's 1955 study of occupational rank and residential segregation. This involves the tabulations of two distributions. The first distribution consists of the proportion of each age group residing in each census tract. The second distribution is obtained by computing the proportion of all other age groups combined, except the group being measured in each tract. The index of residential segregation is then one half the absolute value differences of the two distributions for each age group, taken tract by tract.

Source: Harold Cox and Albert Bhak, "Determinants of Age-Based Residential Segregation," *Sociological Symposium*, no. 29 (January 1980), 35. Reprinted by permission of the authors and *Sociological Symposium*.

received a residential segregation score of 26.5—the highest score of all the groups. The 75-and-older age group received a residential-segregation score of 21.0, which was the second highest score. The 65-to-74 age group received a residential-segregation score of 13.5—the third highest score.

Cox and Bhak's (1980) prediction that the young and old would live in distinctly different zones of the city was also borne out by the data. Their argument was that these two groups, while being defined as dependent, would represent distinctly different status groups, one being in the preoccupational category and the other in the postoccupational category. To test the validity of this hypothesis, the researchers divided the city's Standard Metropolitan Statistical Area into concentric zones in much the same manner suggested by Park and Burgess (1925). Zone 1 represented the central city and zone 7 the regions farthest from the central city; the intermediate zones (2–6) fell in between. As Table 10–2 indicates, a clear pattern emerged. The 20-to-24 age group was most heavily concentrated in zone 1, the 65-to-74 age group in zone 3, and the 75-and-above age group in zone 2. The dependent groups were least likely to live in zone 7—the suburbs and outskirts of the city. This pattern was considerably stronger for the two older age groups. Cox and Bhak argued that the zones of low population density are too isolated and devoid of the minimum social interaction that seems to be desired by members of the older age groups. This study found further that as early as age 55, changes in housing are being seriously considered by older persons as they begin to anticipate retirement and alterations in their lifestyle.

There appear to be two different flows of elderly migration in relation to retirement. The more prevalent flow is out of metropolitan areas to nonmetropolitan areas. This pattern most often involves a decision by the older person to move to a more desirable location, frequently one with a more favorable climate, better recreational amenities, or a more scenic environment.

The second flow of elderly migration is from nonmetropolitan to metropolitan areas and is a less desirable decision often made under stress. The move is usually from an independent to a dependent living arrangement, and most often comes about at a time of crisis, such as the loss of a spouse, declining income, or the onset of a health problem. The destination is frequently congregate housing or a nursing home.

Older persons are found in disproportionate numbers in large urban com-

TABLE 10–2 Differences in Mean Residential-Segregation Scores for Selected Age Groups by Ecological Zones*

Age Group	Ecological Zone						
	1	*2*	*3*	*4*	*5*	*6*	*7*
20–24	26.00	13.00	8.25	16.25	10.50	15.00	10.50
65–74	16.50	22.25	24.50	14.75	15.00	9.25	4.25
75+	16.25	24.75	21.50	14.25	8.25	11.00	5.50

*Ecological zones, comprised of configurations of census tracts concentric with the center of the city, move outward from Zone 1 to Zone 7.

Source: Harold Cox and Albert Bhak, "Determinants of Age-Based Residential Segregation," *Sociological Symposium*, no. 29 (January 1980), 36. Reprinted by permission of the authors and *Sociological Symposium*.

munities and in small towns throughout the country. Their location in zones surrounding the downtown districts in the urban community provides maximum access to the concentration of local services essential to the regular needs of the elderly, such as grocery stores, pharmacies, hospitals, banks, and bus services. The widely spread suburbs make services needed by the elderly less accessible.[12]

But the urban community also carries some undesirable aspects for its elder residents. For one thing, urban communities are designed for the average 30-year-old male who is healthy, strong, mobile, and thereby capable of negotiating the environment with ease. Such an environment presents many barriers for older persons, including irregular surfaces, long flights of stairs, and crowded buses with high steps, as well as high crime rates.[13] The cultural diversity that young people find attractive in urban communities may be a further source of insecurity and fear for the elderly. In addition one finds low-quality housing, deteriorating neighborhoods, crowding, congestion, and noise in the urban community.

The small town is heavily inhabited by farm families who have found their farms too isolated in later life, as well as by some urban residents who have retired to their hometowns because it is cheaper to live there. These communities are likely to provide easy access to grocery stores, pharmacies, and restaurants. They are, moreover, relatively free of crime. They are primarily homogeneous: Most of the residents are white, of northern European descent, and largely Protestant. They provide for older persons a quiet, secluded enclave in which they can feel secure from many of the stresses that accompany the diversity and speed of social change in the large urban community. Unfortunately, government programs for older Americans are often not available in these small, geographically isolated towns.

DESIGN AND ENVIRONMENTAL FACTORS IN SENIOR HOUSING

Architects have designed houses and apartments for senior citizens that have adequate temperature and climate control year-round, adequate sun and artificial light, and adequate control of noise. They have simultaneously kept the living space small and easy to maintain. Inside they have tried to minimize the need to lift, bend, pull, or climb. Bathrooms and showers have had safety features added to minimize falls and the rise of bodily injury. While these design features are helpful and a decided improvement, it must be remembered that the house, apartment, or living space of an older person is but one part of an environment that includes neighborhoods and communities.

Kalish (1975) argues that what the older person needs is a sense of place, a feeling of relatedness, a sense of environmental mastery, privacy, and psychological stimulation.[14] Following Fromm's (1963) work, Kalish maintains that the homes of the elderly should satisfy their need to identify with a place, dwelling, neighborhood, village, city, or landscape. People of all ages need to be able to interact frequently with other human beings, but older persons in particular need this opportunity in order to keep from becoming lonely, depressed, isolated, and preoccupied with themselves. Carp (1966) found that older residents of an enriched environment seemed to respond to their housing by reengaging in social life.[15]

Failure to master and control one or more aspects of one's environment can lead to a growing sense of inadequacy, incompetency, and self-doubt by older persons. A supportive environment, on the other hand, can enhance one's sense of competency, which in turn tends to help older persons to remain independent for as long as possible.

People at any age in life need psychological stimulation. Older persons, because of declining health, widowhood, or any of a variety of other losses, may not be able to look forward to a better tomorrow. Psychological stimulation and diversion, therefore, may prove to be a significant booster of the morale and outlook of these persons. Lack of enough to do and lack of new, stimulating experiences result in older persons having too much time to become preoccupied with themselves and their problems.

Finally, persons of all ages need periods in which they can withdraw from others, as well as from the stimulation and stress of their environment, in order to regroup their energy and restructure their thoughts before meeting any new challenges. They need privacy and a time to be with themselves. Privacy can be an expression of territoriality for human beings.

The designers of homes for the elderly, then, must be aware of both the physiological and psychological needs of older persons. They must take into account the total environment of the homes they are constructing. Unfortunately, architects and behavioral scientists do not always speak the same language, or even attempt to communicate. Therefore, from the point of view of the behavioral scientists, the homes constructed for older persons often leave much to be desired.

Since the health, energy, competence, and life space of older persons are often declining, the environments created for them should support their competence and confidence as much as possible. Unfortunately gerontologists have not always been able to agree on which environmental factors are most desirable. The question of age homogeneity versus age heterogeneity in the neighborhoods of older people is a case in point. Irving Rosow (1967), in a study of older persons living in apartments in Cleveland, concluded that friendship patterns varied in direct proportion to the number of aged peers living nearby. Age homogeneity yielded the larger number of friendships and increased the amount of visiting. Rosow's work strongly supports the notion that age segregation is good for the older person.[16]

The concept of segregation does not fit well, however, with the American ideals of democracy, equality, and social justice. Segregation of any kind is assumed to be bad. Moreover, some have argued that being in contact only with other old people is depressing. One cannot help but be aware that one's friends are aging and dying. A social group made up of just older persons carries the constant reminder of one's own declining health and ultimate death. Gerontologists frequently argue that age-integrated neighborhoods should produce higher morale and greater stimulation for the older person.

Studies that systematically attempt to solve this question seem always to conclude that the age-segregated environment is best for the older person. Powell Lawton (1976), in discussing the movement of older persons to senior housing, cites studies showing

> that to varying degrees a favorable change is experienced by elderly people during the year following such a move, particularly in the areas of organization activity,

social interaction and perceived changes in life satisfaction. Finer detailed examination of some of the processes involved in such an increase in well-being seems to indicate that the physical proximity of age peers and the establishment of a normative system appropriate to the level of competence of the average elderly tenant are major factors in beneficial effect.[17]

Similarly, Bultena and Wood (1969) compared men who lived in four age-segregated communities in Arizona with men of the same age who had remained in integrated communities. Their results indicated that the morale of those living in the retirement communities was significantly higher.[18]

It is the general belief of gerontologists that the older one becomes the more crucial are the environmental factors in determining one's degree of life satisfaction. In discussing this matter, Lawton (1976) proposes an *environmental docility hypothesis*, which in its simplest form states:

> The less competent the individual in terms of personal disability or deprived status, the more susceptible is his behavior to the influence of immediate environmental situations.[19]

Even competent older persons are influenced by environmental factors. Frances Wiltzius and Steven Gambert (1981) studied what happened to competent nursing home patients when they were placed with a confused and mentally incompetent roommate. They found that such placements had many undesirable effects on the competent subjects, including loss of recent memory, passive aggressiveness, and increased anxiety. Most of the subjects became less friendly, more remote, and depressed.

Lawton (1983) has attempted to describe how four components of what he defines as "the good life" can influence one's self-concept. These four critical factors are behavioral competence, psychological well-being, perceived quality of life, and objective environment. The area where the factors overlap is the self (Figure 10–1). Lawton points out that each of these four factors involves individual and social goals that are defensible without regard to how much the effect of change in one is reflected in change in another. Lawton argues that all factors influence the self, which in turn reenergizes the four factors. The exact means by which this occurs is not specified, however.

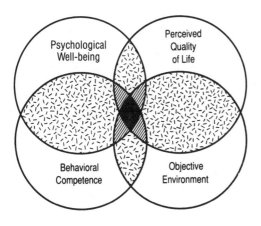

FIGURE 10–1
Four Sectors of the Good Life

Source: M. Powell Lawton, "Environment and Other Determinants of Well-Being in Older People," *Gerontologist*, 23, no. 4 (1983), 355.

Attempts to improve the lives of older persons through environmental manipulation can be seen, and are instituted, in four different ways, according to Lawton (1976). In the first approach, it is the individual who both initiates the change and is the point of its application. Older persons who follow this pattern actively seek stimulation, strive toward self-determined goals, and are alert to the need for change in themselves, Lawton believes. In the second pattern, the individual initiates the change but the point of application is the environment. This approach is an attempt to redesign one's environment in such a way as to maximize the congruity between one's needs and the offering of the environment. Migration to a pleasanter climate or to a neighborhood or community where health care is more readily available would be an example of this kind of environmental improvement. In the third technique, the individual responds to treatment applied individually by a therapist. This involves the person's being a good cotherapist. What distinguishes this type of change from growth is the participation of a professional in the change. In the final pattern, the individual responds to a change applied to the environment. Social designers and architects have attempted with varying success to construct need-fulfilling environments. Studies have indicated that a change in environment will be most effective in changing behavior when the individual is at a threshold level of competence. Consider the individual who is about to lose his or her physical or financial ability to maintain a lifelong home and therefore must move to a smaller and more easily kept apartment. Since this person is at a threshold level of ability in terms of maintaining a home, a change to a more manageable apartment might increase his or her sense of competence and independence.

Victor Regnier (1975) has developed a table indicating the age-related losses that older persons are likely to experience and the changes that may be required in one's environment if one is to adjust to these losses (Table 10–3).[20]

TABLE 10–3   Age-Related Environmental Changes and Personal Losses

50–65	65–75	75–79	80+
Loss of relationship to younger friends and acquaintances of children. Loss of neighborhood role to schools and youth. Home is too large, but mortgage payments are low and equity high.	Loss in relation to work environment, loss of mobility due to lessened income. Dissolving of professional work associations and friendships. Move to apartment, smaller home, or struggle with increased maintenance costs of larger home.	Loss of ability to drive independently. Must rely on bus or relatives and friends. Connections with community, church associations slowly severed. Move to more supportive housing, such as apartments with meals and maid service. Maintenance costs for single-family house unmanageable.	Loss of ability to navigate in the environment. Loss of strong connection with outside neighborhood. Dependence on supportive services. Move to supportive environment necessary, such as nursing home, home for the aged, or siblings' home.

Source: Victor Regnier, "Neighborhood Planning for the Urban Elderly," in *Aging: Scientific Perspectives and Social Issues*, eds. Diana S. Woodruff and James E. Birren (Belmont, Calif.: Wadsworth, 1975), p. 299.

A word of caution might be appropriate at this point. The solution to all older persons' personal losses is not necessarily a move to a different and more manageable and supportive environment. John Briggs (1968) has pointed out that movement from a familiar to a strange environment induces numerous stresses. There is most often a strong attachment by the person to the familiar living arrangements. Present arrangements, while leaving something to be desired, are most often predictable and have been a part of the older person's life for a long time. Moving requires adjustments and is somewhat traumatic for persons of all ages. Elders may simply not be able to withstand another adjustment if they have recently experienced a series of personal losses.

HOUSING AND COMMUNITY CHOICES OF OLDER AMERICANS

Many older persons have no choice regarding where they will live. They are so poor that they must try desperately to hold on to whatever meager quarters they have at the present. For middle- and upper-income elderly, however, there are probably more choices of housing and neighborhoods available to them than ever before. Moreover, Kenneth Ferraro (1982) has found that voluntary moves have no adverse effects on the health of the elderly. Moves to more desirable climates may actually improve their health.

Many elderly who can well afford to move ultimately decide to remain in their current home because of what it represents to them. It is here that they raised their children, entertained, visited with neighbors, loved, fought, and struggled with life's many problems. Their current homes are filled with family traditions and sentiments, which they may not want to break. The choice to remain where one has lived most of his or her life allows the person to continue living in a familiar environment, interacting with familiar neighbors and lifelong friends in a neighborhood they know well. In fact, O'Bryant and Nocera (1985) found that widows' homes became significantly more important and meaningful to them following the death of their husbands. The importance of the home for the widows reported seemed to be a result of their sentimental attachment to the past marital happiness and family experiences. Moreover, the stores are familiar and the service centers accessible. To move entails a variety of adjustments to a new neighborhood. It is easy to see why many older persons choose to remain where they are.

If the decision is made to move out of the old house and neighborhood, however, a variety of choices are available to the older person. It is probably good advice for the older person not to make a decision to move until thinking it over carefully for several weeks or longer, and never to make a decision to move during a time of stress, such as the death of a spouse. No decision should be made for six months after the death of one's husband or wife. A wrong decision, made under traumatic conditions, may be impossible to reverse.

One choice often made by middle-class Americans is to move to a retirement community. This usually involves a move to a different state, since many of the retirement villages are located in such Sun Belt states as Florida, Texas, Arizona, and California.

Many retirement communities are almost self-contained. They include shopping centers, churches, restaurants, recreation centers, golf courses, swimming pools, and sometimes medical centers. The advantages of retirement communities include accessibility to needed services, limitless possibilities for social contacts and friends, and independence and privacy. The major drawback of retirement communities is the cost, which often puts them out of reach of any other than the most affluent older Americans. James Peterson and Culi Larson (1972), in a study of Sagina Hills in Southern California, found that 55.4 percent of the residents had been engaged in professional or managerial occupations before retirement, compared with the 25.3 percent of such professionals within the population at large.[21]

Bultena and Wood (1969) found that residents of retirement communities admit to having less contact with family members than do elderly residents of the general community, but they seem to have more friends available, they have generally higher morale, and they perceive their own health to be better.[22] Eileen Crimmins and Dominique Ingegneri (1990) compared family interaction patterns of adult children and their aging parents between 1962 and 1984. They found fewer parents and children coresiding in 1984. Over the same period there was a continued reduction in the number of days per year that parents and their children who do not live together see each other. Crimmins and Ingegneri (1990) believe that in the future, older persons are going to have fewer children, be more educated, and live at greater distances from their children. All of these factors should result in decreased interaction between older parents and their adult children. If the pattern of high morale for older persons in retirement communities that was found by Bultena and Wood (1969) continues, the decrease of interaction with one's children will not necessarily be a negative factor in one's overall life satisfaction.

John Krout (1983) points out that a significant number of the elderly engage in "seasonal migration" referred to as *snowbirding*. This migration is labeled *snowbirding* because it occurs in the winter months and follows the paths of many birds that migrate south at that time. The elderly migrate from the Northeast and North Central states to the Sun Belt. The Southern states that have received the largest number of migrants are Florida, California and Arizona. *Snowbirding* is probably the wrong name for these migrants. They actually should be labeled *sunbirds* since they avoid the snowy winter months of the Northern states and flock to the warm climates and sunshine of the Southern states.

Mobile-home parks are often available to persons who can't afford retirement communities but want to move to the Sun Belt. Residents usually pay a monthly rate, which includes trailer space, utilities, laundry, and recreational facilities. Most trailer parks have swimming pools, recreation rooms, and organized social activities.

Many of the residents of mobile-home parks originally intended to live there only during the winter but later decided to remain year-round. Hoyt (1954) found in a study of mobile-home residents that 12 percent remained for ten months or more each year. Fifty-eight percent owned the same homes they owned during their working years and returned to them during the summer. An additional 10.3 percent had purchased a different home but also returned to it during the summer months. Thus the majority of the residents of mobile-home parks live there during the winter and return to their original homes for the summer.[23]

Hoyt (1954), whose study took place at a trailer park in Bradentown, Florida, found that the residents were not integrated into the larger community but were integrated into the social structure of the trailer park. Eighty-two percent of the residents reported that they obtained all or most of their recreation within the park. Many reported that they originally moved there because of climate but that they stayed for social reasons.

When asked why they preferred living in the trailer park, a variety of reasons were given. The two most common responses were sociability (46.4 percent) and same status and interests (42.6 percent). Other reasons included "more and better activities" (28.4 percent), "not so lonesome" (14.8 percent), "everyone's the same age" (7.7 percent), "mutual aid" (42.6 percent), and "less disturbance" (18.7 percent). Thus a variety of factors make trailer parks attractive to retired persons.

Full-timing as a way of life during the retirement years is being chosen by an ever-larger number of retirees according to Gail Hartwigsen and Roberta Null (1989). Full-timing is defined as residing in a residential vehicle year-round. Full-timers travel by way of a travel trailer, a fifth wheel or motor home. The reason the full-timers give for choosing this lifestyle is that they like to travel and be outdoors. In actuality the lifestyle of many of the full-timers is not that much different from that of the seasonal migrants. Mr. Thompson is a full-timer who spends from November until May of each year residing in his motor home in a trailer park in Galveston, Texas. In May he travels from Galveston to a lake in central Michigan where he parks his mobile home and lives during the summer months.

A number of church groups sponsor retirement houses for the aged. The accommodations range from modest to very elaborate. These homes generally offer a life-care arrangement in which the tenant pays a founder's fee upon moving in and monthly rent thereafter. Most of these homes, like those in the retirement communities, are so expensive as to be out of the reach of the majority of older Americans.

The federal government, through the office of Housing and Urban Development (HUD), has made funds available for the construction of high-rise apartments for senior citizens across the country. The relatively small amount of land required makes it possible to build these complexes in large urban areas and near shopping centers and needed services. These apartments are inhabited mainly by the less affluent older Americans.

Another choice for the less affluent older person is the retirement hotel. This is usually an old hotel or apartment house located near the downtown area of the city. It may provide maid service and have a common dining room. It offers the older person ample social contact and simultaneously the opportunity for privacy. Unfortunately, these hotels are often located in poor neighborhoods in which the elderly are much more likely than elsewhere to be the victims of crime.

HOUSING COSTS

Rosow (1967) has found that the older persons who are most dissatisfied with their housing are those in the low-income brackets. Economic problems are at the core of the housing problems of older Americans, he concluded.

Since the average older family's income is about half as large as that of younger families, it is easy to understand why the older family spends a larger percentage of its total income on housing. In actual dollars, however, the older family spend less on housing than young families do. Most often this means that older families live in less desirable homes than their younger counterparts.

While many older families simply do not have enough income to maintain their current housing, they most often have too much income to gain entry into public housing which requires that income be less than a designated figure as a condition for residency. This situation is especially true of middle-income older persons.

Charles Harris (1978) found that in 1973, 65 percent of the housing units in the United States were owner-occupied. For the over-65 population 70 percent of the houses were owner-occupied. The older one becomes, however, the less likely one is to live in one's own home. The 1970 census indicated that of the dwellings occupied by 60-to-64-year-olds, 71 percent were owner-occupied; among those of 65-to-74-year-olds, 68 percent were owner-occupied; and for the 75-and-above group, 66 percent were owner-occupied. Older persons are often ultimately forced to give up on maintaining their own homes and to move into some other arrangement, such as government housing or housing with other family members. Harris found further that 82 percent of the owner-occupied housing was free and clear of any mortgage.[24] Harris (1978), in comparing black and white home ownership, states,

> The black aged are only slightly more likely to own (57%) their homes as to rent (43%), compared to white elderly households, of whom, 71% lived in their own homes.[25]

Older persons who rent their homes are much more likely than the general population to be paying 25 percent or more of their income in rent (Figure 10–2).

In the past, when older persons became too ill, too feeble, or too poor to maintain their own home, they moved in with their children. A study by Crimmins and Ingegneri (1990) indicates that moving in with children is becoming increasing less likely in the modern world. Crimmins and Ingegneri compared

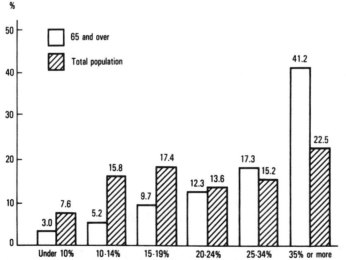

FIGURE 10–2   Gross Rent as Percentage of Income by Age, 1973

Source: Charles Harris, *Fact Book on Aging: A Profile of America's Older Population* (Washington, D.C.: National Council on the Aging, 1978), p. 179.

the years 1962 and 1984 and found that during that time the number of parents and children living together had decreased significantly. The data further indicated that parents and children increasingly were living farther apart and seeing each other less frequently. Family assistance patterns are declining in an increasingly cosmopolitan world. Older persons are increasingly going to have to be able to maintain their own home or move into an institutionalized arrangement such as congregate housing or nursing homes.

In terms of the quality of their homes, the elderly are slightly more likely than the total population to live in housing units lacking some or all plumbing features. This is more often the case for blacks than for whites and more frequently true in rural areas. James Montgomery, Alice Stubbs, and Savannah Day (1980) found in their study of housing in rural America that federal programs designed to assist the rural elderly in home improvements simply were not being effectively implemented. They concluded that the rural elderly were not inclined to seek assistance from the government and that federal programs such as the Cooperative Extension Service, the Farmers Home Administration, and the Federal Housing Administration were not actively offering them any assistance.

Housing costs take a substantially larger share of the incomes of older persons and therefore become more of a burden for several reasons, according to Harris (1978):

1. The inflation of real estate prices means that the elderly are unlikely to be able to sell their homes and find new houses they can afford to buy.

2. The average homeowner pays 3.4 percent of his income in property taxes while the older homeowner pays 8.1 percent.

3. Higher utility costs and the current energy shortages have hit those with fixed incomes the hardest.

4. Maintenance costs for all homeowners have risen dramatically, but this has most affected the older person, who is frequently living in older housing.

5. There is age discrimination in mortgage regulations, which work against the old.

6. The elderly are required in some states to sign over their homes to state welfare departments in order to obtain old age assistance.[26]

It is wrong to assume that the housing needs of the individual are likely to remain constant over the entire life cycle, or that the homes the elderly live in are ideally suited to them. Whereas younger families may have a problem of overcrowding, older families may have a problem of undercrowding if they attempt to live in housing too large for them to maintain and afford.

The Federal Housing Program has addressed some of the housing problems of older Americans. As of 1975 about one fourth of federally sponsored housing units were designed specifically for the elderly. Section 8 of the Federal Housing Program provides assistance for low-income housing. Families assisted under this program may pay no more than 25 percent, perhaps as little as 15 percent, of their gross incomes for rent. Section 8 is also the first housing program that permits the construction of congregate housing units, which are most needed by older Americans whose health or finances no longer permit them to live independently.

SOCIABILITY

It is apparent that housing and neighborhood choices affect older Americans' opportunities for social interaction. Rosow (1967), in discussing the social integration of neighborhoods, believes that the critical factors for integration are long-term residence, neighborhood stability, social homogeneity, and intact primary groups. Moreover, the number of old people's friends will vary with the proportion of their neighbors who are older. Regardless of the number, these friends will consist disproportionately of older rather than younger neighbors.

Rosow's (1967) arguments regarding neighborhood friendship patterns are apparently more true for lower-class persons than for middle-class persons.[27] Rosow (1967) found that the middle-class older person is significantly more likely to have more than one friend than is the working-class older person. There is greater local dependency for friendship in the working class than in the middle class. While the middle-class older person has more friends both generally and specifically in his or her section of town than the working class, the working class is far more dependent on neighbors as a source of friendship and social life.[28]

Rosow's (1967) work indicates that the older person's local friends vary with the proportion of old neighbors, and these friends are drawn basically from older neighbors. Regardless of the number of friends, the aged select their friends most often from older rather than younger neighbors, and this tendency increases with the residential density of old people.[29]

Charles Berresi and his colleagues (1983–84) found that older women are affected more positively by what they consider to be the sociability of their neighbors. Older men are affected more positively by the frequency of interaction with their neighbors.

The friendship patterns of older persons are very similar, then, to those of all age groups. Friendships are most often formed between persons of similar status, notably of age, but also of sex, marital status, social class, beliefs, and lifestyle. Proximity to persons of similar status is a facilitator of social involvement for older Americans.

While social involvement may be more or less desired by persons at any age in life, Rosow (1967) described different social participation types in the sample he studied:

1. Cosmopolitans (32%). This group, which was largely middle class in background, had the least contact with neighbors, and no desire for more friends.

2. Phlegmatic (4%). This group had low contact with neighbors, no good friends, and wanted no friends.

3. Isolated (19%). This group had low contact with neighbors and strongly wanted more friends.

4. Sociable (25%). This group had high contacts with neighbors and wanted no more friends.

5. Insatiable (20%). This group had high contacts with neighbors but still wanted more friends.[30]

The neighborhood environment, and opportunity for social interaction, is evidently much more important for lower-class persons than it is for middle-class persons. Throughout their lives lower-class persons seem to be less integrated into the total community and therefore have fewer resources on which they can draw, other than from the neighborhood, in order to establish friends. This problem becomes more pronounced in later life.

INSTITUTIONALIZATION

While approximately 5 percent of the older population reside in a nursing home at any one time, eventually 25 percent of all older persons will do so at some point. Gottesman, Quarterman, and Cohn (1973) report that of all older persons currently institutionalized, one in seven are in a psychiatric facility; all the rest are in nursing homes.[31]

It is a mistake to assume that the only persons who enter nursing homes are those who are very sick or dying. Often people enter nursing homes when their support system in the community breaks down. This may occur when one's spouse dies and one realizes that it is no longer possible to maintain one's home or to live independently. If no family members live in the immediate area, the individual often comes to realize that he or she has no other choice except a move to a nursing home. Studies have shown that many of those who enter a nursing home have been unable to cope adequately with the outside world during most of their later years and have been unable to utilize either family or community support systems to maintain their independence.

Nursing homes, like prisons and mental hospitals, are *total institutions*. That is, they have control over the entire life of the individual. They are places where a large number of like-situated individuals together lead an enclosed, supervised, and carefully administered life. Goffman (1961) labels them *inmates* because they lose control of so much of their lives and environment upon entering the institution.[32] They most often lose control of their personal property and sometimes even their full name. The insult to one's self-concept and confidence is extensive. New residents often react by disidentifying—stating that they don't belong there. They are often treated as equals, however, with those they believe to be considerably less competent.

The depersonalization of persons in nursing homes often includes feeding and bathing them in assembly-line fashion, treating them all alike, with no regard for individual differences, not calling them by their first names, completely disregarding their sentiments or complaints, speaking to them only to give orders, and tying them to their beds if they cause trouble.

There is a kind of circular process by which one who is already disoriented is inculcated into the total institution and as a result further loses his or her identity. Dress, manners, and conversations are constantly scrutinized. The result is almost total visibility and a complete lack of privacy. Most total institutions tend to be operated under the caste system model. The staff is in total control and constantly disciplines the residents.

Psychologists and psychiatrists have developed a description of the neurotic syndrome that tends to develop in residents of total institutions. The person is characterized as apathetic, expressionless, disinterested. Deterioration in the person's dress, cleanliness, and personal appearance often follow.[33] It is well recognized by psychiatrists today that behaviors previously believed to be manifestations of senility are often instead symptoms of neuroticism, anxiety, and lack of ego strength—all of which frequently result from a decline in participation in the environment and induced sensory deprivation.[34]

Barnes, Sack, and Shore (1973) describe in detail the downward spiral of senility, indicating the progressive loss of self-esteem that may occur among older persons. The deterioration begins at point 2 in Figure 10–3, when society demands that the older person relinquish his or her accustomed roles. This leads in turn to a loss of self-esteem (3). This may be accompanied by failing health and pressure to become dependent (4 and 5). Institutionalization (6) may lead to a further loss of self-esteem and personal confusion (6–8). The older person retreats into the more pleasant memories of the past (9), and is now considered beyond hope by others (10). The spiral eventually terminates with death (11 and 12).

The morale and self-concepts of personnel working in nursing homes may be determined in part by the negative attitudes of the public toward nursing homes. Nursing home staff are frequently seen as caretakers of places where people go to die. Kalish (1975) quotes expressions by staff members such as "time to water the vegetables" and mentions a nursing home administrator who referred to himself and his colleagues as "human garbage collectors." Such comments seem to

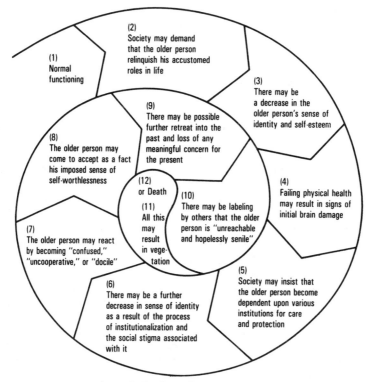

FIGURE 10–3   The Spiral of Senility

The patient may not go through all the stages shown or go through them in the order shown; however, all stages have been observed clinically in different patients at different times. Note that a consistently observed pattern in the spiral is the progressive decrease in self-esteem, ending in death.

Source: K. Barnes, A. Sack, and H. Shore, "Guidelines to Treatment Approaches," *Gerontologist*, 13 (1973), 513–27. Reprinted by permission of *The Gerontologist*.

reflect the fact that society does not place a high value on caring for its older and sometimes dying members. Thus nursing home personnel have difficulty maintaining pride in the important tasks they are required to perform.[35]

Because nursing homes are expensive to operate and many families simply do not have the funds to pay for the care of their elderly members, many facilities cannot afford to hire the additional staff that would enable them to provide intellectual or sensory stimulation for their patients. The advent of the federal medicare and medicaid programs has helped many older persons and their families bear some of the expenses of nursing home treatment. This has lead to the upgrading of nursing home programs. For example, physical therapists and recreational directors are now found in most large nursing homes.

Industrial sociologists have divided organizational structures into two ideal types—the *bureaucratic model* and the *professional model*. These models are often characterized as opposite ends of the continuum of organizational structure.

The bureaucratic model has been described as a hierarchy of offices and authority with (1) increasing centralization of power; (2) increasing specialization; (3) specification, standardization, and formalization of rules; (4) authority residing in the office; (5) impersonal operation; and (6) merit appointment. It is essentially a "closed system."[36]

The professional model, by comparison, includes the following characteristics: (1) horizontal patterns of authority with a minimum of centralized authority; (2) a division of labor based on professionalization of authority; (3) authority resting on professional expertise and competence rather than on the sacredness of the office; (4) considerable autonomy given to the units of the organization; (5) stress on employee commitment to organizational goals; (6) stress on informal rules and primary relations; and (7) responsibility delegated to the lower levels of the organization. This model is essentially an "open system."[37]

Ronald Corwin (1970) has pointed out that employee roles in bureaucratic organizations are likely to stress uniformity of the clients' problems, uniform rules and work procedures, little responsibility of the employee for decision making, and primary responsibility to the organization and administration. Professional roles depend on the opposite conditions, which include stress on informal rules and regulations, horizontal patterns of authority, the uniqueness of clients and of the skills of the personnel, and primary loyalty to clients and colleagues rather than to the organization.[38]

Nursing homes currently seem to approximate the bureaucratic model in both organizational structure and employee attitudes toward their roles. The client in the nursing home would be much better served if both the organizational structure of nursing homes and employee beliefs about their legitimate occupational roles could be moved in a more professional direction. There is certainly room for improvement. As Kalish (1975) reports,

> most nursing home staff members have had no training in the field before coming to their home, receive little or no in-service training and are very poorly paid. Relatively few of them enjoy the task they are required to perform and many are not particularly attracted to working with people.[39]

RELOCATION

Relocation from a familiar to a strange environment involves some stress and numerous adjustments at any age. For the very old, who may be already confused and experiencing several other problems simultaneously, a move can be overwhelming. The older person who moves leaves behind living arrangements that have been comfortable and predictable and enter a new environment that is different and initially somewhat unpredictable.[40]

Earlier research had tended to indicate that the mortality rates for elderly moving to and between nursing homes were substantially higher than actuarial expectations for their age group and higher than the death rate for those on the waiting list.[41] The more recent work of Jerry Borup, Daniel Gallego, and Pamela Hefferman (1979), however, indicates that this is not the case:

> Programs developed for the purpose of reducing mortality of relocated patients should focus on those factors which extend the life of the elderly rather than focus on the stress of relocation since relocation does not cause an increase in mortality. This is not to minimize the need for programs which attempt to reduce stress since relocation is a stress experience for most patients. However, it should be remembered that the stress of relocation does not bring about an increase in mortality.[42]

In any case, Marvin Horowitz and Richard Schuly (1983) argue that research that either supports or refutes the assertion that relocation increased the mortality rates of elderly residents is so methodologically flawed that it is virtually useless.

Thus, the evidence of the negative effects of relocation of older Americans is controversial at present. There seems little doubt that stress is involved and that adjustments have to be made. Whether this stress is serious enough to cause death is not certain. The work of Borup and his associates (1979) suggests that it is not.

CONCLUSION

Research data indicate that there is a direct link between physical space and social distance. In other words, as the work of social ecologists has indicated, where a person lives in the urban community indicates a great deal about his or her status and position in society (McKenzie, 1927; Park, 1952; Laumann; 1966). Coleman and Neugarten (1971) found that respondents referred to the resident's geographic location in the urban community in terms indicating that it was a complex stratification system.

Those older residents in the urban community are most likely to be located immediately around, but not in, the downtown district. These locations seem to offer the older person the maximum access to needed services and transportation with the minimum of effort. Unfortunately, urban areas are often zones of high crime and congestion, and their physical environment is structured primarily for healthy 30-year-olds. Such aspects of the urban environment carry undesirable side effects for older Americans. Even so, the elderly seem to shy away from the more sparsely settled and spacious suburban zones.

For the elderly living in rural areas the small towns seem to be the preferred location. Residence in a small town tends to keep farm families in closer proximity to friends, family members, and the community and to avoid the isolation of remaining on the farm. Small towns provide easy access to grocery stores, pharmacies, and restaurants. Moreover, one is near a group of persons of similar age, status, and life history. Sociability is maximized. Some urban residents have found that moving to a small town reduces the cost of living considerably.

Beyond the urban–rural choice of older Americans is a range of other choices. The person planning for retirement may decide to remain in his or her current house and neighborhood with its long history and personal value, move to a smaller house or apartment, or perhaps move to a retirement community in the Sun Belt. Inevitably there are advantages and disadvantages of any decision that is made. Hoyt (1954) found in his study of trailer-park residents that most returned to their original homes during the summer months.

One problem for the elderly in choosing the house and community where they will live is cost. Most residents of retirement communities have been found to have been professional or managerial workers and to have had considerably higher incomes than the average old person. For the very poor, government housing through HUD programs has often been the solution. Middle-income older persons often have too high an income to gain admission to government-sponsored housing but are not wealthy enough to move to the more exclusive retirement communities. The financial strain of keeping up their current homes may be the greatest for this group.

The debate over age-segregated versus age-integrated housing and communities now seems to favor the former. Generally speaking, older persons in age-segregated communities have more friends, more informal visiting, and higher morale. This is more true for blue-collar workers, who have fewer resources, financial or social, to maintain contacts outside of their immediate neighborhood.

Nursing homes are generally viewed negatively by older persons because they represent a loss of independence and ultimately death. Less than 5 percent of persons over 65 actually reside in nursing homes at any one time. Residents are often marginal in terms of their ability to maintain community or family support for their independent living. The death of a spouse or the tearing down of the apartment or hotel where they lived often precipitates the move to an institution. Thus, most residents of nursing homes entered at a time when their support system broke down. Whether the nursing home environment is desirable is a topic of debate at present. Gerontologists do not have enough information to give a definitive answer. In any event, older persons may decline in health to the extent that their family can no longer provide for them. At that point placing the person in a nursing home is the only reasonable choice the family can make.

KEY TERMS

bureaucratic organizational model
environmental docility hypothesis
professional organizational model
residential segregation
snowbirding

social participation types:
  cosmopolitan
  phlegmatic
  isolated
  sociable
  insatiable
Spencerian principle
total institutions

REFERENCES

BARNES, E. K., A. SACK, and H. SHORE, "Guidelines to Treatment Approaches," *Gerontologist*, 13 (1973), 513–27.

BERRESI, CHARLES M., KENNETH F. FERRARO, and LINDA L. HOBEY, "Environmental Satisfaction, Sociability and Well Being Among Urban Elderly," *International Journal of Aging and Human Development*, 18, no. 4 (1983–84), 277–84.

BORUP, JERRY H., DANIEL T. GALLEGO, and PAMELA G. HEFFERMAN, "Relocation and Its Effect on Mortality," *Gerontologist*, 19, no. 2 (1979), 135–40.

BRIGGS, JOHN C., "Ecology as Gerontology," *Gerontologist*, 8, no. 2 (1968), 78–79.

BROTMAN, H. B., *Facts and Figures on Older Americans: An Overview, 1971*. Washington, D.C.: Department of Health, Education and Welfare, 1972.

BULTENA, G. L., and V. WOOD, "The American Retirement Community: Bane or Blessing?" *Journal of Gerontology*, 24 (1969), 209–17.

CARP, F. M., *A Future for the Aged: Residents of Victoria Plaza, Austin*. Austin: University of Texas Press, 1966.

CARP, FRANCES, "Life Style and Location Within the City," *Gerontologist*, 15 (February 1975), 27–34.

COLEMAN, RICHARD P., and BERNICE L. NEUGARTEN, *Social Status in the City*. San Francisco: Jossey-Bass, 1971.

CORWIN, RONALD G., *Militant Professionalism*. New York: Appleton-Century-Crofts, 1970.

COWGILL, DONALD J., "Segregation Scores for Metropolitan Areas," *American Sociological Review*, 27 (June 1962), 400–402.

COX, HAROLD, and ALBERT BHAK, "Determinants of Age-Based Residential Segregation," *Sociological Symposium*, no. 29 (January 1980), 27–41.

CRIMMINS, EILEEN, and DOMINIQUE G. INGEGNERI, "Interaction and Living Arrangements of Older Parents and Their Children," *Research on Aging*, 12, no. 1 (March 1990), 3–35.

DUNCAN, OTIS D., and BEVERLY DUNCAN, "Residential Distribution and Occupational Stratification," *American Journal of Sociology*, 60 (March 1955), 493–503.

EISENSTADT, S. N., *From Generation to Generation: Age Groups and Social Structure*. New York: Free Press, 1956.

FELDMAN, A. S., and C. TILLY, "The Interaction of Social and Physical Space," *American Sociological Review*, 25 (December 1960), 877–84.

FERRARO, KENNETH F., "The Health Consequences of Relocation Among the Aged in Their Communities," *Journal of Gerontology* (1982), 90–96.

FINKELHOR, DAVID, "Common Features of Family Abuse," in *The Dark Side of Families: Current Family Violence Research*, ed. D. Finkelhor et al. Beverly Hills, Calif.: Sage, 1983.

FOOTE, NELSON, and OTHERS, *Housing Choices and Constraints*. New York: McGraw-Hill, 1960.

FROMM, ERICH, *The Art of Loving*. New York: Bantam, 1963.

GOFFMAN, E., *Asylums*. New York: Doubleday, Anchor, 1961.

GOLANT, STEPHEN M., *The Residential Location and Spatial Behavior of the Elderly*. University of Chicago, Department of Geography, Research Paper No. 143. Chicago, 1972.

GOLDSCHEIDER, CALVIN, *Population, Modernization, and Social Structure*. Boston: Little, Brown, 1971.

GOTTESMAN, L. E., C. E. QUARTERMAN, and G. M. COHN, "Psychosocial Treatment of the Aged," in *The Psychology of Adult Development and Aging*, ed. C. Eisdorfer and M. Lawton, p. 56. Washington, D.C.: American Psychological Association, 1973.

HANSEN, G. D., "Meeting Housing Challenges, Involvement: The Elderly," in *Housing Issues: Proceedings of the Fifth Annual Meeting, American Association of Housing Educators*. Lincoln: University of Nebraska Press, 1971.

HARRIS, CHARLES, *Fact Book on Aging: A Profile of America's Older Population*. Washington, D.C.: National Council on the Aging, 1978.

HARTWIGSEN, GAIL, and ROBERTA NULL, "Full-Timing: A Housing Alernative for Older People," *International Journal of Aging and Human Development*, 29(4) (1989), 317–28.

HOROWITZ, MARVIN, and RICHARD SCHULY, "The Relocation Controversy: Criticism and Commentary on Five Recent Studies," *Gerontologist*, 23, no. 3 (1983), 229–33.

HOYT, G. C., "The Life of the Retired in a Trailer Park," *American Journal of Sociology*, 59 (1954), 361–70.

KALISH, RICHARD A., *Late Adulthood: Perspectives on Human Development*. Monterey, Calif.: Brooks/Cole, 1975.

KROUT, JOHN A., "Seasonal Migration of the Elderly," *Gerontologist*, 23(3) (1983), 295–99.

LAUMANN, E. O., *Prestige and Association in an Urban Community*. Indianapolis: Bobbs-Merrill, 1966.

LAWTON, M. POWELL, "Environment and Other Determinants of Well-Being in Older People," *Gerontologist*, 23, no. 4 (1983).

LAWTON, POWELL, "Social Ecology and the Health of Older People," in *Aging in America: Readings in Social Gerontology*, ed. Cary S. Kart and Barbara B. Manard, p. 320. Sherman Oaks, Calif.: Alfred Publishing, 1976.

LIEBERMAN, M. A., "The Relationship of Mortality Rates to Entrance to a Home for the Aged," *Geriatrics*, 16 (1961), 515–19.

MCKENZIE, R. D., "Spatial Distance and Community Organization Patterns," *Social Forces*, 5 (June 1927), 623–38.

MILLER, SHEILA J., "Segregation of the Aged in American Cities." Unpublished paper, Wichita State University, 1967.

MONTGOMERY, J. E., *Social Characteristics of the Aged in a Small Pennsylvania Community*. College of Home Economics Research Publication no. 233. State College, Pa.: Pennsylvania State University, 1965.

MONTGOMERY, JAMES E., ALICE C. STUBBS, and SAVANNAH S. DAY, "The Housing Environments of the Rural Elderly," *Gerontologist*, 20, no. 4 (1980), 444–51.

O'BRYANT, S. L., and D. NOCERA, "Psychological Significance of 'Home' to Older Widows," *Psychology of Women Quarterly*, Vol. 9 (1985), 403–12.

PARK, R. E., and E. W. BURGESS, *The City*. Chicago: University of Chicago Press, 1925.

PARK, ROBERT E., *Human Communities*. New York: Free Press, 1952.

PETERSON, JAMES A., and CULI E. LARSON, "Socio-Psychological Factors in Selecting Retirement Housing." Revised version of a paper read at the Research Conference on Patterns of Living and Housing of Middle Age and Older People, Washington, D.C., 1972.

REGNIER, VICTOR, "Neighborhood Planning for the Urban Elderly," in *Aging: Scientific Perspectives and Social Issues*, ed. Diana S. Woodruff and James E. Birren. Belmont, Calif.: Wadsworth, 1975.

ROSOW, IRVING, *The Social Integration of the Aged*. New York: Free Press, 1967.

SPENCER, HERBERT, *First Principles*. New York: D. Appleton and Co., 1896.

STEINFELD, EDWARD, JAMES DUNCAN, and PAUL CARDELL, "Toward a Responsive Environment: The Psychosocial Effects of Inaccessiblity," in *Barrier Free Environments*, ed. Michael Bednar. Stroudsburg, Pa.: Dowden, Hutchinson, & Ross, 1977.

TAUMANN, E. O., *Prestige and Association in an Urban Community*. Indianapolis: Bobbs-Merrill, 1966.

THOMPSON, JAMES D., *Organization in Action*. New York: McGraw-Hill, 1967.

WEBER, MAX, *The Theory of Social and Economic Organization*, trans. A. M. Henderson and Talcott Parsons. New York: Oxford University Press, 1947.

WEINER, MARCELLA B., ALBERT J. BROK, and ALVIN M. SANDOWSKY, *Working with the Aged*. Englewood Cliffs, N.J.: Prentice Hall, 1978.

WILTZIUS, FRANCES, and STEVEN GAMBERT, "Importance of Resident Placement Within a Skilled Nursing Facility," *Journal of American Geriatric Society*, 29 (September 1981), 418–21.

ZUSMAN, J., "Some Explanations of the Changing Appearance of Psychiatric Patients," *International Journal of Pscyhiatry*, 4 (1967), 216–37.

NOTES

1. G. D. Hansen, "Meeting Housing Challenges, Involvement: The Elderly," in *Housing Issues: Proceedings of the Fifth Annual Meeting, American Association of Housing Educators* (Lincoln: University of Nebraska Press, 1971).

2. Charles Harris, *Fact Book on Aging: A Profile of America's Older Population* (Washington, D.C.: National Council on the Aging, 1978), p. 185.

3. Ibid.

4. J. E. Montgomery, *Social Characteristics of the Aged in a Small Pennsylvania Community: State College, PA*, College of Home Economics Research Publication no. 233 (State College, Pa.: Pennsylvania State University, 1965).

5. Erich Fromm, *The Art of Loving* (New York: Bantam, 1963).

6. Richard A. Kalish, *Late Adulthood: Perspectives on Human Development* (Monterey, Calif.: Brooks/Cole, 1975), p. 97.

7. R. D. McKenzie, "Spatial Distance and Community Organization Patterns," *Social Forces*, 5 (June 1927), 623–38; Robert E. Park, *Human Communities* (New York: Free Press, 1952); E. O. Laumann, *Prestige and Association in an Urban Community* (Indianapolis: Bobbs-Merrill, 1966).

8. Otis D. Duncan and Beverly Duncan, "Residential Distribution and Occupational Stratification," *American Journal of Sociology*, 60 (March 1955), 493–503.

9. A. S. Feldman and C. Tilly, "The Interaction of Social and Physical Space," *American Sociologial Review*, 25 (December 1960), 877–84.

10. Richard P. Coleman and Bernice L. Neugarten, *Social Status in the City* (San Francisco: Jossey-Bass, 1971).

11. S. N. Eisenstadt, *From Generation to Generation: Age Groups and Social Structure* (New York: Free Press, 1956).

12. Frances Carp, "Life Style and Location Within the City," *Gerontologist*, 15 (February 1975), 27–34.

13. Edward Steinfeld, James Duncan, and Paul Cardell, "Toward a Responsive Environment: The Psychosocial Effects of Inaccessiblity," in *Barrier Free Environnents*, ed. Michael Bednar (Stroudsburg, Pa.: Dowden, Hutchinson, & Ross, 1977).

14. Kalish, *Late Adulthood*, p. 255.

15. F. M. Carp, *A Future for the Aged: Residents of Victoria Plaza, Austin* (Austin: University of Texas Press, 1966).

16. Irving Rosow, *The Social Integration of the Aged* (New York: Free Press, 1967).

17. Powell Lawton, "Social Ecology and the Health of Older People," in *Aging in America: Readings in Social Gerontology*, ed. Cary S. Kart and Barbara B. Manard (Sherman Oaks, Calif.: Alfred Publishing, 1976).

18. G. L. Bultena and V. Wood, "The American Retirement Community: Bane or Blessing?" *Journal of Gerontology*, 24 (1969), 209–17.

19. Lawton, "Social Ecology," p. 317.

20. Victor Regnier, "Neighborhood Planning for the Urban Elderly," in *Aging: Scientific Perspectives and Social Issues*, ed. Diana S. Woodruff and James E. Birren (Belmont, Calif.: Wadsworth, 1975), p. 303.

21. James A. Peterson and Culi E. Larson, "Socio-Psychological Factors in Selecting Retirement Housing" (revised version of a paper read at the Research Conference on Patterns of Living and Housing of Middle Age and Older People, Washington, D.C., 1972), pp. 8–9.

22. Bultena and Wood, "The American Retirement Community."

23. G. C. Hoyt, "The Life of the Retired in a Trailer Park," *American Journal of Sociology*, 59 (1954), 361–70.

24. Harris, *Fact Book on Aging*, p. 183.

25. Ibid., p. 185.

26. Ibid., pp. 192–93.

27. Irving Rosow, "Patterns of Living and Housing of Middle-Aged and Older People," in *Proceedings of Research Conference* (Washington, D.C.: Department of Health, Education and Welfare, 1965), pp. 47–57.

28. Ibid., p. 51.

29. Ibid., p. 56.

30. Ibid., p. 55.

31. L. E. Gottesman, C. E. Quarterman, and G. M. Cohn, "Psychosocial Treatment of the Aged," in *The Psychology of Adult Development and Aging*, ed. C. Eisdorfer and M. Lawton (Washington, D.C.: American Psychological Association, 1973), p. 56.

32. E. Goffman, *Asylums* (New York: Doubleday, Anchor, 1961), p. 1.

33. J. Zusman, "Some Explanations of the Changing Appearance of Psychiatric Patients," *International Journal of Psychiatry*, 4 (1967), 216–37.

34. Marcella B. Weiner, Albert J. Brok, and Alvin M. Sandowsky, *Working with the Aged* (Englewood Cliffs, N.J.: Prentice Hall, 1978), p. 38.

35. Kalish, *Late Adulthood*, p. 110.

36. Max Weber, *The Theory of Social and Economic Organization*, trans. A. M. Henderson and Talcott Parsons, ed. Talcott Parsons (New York: Oxford University Press, 1947), p. 38.

37. James D. Thompson, *Organizations in Action* (New York: McGraw-Hill, 1967), pp. 4–7.

38. Ronald G. Corwin, *Militant Professionalism* (New York: Appleton-Century-Crofts, 1970), p. 63.

39. Kalish, *Late Adulthood*, p. 100.

40. John C. Briggs, "Ecology as Gerontology," *Gerontologist*, 8, no. 2 (1968), 78–79.

41. M. A. Lieberman, "The Relationship of Mortality Rates to Entrance to a Home for the Aged," *Geriatrics*, 16 (1961), 515–19.

42. Jerry H. Borup, Daniel T. Gallego, and Pamela G. Hefferman, "Relocation and Its Effect on Mortality," *Gerontologist*, 19, no. 2 (1979), 135–40.

11

Death and Dying

Epicurus is quoted as having said,

> Thus, that which is the most awful of evils, death, is nothing to us, since when we exist there is no death, and when there is death we do not exist.[1]

Although Epicurus appears to have philosophically accepted death as something that need not concern the living, many people experience some anxiety over the thought of dying and most must find adequate means of coping with this anxiety.

Throughout history, death has been a distinct possibility for all age groups and has commonly occurred at any point in the life cycle. Until the last century the highest percentage of deaths occurred within the first ten years of life. This mortality rate is still found in many primitive cultures throughout the world. Robert Blauner (1966) points out, for example, that

> among the Sakai of the Malay Peninsula, approximately 50 percent of the babies born die before the age of three; among the Kwinai tribe of Australia, 40–50 percent die before the age of 10.
>
> Fifty-nine percent of the male deaths in Nigeria among the "indigenous" blacks were children who had not reached their fifth birthday. Thirty-five percent of an Indian male cohort born in the 1940's died before the age of 10.[2]

The Industrial Revolution, accompanied by an ever-advancing medical technology, has reduced death among children, teenagers, and young adults. Death in industrial societies is most common among those who have retired from work, who have completed their parental responsibilities, and who are beyond the age of 60.

Since death most often occurs among the old in industrial nations, the majority of the adult population have been able to reduce their anxieties and latent fears about it. While people realize that someday they will die, they can control any lingering concerns they may have about death by removing them from the realm of the immediately probable. Thus death is most often thought of as happening to someone who is very old. It is not going to happen to me today, tomorrow, or even next year. Sometime—40, 50, or 60 years from now—I may die, but that's so far off, why worry about it? Thus fear of death in modern society is more easily managed than in the past.

THE IMPACT OF DEATH ON SOCIETY

The death of those who constitute a social group can cause considerable strain as the group attempts to reorganize itself in the absence of the deceased. Methods of coping with the crisis of death can be seen in smaller groupings, such as families, as well as in larger groups, such as work forces and even societies. Blauner (1966) observes that there are complex relationships among how society is organized, how the death crisis is managed, what its death practices are, and how these practices are linked to the social structure.[3]

Blauner observes further that death is most disruptive in primitive and preindustrial societies primarily because of the ages at which its members are most likely to die. Death that strikes the young and those in their adult years seems more devastating to the social order. In these societies death frequently strikes those who are involved in activities that are critical for the society. Thus, replacements must be quickly found and much effort made to reorganize without the deceased, or an entire way of life is likely to be disrupted.

But in the West and most of the industrial societies, as we have noted, death is more likely to occur among the very old. The United States and other Western nations find death highly concentrated among the elderly. These deaths are much less disruptive to the business and productive forces of the society. Some have argued that mandatory retirement is a convenient way of removing older persons from the labor force so that their death will create no disruption in the flow of goods and services.

The general devaluing of the old in American society is often seen as a means of segregating them and thus reducing the significance of their deaths. Robert Hertz (1960) observes a similar pattern in primitive societies:

> Primitive societies hard hit by infant and child mortality characteristically do not recognize infants and children as people; until a certain age they are considered as still belonging to the spirit world from which they came, and therefore their death is often not accorded ritual recognition—no funeral is held.[4]

From a societal perspective it could be argued that the ideal time to die would be when one's family is raised and one's lifework completed. This would cause the minimum disruption in both family life and the economic system.

If one accepts the argument that disengagement is good for older persons since they supposedly no longer have the energy to compete with younger persons, then disengagement could be seen to be desirable for society as well. The disengagement and segregation of older Americans results in the decreasing likelihood of someone dying on the job or in public places. Furthermore, since World War II there has been a growing tendency to remove death from the home and place it in hospitals and nursing homes. The bureaucratization of all the institutions and activities of modern society that Max Weber (1953) so aptly described has now reached the event of death. *Bureaucratization*, as Weber saw it, is a process of ordering and routinizing both everyday and unusual events in order to make all aspects of life as predictable as possible.

Removing death from the home, replacing the church with the funeral parlor, and secularizing beliefs about death seem to be a part of segregating the dying and bureaucratizing the dying process. Death is a traumatic event that tends to arouse strong emotions among the friends and loved ones of the deceased. Bureaucracies usually attempt to keep their personnel and activities functioning as smoothly as possible. All disruptive problems and contingencies are to have a routine method of handling, according to the bureaucratic model. Thus in modern societies that tend to be bureaucratically structured, there is a desire to make the management of death as routine and systematic as possible, with minimum disruption to the social order. Placing the dying in hospitals and nursing homes under the supervision of a professional medical staff rather than keeping them in the home, where many would prefer to die, is just one example of the bureaucratization of death. Removing the deceased from homes and churches and placing them in funeral parlors is another example. William Kephart (1950), in a study of death in Philadelphia, found that 90 percent of funerals occurred in funeral parlors rather than in homes and churches.

Doctors and nurses also tend to avoid and isolate the terminally ill. Le Shan (1964), observing how quickly nurses responded to the service lights of the sick, found that the nurses were much slower in responding to a summons from a patient defined as terminally ill than to calls from patients not so classified.

Many hospitals will go to great lengths to hide the fact that a patient has died. David Sudnow (1967) observes that the hospital morgue is usually on the ground floor with a private loading platform so that the public need not see the departure of the deceased. Similarly, hospitals protect other patients and the public by moving the dying to another room when the end is foreseen and by not removing the body during visiting hours.

It seems that American society has gone far to bureaucratize the process of dying. From families to medical staffs, the sentiment seems to be to isolate the dying and make death as painless as possible and at the same time to minimally disrupt society. Even the modern funeral has tended to become less emotional and eulogistic and more a reading of scriptures that give a philosophic view of death. Some would argue that the bereaved must experience a certain amount of grief before they can adjust to the death of associates and loved ones. But the current routines surrounding death seem to deny any opportunity for the expression of this human emotion. On the other hand, too much emotion can lead to the exaggerated notion that an irreparable tragedy has taken place. Scripture reading can have the virtue of focusing the bereaved on acceptance, reconciliation, and understanding—all of which can help them adjust to their own ultimate encounter with the experience. One of the most unfortunate aspects of the bureaucratization of death in American society is that the dying must spend much of their last few days in isolation.

ATTITUDES TOWARD DEATH

Perhaps the most widespread attitude toward death is fear. All people, however must at some point see their own death as a part of their life and develop some coping mechanisms to deal with this most undesirable reality. Anthropologists often distinguish the sacred and secular aspects of the cultures they are studying. The *sacred* elements of a culture are usually embodied in its religion and are used by its people to explain aspects of reality that they do not fully understand or control. On the other hand, the *secular* elements (often defined as those relating to the material world) are all those aspects of our environment that we can control. While modern science has dramatically increased the secular aspects

Death in the Past

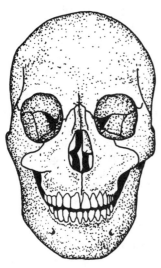

Until the last half of the twentieth century, death was an ever-present part of life. People died at every age, and probably the greatest likelihood of dying occured in the first five years of life.

In the past the aged were most likely to be living with their extended family. Children and grand-children knew them on a personal, intimate basis.

Death Today

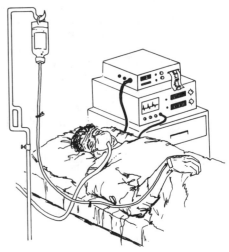

Modern medical technology can now control most of the diseases that killed young people. In modern industrial societies the highest death rate is among the old, so we think that only the old die. Today we see sickness and death as emotionless, sterile, efficient, controlled, and occurring in hospitals.

Old people today live in their own homes. When they become too frail, they are moved to retirement homes or nursing homes. They are not an intimate part of the extended family. They are more likely to be seen as distant relatives who show up at holidays and bring presents.

Death in the Past

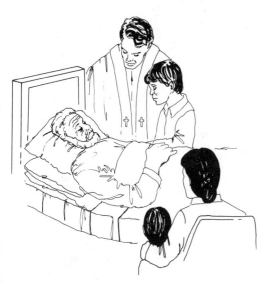

In the past death was most likely to occur in the home. When the elderly were living with their children, the entire family was aware and prepared for the impending death.

Death Today

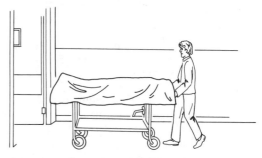

Death today is most likely to occur in a hospital or nursing home. Although most people would prefer to die at home in familiar surroundings, this rarely occurs. Death today is often a lonely event.

In the past the body of the deceased remained in the home, and visitation by friends and family took place there. On the day of the funeral the body was removed to the church for the last rites.

Today the body of the deceased goes directly to the funeral home, where it is prepared for public visitation and the last rites. It remains in the funeral home until it is moved to the burial ground.

of our culture and reduced the sacred, life and death seem to be aspects of reality that defy scientific explanation. Bronislaw Malinowski (1948) believes that hope for a life after death is the only thing that makes the fear of death manageable. Religion reduces the fear of death, for most people, by offering the hope of eternal life:

> Religion steps in, selecting the positive creed, the comforting view, the culturally valuable belief in immortality in the spirit of the body and in the continuance of life after death.[5]

Throughout much of a person's life, death seems remote. Thus, one's anxieties, fears, and apprehensions are kept at the subconscious level of the mind. C. W. Wahl's (1959) view is that death is the cessation of being:

> Death as a cessation of being involves aspects of reality inadmissible to the omnipotent and narcissistic self and for that reason strong defenses are developed against its recognition.[6]

We humans seem to continually develop defense mechanisms by which we psychologically insulate ourselves from the reality of death. We regularly emphasize the accidental causes of death, such as disease, mishaps, or advancing age, and demote death from a necessary reality to a mere accident. More realistically, death, like birth, is a part of life that each individual must experience.

One event that arouses all the latent fears of death is the loss of a close friend or relative. Here we not only feel the loss of a loved one but also come face to face with the fact that all lives must end. All of our fears are brought to the conscious level.

Another event that breaks down our defenses toward death is assassination of a well-known public figure. This was the case with the death of John F. Kennedy. When the President—the most powerful national figure, with whom we have all in some way identified—is cut down in his prime, we cannot help but be aware of how thin the thread is that ties each of us to mortal life. The public reaction to the Kennedy assassination was a reflection of the trauma that death produces among the living. Mourning a well-known public figure or a loved one may be motivated in part by the recognition that someday we too must die.[7] A part of us mourns the deceased, another part of us mourns the fact that someday we must die.

A study by Robert Smith, Martin Sherman, and Nancy Sherman (1982–83) perhaps best illustrates the almost universal fear of death. These researchers asked a sample of young and older persons if they would be willing to assist with a number of volunteer activities for a person with a broken leg and a person dying of cancer. Both the young and the old in this sample preferred to avoid assisting the person dying of cancer, which they perceived would be stressful. While the fear of death appears universal, Jane Myers, Hannalor Wass, and Milledge Murphy (1980) found variation in the degree of fear expressed by different groups. Black elderly males displayed the greatest anxiety, followed by black females, white females, and white males. The researchers offered no logical explanation for this variation.

The acceptance of death is considered a mark of true maturity. Frances Jeffers and Adrian Verwoerdt (1969), in a study of how the old face death, categorized the different ways that people view death. They found that some people viewed it as the cessation of this life but also as a steppingstone to another life. Others viewed it as an enemy that was disrupting their life pattern. Another group saw death as an opportunity for reunion with departed friends and relatives. Some saw death in terms of reward or punishment—as a transition to a better state if they had lived their life well or to a worse state if they had lived poorly. Others were sincerely curious about death. Its unknown, uncertain nature seemed to intrigue them. A final group saw death with a sort of resignation. They believed that death was the end and that there was nothing to follow.

Jeffers and Verwoerdt (1969) found six different mechanisms people use to cope with their fear of death:

1. Strong religious beliefs
2. Acceptance derived from positive relationships with one's children and grandchildren, which connect one's family with the next generation and thus give meaning to one's life
3. Inheritance planning, which shows an acceptance of death (Not planning might indicate superstition—for example, the belief that making out a will brings about an early death.)
4. Denial of impending death through rationalization, suppression, and extenuation (treating death as of small importance)
5. Retreat from the source of the anxiety. This may take the form of avoiding other people and declining social roles and responsibilities, thereby protecting oneself from the painful loss of significant others. Drugs or alcohol may be used to insulate oneself from the pain.
6. Mastery of death through attempted resolution of the crisis. This may take the form of counterphobic mechanisms; attempts to appear young; hyperactivity (becoming so involved in life and engaged in so many social roles that there is no time to think about death); introspection and review of one's life in order to develop a sense of self-meaning so that both successes and failures can be realistically accepted.

In terms of realistic acceptance of death, Wendell Swenson (1961) found that persons with more fundamental religious convictions looked forward to death more than those who have less fundamental religious beliefs. Persons residing in nursing homes have more positive, forward-looking attitudes than those who live alone. Nursing home residents regularly see their friends die. They can also see some of those around them linger on when death would be less painful. Therefore, they are more inclined to accept death as a desirable end for many older persons. Less educated persons in the Swenson study were more likely to be evasive about death, which probably indicates an inability to resolve the anxieties surrounding death. Widowed persons were more likely than single, separated, or married persons to evade the issue of death. Why widows would be more fearful of death is difficult to explain. Those persons who indicated they had a large number of outside interests tended to be actively evasive about death. It would appear that older persons who feel they have much to live for would like to avoid the reality of their own death. Those who report good health are most often actively evasive about death, while those who report poor health look forward to death in a more positive manner.

Scientific studies of the effect of a person's religious beliefs on his or her attitude toward death are inconclusive. While most studies report that religious convictions tend to reduce one's fear of death, Alexander and Adlerstein (1960), in their studies on the psychology of death, report that manifest anxiety about death is found to be significantly higher among the religious. Frances C. Jeffers, Claude Nichols, and Carl Eisdorfer (1961), on the other hand, report that fear of death seemed to be more pronounced in those who consider themselves nonreligious. Among the respondents in their study, 77 percent stated they were sure of an afterlife, 21 percent stated they were not sure, and 2 percent said there was no afterlife. Apparently, many of the self-described nonreligious still believe in afterlife. In any event, it may be wrong to jump to the conclusion that belief in an afterlife will alter one's fear of death.

Assuming that the acceptance of one's death is a sign of emotional maturity, is the choice that one might make about when one will die also a sign of maturity? The following is an illustration of the choice that one couple made about their own death:

> The woman was dying of cancer. Her husband did not want to live without her. They borrowed a car from their neighbor, parked it behind their house and ran a hose from the exhaust pipe into one of the windows. With rags they sealed themselves inside, airtight, and started the engine. In the note they left behind they promised not to leave the motor running. They didn't. As soon as the car was filled with carbon monoxide, they turned off the engine.[8]

The prevailing ethical and religious values in American culture tend to encourage one to view suicide as an irrational and unpardonable act committed by persons who are emotionally distraught. One is not inclined to think of a suicide being committed by a person who has carefully analyzed the circumstances of his or her life and concluded that death is the most reasonable choice available. In the preceding example the husband apparently felt that to continue living without his wife would be meaningless. Therefore, to him death was the most reasonable choice.

THE MEANING OF DEATH

Our forebears had an unwavering belief in a kind of personal afterlife, a concept of eternity as sacred time. Death to them was always accompanied by the possibility of atonement and salvation.

Modern society, having become more secular, has seen the waning of the traditional belief in personal immortality and of the transcendent significance of death. For many people death is not a transition to an afterlife but rather the end of the line. For these persons death has become a wall rather than a door. It is often seen as a loss of identity, an extinction.

In a society that emphasizes the importance of the future, the prospect of no future is to some people an abomination. For such people, death and dying invite hostility, recrimination, and denial.

American culture has attempted to cope with death by disguising it and pretending it does not exist. Those with strong religious convictions speak of the deceased as passing on or joining their ancestors. To those without religious conviction this is euphemistic language; they believe we should speak of the deceased merely as dead.

Robert Kastenbaum (1991), in attempting to explain all the possible meanings of death, discusses four different views of it. The first is that death is the great leveler. Though all societies are stratified and offer different rewards for those considered to be of greater or lesser importance, death terminates all such distinctions. The rich and the poor, the powerful and the weak, the lord and the servant—all eventually die. In Kastenbaum's view, death warns those who set themselves above others to keep their pride and ambition within limits.

In opposition to this view is that of death as the great validator. Death from this view confirms the status or distinction of the individual while alive. Thus, the rich have elaborate funerals with much ceremony and many expensive trappings; the poor have much more humble funerals. Burial plots themselves are often more or less expensive to purchase. That many cities have cemeteries in which blacks and whites are buried in different places reflects a belief in death as a validator of one's existence.

The third view of death is that it is a radical alteration of one's relationships. One part of this change consists in a reunion with deceased relatives and friends. This reflects the desire to be rejoined with people from one's life who have gone before. The other part of the change consists in one's separation from living friends and loved ones. Knowledge of one's impending death may prove painful for the individual or loved ones because of the implicit separation.

In the fourth view, death is the ultimate solution or the ultimate problem. Both at the individual and group levels, annihilation of the perceived opponent can be one solution to a situation of prolonged stress or conflict. Thus one individual may take another's life as well as his own, and nations go to war against other nations. On the other hand, the view of death as the ultimate problem can be seen in the feeling that death can threaten society as a whole. Death is an end of one's opportunity to experience, to achieve, and to exist.

That death has such paradoxical meanings is a reflection of its defiance of intellectual understanding and explanation. Many individuals embrace different views of death at different points in time, not realizing the inconsistency of their thoughts on the matter.

Regardless of the meaning one attaches to death, whether religious or nonreligious, whether in the context of an afterlife or not, one must come with age to accept the reality of one's own impending death. At any age in life there may be adjustments that have to be made to death. Sometimes the individual must face the death of friends and loved ones, sometimes the effect of his or her own death on loved ones.

Victor W. Marshall (1975) found that most of the residents of Glen Brae, a retirement community, had come to accept and even legitimize their impending death. In discussing the legitimation of death, Marshall states that

> All legitimations of death must carry out the same essential task—they must enable the individual to go on living in society after the death of significant others and to anticipate his own death with, at the very least, terror sufficiently mitigated so as not to paralyze the continued performance of the routines of everyday life.[9]

Marshall gives examples of the manner in which Glen Brae's residents have come to legitimize their own death. An 81-year-old widow, when asked how old she wanted to live to be, answered,

> Heavens! I've lived my life. I'd be delighted to have it end. The sooner the better. I nearly went with a heart attack. It would have been more convenient to go when my daughter was in _____ rather than in _____. I feel I've lived my life and I don't want to be a care to anybody. That's why I'm glad to be here [Glen Brae]. No, I don't want to mourn when I go. I've had a good life. It's time.[10]

Of 79 residents at Glen Brae who were asked if they would like to live to be 100, none gave an unconditional "yes." Nineteen residents gave conditional "yes" answers, the conditions most often being good health and the absence of a burden on others. Sixty of the residents answered with an unconditional "no." One resident responded to the question of whether it would be desirable to live to be 100 by saying,

> No point, I have no one to depend on me. And I've looked after the few descendants I have. And I haven't any great problem to resolve.[11]

Arlie Hochschild (1972) believes that the acceptance of death by older persons is often a process of role modeling in which they see their friends and acquaintances die and come to realize how it will be for them. The legitimation of death for older persons often involves the acceptance of a shared system of meanings regarding the importance of life and death. Peter Berger and Thomas Luckmann (1967) maintain that the legitimation of death, like any other process, is best accomplished by the expression and sharing of attitudes, values, and beliefs among members of the group. Having significant others to discuss death with seems critical to the acceptance and legitimation of one's own death. For values and meanings about significant life events to become accepted, they must be shared.

CRITICAL QUESTIONS ABOUT DEATH

Human anxiety about death has made it difficult to discuss rationally when, where, why, and how people die. The prevailing attitude of the general public seems to be that one should cling to life as long and as desperately as possible. Suicide by a friend or loved one is most often met with shock and disbelief by the living.

Reconciliation

Arnold Toynbee and colleagues (1976), in discussing the various ways people have come to reconcile themselves to death, see two basic methods in which people attempt to resolve their fears. The first, *hedonism*, involves enjoying life as much as possible before death snatches it from us. "Let us eat, drink, and be merry, for tomorrow we may die" best expresses this philosophy. The problem Toynbee sees with hedonism is that instead of leading to a good life it often leads to anxieties, fatigues, and maladies that if severe and drawn out long enough may actually make the person look forward to death.

The second philosophical approach to the resolution of death is pessimism. Basically, pessimists conclude that life is so wretched that death is the lesser evil. The Greek poet Sophocles wrote that "it is best to have never been born, but second best to go back again as quickly as possible to whence one has come."[12]

Suicide

One indicator of pessimism might be suicide. If life is of such little value, then suicide might be an acceptable means of ending it. In some instances one might consider suicide meritorious. While no stigma was attached to suicide in the Greco-Roman world, the practice was not nearly as common as it has been in East Asian countries.

Hindu society practiced a form of suicide called *suttee*, by which it was deemed meritorious for a widow to immolate herself on her husband's funeral pyre. During the Vietnam War, Buddhist monks and nuns burned themselves to death as a form of political protest.

Christianity, of Jewish origin and firmly planted in the Greco-Roman world, has always been strongly opposed to suicide. Christians have generally deprived suicides of burial in consecrated ground. For Christians death is exclusively God's prerogative, and hence human intervention is wrong. The Christian prohibition of suicide discourages the terminally ill from considering taking their own lives to avoid further pain. As Toynbee and colleagues (1976) state,

> the Christian inhibition against suicide applies, a fortiori, to giving incurably and painfully ailing human beings the merciful release that humane Christians give, as a matter of course, to animals when they are in the same plight.[13]

Medical doctors who are fully aware of the patient's terminal disease are often put in the awkward position of deciding whether to give the patient just enough drugs to relieve the pain without harm, or to give the patient the means to end his or her life. Thus a doctor, upon visiting a patient who was dying and in pain, disseminated four pills to the patient with the instruction "These pills will relieve your pain if you take one every four hours. Do not, however, take all four of them at once or they will kill you." The doctor by prescribing the four pills has been ethical in attempting to alleviate the patient's suffering. Simultaneously, however, the doctor has made it possible for the patient to end his or her own life, which is not considered ethical or consistent with the Hippocratic oath that commits doctors to assist the patient to good health. Dr. Jack Kevorkian of Pontiac, Michigan, was charged with murder when he assisted Janet Adkins, a dying patient, in using his suicide machine which allowed her to administer an injection of a lethal drug to herself. The court dismissed the murder charge against Dr. Kevorkian stating that Michigan has no law against assisted suicide. The judge, however, did order Dr. Kevordian never to use or make available to other patients his suicide machine. This case indicates the ambiguity of the law and the judicial system on the matter of assisted suicide.[14]

Euthanasia

The word *euthanasia* in a more traditional interpretation means dying without pain or suffering. Today it has come to mean the deliberate shortening of a person's life to relieve suffering. Modern American society, heavily imprinted with Judeo-Christian traditions, has approached the subject of euthanasia (mercy killing) with considerable anguish and trepidation. David Jorgenson and Ronald Neubecker (1980), in a study of attitudes toward euthanasia, found that persons with strong religious convictions were more likely to believe that life should be maintained regardless of its condition. The termination of life by any means or for any reason is still considered to be God's province. There is some inconsistency in this logic, in that few oppose the use of medical technology to save or prolong life, which would seem to be equally an invasion of God's province. Thus the prevailing view seems to be that prolongation of life, in whatever state, is the province of humans (aided by medical technology) but the ending of life is God's province. In the United States, laws prohibit killing for any reason, whether merciful or malicious.

The capacity of medical technology to prolong physical life long after the individual is unconscious and when he or she has no hope of improvement has forced the subject of euthanasia into the world's consciousness. Modern proponents of euthanasia have raised the following questions:

1. Should stroke victims whose brains function only at an autonomic (nonvoluntary) level, and who have no hope of improving, have their lives terminated in the most merciful way available?

2. Should a severely defective fetus be aborted medically if it does not abort spontaneously?

3. Should profoundly retarded persons who are totally dependent on others for all their needs have their lives terminated mercifully?

4. Should persons suffering from advanced senility who have no hope of recovery have their lives terminated in the most merciful way available?[15]

While the question of euthanasia applies to persons at every age, it is likely to apply most frequently to older Americans, who find themselves in various states of declining health.

The proponents of euthanasia are increasing. Wayne Sage (1978) found that 77 percent of the members of the American Association of Professors of Medicine favored the practice. Fifty-four percent of a sample of college students accepted the idea. The only ones against euthanasia were patients themselves; most of a sample of nursing home patients wanted to be allowed to die normally.

There are basically three kinds of euthanasia: passive, active, and voluntary. In passive euthanasia you know the patient is going to die if he or she is not placed on the resuscitator but you do nothing and allow the patient to die. In active euthanasia you know the patient is in pain and is ultimately going to die, and you either give the patient a lethal dose of a drug or injection or allow the patient to give it to himself or herself. In voluntary euthanasia the patient asks to be taken off all machines or medication and to disconnect all of the medical support systems.

To safeguard against abuses of voluntary euthanasia, proponents of the practice have suggested that any forthcoming legislation on the matter requires that the patient, who must be over 21 years old, give his or her consent, and that the agent of euthanasia be a physician who shall have consulted with another physician or some specified authority. Some would argue for a minimum period between the request for euthanasia and the act itself, during which the patient could change his or her mind.

The proponents of legislation allowing euthanasia argue that it is cruel to prolong intense suffering in someone who is mortally ill and desires to die. They argue further that a person has the right to decide whether he or she should continue to live and that such a decision can be reached after rationally weighing the benefits of continued life against the suffering involved.

The opponents of euthanasia argue against any change in the current law. First, they doubt that acts of killing would always truly be merciful for the patients requesting them. Second, they argue that a patient's desire for a merciful death might justify suicide and the withholding of life-prolonging treatment but not an act of killing. They argue further that very few people would actually be helped by new legislation, since those not competent to make the decision (because of the psychological effects of pain, medication, or whatever even over age 21, would not be allowed to request euthanasia). Finally, they warn against abuses and errors that might result from a relaxation of the present strong prohibition against killing.

Ruth Russel, in *Freedom to Die* (1975), has proposed the following solutions to the difficulties of euthanasia:

1. Ratification of a constitutional amendment that would recognize the right to death in addition to the rights to life, liberty, and the pursuit of happiness.

2. Amendment of the suicide laws so as to allow a doctor to provide the patient with the means to end life (this, of course, would not help the unconscious, paralyzed, or mentally deficient).

3. Amendment of the criminal code so that euthanasia would not be defined as murder. Euthanasia could then be considered a compassionate rather than a criminal act.

4. Contest, through litigation, the right of the state to deny a person the right to euthanasia.

5. Inclusion in the definition of death the state of brain death. This would allow euthanasia to be administered to persons who could never recover from an illness or deformity that had reduced them to a passive physical state.

6. Enactment of a euthanasia law that would protect from prosecution for murder those doctors who performed passive euthanasia by not prescribing life-sustaining medicine for a patient who is not of "testamentary capacity."

7. Legalization of active euthanasia for a patient who had made a written declaration for euthanasia.

The critical point of the euthanasia debate for older Americans is the question of when a person should be allowed to die. Mostafa Nagi and Neil Lazerine (1982) report that the clergy they sampled believed that patients fear a prolonged illness more than death itself. Similarly, most do not want to be a burden to their families. Lingering illnesses tend to drain the family both financially and emotionally.

Victor Marshall (1975) quotes some residents of Glen Brae on how they would prefer to die:

1. "I hope . . . when the end comes, it'll be snappy. You know, I know one person here who carries a cyanide pill with him. . . . I think he dreads a terrible siege."

2. "I hope when the time comes it will come fast. I've given the doctors instructions that way."

3. "I'd just like to go to sleep and never wake up. Kind of cowardly but I haven't anyone to say goodbye to."[16]

Aware of the nearness of their death, they want their dying to be of no trouble to themselves or anyone else.

The physician is often left with an impossible dilemma in serving older patients. In most states, to remove an intravenous tube from a dying patient is currently defined as murder. The act of not inserting it in the first place is not defined as murder. Dr. Christiaan Barnard (1986) notes another irony:

> In a nation where doctors may, through abortion, end what could be a productive life, they would be charged with murder for doing so where hope no longer exists.[17]

Changing Public Attitudes toward Euthanasia

As a general rule state legislatures have been reluctant to move very rapidly in changing laws related to euthanasia. Politicians frequently lag behind public opinion on controversial issues out of their desire to avoid conflict and thereby be reelected. They cannot, however, lag too far behind public opinion or that in itself becomes a problem for them. A recent Times Mirror Center survey (1990) indicates considerably more acceptance by the public for the practice of euthanasia than anyone might have believed. Some of the more interesting results of this survey are as follows:

1. Eight out of ten Americans agree that there are circumstances when a person should be allowed to die.

2. Six out of seven persons believe that people have the right to make their own decisions about receiving life-sustaining treatment.

3. Seventy-five percent of the respondents agreed that the closest family member should be able to decide whether or not to continue medical treatment for a terminally ill person who is not able to communicate and whose wishes were not known in advance.

4. Seven out of ten people believe that it is sometimes justified for a person to kill his or her spouse because he or she was suffering terrible pain from a terminal disease.

5. Eight out of ten people believe that medical treatment for a terminally ill patient should be withdrawn or withheld if that is what the patient wishes.

The public seems to be moving in a direction of accepting voluntary euthanasia. The last few years have seen several state legislatures legalize living wills, which indicates they are moving in the same directions as the general public on this issue.

One area of some disagreement between the older patient and the general public was on the issue of the person being a burden on the family. Many older people state that they don't want life-sustaining measures taken on their behalf if they are terminally ill or a burden on their family. By an eight to five margin, the respondents indicated the person had a right to end his or her life if he or she were terminal and in pain. On the other hand, two out of three respondents felt that the individual had no right to end his or her life because it has become burdensome on oneself or one's family.

The Times Mirror Center survey (1990) indicates that there is general movement toward rejecting the view that every possible effort must be made to sustain life under all circumstances. Moreover, an increasing number of people believe that individuals should have the opportunity to state their preferences and participate in making life and death decisions that directly affect them.

Critical Questions for Older Patients

Richard Kalish (1965) has discussed the inevitable questions that older persons, their families, and their doctors must ultimately decide. The first of these is where to die. While most older people would prefer to die in their homes amid familiar surroundings, as observed earlier in this chapter, the trend has been for more and more of them to die in hospitals and nursing homes. This undoubtedly has come about partly because hospitals and nursing homes are better equipped to deal with the dying person. Simultaneously, however, it removes from the family the considerable strain of caring for a dying family member in the home. Because of this strain, most families probably prefer that a terminally ill older member not remain in the home. Kalish quotes one highly emotional housewife who exclaimed that she would never be able to live in her home again if her aged father died there.

Thus while the elderly most often prefer to die at home in the presence of loved ones, among their possessions, they are not likely to be allowed to do so. A variety of medical, family, and financial pressures often result in a decision to allow them to die in hospitals and nursing homes. Marty Zusman and Paul Tschetter (1984) point out that to die at home requires substantial resources including money, time, and space. They found that the well-to-do were sometimes allowed to die at home because of their private health insurance, money, and private control. Those less well off who wanted to die at home had to rely on medicaid and family support. Many simply could not afford the luxury of dying at home.

A second critical question is whether older patients have a right to know when they are dying. Some argue that they should be informed of their condition. This, it is felt, will lead to a more natural relationship between the patient and friends and loved ones, since no one will have to pretend that everything is all right and the patient is going to recover. Simultaneously, it allows the patient some time to make final preparations for death—dispensing property, arranging finances and otherwise planning for family members. Others believe, however, that the patient should be protected against such knowledge, which might close out hope and perhaps hasten death. They feel that many patients simply would not be able to adjust to the knowlege of their impending death, and that instead of giving them time to make any final arrangements that knowledge would merely put them in a state of depression during their final days.

The final question for the older patient, according to Kalish (1965), is "At what point do you cease to be yours?" In other words, "When are you no longer responsible for what is happening to you?" At some point many dying patients become either semiconscious or unconscious. Inevitably, decisions have to be made by family members or medical personnel regarding the effort to be made to keep the patient alive. The physician's ability to reduce discomfort through sedation sometimes results in a vegetablelike existence for the patient.

Our knowledge of how to prolong life has resulted in the ultimate question of when it is unwise to prolong it further. Earl MacQuarrie's story is an example of the decision that must sometimes be made regarding this question. Earl was admitted to the hospital to undergo open-heart surgery. Shortly after receiving a blood transfusion to build him up for the surgery, Earl suffered a stroke. The stroke was a serious one which dramatically altered Earl's state of health. In his current condition, his doctors knew that they could not operate with any reasonable hope of success. After carefully examining Earl for the next 48 hours, the doctors advised Earl's wife that they could probably keep him alive for six months to a year with respirators and other machines that would assist his body in all functions. On the other hand, if they did nothing other than sedate him, he would die within a week. The doctors left the decision of whether or not to put Earl on the life-sustaining medical equipment to his wife. Earl's wife bravely recommended that Earl be allowed to die naturally with no special efforts made by doctors to prolong his life. Earl died four days later.

ADJUSTMENTS TO DYING

Each individual at various times in life develops various means of coping with the inevitability of his or her own death. Most people, while recognizing the finiteness of mortal life, still consciously or subconsciously resist information that suggests that their death is imminent. What happens to people who are told that the time has come and that they are dying?

Elisabeth Kubler-Ross (1969), in working very closely with dying patients, concluded that people go through five stages in attempting to adjust to their death. The first of these is denial. People refuse to believe they are dying and attempt to insulate themselves from anyone or anything that indicates they are dying. The second stage involves the gradual recognition that they are dying: They can no longer deny the evidence, and they become angry and resentful. Many questions arise, most of which center in the theme, "Why is this happening to me?" The third stage of adjustment is an attempt to postpone the inevitable. People bargain with their maker, asking (consciously or subconsciously), "If I do such-and-such, God, will you let me live?" In the fourth stage a sense of depression and loss sets in. People have come to realize that they are dying and that there is nothing they can do to bypass the inevitable. The fifth stage is acceptance, in which one attempts to utilize the remaining time to set one's affairs in order.

While Kubler-Ross is to be credited with pioneering work on the adjustments of the dying, certain questions are being raised about her work. Some gerontologists wonder whether each patient must go through these five stages in exactly the manner Kubler-Ross predicted and whether each patient must go through all of them. Others wonder whether the stages have been adequately examined and empirically tested for their accuracy. Whether they are accurate or not, it would be a mistake to expect every single dying person to progress through them in a timely, predictable manner.

The problem of adjustment to dying is first of all a problem for the dying, but it is secondly a problem for those who must interact with them therapeutically or socially. Doctors and nurses have been trained primarily to save and prolong life. To them, the dying person may represent a failure of their science. Moreover, professionals who have not resolved their own anxiety about death may avoid the dying patient because of that anxiety.

When informed of the results of the Le Shan (1964) study, nurses were surprised to learn how much longer it took them to respond to the calls of the terminal patients. Wilber Watson (1976), in a study of nursing homes, found that 90 percent of dying patients were placed in the rooms farthest from service, office, or assistance centers. Similarly Kubler-Ross (1969), in a study of senior medical students, found that the students complained that the physicians avoided the terminally ill on their rounds. Avoidance of the dying is one way of insulating oneself from both a sense of powerlessness to help and the inevitability of death as a part of life.

Family members' adjustment to the knowledge that a loved one is dying is similar to that of the dying person. Shock and disbelief are common early reactions. How can this be true? Often family members deny the facts of the diagnosis and shop around for a doctor who might give a different diagnosis. Some turn to fortunetellers and faith healers. They may take the patient to expensive clinics. Ultimately, if the second opinion is the same as the first one, they must accept reality.

Ideally the physician, the family, and the patient should be able to discuss the patient's dying in a meaningful, sympathetic, and supportive manner. This, however, depends on the acceptance by all three of the dying person's condition. If the family and the dying person, or the doctor and the dying person, try to keep this condition a secret from each other, the resulting barrier between them will make it more difficult for both. Kubler-Ross (1969) believes that the patient and the family will both be able to adjust to, and deal more realistically with, a problem that they can openly discuss.

Avery Weisman (1976) believes that the doctor is crucial to the patient's acceptance of his or her death. He argues that if the doctor has a misconception of death, it may distort the dying patient's image of death. Weisman lists seven widespread fallacies about death that he has found:

1. Only suicidal and psychotic people are willing to die. Even when death is inevitable, no one wants to die.

2. Fear of death is the most natural and basic fear of man. The closer one comes to death, the more intense the fear becomes.

3. Reconciliation with death and preparation for death are impossible; therefore one should say as little as possible about it to dying people, turn their questions aside, and use means to deny, to dissimulate, and to avoid open confrontation.

4. Dying people do not really want to know what the future holds, otherwise they would ask more questions. To force a discussion or to insist on unwelcome information is risky. The patient might lose all hope. He might com-

mit suicide, become depressed, or even die more quickly.

5. After speaking with family members, the doctor should treat the patient as long as possible. Then, when further benefit seems unlikely, the patient should be left alone, except for relieving pain. He will then withdraw and die in peace, without further disturbance and anguish.

6. It is reckless, if not downright cruel, to inflict unnecessary suffering on the patient or his family. The patient is doomed; nothing can really make any difference. Survivors should accept the futility but realize that they will get over the loss.

7. Physicians can deal with all phases of the dying process because of their scientific training and clinical experience. The emotional and psychological sides of dying are vastly overemphasized. Consultation with psychologists and social workers is necessary. The clergy might be called upon but only because death is near. The doctor has no further obligation after the patient's death.[18]

These fallacies, according to Weisman, become reasons for not getting involved with the dying. Weisman believes that the first three are used to justify withdrawal and the establishment of more distance between doctor and patient. The fourth implies that the patient doesn't want to talk about death. The fifth and sixth presume that the patient is not responsible; the patient's silence suggests ignorance and complacency. The final fallacy assumes that physicians are all-knowing about both their own feelings and those of their patients. Weisman argues that the professional must deal with fallacies such as these and treat each dying patient as an individual, not as a member of a stereotyped group.

The rapidly expanding hospice movement in Western Europe and the United States advocates caring for the terminally ill in a humane manner. Hospices aim at (1) lightening the burden for both the dying patient and his or her family, (2) helping the patient maintain dignity, and (3) minimizing the trauma for remaining family members. Lynette Jordan (1977) advocates hospices as special places for treating the terminally ill that constitute an alternative to allowing them to die in their homes or in hospitals. A specially trained staff assists the terminally ill person psychologically, spiritually, and personally.

St. Christopher's Hospice in London is considered a model of its kind. The staff attempts to care for not only the patient's physical, psychological, and spiritual needs but also the needs of family members. Each patient at St. Christopher's controls his or her own intake of drugs so as to remain an integrated and functioning individual as long as possible. The length of stay at St. Christopher's is two to three weeks on the average; 16 percent die about 26 hours after admission.

GRIEF

The death of a friend, lifelong spouse, or other loved one is difficult to accept. One's sense of powerlessness can be heightened since obviously one was unable to prevent the death. The feeling of powerlessness is accompanied by a sense of loneliness, loss, and social isolation. These are the beginnings of the human emotion called grief.

Grief is best described as a physiological, psychological, and sociological reaction to loss. Physiologically, the individual may suffer from crying spells, upset stomach, headaches, fainting, diarrhea, and profuse sweating. Psychologically, the individual goes through various stages of adjustment to the loss, ranging from disbelief to despair. Sociologically, family and friends may grieve together for the deceased and thus share the experience. The social significance of the event may be the most far-reaching. A wife is a widow, a husband a widower; the company is without an employee, the city council without a member. In one or another way the entire world is changed by every death.

That grief is difficult for those who experience it can be seen in the results of a study by Bernard Benjamin and Chris Wallis (1963) on the mortality of widows and widowers. The six months immediately following the death of a wife was followed by a 40 percent increase in the death rate of a sample of adult men. The death rate then returned to that of married men. Apparently the shock of widowhood weakens resistance to other causes of death. Howard Becker (1933), discussing bereavement, says

> The sorrow of love is ever attached to the beloved object, and in diverse ways, strives to maintain all that remains of the former union.[19]

Persons experiencing grief tend to go through somewhat predictable responses as they attempt to adjust. These include protest, despair, detachment, and reorganization. The protest reaction immediately follows the death and includes the emotions of denial, disbelief, and anger. This is often accompanied by a feeling of numbness, weeping, and bodily complaints.

The next stage is despair, characterized by considerable restlessness, disorganization, and searching. The restless behavior is characterized by pacing or walking in a disorganized manner. The individual searches for the lost person for a variety of reasons. For example, there is a need to confirm that the person is gone, and a need to use the lost person as the basis for one's grief.

Detachment is the stage in which the bereaved begins to pull back from the lost person. The bereaved has now begun to recognize the reality of his or her loss. Some of the former ties are now beginning to be broken; energies are beginning to be directed to other areas of concern. Often the bereaved will withdraw from others and from everyday duties. This period of being alone is a time for doing one's final grieving. It is often a time of forgetfulness; the bereaved may go to the store and forget why he or she went. However, these are the grieving person's attempts to return to normal tasks and should not be viewed negatively.

The final stage of adjustment to the loss of a loved one is reorganization. A sign that reorganization has occurred is the ability of the grieving person to talk about the lost person without severe emotional upheaval. The ability to remember the deceased in favorable terms without continual crying is another sign of final adjustment. The individual will at this time begin to return to former roles, including job, social groups, and community activities. W. M. Lamers (1969) has observed the therapeutic value that funerals have for helping the bereaved person resolve grief.[20] While grief may eventually be resolved, many bereaved maintained persistent ties of affection for their deceased partners, sometimes for years after their death (Moss & Moss, 1984–85).

The time necessary for grieving is difficult to determine and obviously subject to individual differences. Grieving is complete when the person returns to a normal living pattern with no lingering guilt. Many people in the United States today feel that one year is an appropriate time, and that "heavy" decisions— selling one's house and moving, remarrying, or taking a job (or changing jobs)— should be postponed for at least that long after the death of a spouse. Hurried decisions during the grieving period are often wrong decisions.

For most people today, dying takes place over a longer period than in the past. This causes numerous problems for family members and the patient. During a long illness a family member grieves as a mother is taken from the home to the hospital; the husband and children grieve because they have lost a wife and mother. Such grief over the impending loss of a loved one is called *anticipatory grief.* K. C. Aldrich (1974), in comparing anticipatory and conventional grief, says,

> Conventional grief can be prolonged indefinitely. Anticipatory grief, on the other hand, has a finite endpoint dependent on external circumstances of the physical occurrences of the anticipated loss. Also, conventional grief decelerates or diminishes in degree as time passes, while anticipatory grief theoretically should accelerate.[21]

A period of anticipatory grief may also produce feelings of guilt, however, and thereby complicate the working-through process. The individual who anticipates the death of a loved one may experience considerable emotional strain. Prolonged illness in which death is anticipated and considerable grieving occurs beforehand may result in the family being "all grieved out" by the time of the death. While social custom demands further grieving, the family may feel only relief. Kenneth Doka (1984–85) found that expectation of death was significantly related to subsequent grief adjustment.

The grieving person can be considerably aided by friends and family. David Maddison and Wendy Walker (1967) found that the widows who made the best adjustment to the death of a spouse were those who perceived their social environment as an active and helpful one. Widows without a supportive social network experienced greater difficulty with their grief.

Some societies have developed formal customs to help the grieving person recover from his or her loss. The "Irish wake" involved much ceremony surrounding the burial and was followed by a period of drinking and brawling (Kane, 1968). This was a time of considerable social support for the grieving individual. More recently the United States has seen the emergence of widow-to-widow programs by which someone who has experienced considerable grief in the past attempts to help a person currently grieving to adjust to his or her loss (Silverman, 1976).

CONCLUSION

In all probability, human beings since prehistoric times have been awed by the gift of life and dismayed by the presence of death. Although modern science has enabled people to develop some control over the conception of children and to prolong life, life itself and death are subjects that defy scientific explanation and reason.

People's fear of death and the capacity of science to prolong life (even if only in a sedated and vegetable-like state) have created some difficult questions for modern society concerning when, where, how, and why people die. There has been a tendency to bureaucratize death. The old are more likely to die in hospitals and nursing homes and less likely to die at home. Similarly, funerals are more likely to take place in a funeral parlor and less likely to be held in a home or church. We have chosen to let modern society turn the dying and the dead over to specialists. This means that the generation of Americans currently growing up are less likely to have to confront the issue of death directly in their own homes.

The fear of death seems almost universal and is something everyone must ultimately deal with. Vern L. Bengtson and his colleagues (1977) found age to be a critical factor in coming to terms with death. The young perceive death as so far in the future that it evokes little concern. The middle-aged are likely to be increasingly aware of the slowing of certain biological functions and the finiteness of their lives but often have not had time to resolve their fear of death. The old have more frequently come to accept death as inevitable and evidence fewer anxieties about it.

The death of acquaintances, friends, and loved ones arouses many latent fears of death in humans. During times of mourning, we grieve not only for the dead but also for ourselves and the fact that someday we must die. The period of grieving is a necessary part of the adjustment of an individual to the loss of a significant other, an adjustment that is helped if the situation surrounding a death encourages the necessary grieving. Much of the ritual surrounding funerals is designed to assist the grieving individual. One's own grief is best resolved in a supportive environment in which the assistance of others is readily available. Family, friends, and religious convictions often help an individual adjust to the loss of a loved one.

KEY TERMS

anticipatory grief
bureaucratization
euthanasia
grief

hedonism
sacred
secular

REFERENCES

ALDRICH, K. C., "Some Dynamics of Anticipatory Grief," in *Anticipatory Grief*, ed. B. Schoenberg and others, pp. 3–9. New York: Columbia University Press, 1974.

ALEXANDER, I. E., and M. M. ADLERSTEIN, "Studies in the Psychology of Death," in *Perspectives in Personalty Research*, ed. H. P. David and J. C. Brengelmann, pp. 65–92. New York: Springer, 1960.

BARNARD, CHRISTIAAN, "First Word," *Omni*, March 1986, p. 6.

BECKER, HOWARD, "The Sorrow of Bereavement," *Journal of Abnormal and Social Psychology*, 27 (1933), 391–410.

BENGTSON, VERN L., JOSE B. CUELLAR, and PAULINE K. RAGAN, "Stratum Contrasts and Similarities in Attitudes toward Death," *Journal of Gerontology*, 32, no. 1 (January 1977), 76–89.

BENJAMIN, BERNARD, and CHRIS WALLIS, "The Mortality of Widowers," *Lancet*, 2 (August 1963), 454–56.

BERGER, PETER, and THOMAS LUCKMANN, *The Social Construction of Reality: A Treatise in the Sociology of Knowledge*. Garden City, N.Y.: Doubleday, Anchor, 1967.

BLAUNER, ROBERT, "Death and Social Structure," *Psychiatry*, 29 (1966), 378–94.

BLUESTEIN, VENUS W., "Death-Related Experiences, Attitudes, and Feelings: Reported by Thanatology Students in a National Sample," *Omega*, 6, no. 3 (1975), 207–18.

BOWERS, M., and OTHERS, *Counseling the Dying*. New York: Thomas Nelson, 1964.

COX, HAROLD, "Mourning Populations: Some Considerations of Historically Comparable Assassinations," *Death Education*, 4, no. 2 (Summer 1980), 125–38.

DOKA, KENNETH, "Expectation of Death, Participation in Funeral Arrangements, and Grief Adjustment," *Omega*, 15, no. 2 (1984–85).

ELLIOT, T. O., "Bereavement: Inevitable, but Not Unsurmountable," in *Family Marriage and Parenthood* (2nd ed.), ed. H. Becker and R. Hill. Lexington, Mass.: Heath, 1971.

EPSTEIN, CAROLE, ESTER BALHIN, and DAVID BUSH, "Attitudes Toward Classroom Discussions of Death and Dying Among Urban and Suburban Children," *Omega*, 7, no. 27 (1976).

FEIFEL, H., and A. B. BRAUNSCOMB, "Who's Afraid of Death?" *Journal of Abnormal Psychology*, 81 (1973), 282–88.

GLASER, BARNEY G., and ANSELM L. STRAUSS, *Awareness of Dying*. Chicago: Aldine, 1965.

HERTZ, ROBERT, "The Collective Representation of Death," in *Death and the Right Hand*, trans. Rodney and Claudia Needham. Aberdeen: Cohen & West, 1960.

HOCHSCHILD, ARLIE, *The Unexpected Community*. Englewood Cliffs, N.J.: Prentice Hall, 1972.

JACKSON, N. EDGAR, *When Someone Dies*. Philadelphia: Fortress Press, 1973.

JEFFERS, FRANCES C., CLAUDE NICHOLS, and CARL EISDORFER, "Attitudes of Older Persons toward Death: A Preliminary Study," *Journal of Gerontology*, 16, no. 1 (January 1961), 53–56.

JEFFERS, FRANCES C., and ADRIAN VERWOERDT, "How the Old Face Death," in *Behavior and Adaption in Later Life*, ed. Ewald Busse and Eric Pfeiffer, pp. 142–58. Boston: Little, Brown, 1969.

JORDAN, LYNETTE, "Hospice in America," *CoEvolution Quarterly*, Summer 1977.

JORGENSON, DAVID E., and RONALD C. NEUBECKER, "Euthanasia: A National Survey of Attitudes Toward Voluntary Termination of Life," *Journal of Death & Dying*, 11, no. 4 (1980–81), 201–92.

"Judge: Doctor Can't Help Out with Suicides," *The Des Moines Register*, February 6, 1991.

KALISH, RICHARD A., "The Aged and the Dying Process: The Inevitable Decisions," *Journal of Social Issues*, 21 (1965), 87–96.

KANE, JOHN J., "The Irish Wake: A Sociological Appraisal," *Sociological Symposium*, 1 (Fall 1968), 11–16.

KASTENBAUM, ROBERT J., *Death, Society, and Human Experience*. Columbus, Oh.: Merrill Publishing Co., 1991.

KEPHART, WILLIAM K., "Status After Death," *American Sociological Review*, 15 (1950), 635–43.

KUBLER-ROSS, ELISABETH, *On Death and Dying*. New York: Macmillan, 1969.

LAMERS, W. M., "Funerals Are Good for People—M.D.'s Included," *Medical Economics*, 46 (June 24, 1969), 104–7.

LE SHAN, L., "The World of the Patient in Severe Pain of Long Duration," *Journal of Chronic Diseases*, 17 (1964), 119–26.

LEVITON, DANIEL, "Death Education," in *New Meanings of Death*, ed. Herman Feifel, pp. 253–72. New York: McGraw-Hill, 1977.

MADDISON, DAVID, and WENDY L. WALKER, "Factors Affecting the Outcome of Conjugal Bereavement," *British Journal of Psychiatry*, 113 (1967), 1057–67.

MALINOWSKI, BRONISLAW, *Magic, Science, and Religion and Other Essays*. New York: Free Press, 1948.

MARSHALL, VICTOR W., "Socialization for Impending Death in a Retirement Village," *American Journal of Sociology*, 80 (1975), 1124–44.

MOSS, MIRIAM S., and SIDNEY Z. MOSS, "Some Aspects of the Elderly Widower's Persistent Tie to the Deceased Spouse," *Omega*, 15, no. 3 (1984–85).

MYERS, JANE E., HANNELOR WASS, and MILLEDGE MURPHY, "Ethnic Differences in Death Anxiety Among the Elderly," *Death Education*, 4 (1980), 237–44.

NAGI, MOSTAFA H., and NEIL G. LAZERINE, "Death Education and Attitudes Toward Euthanasia and Terminal Illness," *Death Education*, 6 (1982), 1–15.

OBERSHAW, RICHARD J., *Death, Dying, and Funerals*. Burnsville, Minn.: Grief Center, 1976.

PENNISTON, D. H., "The Importance of Death Education in Family Life," *Family Coordinator*, (1963), 15–21.

"Reflections of the Times: The Right to Die." Washington D.C.: Times Mirror Center for the People and the Press, 1990.

RUSSEL, O. RUTH, *Freedom to Die: Moral and Legal Aspects of Euthanasia*. New York: Human Sciences, 1975.

SAGE, WAYNE, "Choosing the Good Death," in *Focus: Aging*, ed. Harold Cox, pp. 188–94. Guilford, Conn.: Dushkin Publishing Group, 1978.

SCHNEIDMAN, EDWIN S., *Death: Current Perspectives*. Palo Alto, Calif.: Mayfield, 1976.

SELDES, GEORGE, ed., *The Great Quotations*. New York: Simon & Schuster, 1967.

SHEATSLEY, PAUL B., and JACOB FELDMAN, "The Assassination of President Kennedy: A Preliminary Report on Public Reactions and Behavior," *Public Opinion Quarterly*, 28 (Summer 1964).

SILVERMAN, PHYLLIS ROLFE, "The Widow to Widow Program: An Experiment in Preventive Intervention," in *Death: Current Perspectives*, ed. Edwin S. Schneidman, pp. 356–66. Palo Alto, Calif.: Mayfield, 1976.

SMITH, ROBERT J., MARTIN F. SHERMAN, and NANCY C. SHERMAN, "The Elderly's Reaction Toward the Dying: The Effects of Perceived Age Similarity," *Omega*, 13, no. 4 (1982–83), 319–31.

SMITH, T. E., "The Cocos-Keeling Islands: A Demographic Laboratory," *Population Studies*, 14 (1960), 94–130.

SUDNOW, DAVID N., *Passing On: The Social Organization of Dying*. Englewood Cliffs, N.J.: Prentice Hall, 1967.

SWENSON, WENDELL M., Attitudes Toward Death in an Aged Population," *Journal of Gerontology*, 16, no. 1 (January 1961), 49–52.

TOYNBEE, ARNOLD, and OTHERS, "Man's Concern with Death," in *Death: Current Perspectives*, ed. Edwin Schneidman. Palo Alto, Calif.: Mayfield, 1976.

WAHL, C. W., "The Fear of Death," in *The Meaning of Death*, ed. Herman Feifel. New York: McGraw-Hill, 1959.

WATSON, WILBER H., "The Aging, Sick and the Near Dead: A Study Distinguishing Characteristics and Social Effects," *Omega*, 7, no. 2 (1976), 115–24.

WEBER, MAX, *Essays in Sociology*, trans. and ed. H. H. Gerth and C. Wright Mills, pp. 196–98. New York: Oxford University Press, 1953.

WEISMAN, AVERY, "Common Fallacies About Dying Patients," in *Death: Current Perspectives*, ed. Edwin Schneidman, pp. 443–52. Palo Alto, Calif.: Mayfield, 1976.

ZEIGENBERG, LOMA, and ROBERT FULTON, "Care of the Dying: A Swedish Perspective," *Omega*, 8, no. 3 (1977), 215–29.

ZUSMAN, MARTY E., and PAUL TSCHETTER, "Selecting Whether to Die at Home or in a Hospital Setting," *Death Education*, 8 (1984), 365–81.

NOTES

1. George Seldes, ed., *The Great Quotations* (New York: Simon & Schuster, 1967), p. 252.
2. Robert Blauner, "Death and Social Structure," *Psychiatry*, 29 (1966), 378–94. Blauner includes a long footnote concerning the source of his statistics. See also Krzywicki, *Primitive Society*, pp. 148, 271; and T. E. Smith, "The Cocos-Keeling Islands: A Demographic Laboratory," *Population Studies*, 14 (1960), 94–130.
3. Blauner, "Death and Social Structure," p. 531.
4. Robert Hertz, "The Collective Representation of Death," in *Death and the Right Hand*, trans. Rodney and Claudia Needham (Aberdeen: Cohen & West, 1960), pp. 84–86.
5. Bronislaw Malinowski, *Magic, Science, and Religion and Other Essays* (New York: Free Press, 1948), p. 26.
6. C. W. Wahl, "The Fear of Death," in *The Meaning of Death*, ed. Herman Feifel (New York: McGraw-Hill, 1959), p. 26.
7. Harold Cox, "Mourning Populations: Some Considerations of Historically Comparable Assassinations," *Death Education*, 4, no. 2 (Summer 1980), 125–38.
8. Wayne Sage, "Choosing the Good Death," in *Focus: Aging*, ed. Harold Cox (Guilford, Conn.: Dushkin Publishing Group, 1978), pp. 188–94.
9. Victor W. Marshall, "Socialization for Impending Death in a Retirement Village," *American Journal of Sociology*, 80 (1975), 1125.

10. Ibid., p. 1127.
11. Ibid., pp. 1127–28.
12. *Oedipus Coloneau*, ll. 1224–26; Quoted by Arnold Toynbee and others, "Man's Concern with Death," in *Death: Current Perspectives*, ed. Edwin S. Schneidman (Palo Alto, Calif.: Mayfield, 1976), p. 19.
13. Toynbee and others, "Man's Concern with Death," p. 19.
14. "Judge: Doctor Can't Help Out with Suicides," *The Des Moines Register*, February 6, 1991.
15. John A. Behnke and Sissela Bok, eds., *The Dilemma of Euthanasia* (Garden City, N.Y.: Doubleday, Anchor, 1975).
16. Marshall, "Socialization for Impending Death," p. 1138.
17. Christiaan Barnard, "First Word," *Omni*, 1986, p. 6.
18. Avery Weisman, "Fallacies About Dying Patients," in *Death*, ed. Schneidman, pp. 439–40.
19. Howard Becker, "The Sorrow of Bereavement," *Journal of Abnormal and Social Psychology*, 27 (1933), 399.
20. W. M. Lamers, "Funerals Are Good for People— M.D.'s Included," *Medical Economics*, 46 (June 24, 1969), 104–7.
21. K. C. Aldrich, "Some Dynamics of Anticipatory Grief," in *Anticipatory Grief*, ed. B. Schoenberg and others (New York: Columbia University Press, 1974), p. 5.

12

The Economics of Aging

ECONOMIC NEEDS OF OLDER AMERICANS

In order to discuss the adequacy of the economic resources of the elderly we must first determine the specific characteristics and needs of this group. Using 65 and above as our definition for old, we find a group of persons who generally have no children remaining at home, who are retired, who own their homes, and whose expenses are likely to be lower than they were during their middle years—except for medical expenses, which are likely to be higher and to climb steadily as one ages. Schulz (1988) has observed that when one gets very old, one is likely to experience exceptionally higher expenditures for chronic illness, hospitalization, and sometimes institutionalization. Declining health and increasing medical expenses can destroy savings and raise the economic needs of older Americans dramatically. Further, the newly retired, sometimes referred to as the *young-old*, are likely to have more adequate incomes than the *old-old* (those 75 and above).

Today's retirees, many of whom experience economic deprivation, have been a relatively quiet, noncomplaining group. They are fairly hardened to their deprivation by having lived in a historical and cultural environment that included two world wars and a major depression. Many of the current retirees have lived on limited resources throughout much of their lives. Moreover, they are generally more conservative in their attitudes toward government services than is the adult population today. They often consider government services to be welfare and are opposed to being the recipients of welfare programs.

In Chapter 10 we observed that less than 5 percent of elderly Americans are living in nursing homes. A survey of older Americans in the Midwest found that 44.3 percent of the noninstitutionalized sample were living alone, 41.3 percent were living with a spouse, 4.4 percent were living with children, 0.8 percent were living with a spouse and children, and 1.2 percent had some other living arrangement.[1] Thus the great majority of this sample of older Americans were either living with a spouse or living alone. Those living independently have the

I would like to express my appreciation to Philip Bibo, associate professor of economics at Indiana State University, for his assistance as the coauthor of this chapter.

same needs for housing, clothing, transportation, and utilities as younger persons in the population.

Although they have fewer expenses than they had during their child-rearing years, the elderly have the same individual needs as any other adults. In terms of medical costs, their needs are greater than others in the adult population. The basic problem for the elderly, then, is to maintain an adequate standard of living on a relatively unchanging retirement income. This problem is compounded by the fact that older persons

1. Generally receive considerably less income than those in their working years
2. Are living in a country in which inflation is relatively constant and quite variable over the long run (the rate has varied from 13.3 percent in 1979 to 1.1 percent in 1986)
3. Have no means of increasing their income at this stage of life

It is easy to understand why some older Americans become depressed during later life. They may feel that they are economically deprived and all they have to look forward to is the same income and reduced purchasing power.

INCOME

The income of older Americans consistently falls below that of other age groups in the adult population. Older persons usually see their incomes reduced by about half when they retire. Figure 12–1 points out the differences in median income of family heads over and under 65 years of age and unrelated individuals over and

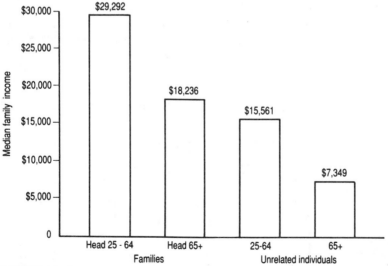

FIGURE 12–1
Median Family Income, Older and Younger Families and Unrelated Individuals, 1984

Source: Unpublished data provided by the U.S. Bureau of the Census, September 1985

under 65. For family heads 25 to 64 the median (average that divides the group in half) was $29,292. The median income of family heads 65 and above was $18,236. The median income for unrelated individuals 25 to 64 was $15,561. The median income for unrelated individuals 65 and above was $7349. It is clear from these figures that older Americans must be content to live on incomes considerably smaller than those of people in their working years.

Currently data from the Social Security Administration indicates that the older the individual, the lower his or her income is likely to be (Table 12–1). Ignoring their family status and just looking at the income of individuals, we see that the median income for individuals 55 to 61 is $23,340, for those 62 to 64 the median income is $18,190, for individuals 65 to 69 the median income is $14,540, for those 70 to 74 the median income is $12,430, for individuals 75 to 79 the median income is $9570, and for those 80 and older the median income is $7620. It is clear that the longer you live the poorer you become.

Regardless of the year calculated, such data indicate some consistent income patterns. Those under 65 consistently earn more than those over 65, married couples consistently earn more than single persons, men consistently earn more than women, and whites consistently earn more than blacks. White males 60 to 64 in 1987 had a mean income of $26,642 compared to $14,517 for black men. White women 60 to 64 had a mean income of $10,811 compared to $8279 for black women (Table 12–2). Looking carefully at the range of incomes from those families who earn $50,000 or more down to those families who earn less than $5,000, the pattern is clear (Figure 12–2). Approximately twice as many of the nonaged families earn $30,000 to $49,999. Approximately twice as many of the nonaged families earn $50,000 or more. About an equal number of aged and nonaged families earn from $20,000 to $29,999. In the next three categories, $15,000 to $19,999, $10,000 to $14,999 and $5000 to $9999, we find approximately twice as many aged families as nonaged families. Only at the very lowest category of those earning less than $5000 do we find more nonaged families. The fact that fewer aged families fall in the less than $5000 income category shows the effect of social security payments on keeping older families out of the extreme poverty categories. The overall pattern is clear. Nonaged families are most heavily represented in any income group above $30,000 per year. Leaving out the less than $5000 per year income, in any income category below $30,000 a year the

TABLE 12–1 Money Income of Aged Units (Married and Nonmarried), Age 55 and Older, 1986

Age	Median Income	Less than $5,000	$5,000– $9,999	$10,000– $14,999	$15,000 or More	Total Percent
55–61	$23,340	13%	11%	11%	66%	100[a]
62–64	18,190	13	15	14	58	100
65–69	14,540	13	22	17	49	100
70–74	12,430	15	26	17	42	100
75–79	9,570	18	34	18	31	100
80 and older	7,620	24	38	16	22	100

[a]May not add to 100 percent due to rounding.

Source: Susan Grad, *Income of the Population 55 or Over, 1986* (Washington, D.C.: Social Security Administration, 1987).

TABLE 12–2 Mean Income by Age, Gender, and Race, 1987

	60–64	65–69	70+
Male Income			
Total	$25,531	$18,821	$15,042
White	26,642	19,598	15,660
Black	14,517	10,526	8,412
Female Income			
Total	10,570	9,768	9,443
White	10,811	10,184	9,886
Black	8,279	6,024	5,264

Source: U.S. Bureau of the Census, 1989

aged families are most heavily represented. Older persons consistently earn less than the rest of the adult population as a group.

Although the older population in general is economically disadvantaged when compared with other age groups in the general population, its gains in income since 1960 have been more rapid than those of any other age group. Carole Allen and Herman Brotman (1981) explain:

> Between 1960 and 1979 alone, the median income of families headed by a person 65 or older increased nearly fourfold (3.9 times), a rate somewhat greater than that of younger families, whose income increased 3.6 times. As a result, the median in-

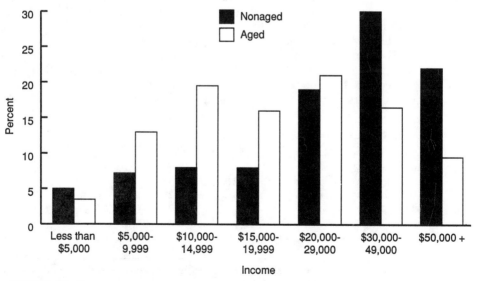

FIGURE 12–2
Comparison of Total Money Income, Aged and Nonaged Families, 1986

Source: U.S. Bureau of the Census, *Money Income and Poverty Status of Families and Persons in the United States: 1986, Current Population Reports*, P-60, no. 157 (Washington, D.C.: U.S. Government Printing Office, July 1987), Table 6.

comes of old families rose from 49 percent to 53 percent of the younger families during this time period. The rate of increase for individuals 65 and older was even greater—their median income rose from 41 percent to 48 percent of the younger persons.[2]

Despite this distinct improvement, in 1979 the median incomes of older families and individuals alike were still roughly half to two thirds those of their younger counterparts. The fact that older persons most often own their own homes and have their children raised alleviates some of the burden of their lower incomes. Moreover, we can expect their retirement incomes to continue to improve over the next few decades. Since women are entering the work force earlier and working longer we can anticipate that more of them are going to qualify for both social security and private pension programs. This will mean improved incomes in the future for older women (and their families, if they are married). Since more companies now are investing part of their employees' salaries in private pension programs, we can expect both men and women in the future to have a private retirement pension in addition to social security.

POVERTY

The poverty index for a nonfarm two-person family with a head age 65 or more was $6630 in 1986. The one-person poverty level was $4255 in 1986. The poverty index is calculated by determining the minimum amount of adequate food for the family, and then the cost of the food at prevailing prices is determined by pricing foods in retail stores. James Schulz (1988) observes that this food allotment was originally devised for emergency periods only and that no one is expected to have to live for a long period on these very minimal amounts. He believes that these food diets would be detrimental to health over extended periods.[3]

It is apparent from Table 12–3 that poverty for all age groups has been going down for three decades. When observing the entire population we see that 22 percent of the population fell below the poverty line in 1959. This figure had dropped to 14 percent in 1986. During the same period of time the elderly saw

TABLE 12–3 Poverty Rates, 1959–1986[a]

	1959	1968	1977	1981	1986
All persons in United States	22%	13%	12%	14%	14%
All persons age 65 and over	35	25	14	15	12
White aged	33	23	12	13	11
Nonwhite aged	61	47	35	c	c
Black				39	31
Hispanic[b]				26	23

[a]The percentages in this table are rounded to the nearest percent and therefore differ slightly from published official government statistics.

[b]Persons of Hispanic origin may be of any race.

[c]Percent not available.

Source: Based on data in U.S. Bureau of the Census, *Consumer Income, Current Population Reports*, Series P-60 (Washington, D.C.: U.S. Government Printing Office, various years).

an even bigger drop in terms of the percent that fell below the poverty line. In 1959 35 percent of the 65 + age group fell below the poverty line, and this figure had dropped to 12 percent in 1986. Thus the elderly made more rapid economic gains than the general population in this time period.

Moreover, specific groups of the 60 + population are considerably poorer than other groups. Hispanics, blacks, those living alone, those with less than eight years of school, those living in central cities, and black women living alone are considerably poorer than the general 60 + population (Figure 12–3). Both the

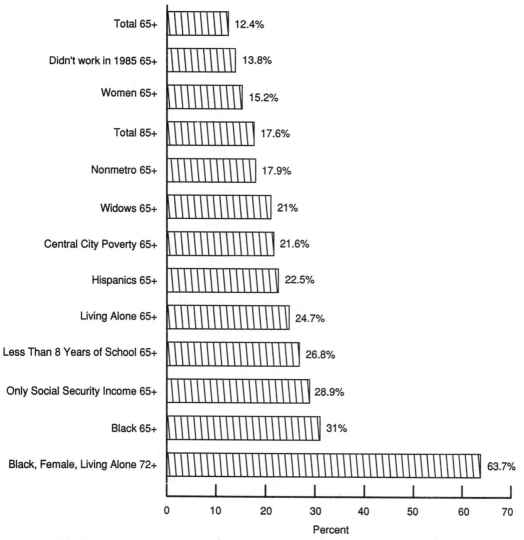

FIGURE 12–3
Percent of Elderly Below the Poverty Level by Selected Characteristics, 1986

Source: U.S. Bureau of the Census, *Poverty in the United States: 1987*, Current Population Reports, Series P-60, no. 163 (Washington, D.C.: Government Printing Office).

increases in median income of older persons and the decreases in the percentage of those falling below the poverty level have occurred primarily because of increases in social security benefits mandated by Congress and increases in the number of persons receiving private pensions.

Rather than just looking at a poverty level, the U.S. Bureau of Labor Statistics developed a retired couples budget in 1966. It was assumed by the creators of this budget that the retired couple was a husband and wife 65 or over who were living independently, self-supporting, in reasonably good health, and able to take care of themselves.

Ultimately three retired couples budgets were developed for lower, intermediate, and higher income levels. The typical family in each of these budgets is assumed to have for each budget level, average inventories of clothing, house furnishings, major durables, and other equipment. The budget was defined for urban families. This budget is purported by the Department of Labor Statistics to be a representative list of goods and services reflecting the collective judgments of families as to what is necessary and desirable to meet the conventional and social as well as the physical needs of families.[4]

The Bureau of Labor Statistics because of economic cutbacks last calculated the retired couples budget for 1981. In 1981 they set the lower-level retired couples budget at $7226, the intermediate at $10,226, and the higher at $15,078.

Yung-Ping Chen (1984) calculated the percent of retired couples with incomes that fell below the low and intermediate retired couples budgets as follows:

Year	Below Lower Level	Below Intermediate Level
1970	29%	49%
1975	21	42
1980	18	35

While the data clearly indicate the improving economic conditions of the elderly, we still see that 35 percent of the elderly fell below the intermediate level income in 1980.

SOURCES OF INCOME

The major sources of income for the elderly are very difficult to determine precisely. Figure 12–4 is an update of an earlier survey done by the Social Security Administration. It is broken down into families and unrelated individuals. We can see from this chart that Social Security and Railroad Retirement combined is the biggest source of income for most older Americans, with over 90 percent of them receiving some benefits. This is followed by income from property (assets), which 64.4 percent receive; wage and salary income (earnings), 41.7 percent; and retirement income in the form of private pension plans and annuities, 35.7 percent.

Whereas Figure 12–4 represents the percentages of families and individuals receiving income from various sources, Figure 12–5, based on Susan Grad's (1986) report for the Social Security Administration, breaks down the total income of older persons by source. While 90 percent of older persons receive some social security benefits, these benefits account for only 38 percent of the total earnings

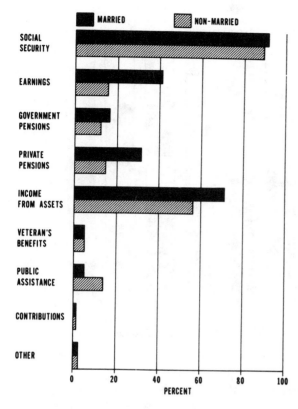

FIGURE 12–4
Percentage of Older Persons Receiving Money Income from Each Source, 1978

Source: U.S. Bureau of the Census

of older Americans. In addition, asset income accounts for 26 percent, earnings for 17 percent, private pensions for 7 percent, government pensions for 7 percent, and other sources for 5 percent.

The higher the income of the older person, the less likely social security is to be the major source of income. As Figure 12–6 indicates, for the poorest

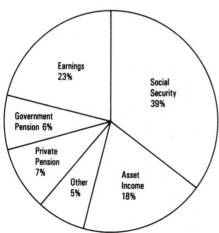

FIGURE 12–5
Sources of Aged Money Income, 1986

Source: Susan Grad, *Income of the Population 55 or Over, 1986* (Washington, D.C.: U.S. Social Security Administration, 1987), Table 47.

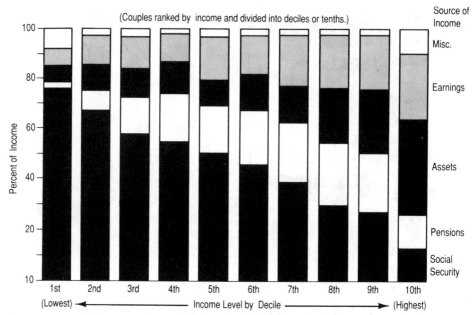

FIGURE 12–6 Sources of Monthly Income of Older Married Couples, 1982

Source: Social Security Administration, Department of Health and Human Services

(lowest-decile) group, social security provided three fourths (approximately 77 percent) of the total income. As income increases, social security accounts for a much smaller proportion of the total and pensions, assets, and earnings account for more. Social security benefits accounted for half or more of total income for approximately 45 percent of the couples and were the dominant source of income through the eighth decile. Social security accounted for only 13 percent of the income for those in the highest decile. The largest source of income for this group is assets (39 percent), followed by earnings (27 percent) and pensions (14 percent).

Schulz (1988) points out that the aged are not a homogenous group, and that to lump them all together tends to give the impression that the entire group is living under the same less fortunate circumstances. Obviously, the great majority of older Americans have incomes that place them above the poverty level. Most are secure enough economically to be able to maintain a desired style of life during their later years.

One often hears the argument that the family, and not government, should take care of its older members. This seems an unlikely prospect: Harold Cox and associates (1978) found that only 10 percent of the older persons in their sample received benefits from family.

There is frequent concern expressed by economists that the social security tax will become such a burden on younger taxpayers that there will be organized opposition to any further increases. Since its inception the trend in social security has been to have fewer people in their working years supporting more people who are receiving social security benefits. In 1960 there were 5 persons working supporting 1 in retirement; in 1984 the ratio was 3.3 to 1. By the year 2034 it is predicted to be 2 to 1 (Figure 12–7). There has, however, been no real threat of a revolution against social security. First, practically every taxpayer has an older family member receiving social security benefits. Second, each taxpayer hopes to be able to draw a social security check upon retirement. Thus, while the Social Security Administration may have to exercise some creative financing to keep the program solvent, a taxpayer's revolution does not seem likely.

In 1972 Congress legislated a *Supplemental Security Income* program (SSI), to be administered by the Social Security Administration. This program provides a national minimum level of income for the aged, blind, and disabled. In 1982 SSI guaranteed $284.30 monthly income ($3411.60 yearly) for individuals and $426.40 per month ($5116.80 yearly) for an elderly couple.

A very small proportion of persons over age 65 work, and their income is considerably higher than those who do not work. As Table 12–4 indicates, the median income of aged family householders who did not work was $11,632, for those who worked part-time was $14,729, and for those who worked full-time was $26,671. Similarly for unrelatd individuals who did not work the median income was $4948, for those who worked part-time $6203, and for those who worked full-time $12,476. Continuing to work dramatically improves the incomes of older persons and their families.

Private pension programs are not as widespread or as adequate a source of income for the current generation of retirees as they may be for future genera-

Social security burden

A dwindling number of workers pay into the pool of Social Security funds that support retirees, the disabled and other recipients: In 1950, 16 workers paid Social Security taxes for each beneficiary. Today, only 3.3 workers support each beneficiary and by 2034 just 2 will carry the burden.

RATIO OF WORKERS TO SOCIAL SECURITY BENEFICIARIES

Ratio by year:

5 to 1

1960

3.3 to 1

1984

2 to 1

2034

FIGURE 12–7
The Burden of Social Security

Source: Board of Social Security Trust Funds

TABLE 12–4 Money Income of Aged[a] Families and Unrelated Individuals, by Work Experience of Householder[b], 1981

Work Experience Last Year	Median Income	Less than $5,000	$5,000– $14,999	$15,000 or more	Total Percent
Families					
Householder did not work	$11,632	16%	47%	37%	100
Worked part-time	14,729	12	40	48	100
26 weeks or less	12,825	19	40	41	100
Worked full-time	26,671	2	17	81	100
26 weeks or less	12,722	16	43	41	100
Unrelated individuals					
Householder did not work	4,948	51	42	7	100
Worked part-time	6,203	38	50	12	100
26 weeks or less	4,040	60	36	4	100
Worked full-time	12,476	14	45	41	100
26 weeks or less	5,425	46	45	9	100

[a]Age 65 or older.

[b]Householder is a Census Bureau definition for the person (or one of the persons) in whose name the home is owned or rented. If the unit is jointly owned, either husband or wife may be listed first.

Source: Based on data in U.S. Bureau of the Census, "Money Income of Households, Families, and Persons in the United States: 1981," *Consumer Income. Current Population Reports*, Series P-60, no. 137 (Washington, D.C.: U.S. Government Printing Office, 1983), Table 36.

tions. As we observed in Chapter 9, most workers have to stay with a company throughout their career in order to receive such benefits. Also the company has to remain in business after the worker retires. Any disturbances in either the worker's career or the company's business generally terminates the pension. William Greenough and Frances King (1976) found that private pensions tend to be fixed permanently, with no compensation for inflationary factors, and they generally offer no coverage for the spouse after the husband's death.

Older persons' assets may include such things as stocks and bonds, farmland, and houses. For the great majority of older Americans, homeownership is their only asset. Schulz (1988) speaks of housing as being a "locked-in," *nonliquid asset*.[5] The elderly cannot quickly turn equity in their homes into cash for day-to-day use, as they can with *liquid assets* such as an interest in a business or stocks and bonds. On the other hand, the fact that many older Americans own their own homes and are thus living without any mortgage or rent payments means that they require less income than a younger person might need to maintain the same standard of living.

In terms of home equity 27 percent of the elderly have no home equity. An additional 8 percent have equity in a home that is less than $20,000. At the other extreme 22 percent have home equity of $100,000 or more (Table 12–5). Home ownership tends to be the major asset of older persons.

Ignoring equity in a home and looking at just financial assets a different picture emerges. Table 12–6 indicates the large proportion of older persons who have few if any financial assets in the form of money, stocks, bonds, or mutual funds. Fourteen percent of married couples have no financial assets, 23 percent

TABLE 12–5   Home Equity[a] of Elderly Households[b], 1984

Equity	Percent
None	27%
$1–$19,999	8
$20,000–$39,999	13
$40,000–$59,999	13
$60,000–$79,999	11
$80,000–$99,999	7
$100,000–$149,999	12
$150,000–$199,999	5
$200,000 or more	5
Total Percent[c]	100%

[a]Equity of elderly persons and, if married, their spouses. Equity of other household members is not included.

[b]Households with at least one elderly member.

[c]Does not add to 100 due to rounding.

Source: James H. Schulz, *The Economics of Aging* (Dover, MA: Auburn House Publishing Company, 1988), p. 39. Author's tabulations of Survey of Income and Program Participation (SIPP), Wave 4.

have less than $3000 in assets, and 37 percent have less than $15,000 in assets. At the other extreme 28 percent of the aged couples have assets of $100,000 or more.

Two other factors must be taken into account in considering the incomes of the elderly—in-kind income and tax breaks. In-kind income consists of services

TABLE 12–6   Financial Assets[a] of the Elderly, 1984

Value of Assets	Married, Both Age 65+	Couples, Only One Age 65+	Unrelated Men, 65+	Unrelated Women, 65+
None	14%	19%	26%	25%
$1–$2,999	9	10	15	19
$3,000–$14,999	14	17	19	18
$15,000–$29,999	11	10	12	13
$30,000–$49,999	9	6	8	9
$50,000–$74,999	9	11	11	9
$75,000–$99,999	7	6	3	2
$100,000–$149,999	10	7	2	3
$150,000–$199,999	9	5	2	1
$200,000–$249,999	3	3	*[b]	*[b]
$250,000 +	6	6	2	*[b]
Total Percent[c]	100%	100%	100%	100%

[a]Interest earning bank accounts, other interest earning assets, and stocks/bonds/mutual funds.

[b]Less than 1 percent.

[c]May not add to 100 percent due to rounding.

Source: James H. Schulz, *The Economics of Aging* (Dover, MA: Auburn House Publishing Company, 1988), p. 41. Author's tabulation of Survey of Income and Program Participation (SIPP).

or goods that older persons may purchase at a reduced price. Older persons are sometimes the recipients of goods and services provided by the government or the business community at a considerably reduced price. Schulz (1988) believes that subsidized government housing is the best example of in-kind income, since one is allowed to pay a price for housing that is below the market value. Schulz reports that 42 major federal programs benefit the elderly over and above those providing direct money income. The largest single government expenditure is for health care. While the aged may have very low money incomes, they may have considerable in-kind incomes.

As for tax breaks, Schulz (1988) believes that the provision permitting persons over 65 to double their personal tax exemption tends to help the higher-income elderly. Stanley Surrey (1973) has estimated that nearly half of federal tax assistance goes to individuals with incomes above $10,000.

EFFECTS OF INFLATION

The economic problems associated with the U.S. population 65 and over are not necessarily different from those of the general population. The principal difference between the 65+ group and the general population is the vulnerability of the former to the effects of *inflation*. These can be much worse for those whose money incomes are relatively fixed than for those who remain in the work force earning a money income geared to the inflation rate. Rising prices versus relatively fixed incomes means either a reduction in the standard of living or the selling of assets accumulated over the working years in order to maintain a given lifestyle. Without earned income to help offset the effects of rising prices, the retired must either reduce their standard of living or draw upon accumulated assets. Liquidation of accumulated assets is an especially difficult choice because of the specter of outliving one's income.

One of the best methods of measuring the effect of inflation on the purchasing power of the American consumer is the Consumer Price Index (CPI), which is presented monthly by the Bureau of Labor Statistics. The index is calculated by determining how much it costs in a particular month to buy a market basket of goods and services that is representative of the buying pattern of consumers. This amount is then expressed in a ratio whose reference point is what it would have cost to buy this same market basket of goods and services in the base period of 1967. This ratio is then multiplied by 100, yielding a percentage. Over 400 items are included in this analysis.[6]

Recently the inflation rate as measured by the CPI has been led by rising food prices, sharply increasing prices for energy, and a continuing escalation of prices for medical care. These three components of the CPI work a much greater hardship in the over-65 non–wage-earning population than on the general population. Higher food prices make maintenance of an adequate diet for those on relatively fixed incomes much more difficult. Rising energy costs have substantial effects on one's ability to live comfortably, especially for those Americans who live in areas subject to cold winters. Finally, and despite such programs as medicare and medicaid, increasing medical costs have been most devastating to those persons 65 and older.

A 1975 Louis Harris and associates survey revealed that inflation (which for the first quarter of 1975 was more than 10 percent) had reduced real income significantly for retired people. Of the respondents to their survey, 34 percent indicated that the quality of their life had deteriorated since retirement. The concern over money replaced fear of crime and poor health as the major problem for retired people, according to the study. Inflationary pressures were seen as the primary motivation for the preference of 46 percent in the survey to be working.

What has begun to be more frequent is for retirement programs to have a cost-of-living escalator built into them to deflect the cost of inflation. Joseph Minarik (1981) reports that about 57 percent of the organized workers under contract have some of their earnings pegged to the CPI. However, there may be a few months' lag before the retirement checks are adjusted to reflect the rising cost of prices. Thus ideally the older persons' purchasing power remains constant.

Unfortunately, solutions to the problem of falling real income that confronts retirees are limited. One set of solutions could be classified as internal. That is, people can control their destinies through their decisions on how to allocate their money for purchases: The retiree sets his or her own priorities. The second set of solutions is external to the retiree: The individual is dependent on alternatives determined by an outside agency, such as government. In general the money value of tangible financial assets tends to increase with inflation, leaving the older persons' wealth unaffected as inflation raises prices. The value of the older persons' house (a tangible) asset increases and their wealth remains constant. Financial assets, however, such as insurance policies, bonds, and savings accounts, tend to decrease in relative value as inflation raises prices. Schulz (1988) reports that when households are grouped according to age of the head that the largest decline in wealth as a result of inflation occurs among elderly families. The largest gains in wealth as a result of inflation occurs among families in the 25 to 34 age group. Those aged with substantial assets in the form of savings are the largest losers in times of high inflation.

Social security benefits were increased by amendments to the social security

Source: Don Wright, *The Miami News.* Reprinted by permission.

laws to help offset the effects of inflation. Benefits, beginning in July 1975, were geared to inflation by an escalator clause. That is, in June of each year benefits are increased when the CPI shows an increase of 3 percent or more. The escalator was, of course, designed to compensate for rising price levels. However, the lag time of one year before benefits are adjusted never allows current payments to reflect current prices. In addition, the poverty-level income of the average social security beneficiary exacerbates the inflationary problem. Finally, it is Congress that decides what the cost-of-living increase shall be.

One of the components of the hypothetical market basket used to determine the consumer price index is housing. Housing as a part of a family's budget is quite significant and thus is given a relatively heavy weight in the makeup of the CPI. Cost-of-living adjustments (COLA) for social security payments are based upon increases in the CPI. Since the majority of the population 65 and over either own their own homes or have accrued a substantial equity in their homes, the use of the CPI for COLAs may provide a modest windfall in social security payments.

More recently the inflation rate has dropped appreciably, from 13.3 percent in 1979 to the 1.1 percent of the 1980s. Lower rates of inflation make the fixed incomes of many older persons more dependable in terms of purchasing power. Low inflation means stable or very slowly rising prices. Under these conditions people may well retire at age 65 and 10 years later still find that they have enough money to live comfortably. The inflation rate, however, if returned to the 13 percent or higher of the late 1970s, could once again impose hardship on older Americans. The escalator clause should be helpful. Moreover, as Robert Clark and Daniel Sumner (1985) point out, older Americans with accumulated assets and investments will see their incomes rise as prices rise. Thus the more affluent older persons are less affected by inflation than the less affluent. Should the inflation return to the double-digit figures of the late 1970s, the only alternative for older Americans without accumulated assets or investments wishing to increase their earnings would be to reenter the job market. Entering the job market is often difficult or impossible for older Americans because of their poor health, lack of skill, or discrimination by employers.

CONCLUSION

The great majority of older Americans live on incomes about half those they were earning prior to retirement. Even so, most initially believe that their income is enough for them to maintain their preretirement standard of living, for their families are raised and they usually own their homes. Many older Americans are therefore able to maintain their preretirement lifestyle during their retirement years. For those who were earning low incomes during their working years, the reduction of income at the time of retirement can place them in a state of poverty. To reduce by half an already inadequate income can be catastrophic.

Of those 60 and above, 13.6 percent fell below the poverty line in 1982. Women's incomes are more likely than men's to fall below the poverty line, and blacks' are more likely to do so than whites'. Black women are the poorest group of all.

Many older Americans are concerned that their incomes, which may be adequate when they retire, will not be adequate ten years later as a result of inflation and rising prices. The data indicate, however, that older persons with accumulated assets and investments will find their incomes rising as prices rise. Older Americans who have few assets and depend almost entirely on social security are the focus of recent changes in the law that are designed to reduce inflationary pressures. Congress, in an attempt to alleviate the economic woes of older Americans, has provided an escalator clause that allows social security payments to be increased whenever the Consumer Price Index shows an increase of more than 3 percent per year. This helps—but does not entirely solve the problem of inflation, since Congress determines how much the increase will be, and the increases are sometimes lower than the rate of inflation.

For older persons who fall below the poverty line, however, the picture is bleak. Realistically, there is little opportunity for them to return to the labor force—their only means of increasing their income.

While the incomes of older persons are considerably lower than those of the general population, they have made significant gains in purchasing power since 1960. Allen and Brotman (1981) observe that while the Consumer Price Index rose by 145 percent from 1960 to 1979, the income of older families rose by 291 percent, compared with 259 percent for younger families. Older individuals' income in the same period rose by 343 percent, compared with 278 percent for younger individuals. These improvements, as we have observed, have come about because of such factors as increased social security benefits, the greater number of persons qualifying for these benefits, and the increasing number of retirees covered by private pension plans. While older persons will continue to have lower incomes than younger age groups they have made more rapid gains than younger people in their standard of living. They are represented in Washington by a variety of interest groups and they are a large enough voting block to carry considerable political clout. They are likely to continue to improve their economic position in our society.

KEY TERMS

Consumer Price Index
inflation
liquid assets

nonliquid assets
poverty index
Supplemental Security Income

REFERENCES

ALLEN, CAROLE, and HERMAN BROTMAN, *Chartbook on Aging.* Washington, D.C.: White House Conference on Aging, 1981.

BROTMAN, HERMAN B., "Income and Poverty in the Older Population in 1975," *Gerontologist,* 17, no. 1 (1977), 23–26; quoting U.S. Bureau of the Census data.

CHEN, YUNG-PING, "Economic Status of the Aged," in *Handbook of Aging and the Social Sciences* (2nd ed.), ed. Robert H. Binstock and Ethen Shancis. New York: Van Nostrand Reinhold.

CLARK, ROBERT, and DANIEL A. SUMNER, "Inflation and Real Income of the Elderly: Recent Evidence and Expectations for the Future," *Gerontologist,* 25, no. 2 (1985), 146–51.

COX, HAROLD, GURMEET SEKHON, and CHARLES NORMAN, "Social Characteristics of the Elderly in Indiana," *Proceedings/Indiana Academy of the Social Sciences,* 8 (1978), 186–97.

FOWLES, DAN, "Assets of Older Americans," *Aging,* No. 351 (1985), 32–55.

FOWLES, DAN, "Poverty and Plenty: A Paradox," *Aging,* No. 345 (1984), 46–47.

GRAD, SUSAN, *Income of Population 55 or Over, 1986.* Washington, D.C.: U.S. Social Security Administration, 1986, p. 47.

GREENOUGH, WILLIAM C., and FRANCES P. KING, *Pension Plans and Public Policy.* New York: Columbia University Press, 1976.

HARRIS, CHARLES, *Fact Book on Aging: A Profile of America's Older Population.* Washington, D.C.: National Council on the Aging, 1978.

HARRIS, LOUIS, and ASSOCIATES, *The Myth and Reality of Aging in America* (2nd ed.). Washington, D.C.: National Council on the Aging, 1975.

MANSFIELD, EDWIN, *Economics: Principles, Problems, Decisions* (3rd ed.). New York: W. W. Norton, 1977.

MINARIK, JOSEPH J., Testimony Before the U.S. Senate Special Committee on Aging. Hearings on "Social Security Oversight: Cost-of-Living Adjustments." Part 3. Washington, D.C.: U.S. Government Printing Office, 1981.

SCHULZ, JAMES, *The Economics of Aging* (4th ed.). Belmont, Calif.: Wadsworth, 1988.

SURREY, STANLEY, *Pathways to Tax Reform: The Concept of Tax Expenditures.* Cambridge, Mass.: Harvard University Press, 1973.

THOMPSON, GAYLE B., "Pension Coverage and Benefits: Findings from the Retirement History Study," *Society Security Bulletin*, 41 (February 1978), 3–17.

U.S. BUREAU OF THE CENSUS, "Consumer Income," *Current Population Reports*, Series P-60, no. 116. Washington, D.C.: U.S. Government Printing Office, 1978.

U.S. BUREAU OF THE CENSUS, "Demographic Aspects of Aging and the Older Population in the U.S.," *Current Population Reports*, Series P-23, no. 59. Washington, D.C.: U.S. Government Printing Office, 1976.

NOTES

1. Harold Cox, Gurmeet Sekhon, and Charles Norman, "Social Characteristics of the Elderly in Indiana," *Proceedings/Indiana Academy of the Social Sciences*, 8 (1978), 186–97.
2. Carole Allen and Herman Brotman, *Chartbook on Aging* (Washington, D.C.: White House Conference on Aging, 1981), p. 54.
3. James Schulz, *The Economics of Aging*, 4th ed. (Belmont, Calif.: Wadsworth, 1988), p. 52.
4. Ibid., p. 51.
5. Ibid., p. 52.
6. Edwin Mansfield, *Economics: Principles, Problems, Decisions*, 3rd ed. (New York: W. W. Norton, 1977), pp. 177–78.

13

Exploitation of the Aged: Crimes, Confidence Games, and Frauds

FEAR OF CRIME

In a 1975 Louis Harris survey, fear of crime ranked above health, money, and loneliness in a list of the major concerns of older Americans. Carl Pope and William Feyharm (1976), and Alan Malinchak (1980) have also found that fear of crime is one of the major concerns of older Americans.[1] Frank Clements and Michael Kleiman (1976), documenting the fear of crime among the elderly, found that 52 percent of respondents aged 65 and over said they were afraid of crime versus only 41 percent of the under-65 group. A survey conducted by Erikson (1974) indicated that women are more likely to express fear of crime than are men. This may be a result of the fact that men are more reluctant to admit fear than women.[2] Clements and Kleiman (1976) reported that only 19 percent of all males in their sample reported fear of crime. When broken down by age, however, 34 percent of the elderly men admitted to such a fear.[3]

In examining race, Clements and Kleiman (1976) found that blacks are considerably more afraid of crime than are whites. This fear, which held for all age categories, was particularly strong among the aged. Whereas about 47 percent of the white elderly were afraid to walk alone in their neighborhood at night, 69 percent of the black aged expressed the same fear.

Clements and Kleiman (1976) also found that among the elderly, poor people are more fearful of crime than are the more affluent. Fifty-one percent of those with incomes of less than $7000 per year expressed fear of crime in comparison with 43 percent of those with $7000 or more in income.[4]

Residents of large cities tend to be more fearful of criminal victimization than people in smaller towns and rural areas. In large cities, 76 percent of the elderly expressed fear of crime, compared with 68 percent in medium-size cities, 48 percent in suburbs, 43 percent in small towns, and 24 percent in rural areas.[5] Elderly residents of cities of 50,000 + population show significantly greater fear of crime than do either younger persons or their counterparts in suburbs, small towns, and rural areas.

The picture, then, is quite clear concerning who is more fearful of crime. Older persons as a rule are considerably more afraid of crime than are any of the younger age groups. Women are much more likely to express a fear of crime than are men. Blacks are more fearful of crime than are whites. Older persons on incomes of less than $7000 are more fearful of crime than are those with incomes above that figure. Finally, residents of large cities are more fearful of crime than those living in suburbs, smaller cities, and rural areas. It would follow, then, that poor, black, older women living in large urban areas are likely to be the most fearful of crime.

VICTIMIZATION BY CRIME

While the data clearly indicate that older persons are more fearful of crime than are other age groups, it is not quite clear whether this fear is justified. Many studies have indicated that in fact older persons are the least likely to be victimized. Others indicate that there are certain kinds of crimes in which the elderly are most likely to be victimized.

Fay Cook (1976), in examining statistics on criminal victimization, concluded that of all age groups, older persons are the least likely to be victims of both personal and household crimes.[6] Table 13–1 indicates that the crime rate decreases with age across all age groups. For personal crimes, 15 older persons per 1000 were victims, whereas the rate was 98 per 1000 for persons 20 to 24 and 67 per 1000 for persons 25 to 34. A similar pattern is found for crimes against households (Table 13–2). Among the elderly, 55 per 1000 were victims, as opposed to 140 per 1000 for 20-to-34-year-olds and 114 per 1000 for 35-to-49-year-olds. The elderly, then, are significantly less likely than other age groups to be victims of the nine classifications of crime in Tables 13–1 and 13–2.

Other studies have come to different conclusions, however. Jack Goldsmith and Noel Thomas (1974) argue that the underreporting of crime by the elderly results in inaccurate projections based on standard police and FBI statistics.[7] Another problem is that many police departments do not routinely list the victim's age. And even when they do, they do not necessarily classify crimes the way departments in other cities do. As Table 13–3 indicates, Miami delineates crimes against older persons but includes only the more serious aggravated assault cases.

TABLE 13–1 Crimes Against Persons by Age of Victim per 1000 Population

Both Sexes, Age	Total	Rape	Robbery With Injury	Robbery Without	Assault Aggravated	Assault Simple	Personal Larceny
12–15	126.4	0.7	1.6	4.8	7.7	18.3	93.4
16–19	122.1	1.4	1.9	3.2	11.9	17.2	86.5
20–24	98.0	1.4	1.9	3.9	10.3	13.8	66.7
25–34	67.0	0.6	1.2	2.3	5.9	8.1	48.8
35–49	46.7	—	0.9	1.6	3.3	5.1	35.6
50–64	30.0	—	0.6	1.1	1.4	2.5	24.3
65 and over	15.1	—	1.0	1.5	0.8	1.1	10.6

Source: Criminal Victimization in the United States, January–June, 1973: A National Crime Panel Survey Report. U.S. Department of Justice, Bureau of Justice Statistics.

TABLE 13–2   Crimes Against Households by Age of Household Head per 1000 Population

Age	Total Crimes	Burglary	Household Larceny	Motor Vehicle Theft
12–19	236.6	106.0	105.4	25.3
20–34	140.9	56.9	71.0	13.0
35–49	114.0	46.4	58.4	9.3
50–64	83.1	35.9	40.4	6.9
65 and over	55.3	28.5	24.8	2.0

Source: Criminal Victimization in the United States, January–June, 1973: A National Crime Panel Survey Report. U.S. Department of Justice, Bureau of Justice Statistics.

One would guess that most assaults against older persons are not aggravated assaults.

In order to determine the actual rate of criminal victimization in the nation's larger cities, given the problems of the standard police statistics and the number of crimes that go unreported, the Law Enforcement Assistance Administration conducted a research survey of criminal victimization in 26 cities. The data from this survey indicated that anywhere from one half to two thirds (depending on the type of crime) of all the crimes committed against victims of any age group go unreported and that older persons (65+) are slightly more likely than younger persons (12–64) to report victimization to the police.[8]

The LEAA survey, which included both reported and unreported crimes, indicated that the two most frequent crimes committed against older persons are robbery and personal larceny with contact (purse snatching and pocket picking) (see Table 13–4). The elderly rank the highest of all age groups in terms of being victimized by purse snatching and in terms of personal larceny with contact in

TABLE 13–3   Crimes Against the General Population (Under 60) and the Elderly (60 years or older)* for a Six-Month Period in Miami, Florida, 1976

Crime	General Population	Elderly
Homicide	5	0
Rape	2	0
Robbery	81	53
Assault**	51	7
Burglary	912	364
Larceny	1,761	434
Auto theft	145	34
Pickpockets	116	99
Purse snatching	87	64

*Approximately 59 percent of Miami Beach's permanent residents are over age 60.

**Simple assaults not counted—only aggravated assaults or worse.

Source: Adapted from John H. Tighe, "A Survey of Crimes Against the Elderly," Police Chief, February 1977, p. 19.

TABLE 13–4 Estimated Rates (per 100,000 Persons 12 Years of Age or Older) and Percentage Distribution of Personal Victimization, by Type of Victimization and Age of Victim; Aggregate Data for 26 Cities, 1974, 1975

| | Age of Victim | | | | |
	65 or Older	50 to 64	35 to 49	12 to 34	Estimated Totals[a]
Population base	3,167,119	4,475,746	3,475,024	10,702,641	22,720,530
Rape	19	30	85	313	173
	0%	1%	2%	4%	3%
	(610)	(1,377)	(3,841)	(34,339)	(40,167)
Aggravated assault	288	560	957	2,265	1,402
	7%	12%	19%	26%	21%
	(9,303)	(25,489)	(42,601)	(247,583)	(324,977)
Simple assault	377	729	1,143	2,409	1,551
	9%	16%	22%	27%	24%
	(12,124)	(33,142)	(50,189)	(263,606)	(359,693)
Robbery	1,615	1,742	1,926	2,794	2,255
	40%	39%	38%	32%	34%
	(51,875)	(79,147)	(85,524)	(304,463)	(521,023)
Larceny with contact	1,752	1,442	1,050	999	1,201
	43%	32%	20%	11%	18%
	(56,488)	(65,524)	(46,792)	(109,278)	(278,093)
Estimated totals[a]	4,053	4,503	5,162	8,780	6,582
	100%	100%	100%	100%	100%
	(130,406)	(204,679)	(229,577)	(959,269)	(1,523,932)

[a]Categories may not sum to total due to rounding.

Source: Ellen Hochstedler, *Crime Against the Elderly in 26 Cities* (Albany, N.Y.: Criminal Justice Research Center, 1981).

general. If we lump all of the different crimes together, however, we find that the elderly have the lowest rate of victimization. Ellen Hochstedler (1981) reports that theft rather than violence constituted the greater part of the victimization of the elderly; violence without theft was relatively rare. And indeed Table 13–4 indicates that the elderly are most likely to be victims of theft.

The LEAA survey indicated a number of factors related to criminal victimization of the elderly that the more standard criminal statistics did not, such as the following:

1. The rate of theft is higher for the elderly than for any other age group.

2. The poor inner-city elderly suffer from crime more often than their non–inner-city counterparts.[9]

3. Income is negatively related to crimes of violence (the lower the income, the higher the incidence of crime) but positively related to crimes without violence (the higher the income the higher the incidence of crime). (Families with incomes less than $3000 are most likely to have been robbed and assaulted while families with incomes over $15,000 are most likely to have been victims of larceny.)

4. Blacks are more likely to be victimized than whites, especially in the case of robbery and assault.

The data at this point appear confusing. National crime statistics, such as those listed in Tables 13–1 and 13–2, indicate a considerably lower rate of criminal victimization of the elderly than of other age groups. The later studies by the Law Enforcement Assistance Administration, which did not rely only on reported crimes but also surveyed people living in the chosen neighborhoods and communities, found higher rates of theft and larceny with contact among older persons than among the general population.

While the fear of crime among the elderly may be greater than the actual threat of crime, this may be explained in part by the fact that the elderly are more likely to experience larceny with contact and be shoved around or assaulted while having a purse or billfold stolen; thus the potential crime represents a threat to their personal safety. Moreover, the crimes are often committed in or near their homes. Lou Cotton (1979) reports that the perpetrators of crimes against the elderly are most often males who live within ten blocks of the victim. According to George Antunes and associates (1977), this represents a penetration of one's personal life space and is therefore more threatening.[10] Also, both personally and financially, the elderly have few resources in which they can protect themselves or recover from the losses they might incur by being victimized. Therefore when the elderly are the victims of crime, the effect on their lives is likely to be more devastating than for other age groups. Thus their fears can be more easily understood even if the criminal statistics do not always indicate that they are justified. These fears are probably accentuated by the fact that many elderly persons live alone and are often somewhat isolated from neighborhood and community groups. Arthur Patterson (1977) reports that elderly who live alone fear crime more than those who do not live alone.[11] Fear is probably more manageable when it is shared.

Realistically the elderly's fear of crime is difficult to assuage in large part because it grows out of their own sense of weakness and vulnerability. Norton and Courlander (1988) found that education about crime did increase the numbers of steps older persons took to protect themselves and their property, but it also increased their level of fear. The authors postulated that after presentations to the elderly on the possible crimes that they might encounter, they became increasingly conscious of their vulnerability and thus more fearful.

THE OLDER PERSON'S RESPONSE TO VICTIMIZATION

A critical question for people at any age is how to respond to a threat to person or property. Does the average person take precautions before being victimized or only after being victimized? Marlene Rifia (1977) studied people's responses to potential and actual victimization. She found that among a sample of the general population, whether or not they had been victims of crime, 25 percent of the males and 21 percent of the females indicated that they had taken some action to prevent themselves from being victimized. Of those persons who had been victims of crime, 42 percent of the males and 37 percent of the females had acted to make themselves more secure.[12] Thus, persons who have been victims of crime are somewhat more likely to take measures to prevent themselves from being victimized in the future.

As a rule, women are more likely than men to take precautions to prevent criminal victimization (Table 13–5), although there are some notable exceptions.

TABLE 13–5 Responses Taken by Older Persons to Protect Themselves from Criminal Victimization

	Male Percentage	Female Percentage
Don't carry a wallet, money, or purse when out in public	9	12
Avoid going out at night	20	33
Carry a weapon	6	4
Add locks to doors and windows	31	34
Mark property with crime-prevention identification	13	12
Attend a neighborhood crime-prevention meeting	1	5
Keep lights on in the house when gone	20	20
Have a dog or an alarm system	9	6

Source: Marlene Rifia, "The Response of the Older Adult to Criminal Victimization," *Police Chief*, February 1977, pp. 32–34.

Women were more likely not to carry a purse or wallet when in public, to avoid going out at night, to add locks to doors and windows, and to have attended a neighborhood crime-prevention meeting. Men were more likely to carry a weapon, mark property with crime-prevention stickers, and have a dog or an alarm system.

Rifia (1977) found that the four most common patterns of response by older persons to the threat of criminal victimization were

1. Not going out at night
2. Adding locks to doors and windows
3. Leaving some lights on at home when away
4. Marking personal property with crime-prevention identification[13]

Psychologists and anthropologists have for some time discussed the territorial behavior of animals. Their research indicates that animals have a keen sense of territorial rights and will fight fiercely to protect their territory from other animals. Some gerontologists believe that creation of a sense of territory or neighborhood among older persons may reduce their fear of crime.

Patterson (1977) divided respondents on the basis of whether or not they had a high sense of territoriality. He found that males who were highly territorial were markedly less fearful than males who were low on sense of territory. Females who were high on sense of territoriality were only slightly less fearful than females who were low on sense of territory. Thus, the principle seems to hold stronger for males than for females.[14]

Homeowners who lived alone and who were low on territoriality were found by Patterson to be much more fearful than homeowners who lived alone and who were high on territoriality.[15] Those with a high sense of territoriality were significantly less fearful of property loss and personal assault than those with a low sense of territoriality.[16] Those with a high sense of territory were much more likely to feel safe and secure in their homes and neighborhoods.

Older persons at some point may come to feel too weak to be able to control their environment. They become, in the terminology of psychologists, *field-dependent* rather than *field-indepedent*. One would conclude that those older persons who are field-independent—who feel capable of managing their environment—are much less likely to be afraid of crime or of becoming victimized than those who are field-dependent—who do not feel in control of their environment. It may well be that the older one becomes, the more likely one is to shift from field independence to field dependence, thereby becoming more fearful.

CONFIDENCE GAMES AND FRAUDS

Not only are the elderly often the victims of attack on their persons and property but they also can fall prey to a variety of confidence games and frauds designed specifically to exploit them. Also, some business people exploit the emotionally vulnerable in order to make a profit. The elderly, who are frequently lonely, isolated, and fearful, become the target. The following are illustrations of a few of the most common schemes to exploit older persons.

Example A

Mr. Smith, an elderly member of a respectable city neighborhood, is called and told that he will be given a free gift if he will merely provide information about purchasing patterns for a national survey that the caller claims to be conducting. Mr. Smith is asked whether he had made any major purchases recently; he responds that he had bought a new television in the last three months and a new couch in the last six months. Mr. Smith is then asked how the quality of these items compares with that of other home appliances and furniture. As the conversation progresses, Mr. Smith is gradually led into a discussion of most of the major items in his home. Some unique antiques owned by Mr. Smith as well as most of the routine furnishings are described. The caller then thanks Mr. Smith for his assistance and tells him that he will be delivering his gifts—when will he be at home? Mr. Smith unsuspectingly tells the caller when he plans to be at home *and away* for the next several days. The conversation ends cordially with the caller thanking Mr. Smith for his cooperation. By this ruse the criminal now knows the major items of value in Mr. Smith's home and the most likely times to rob Mr. Smith's home. The criminal has successfully misrepresented himself and exploited his victim's trust.

Example B

A Mr. Jones knocks on the door of Mr. Smith, flashes a badge, and identifies himself as an FBI agent. He carefully explains to Mr. Smith that the teller at the First National Bank, where Mr. Smith has his life savings, is suspected of stealing money from the bank. He asks Mr. Smith if he would be willing to help him catch the teller in the act of stealing money. Mr. Jones points out that this would be an act of public service—to the FBI, the bank, and the community. Mr. Smith is by now more than happy to assist the FBI in trapping the crooked bank teller. He is directed to go to the bank and withdraw all of his savings and then meet Mr. Jones outside the bank immediately after the withdrawal. He is asked not to discuss the matter with anyone, for security reasons. Mr. Jones is waiting as Mr.

Smith comes out of the bank with his life savings in hand. Mr. Jones takes the money from Mr. Smith, explaining that the money will be returned to his bank account in the next few days. The two part company exchanging cordial good-byes, and Mr. Smith has a feeling of pride in the good deed he has performed. It may be some time before he realizes that he has been swindled and that his savings will never be returned to the bank.

There are also a variety of dishonest selling practices that are used to persuade older persons to buy products they most often do not need. The following are two examples.

Example C

A salesman shows up at Mr. Smith's door and offers him a reduction in price for aluminum siding on his house if he will allow the salesman to use his house as a model and bring potential clients to look at the siding. Mr. Smith agrees to the plan and is given a contract at a very reasonable price to have his house sided. The salesman then asks Mr. Smith to put new asphalt on his driveway in order to improve the looks of his home. Mr. Smith is given a very inexpensive price for the cost of the asphalt. Upon agreeing, Mr. Smith is quickly presented with a contract. Then Mr. Smith is told that the price will be reduced further if he pays cash for these jobs. Mr. Smith promptly produces the money, upon which the salesman leaves, informing Mr. Smith that his company's work crews will come by in the next few days to do the contracted work. The salesman leaves with Mr. Smith's money. The work crews never appear. Mr. Smith, checking the telephone book, finds that there is no company with the name appearing on the contracts. He realizes he has been swindled.

Example D

A man in a service truck from a plumbing and heating contractor appears at Mr. Smith's door and tells him that for a minimum charge of five dollars, he will inspect his furnace and heating system to make sure that everything is working before winter sets in. Mr. Smith notes that the price is most reasonable and promptly shows the man to the basement. The man then bangs on the furnace and pipes for about fifteen minutes to persuade Mr. Smith that he is doing his job. He reappears upstairs and asks Mr. Smith to return to the basement with him. The furnace man shows Mr. Smith cracks in his furnace and tells him that the furnace is worn out and that if he doesn't have it replaced immediately there is a distinct danger that it could burn down the house when burning at capacity. Mr. Smith fears this danger to his home and gladly agrees to sign a contract for the installation of a new furnace. Within a week the new furnace is brought to Mr. Smith's home and installed. Mr. Smith is pleased with the company's speed in installing his new furnace. He brags to his neighbors about what a good company it is to do business with. What Mr. Smith does not know, and may never realize, is that any furnace will eventually have some cracks in it and that he did not need a new one. The furnace salesman has played on Mr. Smith's fear for his home in order to sell him a furnace he didn't need.

Nine out of 10 victims of consumer fraud, it is believed, do not report it to police; they either are too embarrassed or feel that a report would be of little value. Sadly, it is often true that the police cannot help, partly because some of the practices, though dishonest, are not necessarily illegal. A law has been passed that would prevent a victim from being forced to comply with the terms of a contract if it is canceled within 72 hours of signing. The main protection for older people lies, however, in not allowing themselves to be rushed into signing a contract.

The Wisconsin Bankers Association has developed a customer's release form that advises the depositor of the dangers involved in withdrawing large amounts of money; it is, of course, designed to protect customers against various swindle schemes—something that would seem particularly helpful for older customers.

Eva Kahana and her colleagues (1977) attempted to determine the degree to which older persons felt themselves victims of crime in the private sector, in neighborhoods, and in the public sector. Victimization in the private sector was defined as rejection by friends and family, employment rejection, and problems as consumers in purchase of services or merchandise. Victimization in neighborhoods was defined as being victims of crime or living in undesirable neighborhoods. Victimization in the public sector was defined as problems with social security, taxes, the police, and the like.

Nineteen percent of the sample reported victimization in the private sector, 39 percent victimization in neighborhoods, and 12 percent victimization in the public sector. When questioned regarding whether they thought that their victimization was related to age, approximately 30 percent of those reporting victimization in the private sector attributed it to age, as did 12 percent of those reporting neighborhood victimization and 21 percent of those reporting victimization in the public sector. There is, then, a segment of those persons who are victimized in any of the three sectors who attribute their victimization to age. Thus not only do they fear victimization but they often feel that they are being singled out because of their age.[17]

ABUSE OF THE ELDERLY

Chapter 1 included data indicating the growth in both the numbers and percentage of our total population that are 65 and above. Moreover, the 80-and-above age group is currently the fastest-growing group. The older people become, the more likely they are to be dependent on families and the professional staffs of nursing homes and other service providers. Human beings who are dependent on others for their survival, whether they are children or older persons, are always vulnerable to mistreatment and abuse. As our older population has grown, the number of cases of adult abuse has also grown. Older Americans represent a large, vulnerable group. Moreover, the older they become, the more likely they are to experience the health losses that lead to dependence on others for their care. Independent older people are not likely to be abused, and if they are abused, they are in a better position to seek help and protect themselves from further abuse. Dependent older persons are in no position to protect themselves and if abused are likely to become more submissive in order to protect themselves from the abuser.

Moreover, the older you become the more likely you are to become dependent on others. Eighty-year-olds are more likely to be residing in nursing homes than are 65-year-olds. Karl Pillemer (1989) made a study of abuse experienced by the elderly living in nursing homes. Of the 577 staff members working in a nursing home, 10 percent admitted to one or more abusive acts (pushing, grabbing, pinching, and so on); 2 percent admitted to hitting a patient with an object or trying to do so; and 1 percent had thrown something at a patient.

The staff also admitted to incidence of psychological abuse; 33 percent stated that they had yelled at patients, 10 percent had cursed at patients, 4 percent had denied a patient food or privileges, and 2 percent had threatened a patient.

Joan Krauskopf and Mary Elise Burnett (1983) delineate the kinds of abuse experienced by the elderly:

1. Physical abuse, which includes lack of personal care, lack of supervision, bruises, welts, lack of food, and beatings
2. Psychological abuse, which includes verbal assaults, isolation, and threats
3. Material and financial abuse, including misuse or theft of money or property
4. Unsatisfactory living conditions, such as a dirty and unkept house or apartment or the stench of urine or garbage

Krauskopf and Burnett observe that these kinds of abuse are not mutually exclusive. An older person can simultaneously be experiencing more than one kind of abuse.

Richard Douglas and Tom Hickey (1979) distinguish between passive neglect, which includes being ignored, left alone, or isolated; and active neglect, which includes withholding companionship, medicine, food, or exercise.

Karl Pillemer and Rosalie Wolf (1986) examined five possible causes of elder abuse:

1. Intraindividual dynamics: Some have argued that the abuser has sadistic personality traits and a perverse fascination with punishment as an entity in itself. Some have argued the abusers are more frequently alcohol or drug abusers.
2. Intergenerational transmission of violent behavior: This approach suggests a cycle of violence in abused children who grow up to be child or elder abusers.
3. Dependency: Some have argued that resentment is generated by increased dependency of an older person on a caretaker. Often the caretakers themselves were found to be financially dependent on their victims. David Finkelhor (1983) notes that abuse can occur as a response to perceived powerlessness. Acts of abuse, he observes, seem to be acts carried out by abusers to compensate for their perceived lack or loss of power. Thus spouse abuse has been found to be related to a sense of powerlessness, and child abuse tends to start with a feeling of parental impotence. The powerlessness experienced by an adult child dependent on the elderly parent may be particularly strong because it so opposes society's expectation of normal adult behavior.
4. External stress: A number of studies have found a positive relationship between external stress and wife or child abuse.

5. Social isolation: Social isolation has been found to be characteristic of families in which child and spouse abuse occurred.

In a study to determine individual characteristics that could explain abusive behavior, Pillemer and Wolf (1986) found that abusers had more mental problems than nonabusers and were more likely to have been hospitalized for psychiatric reasons. Therefore, the intraindividual-dynamics explanation of abuse appears to have some validity.

A study of the intergenerational-transmission hypothesis indicated no relationship between being a victim of child abuse and later becoming an abuser oneself. This explanation apparently has little or no validity.

The research findings on dependency indicated that the older person who was abused was not any more dependent than a control group of older persons who were not abused. However, the abusers were significantly more likely to be dependent on their elderly victims than were a control group of nonabusers. The abusers were most often found to be dependent on their elderly victims for housing, financial assistance, and transportation. Apparently the inability of the abuser to succeed at being an independent and self-directing member of society creates in him or her some of the anxiety and frustration leading to emotional outbursts and abusive behavior.

External stress was not found to be related to elder victimization. Elder abusers were not found to be under any more stress than were a control group of nonabusers. Thus the external-stress hypothesis was not proved valid.

Finally, the abuser groups did score more poorly on two social-resource scales. Apparently elder abusers are more socially isolated than a control group of nonabusers. Pillemer and Wolf's (1986) findings indicate that elder abusers are suffering from more mental and emotional problems, are more likely to be financially dependent on the person they abuse, and are more likely to be socially isolated. They are not any more likely to have been abused themselves as children and they are not necessarily experiencing any more external stress than nonabusers in the population.

An emerging area of concern for persons that provide social services to older Americans is the older persons' self-neglect or self-abuse. Some older persons reach a point where they are no longer bathing, dressing, and feeding themselves properly. They seem to give up on living and following the normal daily self-care practices for survival that everyone in one way or another must follow. The Virginia Department of Social Services (1991), in a national survey on self-neglect, found 61 percent of older people who had in one way or another been deprived or abused were self-neglectors. They were no longer capable of caring for themselves or of employing other people to help them care for themselves. Many states now provide Adult Protective Services for the older population, both to detect and prevent cases of abuse of the elderly and to find ways of caring for the self-neglecting elderly who are no longer able to take care of themselves.

CONCLUSION

The data at this point on the criminal victimization of older persons are confusing. FBI and police statistics accumulated on a national or other very broad basis tend to indicate that older persons are the victims of crime much less often than the general population. On the other hand, data gathered by LEAA in selected cities and neighborhoods across the country tend to indicate that older persons are more frequently the victims of certain kinds of crime (crimes involving theft with personal contact between the victim and offender) than other age groups.

It is perfectly clear, however, that older persons are more fearful of crime than any other age group. This may be explained in part by the fact that older persons often feel weak, vulnerable, and isolated. In a case of personal assault or attack, they feel unable to defend themselves. They are also the least likely to have additional resources that allow them to minimize the effect of a loss of money or property.

Goldsmith and Thomas (1974) list a series of reasons why they believe the elderly are more vulnerable to criminal attack:

1. There is a high incidence of reduced or low income among the elderly. Thus the impact of any loss of economic resources is relatively greater.

2. Older people are more likely to be victimized repeatedly, often by the same crime and the same offender.

3. Older people are more likely to live alone and to be socially isolated.

4. Older people have diminished physical strength and stamina; hence, they are less able to defend themselves or to escape from threatening situations.

5. Older people are far more likely to suffer from physical ailments such as loss of hearing or sight, arthritis, and circulatory problems.

6. Older people are physically more fragile and more easily hurt should they opt to defend themselves. For example, bones are more easily broken, and recovery is more difficult. Thus they are less likely to resist attackers.

7. Potential criminals are aware of the diminished physical capacity of the elderly and thus are more likely to seek out an elderly target (whose aged status is easily visible).

8. There is a greater likelihood that older people will live in high-crime neighborhoods rather than in suburbia as a result of diminished income and of being rooted in central cities. Thus they find themselves in close proximity to the groups most likely to victimize them—the unemployed or teenage dropouts.

9. The dates of receipt of mail of monthly pension and benefit checks (and hence the dates when older people are most likely to have cash on their persons or in their dwellings) are widely known.

10. Dependency on walking or on public transportation is more usual among older people, who, for physical, financial, or other reasons, are less likely to drive or own a private automobile.

11. There is evidence that older people are particularly susceptible to frauds and confidence games.

12. Older people have the highest rates of the crime of personal larceny with contact (theft of purse, wallet, or cash directly from the person of the victim, including attempted purse snatching).

13. Awareness of increased vulnerability to criminal behavior has a chilling effect upon the freedom of movement of older Americans. Fear of criminal

victimization causes self-imposed "house arrest" among older people, who may refuse to venture out of doors. Furthermore, even in those situauons where the fear of being victimized may be somewhat exaggerated or unwarranted by local conditions, the effect on the older persons is just as severe as when the fears are justified.

14. Because of loss of status and decreased sense of personal efficacy associated in American culture with being old, older people may be less likely to process complaints through the criminal justice bureaucracy and to draw upon available community resources for protection and redress.[18]

In terms of fear of crime among the elderly, women were found to be more fearful than men, blacks more fearful than whites, inner-city dwellers more fearful than suburban or rural dwellers, and poor people more fearful than persons of middle or upper income. While the initial data indicate the older persons may be more fearful than the likelihood of their being victimized suggests, later refinements of police statistics seem to indicate that it is inner-city residents, women, blacks, and the poor who are most frequently the victims of crime. Thus, it is specifically those categories of old people who are most fearful of crime that are most frequently victimized. Perhaps there is greater justification for older persons' fear than the earlier police statistics tended to indicate. Moreover, the elderly are most often victimized within a few blocks of their homes. This represents an invasion of their personal life space, which is more threatening to them.

A newly emerging phenomenon in the area of crime and the elderly is that of the older person as an offender and not a victim. Jim Le Beau (1982), reporting on crimes committed by seniors, points out that in 1970, 6.6 percent of those 65 and older who were arrested were charged with serious crimes. In 1980, 17.6 percent of the seniors arrested were charged with serious crimes. Le Beau (1982) indicates that the increase in serious crimes (such as murder, robbery, and arson) committed by seniors increased steadily during the 1970s. Future researchers will undoubtedly delve into the causes of this trend.

KEY TERMS

Field-dependent
Field-independent

REFERENCES

ANTUNES, GEORGE E., and OTHERS, "Patterns of Personal Crime Against the Elderly," *Gerontologist*, 17, no. 4 (1977), 321–27.

CLÉMENTS, FRANK, and MICHAEL KLEIMAN, "Fear of Crime Among the Aged," *Gerontologist*, 16, no. 3 (1976), 207–10.

COOK, FAY LOMAX, "Criminal Victimization of the Elderly: A New National Problem," in *Victimization and Society*, ed. Emelio C. Viano. Washington, D.C.: Visage Press, 1976.

COTTON, LOU, *Elders in Rebellion*. New York: Doubleday, Anchor, 1979.

DOUGLAS, RICHARD, and TOM HICKEY, "A Study of Maltreatment of the Elderly and Other Valuable Adults." Ann Arbor: Institute of Gerontology, University of Michigan, 1979.

ERIKSON, H., "The Polls: Fear of Violence and Crime," *Public Opinion Quarterly*, 38 (1974), 131–45.

FINKELHOR, David, ed., *The Dark Side of Families: Current Family Violence Research*. Beverly Hills, Calf.: Sage, 1983.

GOLDSMITH, JACK, "A Symposium on Crime and the Elderly," *Police Chief*, February 1976, pp. 18–20.

GOLDSMITH, JACK, and NOEL E. THOMAS, "Crimes Against the Elderly: A Continuing National Crisis," *Aging*, June-July 1974, pp. 230–37.

HARRIS, LOUIS, and ASSOCIATES, *The Myth and Reality of Aging in America*. Washington, D.C.: National Council on the Aging, 1975.

HINDELANG, MICHAEL, *Criminal Victimization in Eight American Cities*. Cambridge, Mass.: Ballinger, 1976.

HOCHSTEDLER, ELLEN, *Crime Against the Elderly in 26 Cities*. Albany, N.Y.: Criminal Justice Research Center, 1981.

KAHANA, EVA, and OTHERS, "Perspectives of Aged on Victimization, Ageism, and Their Problems in Urban Society," *Gerontologist*, 17, no. 2 (April 1977), 121–29.

KRAUSKOPF, JOAN A., and MARY ELISE BURNETT, *Trial*, 1983, pp. 61–63.

LE BEAU, JAMES, "Increase in Serious Crimes by Seniors," *Terre Haute Tribune Star*, April 7, 1982, p. 3.

MALINCHAK, ALAN A., *Crime and Gerontology*, pp. 39–63. Englewood Cliffs, N.J.: Prentice Hall, 1980.

MALINCHAK, ALAN A., and DOUGLAS WRIGHT,

"The Scope of Elderly Victimization," *Aging*, Nos. 281–82 (April 1978), 12–16.

NORTON, L., and M. COURLANDER, "Fear of Crime Among the Elderly: The Role of Crime Prevention Programs," *Gerontologist*, 22, no. 4 (1988), 388–93.

PATTERSON, ARTHUR, "Territorial Behavior and the Fear of Crime in the Elderly," *Police Chief*, February 1977, pp. 20–29.

PILLEMER, KARL, "Abuse of Patients in Nursing Homes," *Gerontologist*, 29, no. 3 (1989), 314–20.

PILLEMER, KARL A., and ROSALIE S. WOLF, *Elder Abuse: Conflict in the Family*. Dover, Mass.: Auburn House Publishing, 1986.

POPE, CARL E., and WILLIAM F. FEHARM, "A Review of Recent Trends: The Effects of Crime on the Elderly," *Police Chief*, February 1976.

RIFIA, MARLENE A., "The Response of the Older Adult to Criminal Victimization," *Police Chief*, February 1977, pp. 32–34.

TIGHE, JOHN H., "A Survey of Crimes Against the Elderly," *Police Chief*, February 1977, p. 19.

VIRGINIA DEPARTMENT OF SOCIAL SERVICES, "A National Study of Self-Neglecting Adult Protective Service Clients," 1991.

NOTES

1. See Louis Harris and Associates, *The Myth and Realities of Aging in America* (Washington, D.C.: National Council on the Aging, 1975); Carl E. Pope and William F. Feyharm, "A Review of Recent Trends: The Effects of Crime on the Elderly," *Police Chief*, February 1976; and Alan A. Malinchak, *Crime and Gerontology* (Englewood Cliffs, N.J.: Prentice Hall, 1980).

2. H. Erikson, "The Polls: Fear of Violence and Crime," *Public Opinion Quarterly*, 38 (1974), 131–45.

3. Frank Clements and Michael Kleiman, "Fear of Crime Among the Aged," *Gerontologist*, 16, no. 3 (1976), 207–8.

4. Ibid., p. 209.

5. Erikson, "The Polls," p. 144.

6. Fay Lomax Cook, "Criminal Victimization of the Elderly: A New National Problem," in *Victimization and Society*, ed. Emelio C. Viano (Washington, D.C.: Visage Press, 1976).

7. Jack Goldsmith and Noel F. Thomas, "Crimes Against the Elderly: A Continuing National Crisis," *Aging*, June–July 1974, p. 11.

8. Michael Hindelang, *Criminal Victimization in*

Eight American Cities (Cambridge, Mass.: Ballinger, 1976), p. 377.

9. Alan A. Malinchak and Douglas Wright, "The Scope of Elderly Victimization," *Aging*, Nos. 281–82 (April 1978), 12–16.

10. George E. Antunes and others, "Patterns of Personal Crime Against the Elderly," *Gerontology*, 17, no. 4 (1977), 321–27.

11. Arthur Patterson, "Territorial Behavior and the Fear of Crime in the Elderly," *Police Chief*, February 1977, pp. 26–29.

12. Marlene A. Rifia, "The Response of the Older Adult to Criminal Victimization," *Police Chief*, February 1977, pp. 32–34.

13. Ibid., p. 33.

14. Patterson, "Territorial Behavior," p. 27.

15. Ibid., p. 27.

16. Ibid., p. 28.

17. Eva Kahana and others, "Perspectives of Aged on Victimization, Ageism, and Their Problems in Urban Society," *Gerontologist*, 17, no. 2 (April 1977), 121–29.

18. Goldsmith and Thomas, "Crimes Against the Elderly," p. 232.

14

Politics and the Government Service Delivery System

The demographic shifts in the number and percentage of persons 65 and older in our population were discussed in the earlier chapters of this text. These figures must be reiterated at this point because they have direct implications regarding the potential political power of Americans 65 and older. The 3 million 65+ Americans in 1900, representing 4 percent of the population and widely distributed across the country, made few demands for public services and could easily be ignored by the politicians of the day. The 30 million Americans 65 and over in 1988, representing 12 percent of the population, cannot be ignored so easily. Moreover, this 12 percent of the population constitutes 20 percent of the electorate due to the fact that those under age 18 do not vote.

While demographic predictions about what the percentage of those persons 65 and older will be in the year 2000 are risky at best, not even the most conservative of demographers predicts anything other than an even larger percentage of the population being in the older age group. A rapid upturn in the crude birthrate resulting in an unexpected increase in the number of young persons in total population could alter these predictions. This seems unlikely, however, because the current trends are for lower birthrates and the value of having small families is shared by a large percentage of younger persons.

It seems likely, then, that in the foreseeable future the 65-and-over age group is going to make up an ever-increasing number and percentage of the total population and will make greater demands on government resources. What must be remembered is that government never has enough resources to meet all the requests of its citizenry. Those requests that are met are usually related in some way to the receiving group's exercise of political power.

POLITICAL PARTICIPATION

Political participation connects the individual to the decision-making bodies of the country. Political participation includes such things as:

1. Holding opinions on the current issues facing the country
2. Being an opinion leader and convincing others of one's point of view
3. Voting
4. Joining political parties and movements
5. Holding office

Older people are slightly more likely than younger people to hold an opinion on an issue. Norval Glenn and Michael Grimes (1968) found that the better educated and those actively involved in the community were more likely to hold an opinion than the less well educated or the uninvolved members of the community.[1]

Jaber Gubrium (1976) found that older persons were overrepresented among opinion leaders (those whom others turn to for advice on political matters). Young people are more prone to turn to older people for advice on political issues than to their own age group. While 22 percent of the general adult population have been identified as opinion leaders, 35 percent of retired persons were so identified.[2]

The voting patterns of different age groups in the population have been fairly well established by research. While younger people may talk at great length and with considerable emotion about political issues, older people are much more likely to turn out and vote. Campbell (1962) reports that while only about 50 percent of people in their early 20s vote, slightly more than 80 percent of those in their 60s vote and about 75 percent of those in their 70s vote.

The voting patterns outlined by Campbell (1962) in the 1950s and 1960s are still basically the same if we look at the elections that took place in the 1980s. *The Economist* (1988) reports that in the 1980 elections 71 percent of Americans aged 55 to 64 went to the polls compared to 36 percent of those 18 to 20. Moreover, George Engelter (1988) reports that in the 1988 presidential election, voters aged 60 to 69 boasted the nation's highest turnout rate of 72.8 percent. Campbell argues that evidence exists that political involvement generally increases with age. Older people, he believes, are more interested in politics, they follow political activities in the media more closely, and they participate more actively than younger people.[3] Engelter's (1988) description of the political participation by seniors in the 1980s follows this predicted pattern. Engelter reports that while only 28 percent of those 24 or younger say they watch television every night; over three quarters of those over 65 watch on a regular basis. While 70 percent of those over 60 read the newspaper daily, only 39 percent of the younger group do so. As a result of the above patterns, 41 percent of people under 24 report not having enough information on political candidates while only 20 percent of the over-40 group report the same problem.

Persons over 65 are split about equally in their identification with the two major political parties. Since those under 60 are somewhat more likely to be Democrats, this has led some persons to conclude that there is a shift toward the more conservative Republican party in old age. This does not appear to be the case. Those now 65 and over were socialized with political attitudes and ideals before the New Deal. There were at that time about an equal number of Republicans and Democrats. Persons reared since the 1930s and the New Deal legislation are more likely to be Democrats than Republicans. One does not appear to shift parties as one ages. It may well be that a later cohort group of retirees, trained in their political beliefs during and after the 1930s, will be more likely to be Democrats. Not only is there not a tendency to shift one's political party in old age but indeed the older one becomes, the more one becomes committed to the party of choice.

Lane (1959) argues that insofar as voting is a conscious positive commitment of time and energy, older people, in direct contradiction to disengagement theory, display high political involvement and integration into society.[4]

There is much discussion concerning whether older voters are likely to vote as a bloc for issues they perceive to be in their best interest. Campbell (1971) argues that the most important general assertion that can be made is that there is no "aging vote." He claims that elderly voters think more in terms of ethnicity, party, class, and region when they come to the polls and rarely in terms of age.[5] Herman Loether (1967) believes that age does not constitute a primary reference group because voters are more likely to identify themselves with their families, their political parties, their churches, and their social groups.[6] Elizabeth Douglas, William Cleveland, and George Maddox (1976) report that only at the most immediate level—the community—did age enter at all as a significant determinant of political attitudes.[7]

While it may well be that the aged do not always vote as a bloc and that they do hold a variety of cross-cutting loyalties, they do coalesce when they consider an issue vital to their interests. Loether (1967) did find that concentrations of older voters in Miami voted as a bloc when they felt their vested interests could be affected by the outcome of the election. Social security, the Older Americans Act, and medicare are examples of programs that were passed, at least in part, because of the strong support and endorsement of older Americans.

Political participation can include joining a political party in order to campaign for a party platform and candidates with favored political views, as well as joining a social movement whose goal is to change society in one way or another. One advantage that older persons have in either of these endeavors is ample free time. The middle-aged American who is torn among family, work, and community obligations frequently has little time left over for other kinds of commitments. Political participation, whether in political parties or social movements, requires large commitments of time and energy. Research on social movements has indicated that their members tend to be young, unmarried, and frequently without full-time jobs. This means that they have the available time that social movements require.

Becoming active in a political party usually can be seen as a semicareer. Most loyal party members join in their early 20s and remain active throughout their adult lives. One wonders if at 65 persons who have not been politically active throughout their adult lives are likely to do so at this time. On the other hand, those who have been active party members will now find that they have time to become even more involved and therefore can exercise greater influence in political decisions.

Moreover, James Franke (1984) found that activists in such elderly groups as the American Association of Retired Persons (AARP) are able to get their organization to endorse more liberal government policies than the membership actually prefers.

Georgia Barrow and Patricia Smith (1979) argue that social movements don't just happen but rather are the combined results of social, economic, and historical events. Those who are affected negatively by such events usually join forces to change the situation, demanding their rights and pointing out the injustices of the current arrangements. Barrow and Smith, in discussing the historical development of aged-based social movements, state

> This happened in the early 1900s when a large proportion of the aged were living in poverty. Retirement had increasingly become mandatory; yet pensions were not available which often left the aged with neither work nor money.[8]

This kind of deprivation being experienced by large numbers of the elderly resulted in the emergence of a social movement led by a retired physician named Townsend. The Townsend Plan called for the government to pay $200 a month to persons 60 and older with the requirement that they retire from work and spend the money within 30 days. The plan's backers felt it would have two positive results if put into practice. First, it would improve the economic conditions and status of older Americans. Second, it would stimulate a depressed economy. Townsend Clubs sprang up across the country and at their peak in 1936 numbered more than 7000.

As with most social movements that have widespread appeal and backing, one of the two major parties incorporated the suggested changes into its platform. The Democratic New Deal administration in 1935 secured passage of the Social Security Act, which provided a pension for the elderly, thus undercutting the

In 1935 President Franklin D. Roosevelt signed the nation's first major program for the elderly, The Social Security Act.

major thrust of the movement. There seems little doubt that the Townsend movement aided the passage of the Social Security Act.

The Townsend movement has been followed by other movements on behalf of older persons. George McLain in the 1940s led a California-based movement to improve the lives of older Americans. Paul Kleyman (1974) notes that an interesting feature of all these movements was that they extracted great sums of money from the aged themselves. Kleyman (1974) describes the leaders of the movements as "pension panacea peddlers."[9] Social unrest, whether structured into a social movement or not, does most often bring about change. Prolonged social unrest among the elderly ultimately resulted in the passage of the Older Americans Act in 1965 and medicare in 1966. While older persons have not shown any inclination to vote as a bloc except on local community issues, the causes addressed by any of the social movements on their behalf have most often been picked up and endorsed by one or both of the political parties. This almost guarantees legislation on behalf of older persons. The major advantage of a social movement seems to be to increase the public's awareness of a problem. Once political leaders become aware that there is widespread support for change it is very difficult for particular interest groups to block proposed legislation.

Gerontologists, in discussing the power of older Americans' movements, observe that they have yet to lose a major political campaign. The "gray lobby" has taken on the American Medical Association over medicare, the large corporations over mandatory retirement, and taxpayers' groups over social security, and defeated them all.

The 1970s saw the emergence of the Gray Panthers movement led by Maggie Kuhn. Comprising a loose coalition of young and old social activists, this group launched major attacks on the American Medical Association for its lack of attention to the health problems of older Americans and on social values that require older persons to disengage. Pauline Ragan and James Dowd (1977) believe that rather than social change, the focus of the Gray Panthers is more on alternative lifestyles for the aged.[10] As with other social movements on behalf of the aged, the major function of the Gray Panthers seems to be to raise the public consciousness of the problems of older Americans. They have at various times attacked compulsory retirement, advocated pension reform, and proposed the elimination of poverty. Anne Foner (1984) observes that it is not uncommon for social movements to arrive almost simultaneously. She asks whether this occurs because the movements are responding to similar conditions or whether it occurs because one movement stimulates the emergence of other movements.

The Gray Panther movement seems to be following on the heels of the civil rights movement and the women's liberation movement. These movements of the 1950s, 1960s, and 1970s have one thing in common: They all are reflections of a new emphasis on the quality of life in America today. Black people in the civil rights movement were essentially saying, "We want an improvement in the quality of life for blacks. We want more jobs, opportunities for upward mobility, and a larger share of rewards that go with an affluent industrial economy." The women's liberation movement also embodied the quality-of-life demands expressed by a deprived group. These demands were similar to those of the civil rights leaders—greater opportunities for employment and promotion, larger salaries, and protection from discrimination. Women, in essence, want a larger share of the rewards of the system and an improvement in the quality of their lives. The Gray Panther movement can be seen as an expression of older persons' demands for an end to discrimination in employment, for improved pensions, and for a larger share of the nation's resources. Thus their demands can also be seen as an assertion of their rights to an improved quality of life.

There are a variety of more traditional organizations that pursue the interests of older constituents. These include the National Caucus of Black Aged, the National Council of Senior Citizens, the National Retired Teachers Association, and the National Association of Retired Federal Employees. While more traditional and less militant than the social movements, these groups work systematically to improve the life of senior citizens, and because they are more widely accepted they have probably accomplished more. But they are similar to the movements in that one of their major functions is to keep the public and political leaders informed of the plight of older Americans.

Henry Pratt (1974) believes the more traditional associations for older Americans have had greater success than the groups in the 1930s and 1940s because they have had more financial support than solely membership dues. They have had experienced leadership rather than the charismatic leadership of the 1930s and 1940s movements, which relied solely on popular appeal. In addition, the political climate of the 1960s and 1970s has been more responsive to the demands of older Americans.[11]

Most observers of the political power of the aged have concluded that it is not their power as a voting bloc that has brought about legislation and change but rather the fact that interest groups and the efforts of the more traditional associations of older Americans have brought their problems to the attention of the public. As Beth Hess (1978) states,

> If there is any political clout to be claimed for older Americans, . . . this derives from those operating on behalf of the aged but who typically are not yet themselves elderly.[12]

As we pointed out in Chapter 1, demographers have traditionally thought of persons under 18 and over 65 as dependent for their goods and services on those between 19 and 64, who are in essence in their productive years. Donald Cowgill (1977) maintains that the dependency ratio of the U.S. population has not changed dramatically since 1900, even with the dramatic increase in the 65+ group. Since the growing number of older Americans has been accompanied by a decline in the number and percentage of the population under 18, Cowgill (1977) argues, the percentage of the population defined as dependent has not increased but rather has shifted. While maintaining about the same percentage of the population in the dependent category we now have fewer young people and more older persons.[13] There is one big difference, however, in terms of the demands on government: Whereas families consider it a moral obligation to look after their young, they do not consider it their obligation to look after their older family members.

Much of the legislation and governmental programs providing services to older Americans has come with the strong support and endorsement of middle-age voters who are anxious to shift the responsibility for older family members off of themselves and onto the government. Thus, younger family members and organized lobbying groups operating on behalf of older Americans are as much a factor in federal programs in their behalf as the efforts of older persons themselves. Moreover, there is an ever-growing group of service providers, administrators, and scientists whose professional careers are dependent upon further programs and additional government resources for older Americans.

Most social movements that attempt to change society ultimately experience a backlash from elements of society that feel that the change will not be in their interest or that it is excessively costly. Whether the movements for older Americans will experience such a backlash remains to be seen.

There is no doubt that federal expenditures for older Americans have risen at alarmingly fast rates for many taxpayers. The cost of social security alone has risen from $36 billion in 1970 to $90 billion in 1976 to $175.3 billion in 1986. Moreover, future increases are likely to be mandated almost automatically by Congress so that the incomes of older persons can be kept somewhat in line with increasing costs due to inflation. David Fischer (1979) maintains that government spending has moved out of the control of the President and federal administration and into the category of uncontrolled costs. He describes the "graying" of the federal budget and the uncontrollable nature of the increases as the withering away of the ability to govern.[14] The question that must be addressed by advocates for older Americans' programs is this: At what point will taxpayers' lobbies and other groups come to believe that programs for older Americans are becoming too expensive and should therefore be curbed?

In terms of holding political office, older persons tend to be overrepresented in Congress, the presidency, and the Supreme Court. Congressional and Senate subcommittees are usually chaired by their senior members. Because the Constitution does not permit anyone to be elected to the Senate until he or she is 30, and because only the senior members are likely to chair the committees and hold the more important posts, it is easy to see how the older senators exercise considerable power. In 1974 the large number of new and younger members of Congress loosened the hold of the older, experienced members on the committee chairs. The senior members still exercise considerable power, however.

Most Presidents have been between the ages of 50 and 65 when elected. The first four Presidents of the United States were 57 or older. On the other hand, only two Presidents ever entered office after the age of 65—William Henry Harrison and Ronald Reagan, who became President at 68. Several Presidents have turned 65 while in office. The youngest two Presidents have been Theodore Roosevelt, who assumed the office at 42, and John Kennedy (43). While most presidents are older, a youthful image of the President has become popular in the twentieth century.

The position of Supreme Court justice implies experience and wisdom. Those chosen have often been involved in the judicial system for some time and have served as judges in various courts. It is unlikely that a young lawyer would have had the opportunity for the kind of experiences Presidents look for in appointing justices. In 1978 the youngest justice was 54, the oldest 72, and the average age was 65.5.

Thus while most representatives, senators, Presidents, and Supreme Court justices have been in their middle or later years, the United States has not created a gerontocracy. A majority of these offices are still held by persons under the age of 65. A youthful image is a political asset even for older politicians, and even when politicians are old, their age does not appear to be the critical variable affecting their positions on the issues of the day.

INTERGENERATIONAL CONFLICT OR CONSENSUS

Students of political power have, in the past, argued that the old and the young in Western societies are deprived groups that share many of the same deprivations. Both of these groups are not involved in careers and are out of the productive years of their lives. Because of the high value placed on productivity in Western industrial nations, generally the young and the old share positions of low status, privilege, and power in the society. As a result they tend to be more likely to be low income and share fewer of the society's resources. Therefore, many have argued that the young and the old should coalesce to consolidate their position and seek to compete with those in the working years of adult life for a larger share of the social systems resources. This, however, has never happened because the young and the old see themselves at such distinct points in the life cycle that they don't perceive the similarity of their situations. While the young may see themselves as poor and having no secure position in society, they view this as a temporary condition. They believe it will only be a matter of time until they arrive at adult status, enter a career, and assume a secure position in the society. The old, on the other hand, who find themselves poor have little hope of any improvement as they look to the future. All they have to look forward to in countries where inflation is constant is rising prices while they attempt to survive on a fixed income. Moreover, there is little if any opportunity for them to seek employment as a means of increasing their income at this stage of life. Thus, as a result of their distinct positions in the life cycle, there has been no political coalition among the young and the old.

What actually has occurred more frequently in the last two decades is competition between the young and the old for government programs and services. Moreover, groups such as the American Retired Teachers Association and the American Association of Retired Persons have had great success in lobbying for programs and services for older Americans. Seniors, as a result of the advocacy groups lobbying on their behalf, have cost-of-living increases in their social security checks automatically guaranteed by Congress and have witnessed the emergence of a wide range of government programs designed to serve them. These programs include medicare/medicaid, nutrition, transportation, housing, senior employment programs, and others. Thus the 1970s and 1980s have seen Congress approve of an ever-wider range of benefits and services for senior citizens.

As a result of the effectiveness of senior citizens and groups lobbying Congress on their behalf, Johnson, Conrad, and Thompson (1989), and Chris Phillipson (1991) are predicting there will be intergenerational conflict between those in the working years who are paying taxes to support the programs serving those out of the working years. Currently, new groups have emerged lobbying congressional leaders against the cost of senior programs. Their basic argument is that senior service programs are costing too much to those in their working years and therefore they should be terminated. They assert that Congress should be concerned with what they call *generational equity*.

Johnson et al. (1989) asserted that older people have created a comprehensive welfare state for themselves while reducing equivalent resources for young people. Phillipson (1991) outlines the reasons given for predicting intergenerational conflicts from different writers as

1. The older people have been active in designing a welfare state which is largely for their own benefit.

2. The younger people now perceive this to be the case and are beginning to act as a generational group in opposing inequities in welfare resources.

3. The number of older people is itself a factor in generating instability within the system.

4. The original case for extensive welfare benefits for the old is in any case undermined by their increasing propensity in comparison to younger households.[15]

Phillipson (1991) then looks at each of these arguments critically to determine their validity. Reviewing the Social Security Act, the first law passed to benefit the elderly, Phillipson argues that the social security system was created in an attempt to get old people out of the labor force in order to have enough jobs for the young people with family responsibilities. Thus the first step in the creating of what some would label a welfare state for the elderly was done with the intention of providing more jobs for the young. Indeed the elderly by retiring were asked to bear the brunt of the high unemployment of the depression years, according to Phillipson (1991).

Those predicting intergenerational conflict believe the young perceive the inequities of the current welfare system and therefore oppose it. The surveys of public opinion in both Britain and the United States indicate that the young do not oppose government services for the elderly. Phillipson (1991) observes that a survey of British attitudes indicated that 80 percent of the public felt that providing a decent standard of living of the old was "definitely" a legitimate area of state responsibility, while 84 percent felt the state should provide health care for the aged. Only 1 percent were prepared to say that these activities did not fall within the scope of government. Similarly the American Association of Retired Persons reported a survey of American voters which indicated that 90 percent favored continuing support for medicare, and 75 percent believe the program should be expanded to include coverage for long-term care. Eighty percent believe the government is not doing enough for children living in poverty. Ninety percent believe that Social Security is a good program. The AARP concluded that the results of the survey of American voters indicated that the tension is not between generations but between income levels and social classes. The struggle is in reality between the haves and have nots.

Regarding the question of a growing number of old people retiring depending on fewer people working resulting in instability to the system, Phillipson (1991) points out that cutting the unemployment rate could considerably alter the dependency level and deflect any future strain on the pension system. Phillipson (1991), in looking at the problem in the United Kingdom, states

> If employment remained at the level it was in 1985, the ratio of people over 60 to those aged 20–65 would increase 23.2% by 2025. If, on the other hand, unemployment was eradicated, this dependency ratio would actually fall by 66.7%.[16]

Thus if productivity is the goal of Western nations, they could both increase productivity and lower any strain on welfare or pension programs by reducing the level of unemployment of those in their working years.

The final argument asserted by those predicting generational conflict is that the increasing number of older persons in the welfare state are putting undue burdens on younger families as taxpayers. The work of gerontologists indicates that in times of need older persons turn first to their families, then to neighbors, and finally to the bureaucratic agencies because they expect families to help in case of need. Thus government sources of support are only turned to when all others have been exhausted. As a result many people that could legitimately qualify for government services never use them. Lee (1985), however, argues that old people turn first to their families because government services are not believed to be available nor considered a viable option. Lee (1985) believes that the elderly's sense of independence is probably less threatened by dependence on government and more by dependence on their children. Governmental services are seen by the elderly as a right they have earned and paid for by their years of paying taxes. Family support is more subjective and less likely to be viewed as an earned privilege. In terms of the cost of the dependent population to society, Schulz (1988) observes that the cost of rearing a child to age 20 is one quarter to one third higher than needed to support a 60-year-old for the rest of his or her life.

The conclusion would seem to be that a revolution by young taxpayers against social security or the senior service programs of the United States or other Western nations is highly unlikely. Most young people who are actually paying the taxes to support these programs first believe that the elderly who have labored long in the social system have earned the right to pensions and other services. Second, they know that if the government weren't providing these services for family members that they would have to. Finally, the younger people themselves look forward to the time when they will retire and be the recipients of the services. It seems highly unlikely that intergenerational conflict is going to be a threat to government programs for the elderly either now or in the future.

STATUS INCONSISTENCY

Gubrium (1976) states that older persons' political attitudes can perhaps best be understood by assuming that many older persons are experiencing *status inconsistency.* Individuals at any age assume different roles in the various groups of which they are members. Each of these roles carries a status and the commensurate privileges assumed to go with that status. One may be the president of the Lions Club, which implies an important role and accompanying status in the organization, while simultaneously being a junior salesman for a local construction firm. This latter role carries low status. Thus a person may have high status, power, and privilege in one group and low status, power, and privilege in another group. The possession of discrepant ranks in various status hierarchies creates social and psychological strain. This stress causes the individual to try to bring his or her ranks into balance. In other words, individuals are inclined to seek consistency among their ranks and statuses in various groups.

Hughes (1944–45) found that a combination of low racial or ethnic status (ascribed) and a high occupational and educational status (achieved) is found in individuals who are most inclined to be politically liberal.[17] Either consciously or unconsciously they apparently believe that social change would be good for them

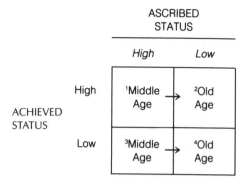

FIGURE 14–1
Status Inconsistency Model

Source: Jaber F. Gubrium, *Time, Roles and Self in Old Age* (New York: Human Sciences, 1976), p. 142. © 1976 by Human Sciences Press.

because it would result in a better balance among their current disparate statuses.

Gubrium (1976) uses the status inconsistency model to explain some of the problems, frustrations, and stresses of old age. Age, he argues, should be considered an ascribed status. He starts with the premise that being old in Western cultures is an unequivocally low status, since youthfulness is highly valued. Following Figure 14–1, Gubrium argues that the profile of a person of higher socioeconomic status (achieved) who moves from cell 1 to cell 2 changes from a consistent to an inconsistent status. Those persons of a lower socioeconomic status (achieved) who move from cell 3 to cell 4 change from inconsistent to consistent status. Moving from cell 1 to cell 2 may be typical of the successful business executive who is forced to retire. (Gubrium argues that to compensate for his low status on the ascribed variable of age, the retired executive may continually remind his aged associates of his former rank and seek the deference that he was accorded earlier.) Moving from cell 3 to cell 4 would seem to be more typical of the unskilled factory worker.[18]

Lenski (1954) observed that persons with low ascribed and high achieved status often see themselves as successful but victimized by the system. These individuals, he found, are likely to be liberal in political orientation and express strong desire for change, which they feel would bring their discrepant statuses into balance. Thus persons of inconsistent status often respond to institutional barriers that block status equilibrium by generating pressures for change within the social structure.[19]

What is not certain is whether older persons experiencing status inconsistency would become liberal advocates of change in order to bring their discrepant statuses into balance, as younger people do, or whether they might become increasingly conservative, seeking to return to the preretirement years when they experienced status consistency. Only future research will be able to answer this question.

AGE AND POLITICAL CONSERVATISM

There is a widespread belief that older persons tend to become more conservative and that the older one becomes, the more conservative one is likely to be. Young people, it is felt, have low status and a low commitment to the current social order. They have little at stake and therefore can afford to be liberal advocates of change. Older persons have a secure status and position in the social system and are likely to see change as undermining their position. Older persons, it is felt, distrust change because they hold valuable the things they currently have. The investments of a lifetime may be lost in radical changes of the system.

The past attitudes and voting records of older persons do not indicate consistently conservative patterns. Campbell (1962) found that older persons supported government programs for full employment and low-cost medical care but did not support government programs to assure equal rights to blacks and to build better schools.[20] It appears, then, that the degree of liberalism or conservatism found among older voters is related more to what they define as their vested interests than to any lifelong liberal or conservative drift.

SOCIAL SERVICES FOR OLDER AMERICANS

The current generation of older Americans were born between 1900 and 1930. They were raised in a period in which only limited government services were available to individuals. Sociologist William Ogburn (1922) coined the term *cultural lag* to describe the process whereby one part, section, or institution in a culture will change and thus require alterations and adjustments in other parts of the culture. Ogburn viewed culture as functioning in much the same manner as a machine or a clock. All the parts of the clock are mechanically synchronized. For the clock to work, all the moving parts must turn at the right time, the right speed, and to the right degree. Ogburn states that because

> the various parts of modern culture are not changing at the same rate, some parts are changing more rapidly than others; and that since there is a correlation and interdependence of parts a change in one part requires readjustments through changes in the various correlated parts of culture.[21]

The considerable time it may take for various elements of a culture to catch up to a change in another part of the culture is referred to as cultural lag.

Between 1850 and 1920 the Industrial Revolution gradually changed the United States from an agricultural to an industrial nation. When the country was agricultural, the family was the unit of production and consumption. All family members worked collectively to accomplish needed tasks, from building barns to planting corn. When the older members of the family were too old to work they were looked after by younger members. There were no government services offered to older Americans, and none were desired. It would have been a threat to one's feelings of self-sufficiency, independence, and usefulness to accept government assistance. Welfare was considered appropriate only for the lazy and shiftless and should provide recipients with barely enough to survive on.

The Industrial Revolution moved work from the home to the factory; families were no longer the basic unit of production. Family members moved to different geographic locations to meet the labor demands of industrial society. Thus dispersed, families could no longer protect their members during times of crisis. There was a considerable lag between the emergence of the Industrial Revolution in the United States, the passage of government assistance programs for older Americans, and the acceptance of these programs by the public. The

Social Security Act was not passed until 1935, and even then it took a major economic depression to create enough public support for change to lead to its passage. This is the kind of cultural lag to which Ogburn (1922) refers.

The current generation of retired Americans was reared with values that were opposed to any kind of government assistance programs. Some of these older people do not utilize the programs available to them because of their belief that acceptance of such assistance makes them welfare recipients. Most, however, have come to accept government services as a right they have earned because of long years of work and service to the country.

Historical Development of Government Services for the Aged

The first major federal legislation that specifically addressed the problems of older Americans was the Social Security Act of 1935. Congress passed this law with the intention that social security provide a supplemental income that could be combined with savings, investments, and other income to make an adequate level of retirement income for qualified older Americans. Social security, however, has become the major source of income for most older Americans, many of whom have no additional savings, investments, or other income. Originally the Social Security Act established the retirement age of 65, which has generally been adopted by business, industry, religious, and government agencies. In 1978 legislation was passed allowing persons to work to age 70 before mandatory retirement policies could be imposed. The long-range trend has been, however, for older persons to retire prior to age 70. Later amendments to the Social Security Act provided old-age insurance and medicare and reduced the age of eligible applicants.

The next major effort by government to confront the problems of older Americans came in 1950, when the first National Conference on Aging was held. Sponsored by the Federal Security Agency, this conference attracted participants from a number of private and federal agencies as well as representatives of the state and federal governments. It led to the establishment in 1951 of the first Federal Administrative Committee on Aging and Geriatrics. The Geriatric Committee was placed under the authority of the Department of Health, Education and Welfare. The committee functioned primarily to create nationwide awareness of the problems of older Americans and their need for services.

The first White House Conference on Aging was held in 1961. The critical issue of the conference was medical problems of the elderly. Medicare was brought forth by this conference as the solution to this problem. While basically an exploratory and information-gathering conference, it did carefully examine the need for a federal agency on aging.

In 1963 the Office on Aging was established, taking over the functions of the Special Staff on Aging from the Welfare Administration. The role of this new office was to collect social welfare programs under a unified authority.

A question that arose in the development of programs was whether needed services for older Americans should be provided through comprehensive programs for people of all ages, or whether separate programs should be developed specifically for older Americans. Congress was convinced that older Americans would always be overlooked in programs designed for all age groups. Therefore it formulated the Older Americans Act of 1965 to insure that all persons over 60 would have programs tailored specifically to their needs. The act established the following statutory entitlements to help reach that goal:

> *Title I:* committed the government to assist the elderly in securing full and equal opportunity in such areas as income, housing, health care, and employment
>
> *Title II:* created the Administration on Aging
>
> *Title III:* provided grants for community planning services and training
>
> *Title IV:* funded research and demonstration projects designed to study the status of the elderly and to develop approaches to improving their living conditions
>
> *Title V:* provided funds for training persons employed in programs assisting older Americans

In 1967 amendments were added to the Older Americans Act that extended existing grants and contract authorities under Titles III, IV, and V and increased funding for the various titles. Further amendments in 1969 authorized additional funds under Title III for areawide model projects. Title VI was added, creating the National Older Americans Volunteer Program. In 1971 control of Title VI was transferred to ACTION, another federal agency. In 1973 Title VI was repealed.

In 1971 the second White House Conference on Aging recommended the establishment of a network of federal, state, and local planning and advocacy agencies to influence the major service providers to provide better services for the elderly. It also recommended the development of a wide range of services to meet specific identifiable needs of older persons.

In 1972, amendments were added to the Older Americans Act creating Title VII, which provided funds for nationwide projects to meet nutritional needs of the aged. Passage of the Older Americans Comprehensive Amendments in 1973

1. Created a national clearinghouse on aging and a Federal Council on Aging under Title II
2. Enabled state and area agencies on aging to develop comprehensive service programs under Title III
3. Provided additional monies for multidisciplinary gerontology centers by combining Titles IV and V
4. Established multipurpose senior centers under Title V
5. Provided for community service employment for older Americans under Title IX

The Social Service Amendments, passed in 1974, established Title XX of the Social Security Act. While directed toward the needs of all age groups, this entitlement included some programs directed specifically toward needs of the elderly. For example, Title XX funds can be used for protective services for adults, housekeeping and homemaker service assistance programs, housing improvement programs, preventive services, transportation, and information and referral services.

The 1978 amendments to the Older Americans Act

1. Required states to develop a comprehensive and coordinated service delivery system for older Americans
2. Required states to create a sole state agency on aging in order to qualify for funds
3. Mandated three-year plans from each area agency on aging
4. Expanded the funds available for the development of multipurpose senior centers

Programs Serving Older Americans

The numerous programs serving older Americans are funded by government, religion, and the private sector of the economy. The following is a brief description of some of the more well-established programs.

Retired Senior Volunteer Program (RSVP). The Retired Senior Volunteer Program was designed to solicit the support of anyone 60 and older who wants to use his or her experience and talents to serve or improve the community. Seven hundred RSVP projects across the country employ more than 50,000 senior volunteers. All kinds of activities are pursued by the volunteers: They serve in schools, libraries, correctional institutions, hospitals, nursing homes, telephone reassurance programs, government agencies, and more. The volunteers in this program receive no pay; however, they are reimbursed for the cost of their transportation to and from their volunteer stations and for the cost of a meal if they are volunteering during mealtime.

Foster Grandparent Program. The Foster Grandparent Program is a double-barreled program designed to assist both low-income elderly and disadvantaged children. Low-income elderly are paid to spend a prescribed amount of time each week working in public and private schools with disadvantaged youngsters. Normally they work 20 hours a week providing individual attention, companionship, advice, and counsel to this group of young people who need special attention. These elderly give of their experiences and talents to a group of children who otherwise might not receive this extra support in the regular school setting. Foster grandparents often help with homework, provide advice about problems, and assist in speech and physical therapy. This program has proved meaningful for both the older person serving and the children being served.

Senior Companion Program. The Senior Companion Program employs low-income older persons to assist other older persons in need, often the sick, the bedridden, the very old, and the infirm. Companionship, concern, housekeeping, cooking, letter writing, and bill paying are just a few of the varied activities taken up by the senior companions. This program is designed to help older persons stay in their homes longer, thus delaying the more expensive alternative of institutionalization.

Friendly Visitor Program. Title XX provides for this program, which matches up a volunteer visitor with a lonely, isolated elderly person. The visitor meets frequently with the elderly person, providing friendship and a helping hand with personal or household problems. The visitor can write letters, take small gifts, run errands, or just give the senior someone to talk with. Those interested in giving of their time but unable to visit can act as telephone visitors by making calls to an older person. Thus the older person has someone to talk to and avoids prolonged isolation. The only reimbursement offered to the friendly visitor is transportation costs.

Senior Community Service Employment Program (SCSEP). The Senior Community Service Employment Program is funded by the Department of Labor. Its goal is to provide employment for economically disadvantaged persons 55 and older. The seniors are paid for part-time community jobs at about minimum wage. Participants often work in parks, hospitals, senior centers, schools, or day-care centers. They receive an annual physical exam, on-the-job training, and related services. Green Thumb is a branch of the program involved in conservation and restoration projects in rural areas. Green Thumb workers can earn up to $1600 per year.

Senior Employment Service. In 1975 Congress passed a Title V older workers' program. This program subsidizes public and private nonprofit organizations that hire unemployed, low-income aged for part-time work.

Nutrition Program. The Older Americans Act provides money to establish and operate programs serving meals to senior citizens. This program provides nutritious low-cost lunches for area seniors. These are usually served Monday through Friday at local neighborhood sites throughout the county. Participants must be 60 years or older (or have a spouse over 60). Home-delivered meals are available on a limited basis. The site of the lunch program is also often a location for after-lunch activities such as bingo and crafts. The program not only provides a hot noon meal but also companionship to many who would otherwise eat alone. People who eat alone or cook for only one do not get as hungry or eat as well as those who eat in a group setting. Eating is a social as well as a physiological event.

No set price is charged. The seniors, however, are encouraged to make a donation. The amount of the donation is left up to the senior and ranges from $.05 to $1.50 per meal. Even though donations are encouraged, no one is left out due to inability to pay.

Transportation. Area agencies can use Title III money provided by the Older Americans Act to either provide transportation by van service or contract with a local taxi company to provide transportation at a discount rate to senior citizens. Federal funds pay for leasing or buying a van or vans and for the driver's salary. No set price is charged for the seniors, although donations are encouraged to cover the cost of gasoline.

This service gives seniors door-to-door transportation to their doctor's office, supermarket, or places where they have personal business to take care of. The van services small communities in outlying areas as well as urban districts.

When a contract is made with a taxi company, the discount coupon method is used. The taxi service is similar to the van service as far as destinations and the opportunity for door-to-door service are concerned. However, the payment for the service is different. Coupon booklets purchased by the senior citizens allow them to hire the cab at a discount rate. For example, two dollars worth of coupons paid to the driver would cost the senior one dollar. The goal of both programs is to help the elderly remain independent.

Multipurpose Centers. The multipurpose centers are designed to provide senior citizens with social, recreational, educational, and nutritional services at a central location. A center may also serve as an Information and Referral Center for the county in which it is located. In the latter case, senior citizens can obtain vital information and needed referrals from a central location in their own county. The center director also refers participants at the center to an outreach program if he or she feels they need further assistance. Center activities include arts and crafts, physical fitness, kitchen bands, field trips, and health screenings. The goal of the multipurpose senior centers is to provide a central location where senior citizens can learn, grow, relax, be creative, and socialize.

Day-Care Centers. Title XX provides funds for the establishment of senior day-care centers. Many older persons are living in the homes of their adult children and receive the kind of attention and support they need from their children during the latter's nonworking hours. Placement in a day-care center during the workday oftens means they can be kept out of retirement homes, hospitals, and nursing homes during their last few years. They are brought to the day-care centers by their children as the children leave for work in the morning and picked up when the children return from work in the evening. The day-care centers usually employ a nurse, who can give the older person needed medication, periodically check up on such things as blood pressure, and help with the common problems of the elderly.

Other staff members at the day-care center plan activities, crafts, and field trips for the clients. Many community service projects are performed by the clients, such as tray favors for hospitals and bandage folding for the Red Cross. This not only makes the elderly person feel useful and involved but makes the community aware of the day-care center.

Information and Referral. The Information and Referral Program is the link between the aging person and the programs for the aging. It provides information to seniors and refers them to services of help for their needs. Information is given out on every subject, from social security insurance to whom to call to have yardwork done to what to do if one runs out of fuel. It is much easier to educate the I & R staff and let them give out information than to try to educate citizens on every number and agency name and service they might ever need.

Most I & R programs distribute booklets to the elderly that include regularly called numbers and emergency numbers for their area. These books are free and often appear in large print to make reading easier for older people.

Programs involving several counties have a toll-free number. This is a great convenience, for elderly people would be less apt to call for information if they had to go through an operator or pay for the call on their limited income.

Protective Care. This program helps elderly persons who are unable to protect their own interests and who may therefore suffer physical or mental injury, neglect, inadequate food or shelter, or loss of resources. The program is designed to provide assistance and intervention in cases of suspected or actual neglect or abuse or health problems that seriously disrupt the elder's living situation.

Ombudsmen.   The Older Americans Act also provides funds for the establishment of an Ombudsman Program. The ombudsman acts as a liaison between a nursing home administrator and the nursing home residents and their families. The ombudsman's duty is to investigate any problems or complaints reported to him or her involving the residents. These problems include such things as mistreatment of patients, poor dietary procedures, or questionable acts by the home's staff.

In most cases handled by the ombudsman, the home's administrator is very cooperative in working out the problem. However, it may be necessary for the ombudsman to seek legal assistance for residents.

Personal Care Assessment.   The basic goal of this program is to locate, assess, and evaluate the needs of the elderly. After the assessment has been made the PCA worker helps the older persons by referring them to the appropriate social service providers. Funded by Title XX, this program was designed to help the elderly remain self-sufficient for as long as possible.

Referrals come to the personal care assessor from many sources—welfare departments, township trustees, hospitals, churches, interested neighbors, sometimes even the clients themselves. This program and the I & R program work hand in hand to refer the elderly to the agency that can best meet their needs.

Handyman and Homemaker Services for the Elderly.   Many older persons, because of poor health, are no longer able to fix leaking roofs, sagging drainpipes, and broken windows. The cost of hiring someone to do these chores can be excessive and can lead the older person to decide to give up his or her home. The Handyman and Homemaker Services are designed to alleviate this problem. They are available to persons over 60.

The handyman can repair broken windows, install and remove storm windows, make plumbing repairs, do light yardwork, repair leaking roofs, and generally maintain the older person's home. The homemakers try to meet the basic household needs of older persons. They do light housework, do the laundry, wash windows, pay bills, and run errands. This service also gives the elderly person someone to look forward to seeing. Many close relationships have come about between homemaker and client.

Medicare.   Medicare was provided by Congress to help alleviate some of the costs of medical expenses incurred by older Americans. Medicare covers about 66 percent of short-term hospital bills. Most persons on social security pay no premiums for medicare. The second part of the program is major medical insurance, for which the individual pays $21.90 per month. This covers the cost of the necessary doctors' services and additional outpatient services.

As a general rule medical care is designed to handle acute conditions but not chronic ones. Unfortunately, many of the problems of older Americans are chronic. Medicare was designed to help pay for services that are reasonable and necessary but not those that are custodial.

Medicare covers several areas:

1. A semiprivate room (two to four beds in a room)
2. All meals, including special diets
3. Regular nursing services
4. Costs of special care units, such as an intensive care unit
5. Drugs furnished by the hospital
6. Lab tests included in the hospital bill
7. X-rays and other radiology services, including radiation therapy, billed by the hospital
8. Medical supplies such as casts, surgical dressings, and splints
9. Use of appliances, such as a wheelchair
10. Operating and recovery room costs
11. Rehabilitation services, such as physical therapy, occupational therapy, and speech pathology[22]

Medicare does not cover the following:

1. Personal convenience items requested by the patient, such as a television, radio, or telephone in one's room
2. Private-duty nurses
3. Any extra charges for a private room, unless the patient needs it for medical reasons
4. The first three pints of blood one receives in a benefit period

In addition, medicare does not cover acupuncture, Christian Science practitioners' services, cosmetic surgery, dental care, drugs or medicines bought without a prescription, eyeglasses, eye examinations, full-time nursing care in the home, and routine physical examinations.

Critics of medicare maintain that it covers only acute health problems and ignores preventive medicine. This is easy to understand since routine checkups are not covered by the program.

Medicaid, available to qualified low-income elderly, pays for several services not covered by medicare. These include eyeglasses, dental care, prescribed drugs, and long-term nursing home care.

Legal Services. Older persons are more likely than any other age group to need the advice of a lawyer. They often experience the death of a spouse and the problems involved in settling an estate. They themselves must plan for the distribution of their property upon their death. They are likely to need to know how to claim their legitimate retirement benefits, to cash in insurance policies, or to invest savings accumulated in an insurance program, and they may need a myriad of other legal questions answered.

Illustrations of Programs

Often a description of government services provided to a certain group of persons leave the reader wondering about the necessity of the programs and their value for clients. The following cases, made available by the social service providers in Area 7 of West Central Indiana, provide some idea of the need for the programs just described as well as the services they render.

Case 1.   Dovie lives on a rural route in an agricultural county. The county seat has a population of approximately 10,000. She was assessed to need a Friendly Visitor. Dovie is in very poor health and almost blind. Her visitor, Mrs. P., came to visit on a July afternoon, and this is what she wrote in her visitor's log:

> Called her the night before, and she told me about her leg and back. I went to the drugstore and got her a tube of Mobisyl Creme and took it to her to rub the affected parts of her body. I also took her some homemade sausage. I called her the next evening and she told me she slept "like a log" and didn't get up until eight o'clock the next morning. She said it really helped her. She even got out in the yard and pulled weeds from her flowers. Said her leg didn't even hurt to walk on it. She liked her sausage also. Now, she is telling everyone she talks to about the Mobisyl Creme because it helped her so much. I am so glad she got relief. Dr. Jones is my doctor and he said it is the only thing he has found that helps *him*. Try it, if you have aches, pains, or sore places. Dovie wanted to pay me for it, but I refused. I told her "that was my good deed for the day."[23]

Case 2.   Early one morning I received a call from the Sullivan County Senior Citizen Center informing me that an elderly lady in Sullivan was having difficulty in obtaining home repairs. I had a difficult time finding her home due to the fact that the front porch had collapsed and the remainder of the house appeared unfit for human life. I asked a neighbor, who directed me to this home, which was the most dilapidated abode I had seen since I have been connected with aging programs. No one was home, except for 10 to 15 cats that were climbing in and out of a couple of broken windows. Since the front porch was unsafe, I went to the back door to meet the lady. The back porch was not much better than the front porch. The floorboards were rotten and in places you could see through to the ground. As I rounded to the front of the building, I saw coming down a side street an elderly crippled lady pushing a grocery cart with a couple of sacks in it. I asked if I might be of assistance to her and if she was Ms. Y. She said she was and she accepted my offer to help. We entered the back door. The odor from the cats was overbearing. Upon entering the living room I saw sunlight streaming through holes in the roof a foot square. How, I wondered, could this lady have survived the severe winters we'd been having?

Our handyman program obviously could not handle a project of such magnitude. However, in concert with other sources of assistance I felt that maybe the network of services could handle the problem.

After returning to the office, I contacted our personal care assessor and asked that he contact the Farmer's Home Administration. They can provide interest-free grants of up to $5,000.00 to eligible senior citizens. This lady only received Supplemental Security Income—approximately $190.00 a month. There was no question of her eligibility for an FHA grant. However, the FHA decided that her home was not worth investing the money in. Without the assistance of the FHA, our handyman program and the winterization program could do nothing. Within 3 months the house was condemned and the lady was placed in a nursing home. I am certain that if she had a home which was livable, and our homemaker service to help with transportation and housework, this lady could have continued to live independently.[24]

Case 3.   Because of a winter snow storm only two staff members could make it into the office. Midmorning I received an anonymous phone call from a nurse at one of our local hospitals stating her concern for an elderly lady they had treated in the emergency room the night before.

This lady had been brought in by ambulance with a cut on her head. Someone had called the ambulance when they saw her lying in the road. She had been treated and released to the care of her guardian. The nurse was not concerned with the cut but during the treatment Gladys said many things that the nurse couldn't block out of her mind. The nurse reported that Gladys had stated she was hungry, that her guardian would not let her keep food in her own house but had to walk up a hill a quarter of a mile to get her meals at the guardian's house. This explained why she was going up the road in such bad weather.

Gladys was really bundled up explaining to the nurse that she had burnt almost all of her coal and it would last longer if she didn't keep it so warm in her house. But she just had to get home because her dog, Tobey, was all alone.

After getting Gladys' approximate address from the nurse, another staff member and I drove the 10 miles out of town to the post office thinking the postman might be familiar with the situation. We were lucky enough to catch the postman there and he drove us to Gladys' house.

We walked back from the road and found an old shack, the elderly lady, and Tobey. The lady was out combing the ground to find small pieces of coal to burn in the stove. She was very glad to see someone and immediately invited us in. The windows of the shack were covered with cardboard, the pipes of the coal burning stove were burnt out and open flames were exposed. The furniture of the house was scarce: a bed, a table, a kitchen chair and the remains of a dresser. The other part of the dresser had been chopped up and used to burn in the stove. The walls of the shack were covered with tar paper; however, there were cracks in the walls where the paper had fallen off. The only food we found in the house were two half-rotten potatoes.

She was very fearful about telling us anything about her guardians; apparently they had mistreated her when she complained about her situation. I could tell the lady was underfed and neglected. We told Gladys we would help her and not to worry about her guardians anymore.

We went to a phone, contacted her doctor, and he agreed to admit her to the hospital because of malnutrition. We went back to get Gladys and to meet the guardian.

When we arrived at the guardian's house we were met at the back door by at least 15 dogs all on the inside of the house. It wasn't until we were asked in did we see the chickens that were also inside. After introducing ourselves and explaining why we were there, the guardian became very defensive. When we said we were taking Gladys with us to the hospital, the guardian said she would sue our agency and us personally for taking Gladys without her consent. The guardian also told us Gladys had no relatives and she was appointed guardian because Gladys was mentally not able to care for her own affairs.

When Gladys left with us to go to the hospital, she padlocked the shack door and trusted me to keep her key. Her whole life's memories of her childhood and her late husband were stored there. Should anything happen to her, she asked me to care for her most valued possessions.

After getting Gladys settled for the weekend, we had at least until Monday morning to decide what to do next. On Monday we checked birth certificates and marriage licenses and found that Gladys had a niece living in a town about 120 miles away. When calling the niece we found Gladys had a living sister, too, and they had always been concerned about this situation but were scared of her guardian.

When the guardian realized that she was really likely to have legal problems herself for receiving Gladys' Social Security checks and not spending it on her, she decided not to sue us but just to bow out of the case as soon and as quietly as she could.

I worked with the niece, who agreed to have Gladys come to live with her and to take care of whatever needed to be done. After one week in the hospital, Gladys was released to go live with her niece. However, she had no clothes because hers had been destroyed upon admission and the ones in her home were very dirty.

Our office asked for donations and finally got her ready to go. Thinking we were on the home stretch we sighed with relief, when we realized Gladys had no transportation to get to her new home. As you can probably guess, I drove her to meet her family, making only one stop on the way. We went by Gladys' old shack to pick up the possessions that she had locked up and Tobey, her pet dog.

Upon arriving at Gladys' new home, it was good to see a family anxiously awaiting a new member. The family accepted Gladys and Tobey with open arms.

That's been 3 years ago and I still hear from Gladys and her family. Her sister has since died but Gladys still stays with her niece and lives a happy life.[25]

Case 4. A minister called our office one morning and gave us the name and address of a man that walked into his church the night before. He said the man was very hard of hearing and was in need of help!

We went to see George and found that he lived in an upstairs apartment in a very run-down house. When we got there the apartment door had a padlock on it and a very nosey neighbor said they had seen him leave a couple of hours ago. We later found out that George had walked about ten blocks in several inches of snow carrying the battery from his car. After leaving the battery at a garage, he walked the ten blocks back in the bitter cold snowy weather.

We went back that afternoon and found George home. As we walked up the steps of the dark apartment building, several doors opened to see who was coming and what we wanted. We pounded on the apartment door and introduced ourselves to George. He was so hard of hearing we had to talk loudly; however, he kept putting his hand to his mouth to give us the quiet sign because he didn't want the neighbors to hear his business through the paper-thin walls. I suggested we communicate by writing and that's when he told me he could neither read nor write.

He said that he had appeared in court the day before because the lady that took care of the apartments wanted him out. They didn't like him, he said, and since they couldn't steal what they wanted from him they would just kick him out. I'm sure there were two sides to this, but right now our only concern was this elderly gentleman. Even though he had gone to court, he said he didn't know what had gone on because he couldn't hear the judge so he was scared as to what would happen next. I gave him my card and said if he needed anything, someone could either dial the number for him or give him directions to the office. In the meantime, I told him I would find out what happened in court and get back with him. The judge was out of his office until the next morning so I could only hope nothing would happen the rest of the day.

The next morning there stood George in front of my office door before 8:00 A.M. He said the police had come at midnight the night before and evicted him from his apartment and took him to the Light House Mission to spend the night. The eviction notice said he would be given three days to remove his belongings and he would have to get the key from the lady who took care of the apartments whenever he wanted to get in and pack. Where do you put a low-income elderly man and three rooms of junk in three short days? And if we had a place, how would we move him?

After begging the judge and the landlord, they jointly agreed to extend the time to a week so we could breathe a little easier. The Light House Mission helped us a lot by providing George a place to eat and sleep until we found an apartment. The Housing Authority worked with us to speed up a Section 8 Application and it was up to me to find an apartment and landlord who would accept a Section 8 applicant (Section 8 is a program which subsidizes people's rent if they meet the income guidelines). After a couple of days and evenings of apartment looking, we finally found a satisfactory place. By this time we only had two days to move so we couldn't waste any time. The apartment chosen was close to a grocery store and laundromat. As soon as we got him moved in we would teach him how to use a washing machine.

Friday was moving day and it was the project of our total staff. We got a truck, a roll of trash bags, and off to George's we went. I tried to explain to him that time was running out, the new apartment was a lot smaller and there is no way we could or would move all that stuff. We filled 27 trash bags with all kinds of things from old clothes to dead dried-up flowers. Much against his better judgment he closed his eyes, protested under his breath, and let us throw away whatever we felt had to go.

We got to the new apartment, hung some pictures, put clean sheets on the bed and halfway unpacked to make him feel at home. We left George on a Friday night to let him get settled and enjoy his new place.

I spent the weekend calling people I knew to get some donated towels, sheets, dishes, and his size clothing. On Monday morning I was off again to George's new apartment, to take these things and to see if he had survived the move and the weekend.

He was pleased with his new home and the things I had brought to him, but he asked if I could do just one more favor. George and I went and picked up his car battery and he got his car running.

We set up the homemaker service and they taught George to use the laundromat and how to keep his house a little cleaner.

George was upset that so much of his stuff was thrown away, but finally realized it had to be done.

That was about a year ago and George still lives in that same apartment but he seems a little happier now. He met the elderly lady in the front apartment and they have started a courtship. Whether it does or does not turn into a more serious relationship, temporarily they are enjoying each other's company.[26]

FUTURE DIRECTIONS OF SERVICE PROGRAMS FOR THE AGED

The 1981 White House Conference on Aging was surrounded with controversy and probably will prove to be the least fruitful of these conferences on aging in terms of promoting the interests of older Americans through federal legislation and program support. The major difference between the 1981 conference and previous White House Conferences on Aging was the attitude of the President and the party in power in Washington at the time. Until 1981 the conferences had received a sympathetic ear from the President and the party in power. The 1981 conference, however, found a President who was committed to a program of curbing inflation by reducing government spending. The reduction of government spending was to be done primarily by reducing social service and entitlement programs. Thus, while the delegates to the 1981 White House Conference on Aging asked for increases in government services for older Americans, the Reagan administration was committed to curbing any further expansion of these programs.

This impasse between the advisory committee of the 1981 conference and the administration became apparent even before the delegates to the conference assembled. Laurie Soriano (1981), in the *Gray Panther Network*, pointed out that minute changes in conference rules and in the selection of committee leaders imposed by the administration would have the effect of bringing the committees more under the control of committee leaders and restricting democratic discussions by the committee members since no subcommittees were to be formed. Soriano (1981) argued that the input of individual delegates would be reduced and become more subject to the interpretation of the committee chair.

Despite the controversy surrounding the structure of the 1981 White House Conference on Aging, the committees did produce 668 separate recommendations. A few of the more important issues can be identified. The two most urgent priorities in the minds of the delegates were the maintenance of current social security benefits and the expansion of health insurance benefits for older Americans.

While maintenance of current social security benefits was agreed upon by all the delegates, they disagreed on how this was to be done. The recommendation of one committee was for Congress not to use general revenue to shore up the depleted social security funds. Another committee recommended just the opposite.

In terms of the delegates' demands for increased health insurance benefits, the committee recommendations emphasized

1. The need to develop a comprehensive long-term care service, to include an array of home-based services
2. The need for medicare coverage to include preventive care and health maintenance (in addition to the current coverage)
3. The need to protect the rights of the institutionalized aged through such mechanisms as a patients' bill of rights, ambulance service, and advocacy councils

The political effect of the 1981 White House Conference on Aging would seem to have been to educate members of Congress and the President of the inadvisability of reducing social security benefits, no matter how great the temptation. On the other hand, it seems unlikely that there will be any expansion of the health insurance program in the near future.

While the early 1980s saw a curbing of the expansion of federally funded social service programs for older Americans, one wonders if this is a temporary or permanent phenomenon. The best guess, given the needs of older Americans and the numbers of voters they represent, is that ultimately there will be an expansion of these programs. This expansion may be some time in coming, however. The major problem facing those advocating an expansion of government services of older Americans is financing. The Reagan administration in the period from 1980 to 1988 was opposed to any expansion of social service programs for any age group; hence there was little if any such expansion in this period. The Bush administration (1988 to 1992) has basically adopted the same policy of opposition to the expansion of social services for any group. Approximately every ten years since 1950 there had been a White House Conference on Aging, which were used as a means of informing government leaders of the needs of senior citizens. Many of the current senior service programs resulted from these conferences. As a result of no expansion of social services policies of the Reagan and Bush administrations, there was no 1990 White House Conference on Aging.

Carroll Estes (1979) has perhaps been most critical of the current government service programs for older Americans. Employing a conflict perspective, Estes argues that the current programs are shortsighted, piecemeal attempts to enhance the social activities and life satisfaction of older persons while ignoring the larger economic, political, and social conditions that determine the quality of their lives. Moreover, she believes the current programs stigmatize the elderly as sick, feeble, dependent, and the cause of their own problems.[27] Estes sees four major problems with the current service delivery programs:

1. The aged are economically prevented from creating their own choices and options and must depend on service providers for minimum assistance and quickly learn to be submissive in order to receive the service.

2. The policies that provide for jurisdictional expansion of service providers and middle-level bureaucrats are likely to increase the public's dependence on the service.

3. Service strategies in general and those for the aged in particular tend to stigmatize their clients as recipients in need, creating the impression that they have somehow failed to assume responsibility for their lives.

4. Service approaches are likely to inhibit thinking about problems of the aged as being related to larger social and economic conditions.[28]

While Estes's (1979) analysis is perceptive, it in essence demands a restructuring of the entire social service delivery system in order to improve the power position and thereby the social status of the elderly. Short of a revolution, societies have not been known to completely restructure any of their institutions in order to improve the social standing of a particular group. This drastic a shift in the current social service delivery seems unlikely at present.

CONCLUSION

The fact that in 1988 persons 65 and above composed 12 percent of the population and 20 percent of the voters has resulted in a great deal of interest in and deference to their wishes by political candidates. This interest, while understandable, may not be entirely deserved. The current group of retirees are about equally divided between the Democratic and Republican parties and are the least likely group to abandon their party because of a particular issue.

In terms of political participation, older persons appear to be the most active of any age group. They follow news about political issues regularly, are more likely than other age groups to hold an opinion on a particular issue, and are disproportionately represented among opinion leaders. They vote more regularly than other age groups. Most of them are long-standing party members. While the United States does not have a gerontocracy, most of the Congress and many Presidents have been middle-aged or old. The Supreme Court, which does not require justices to retire, tends to include several persons over 65. Older political figures, however, tend to vote on the issues more as a result of their political beliefs and ideologies than on the basis of their age.

Older Americans tend to vote more along social-class lines, based on what they believe to be the best interest of their particular socioeconomic group. They are not a homogenous group and apparently have not formed a pervasive subculture. They represent the views of their different class backgrounds and ethnic, racial, and religious identities. They vote as a bloc only when they feel that the issue in question is directly related to the interest of their age group. When they do solidly back legislation that addresses an issue they consider important, they are most often successful. A few examples of their successful efforts include the change in the mandatory retirement age from 65 to 70 (something large corporations and universities clearly did not want); the passage of medicare, which was opposed by the American Medical Association; increases in social security benefits, which some taxpayer groups did not want; and, through the Older Americans Act, a multitude of services for older Americans, which those opposed to large government and a growing federal bureaucracy clearly did not want.

It should be pointed out, however, that these sweeping changes in the form of legislation favoring older Americans seem to have had several causes. First, a variety of organizations and associations brought the problems of the elderly to the public's and political leaders' attention. Second, middle-aged voters wanted to shift the responsibilities for aging family members off of themselves and onto the government. Finally, both big business and labor unions have wanted to encourge older workers to retire early.

Those concerned about the rising costs of social service programs have predicted a backlash against these programs and intergenerational conflict between younger and older age groups. The younger adults are expected to rebel against having to increase taxes to pay for programs benefiting the elderly. Current public opinion polls simply do not find dissatisfaction with these programs or their costs among younger or older voters. A recent Gallup poll indicates that less than 9 percent of the public are in favor of cutting either social security or the medicare programs—two of the more costly senior service programs. The Reagan and Bush administrations, with their focus on reducing government spending for social services, have discouraged any further expansion of senior service programs although these programs are widely supported by the general public.

KEY TERMS

cultural lag
generational equity
Gray Panthers

status inconsistency
Townsend movement

REFERENCES

BARROW, GEORGIA M., and PATRICIA A. SMITH, *Age, Ageism, and Society*, pp. 355–59. St. Paul: West, 1979.

CAMPBELL, A., "Politics Through the Life Cycle," *Gerontologist*, 11 (1971), 112–17.

CAMPBELL, A., "Social and Psychological Determinants of Voting Behavior," in *Politics and Age*, ed. W. Donahue and Clark Tibbitts, pp. 92–105. Ann Arbor: University of Michigan Press, 1962.

COWGILL, DONALD, "Critical Problems of Aging." Lecture given at Indiana State University Workshop, June 1977.

DOUGLAS, ELIZABETH B., WILLIAM P. CLEVELAND, and GEORGE L. MADDOX, "Political Attitudes, Age, and Aging: A Cohort Analysis of Archival Data," *Journal of Gerontology*, 74, no. 26 (1976), 666–75.

The Economist, March 12, 1988, p. 30.

ENGELTER, GEORGE H., "The Impact of Older Voters on the 1988 Elections," *Aging Network News*, IV, no. 11 (March 1988), 1, 6.

ESTES, CARROLL, *The Aging Enterprise*. San Francisco: Jossey-Bass, 1979.

FISCHER, DAVID HACKETT, "The Politics of Aging in America: A Short History," *Journal of the Institute for Socioeconomic Studies*, 4, no. 2 (1979), 51–66.

FONER, ANNE, "Age Stratification as One Form of Social Stratification." Paper presented at Meeting of the American Sociological Association, San Antonio, 1984.

FRANKE, JAMES L., "Representation in Age Based Interest Groups," *Research on Aging* (1984), pp. 346–71.

GLENN, NORVAL D., and MICHAEL GRIMES, "Aging, Voting, and Political Interest," *American Sociological Review*, 33 (1968), 563–75.

GUBRIUM, JABER F., *Time, Roles, and Self in Old Age*. New York: Human Sciences, 1976.

HEALTH, EDUCATION AND WELFARE PUBLICATION NO. (SSA) 78–10050. Washington, D.C.: U.S. Government Printing Office, 1977.

HESS, BETH B., "The Politics of Aging," *Society*, 15, no. 5 (July–August 1978), 22–23.

HUGHES, E. C., "Dilemmas and Contradictions of Status," *American Journal of Sociology*, 50 (1944–45), 353.

JACKSON, E., "Status Consistency and Symptoms of Stress," *American Sociological Review*, 27 (1962), 469.

JOHNSON, P., C. CONRAD, and D. THOMPSON, eds., "Workers Versus Pensioners." Manchester: Manchester University Press in Association with the Centre for Economic Policy Research, 1989.

KLEYMAN, PAUL, *Senior Power: Growing Old Rebelliously*. San Francisco: Glide Publications, 1974.

LANE, R. E., *Political Life*. New York: Free Press, 1959.

LEE, G., "Kinship and Social Support: The Case of the United States," *Aging and Society*, 5, no. 1 (1985), 19–38.

LENSKI, G., "Status Crystallization: A Non-Vertical Dimension of Social Status," *American Sociological Review*, 19 (1954), 204.

LOETHER, HERMAN J., *Problems of Aging*. Belmont, Calif.: Dickenson, 1967.

LOWRY, LOUIS, "Social Welfare and the Aging," in *Social Problems of the Aging*, ed. Mildred Seltzer and others, pp. 300–314. Belmont, Calif.: Wadsworth, 1978.

OGBURN, WILLIAM F., *Social Change*. New York: B. W. Heubsch, 1922.

PHILLIPSON, CHRIS, "Inter-Generational Relations: Conflict or Consensus in the 21st Century," *Policy and Politics*, 19, no. 1 (1991), 27–36.

"Poll Finds Little Friction Between the Young and Old," *AARP Highlights*, 5, no. 3 (July 1987), 1.

PRATT, HENRY J., "Old Age Associations and National Politics," *Annals of the American Academy of Political and Social Sciences* (September 1974), pp. 106–19.

RAGAN, PAULINE, and JAMES DOWD, "The Emerging Political Consciousness of the Aged: A Generational Interpretation," *Journal of Social Issues*, 3, no. 3 (1977), 137–50.

SCHULZ, JAMES H., *The Economics of Aging* (4th ed.). Dover, Mass.: Auburn House, 1988.

SORIANO, LAURIE, "White House Conference: A Political Rodeo," *Gray Panther Network*, November–December 1981, p. 1.

WILENSKY, H. L., and C. N. LEBEAUX, *Industrial Society and Social Welfare* (2nd ed.). New York: Free Press, 1966.

NOTES

1. Norval D. Glenn and Michael Grimes, "Aging, Voting, and Political Interest," *American Sociological Review*, 33 (1968), 563–75.

2. Jaber F. Gubrium, *Time, Roles and Self in Old Age* (New York: Human Sciences, 1976), p. 142.

3. A. Campbell, "Social and Psychological Determinants of Voting Behavior," in *Politics and Age*, ed. W. Donahue and Clark Tibbitts (Ann Arbor: University of Michigan Press, 1962), p. 92.

4. R. E. Lane, *Political Life* (New York: Free Press, 1959).

5. A. Campbell, "Politics Through the Life Cycle," *Gerontologist*, 11 (1971), 112–17.

6. Herman J. Loether, *Problems of Aging* (Belmont, Calif.: Dickerson, 1967), pp. 155–56.

7. Elizabeth B. Douglas, William P. Cleveland, and George Maddox, "Political Attitudes, Age, and Aging: A Cohort Analysis of Archival Data," *Journal of Gerontology*, 74, no. 26 (1976), 666–73.

8. Georgia M. Barrow and Patricia A. Smith, *Age, Ageism, and Society* (St. Paul: West, 1979), p. 356.

9. Paul Kleyman, *Senior Power: Growing Old Rebelliously* (San Francisco: Glide Publications, 1974).

10. Pauline Ragan and James Dowd, "The Emerging Political Consciousness of the Aged: A Generational Interpretation," *Journal of Social Issues*, 3, no. 3 (1977), 137–50.

11. Henry J. Pratt, "Old Age Associations in National Politics," *Annals of the American Academy of Political and Social Sciences* (September 1974) pp. 106–19.

12. Beth B. Hess, "The Politics of Aging," *Society*, 15, no. 5 (July–August 1978), 23.

13. Donald Cowgill, "Critical Problems of Aging" (lecture given at Indiana State University Workshop, June 1977).

14. David Hackett Fischer, "The Politics of Aging in America: A Short History," *Journal of the Institute for Socioeconomic Studies*, 4, no. 2 (1979), 64.

15. Chris Phillipson, "Inter-Generational Relations: Conflict or Consensus in the 21st Century," *Policy and Politics*, 19, no. 1 (1991), 28.

16. Ibid., p. 31.

17. E. C. Hughes, "Dilemmas and Contradictions of Status," *American Journal of Sociology*, 50 (1944–45), 353. See also E. Jackson, "Status Consistency and Symptoms of Stress," *American Sociological Review*, 27 (1962), 469.

18. Gubrium, *Time, Roles and Self*, pp. 128–30.

19. G. Lenski, "Status Crystallization: A Non-Vertical Dimension of Social Status," *American Sociological Review*, 19 (1954), 204.

20. Campbell, "Social and Psychological Determinants of Voting Behavior," p. 152.

21. William F. Ogburn, *Social Change* (New York: B. W. Heubsch, 1922), pp. 200–201.

22. This and the following list are derived from HEW Publication No. (SSA) 78–10050 (Washington, D.C.: U.S. Congressional Budget Office, 1977), p. 13.

23. Case cited by Jane Royse, Director of Transportation, Program Area 7, Agency on Aging, Terre Haute, Ind. Reprinted by permission.

24. Case cited by Rick Jimison, Director of Area 7, Agency on Aging Homemaker and Handyman Services, Terre Haute, Ind. Reprinted by permission.

25. Case cited by Jane Royse.

26. Case cited by Rick Jimison.

27. Carroll Estes, *The Aging Enterprise* (San Francisco: Jossey-Bass, 1979), pp. 221–24.

28. Ibid., pp. 241–45.

15

Religion and Aging

INTRODUCTION

A review of the studies of *religiosity* (commitment to religious beliefs and principles) and aging indicates a number of patterns of church attendance, belief in God, life satisfaction, and personal adjustment. This research indicates that church attendance hits a low point between 18 and 24, remains relatively stable between 25 and 54, rises slightly after 54, and drops slightly after 80. Thus, for most of one's adult life up to age 80 church attendance is fairly stable with a slight rise in the later years. The data indicate that a majority of all age groups express a belief in God, but that the older people become, the more likely they are to do so. A higher percentage of the elderly believe that religion is important in one's life and a higher percentage of them believe in immortality. All of the studies on religiosity and life satisfaction come to the same conclusion: those persons who attend church experience greater life satisfaction and are better adjusted than those who do not. A plausible explanation for the positive value of religious participation in the lives of the elderly is that the church becomes a focal point of social integration and activity, providing them with a sense of community and well-being. This concept of the positive functions the church serves in the lives of the elderly is analogous to Durkheim's (1915) discussion of the church as a moral community.

In reviewing the articles and research reports on religion and aging one cannot help but notice the dearth of materials on the topic. Textbooks on the sociology of religion occasionally mention religious participation over the life cycle, age and religious participation, or differences in religious participation by men and women. But these textbooks are few and the references sparse. In examining research articles in the various gerontology journals one finds a few articles on religion and aging, but the topic has clearly not caught the imagination of very many gerontologists. Since the great majority of older persons profess

I would like to express my appreciation to André Hammonds, professor of sociology at Indiana State University, for his assistance as coauthor of this chapter. Parts of this chapter appeared in "Religion, Aging and Life Satisfaction," *Journal of Religion and Aging,* 4, no. 3 (1988).

some religious belief and when questioned will assert that religion is very important in their lives, the sparsity of scientific writing on this subject is surprising. Richard Crandall (1980), in reviewing some of the studies on religion and aging, observes that many of the best studies have become quite outdated and most make no distinction among religious groups such as Protestantism, Catholicism, and Judaism.

Arthur Schwartz and James Peterson (1979) believe that the seeming disinterest of scientists in the topic of religion and aging can be explained by the fact that religion offers an alternative to the definition of truth provided by the scientific community and therefore the scientists are skeptical. Scientific training encourages the individual to question all knowledge and ways of viewing reality in hopes that new ideas, theories, and solutions to human problems can be found. Frequently only by debunking past beliefs can new knowledge be discovered. Thus, the creative efforts of the scientific community require that scientists approach any source of knowledge with a healthy amount of skepticism. Whereas this intellectual skepticism is a fundamental part of scientific training, religious leaders ask their converts to accept their truth as a matter of faith—something that scientists may find very difficult.

Studies have indicated that as a rule faculty members are less likely to be religious than the general public. Fred Thalheimer (1965) surveyed 741 faculty members at a large West Coast state university and compared responses with those of the general population as revealed in a Gallup Poll and a *Catholic Digest* survey. He found that only 54 percent of the faculty claimed to be affiliated with some church, compared with 97 percent of the general population. Moreover, 86 percent of the general population regarded the Bible as the revealed word of God, versus only 20 percent of the faculty. Similarly, only 47 percent of the faculty indicated a belief in God, compared with 96 percent of the general public.[1]

Edward Lehman and Donald Shriver (1968), in a study of academic religiosity, looked at the extent to which various academic disciplines included the scholarly study of religion. They found that the more removed one's field was from the study of religion, the more religious one was likely to be. Conversely, those professors whose discipline included some study of religion were less likely to accept traditional religious dogma and to report religious experience.[2] Apparently, close scientific examination of religious belief tends to remove the sacredness of the topic and to make one more doubtful.

Both Richard Crandall (1980) and Fred Thalheimer (1965) conclude that the sparsity of scientific studies of religion is a result of the *secularization* of society (a greater emphasis on the present world, or things not religious). Academicians themselves may be the vanguard of the secular view of society, and because they have seen secularization occurring they may have decided not to expend too much effort analyzing an element of society that they believe is becoming less important. Given the limitations just outlined, we will attempt in this chapter to review research on religion and aging and to assess future trends.

CHURCH ATTENDANCE

Among the various methods of measuring a person's religiosity, perhaps one of the quickest and best is church attendance. A number of studies have examined church attendance to determine what pattern was most prevalent over the life cycle. The early studies—those done in the 1950s and 1960s—indicated slightly higher church attendance among older people than among younger people.[3] Studies done in the 1970s did not indicate this pattern.[4] The research findings on church attendance throughout the life cycle are therefore inconclusive and subject to a variety of interpretations. One major problem of interpretation is that most of these studies were cross-sectional, based on interviews and questionnaires given to younger and older persons at a single point in time. In such studies it is impossible to determine whether differences show changes over time or whether the recent generations are simply less religious than earlier ones.

Howard Bahr (1970) reviewed studies of church attendance and developed four different models based on their findings:

1. The traditional model reveals a steady drop in church attendance from age 18 to 35. The lowest point for most people is between 30 and 35, after which attendance increases until old age.

2. The stability model assumes that there is no relationship between aging and church attendance and that the pattern of attendance remains stable throughout one's lifetime.

3. The family cycle model indicates that church attendance is altered by stages of the family cycle. Families peak in church attendance when the children reach Sunday school age. When the children grow up and leave home the attendance of the parents begins to drop.

4. The disengagement model assumes that church attendance, like many other areas of social participation, declines after middle age.[5]

The pattern of religious belief and church attendance found by most of the more recent studies tends to indicate stability of religious belief and church attendance over the life cycle, the only exception being a decline in church attendance among the very old. These were basically the findings of Dan Blazer and Erdman Palmore (1976).[6] Similarly Matilda Riley, Anne Foner and associates (1968), in their inventory of research on religion, observed that church attendance tends to decrease rather than increase in old age. David Moberg (1965) also observed a pattern of declining church attendance among older persons.

The 1975 Harris poll indicates a fairly stable attendance pattern over the life cycle. There is a low in church attendance between ages 18 and 24, a slight increase after the age of 55, and a slight decrease after 80 (Table 15–1). The Harris findings confirmed the findings of Robert Havighurst and Ruth Albrecht (1953) that women attend church more frequently and maintain a higher degree of religious participation for a longer period than men do.[7]

Bernard Lazerwitz (1961) looked at attendance by different religious groups. He found that among persons 65 and over, 66 percent of the Catholics attended church regularly, 46 percent of the Protestants, and 25 percent of the Jews.

While the diverse research findings on age and church attendance do not entirely support any of Bahr's (1970) four models, there do appear to be some common trends. Other than for 18-to-24-year-olds, the pattern of church attendance over the life cycle is fairly stable, with a slight increase after age 55 and a slight decrease after age 80. The low point in church attendance at ages 18 to 24 can perhaps best be explained by the fact that this is a period of transition from

TABLE 15–1 Attendance at a Church or Synagogue

| | When Attended Last | | | | | |
	Attended in Last Year (percent)	Within Last Week or Two (percent)	A Month Ago (percent)	More than 3 Months Ago (percent)	Not Sure (percent)	Other (percent)
Total Public	75	71	13	7	9	*
18 to 64	74	70	14	7	9	*
65 and over	77	79	9	5	7	*
18 to 24	67	60	18	8	14	*
25 to 39	73	72	11	7	10	*
40 to 54	78	70	15	8	7	—
55 to 64	81	79	11	4	6	—
65 to 69	80	79	9	5	6	1
70 to 79	78	79	10	4	7	*
80 and over	68	76	10	6	8	*

*Less than 0.5 per cent.

Source: Louis Harris and associates, The Myth and Reality of Aging in America (Washington, D.C.: National Council on the Aging, 1975), p. 181.

teenage to adult status. People in this age group are frequently moving away from their home communities to go into the service, attend college, or take a job. It takes time to become established in the new community and to reestablish the same religious ties and commitments they had in their home community. The drop in church attendance and activity among the very old that was noted in many of the studies is probably related to poor health and a lack of available transportation to church services. Stephen Ainlay and Randall Smith (1984) observe that while church attendance may decline among the very old, private devotionalism and other kinds of religious commitment actually increase; this group does not disengage from its religious beliefs.

BELIEF IN GOD

Crandall (1980) argues that people's commitment to religious beliefs is important because it tends to shape their attitudes, beliefs, opinions, and values. Simultaneously it provides people a framework for seeing and interpreting events in their world for themselves and others.[8]

Riley and Foner (1968) indicated that the older the person the more likely he or she was to express a belief in God. Seventy-one percent of 18-to-24-year-olds expressed a belief, 80 percent of 25-to-34-year-olds, 81 percent of 35-to-44-year-olds, 85 percent of 55-to-64-year-olds, and 86 percent of the 65 + group.[9]

These results were obtained, however, from cross-sectional data, and it is impossible to determine whether they reflect an increase in religious belief as one ages or merely generational differences in belief. Some would argue that the pattern found by Riley and Foner is a reflection of the secularization of society, by which each succeeding age cohort is somewhat less religious than its predecessors.

TABLE 15–2   The Importance of Religion in One's Life

	18–64	65+	18–24	25–39	40–54	55–64	65–69	70–79	80+
Very important	49	71	34	45	58	65	69	71	73
Somewhat important	33	21	40	35	29	25	22	21	19
Hardly important at all	17	7	25	20	12	10	8	8	6
Not sure	1	1	1	°	1	°	1	°	

°Less than 0.5 per cent.

Source: Louis Harris and associates, The Myth and Reality of Aging in America (Washington, D.C.: National Council on the Aging, 1975).

Louis Harris and associates (1975) asked their respondents how important religion was in their life. The responses were categorized as very important, somewhat important, hardly important at all, and not sure. The top row of Table 15–2 indicates the same pattern these researchers found with religious belief, in terms of what percentages of which age groups considered religion very important: 45 percent of the 25-to-39-year-olds did, 58 percent of the 40-to-54 year-olds, 65 percent of the 55-to-64-year-olds, 69 percent of the 65-to-69-year-olds, 71 percent of the 70-to-79-year-olds, and 73 percent of the 80+ age group.

Harris and associates found that 49 percent of the 18-to-64-year-olds considered religion very important versus 71 percent of the 65-and-older group. Whether this difference is a result of generational differences in religious belief or a gradual shift in religious belief over the life cycle, it does appear that the older persons consider religion more important than those under 65.

BELIEF IN IMMORTALITY

The belief in *immortality* may have special significance for older persons since they must recognize that death for them will occur sometime in the not too distant future. Studies have indicated that most older persons have come to accept the reality of their own death and are not unduly worried about it.

While one's religious faith apparently remains fairly stable over the life cycle, Rodney Stark (1973) hypothesized that belief in immortality, because of its special relevance for the elderly, would increase systematically with age. The data clearly reveal that this is the case for Protestants but not for Catholics. Table 15–3 indicates that for liberal Protestants under age 20 only 38 percent were completely sure that there was life after death; this figure rises to 50 percent for those in their 50s and to 70 percent for those persons 70 and over. Among the moderate Protestants the proportion who are completely sure of life after death rises from 56 percent of those under 20 to 87 percent of those 70 and over. The Roman Catholics, on the other hand, are very certain that there is life after death at age 20, with 90 percent of them stating that this is the case; the figures drop slightly for each succeeding age group through the 40-to-49-year-olds, of whom only 77 percent are certain. There is a slight increase after age 50, but even at 70 it has risen to only 78 percent—still less than the 90 percent of the 20-year-olds.

TABLE 15–3 Age and Belief in Life After Death

	Percentage Who Think It "Completely True" That "There Is a Life Beyond Death"						
Age	Liberal Protestants		Moderate Protestants		Conservative Protestants		Roman Catholics
Under 20	38%	(21)	56%	(16)	87%	(15)	90%	(10)[a]
20–29	41	(95)	62	(99)	90	(89)	84	(93)
30–39	47	(249)	65	(205)	92	(105)	78	(145)
40–49	44	(278)	69	(251)	90	(103)	77	(122)
50–59	51	(169)	75	(149)	99	(68)	80	(87)
60–69	75	(91)	86	(92)	96	(45)	81	(47)
70 and over	70	(52)	87	(59)	100	(20)	78	(18)

[a]Too few cases for a stable percentage, presented for descriptive interest only.

Source: Rodney Stark, "Age and Faith: A Changing Outlook or an Old Process?" in *Religion in Sociological Perspective: Essays in the Empirical Study of Religion*, edited by Charles Y. Glock. Belmont, Calif.: Wadsworth, 1973, p. 54.

As early as 1928, James Pratt, in a study of the psychology of religion, observed that in the modern secular world, religion had lost much of its sacred and supernatural status and that the most important pragmatic value of religion was the belief in a personal future life.[10] Riley and Foner (1968) concluded after a review of the research on religion that belief in God and immortality is firmly ingrained in most older people and in the general public as well.[11]

ORTHODOX RELIGION

Stark (1973) attempted to determine if people became more orthodox in their religious belief as they aged. *Orthodox* religious beliefs were presumed by Stark to be the most conservative beliefs, and he felt that older persons might be more likely to hold these beliefs. The four measures of orthodox belief that Stark (1973) used were a firm belief in a personal God, a belief in the divinity of Jesus Christ, a belief in the authenticity of biblical miracles, and a belief in the existence of the devil. As Table 15–4 indicates, Stark found not a gradual shift toward orthodox religious beliefs as one ages but rather a lower percentage of orthodox believers for the post–World War II generations. The meaningful shift for both moderate and conservative Protestants came between the prewar generations, who were above 50 in age, and those in their 40s and below, who were considered by Stark to be the postwar generations. The Catholics remained fairly orthodox throughout the life cycle. On the other hand, the liberal Protestants were relatively non-orthodox in religious belief throughout the life cycle.

Stark (1973) concluded that post–World War II America was a more urban and a considerably more secular society and as a result less accepting of orthodox religious beliefs:

> World War II was a watershed between the new world and the older America of parochial small-town and rural society. While all the persons in this sample live today in this new America, those past fifty did not grow up in it. This data strongly suggests that in this new America traditional Christian orthodoxy is less powerful.[12]

TABLE 15–4   Age and Orthodoxy

| Age | Percent High on Orthodoxy Index | | | |
	Liberal Protestants	Moderate Protestants	Conservative Protestants	Roman Catholics
Under 20	5	29	a	a
	(19)	(15)	(12)	(9)
20–29	10	26	75	64
	(19)	(95)	(89)	(89)
30–39	10	27	79	66
	(243)	(203)	(101)	(141)
40–49	9	28	78	48
	(262)	(244)	(102)	(124)
Postwar generations				
Prewar generations				
50–59	11	40	94	61
	(157)	(134)	(67)	(83)
60–69	14	49	89	73
	(80)	(79)	(43)	(41)
70 and over	27	45	100	64
	(40)	(51)	(19)	(15)

[a]Too few cases for stable percentages.

Source: Rodney Stark, "Age and Faith: A Changing Outlook or an Old Process?" in *Religion in Sociological Perspective: Essays in the Empirical Study of Religion,* edited by Charles Y. Glock. Belmont, Calif.: Wadsworth, 1973, p. 51.

Wingrove and Alston (1971) noted a similar trend toward *secularization* of society when they concluded that all cohorts reached their peak in religious-service attendance between 1950 and 1960. They found that after 1965 all cohorts showed a decline in religious attendance.[13]

RELIGIOUS RITUALISM AND PRIVATE DEVOTIONALISM

Stark (1973) examined the relationship between age and both religious *ritual* involvement and private *devotionalism.* The relationship Stark found can be seen in Table 15–5. The only noticeable pattern for Protestants was for those persons 70 and over to be more inclined to ritual commitment than those under 70. There seems to be no distinct pattern for those under 70 except that those under 20 are a bit less likely to become involved in ritual than are those over 20. (However, there were so few respondents under 20 that one should be careful in drawing any conclusions.) Other than the under-20 group being less involved in ritual than the rest, there appears to be no noticeable pattern of ritual involvement by age among Roman Catholics.[14]

The most notable result of Stark's (1973) research can be seen in the bottom half of Table 15–5, where private devotionalism seems to increase noticeably with age. Only 34 percent of the liberal Protestants in their 20s scored high on private devotionalism, whereas 48 percent of those in their 50s and 68 percent of those 70 and over did so. For moderate Protestants the comparable figures were 35

TABLE 15–5 Public Ritual Involvement, Private Devotionalism, and Age

Age	Liberal Protestants		Moderate Protestants		Conservative Protestants		Roman Catholics	
	Percent High on Index of Public Ritual Involvement							
Under 20	19%	(21)	38%	(16)	36%	(14)[a]	30%	(10)[a]
20–29	23	(97)	40	(99)	73	(89)	46	(92)
30–39	38	(247)	45	(208)	73	(107)	47	(146)
40–49	28	(282)	46	(258)	75	(104)	46	(129)
50–59	24	(168)	41	(146)	83	(65)	43	(94)
60–69	24	(95)	47	(90)	75	(43)	54	(46)
70 and over	54	(54)	53	(60)	90	(21)	41	(22)
	Percent High on Index of Private Devotionalism							
Under 20	37%	(19)	29%	(14)[a]	64%	(14)[a]	56%	(9)[a]
20–29	34	(90)	35	(97)	62	(87)	58	(93)
30–39	41	(237)	43	(204)	75	(105)	63	(142)
40–49	35	(268)	46	(246)	79	(104)	62	(125)
50–59	48	(163)	58	(148)	88	(68)	74	(91)
60–69	51	(94)	71	(93)	93	(45)	77	(47)
70 and over	68	(53)	81	(57)	96	(21)	75	(20)

[a]Too few cases for a stable percentage, presented for descriptive purposes only.

Source: Rodney Stark, "Age and Faith: A Changing Outlook or an Old Process?" in *Religion in Sociological Perspective: Essays in the Empirical Study of Religion*, edited by Charles Y. Glock. Belmont, Calif.: Wadsworth, 1973, p. 55.

percent, 58 percent, and 81 percent, respectively. The proportions of conservative Protestants in these same age groups who engaged in private devotionalism were 62 percent, 88 percent, and 96 percent, respectively. Among Roman Catholics the same pattern is found—58 percent for 20-year-olds to 74 percent for 50-year-olds to 75 percent for those 70 and above.[15]

David Moberg (1965) and Philip Hammond (1969) both found a similar pattern of private devotionalism and age. They concluded that although church attendance, or "external" religious practices, declines with age, "internal" religious practices such as reading the Bible at home, praying, and listening to or watching religious programs on radio and television all increase. This turning inward to personal religious practices that several researchers have found would seem to be consistent with the psychological studies of personality changes in later life that indicate a closure of personality in old age and less need for group support and external sanctions for one's behavior. This is consistent with the findings of Gay Young and Winifred Dowling (1987). Their data indicated that the "young old" participated more in formal religious activities, while the "old old" participated more in private devotionalism.

RELIGIOSITY AND LIFE SATISFACTION

A number of scientists have observed the potentially positive value that religious faith and activities can have on the lives of older Americans. Milton Barron (1961) notes that the psychological supports religion provides older persons help them

(1) face impending death; (2) find and maintain a sense of meaningfulness and significance in life; (3) accept the inevitable losses of old age; and (4) discover and utilize the compensatory values that are potential in old age.[16]

Socially the church also provides a number of functions that can be particularly useful for older Americans. For one thing, it provides a variety of social activities that bring people of all ages and backgrounds together. The social interaction that ensues tends to reduce the individual's social isolation. These activities can involve older persons in community concerns and current issues, which will inevitably be discussed on such occasions. Moreover, the interest shown the individual by other participants becomes a source of social support. Young and Dowling (1987) found that frequent interaction in social networks contributes to the spiritual well-being of elderly persons; that is, it affirms the wholeness of their lives. In addition, such activities draw the older person's attention away from self and to the problems and concerns of others. All of these things have positive consequences for older people and are likely to improve their outlook on life. Kurt Wolff (1959) found that religious belief, prayer, and faith in God all helped the aged to overcome many of the common problems of old age, such as loneliness, grief, and unhappiness.[17]

A number of studies have attempted to determine if there is a positive relationship between religion and life satisfaction for older Americans. David Moberg and Marvin Taves (1965), in a study of church participation and life adjustment in old age, questioned 5000 persons over 65 in four Midwestern states. They found that church members had higher personal-adjustment scores than nonmembers and that church leaders and officers had higher adjustment scores than other church members. They concluded that their evidence convincingly indicated church participation was related to good personal adjustment in later life.[18] Moberg and Taves did observe that the direction of this relationship was difficult to determine. Do those who are well adjusted choose to engage in many religious activities, or does engaging in many religious activities lead one to be well adjusted?

Studies by Edwards and Klemmack (1973) and Spreitzer and Snyder (1974) came to the same conclusion regarding the value of religious participation for older persons. Their evidence indicated that religiosity was related to life satisfaction and other measures of well-being for older persons.[19] Similarly, Blazer and Palmore (1976) found that happiness and a sense of usefulness and personal adjustment are significantly related to religious activity and attitudes.[20]

Rebecca Guy (1982), in a study of religion and life satisfaction, found that the group scoring the highest on life satisfaction was the one that reported attending church more frequently at the time of the study than 15 years before. Closely behind was the group whose church attendance had remained relatively stable. Respondents attending church less at the time of the study than 15 years previous scored lower than the other two groups on life satisfaction, with the lowest scores being made by those who never attended church. Similarly, Kyriakos Markides (1983), in a study of the role of church attendance, self-rated religiosity, and practice of private prayer in life satisfaction, found only church attendance to be significantly related to life satisfaction. It appeared to Markides that the integrative function of religion rather than its spiritual function was the crucial determinant of life satisfaction.

Suzanne Ortega, Robert Crutchfield, and William Rushing's (1983) findings in a study of race differences and personal well-being of the elderly would tend to support Markides's conclusion about the integrative function of the church. Ortega and her colleagues found elderly blacks reporting higher life satisfaction scores than elderly whites. After introducing a multitude of control variables to explain the race differences in life satisfaction scores they concluded

> that control with friends mediates the relationship only where friendships have the church as their locus. It appears that the association between race and life satisfaction is due, at least in part, to greater church related friends among the black elderly.[21]

One possible explanation they suggest for their findings is that the black church in the South forms a focal point of the community, serving as a pseudoextended family, particularly for the aged. This argument is very similar to Markides's (1983) hypothesis about the integrative function of religion.

Studies, then, overwhelmingly confirm a positive relationship among religious belief, religious participation, and life satisfaction in later life. While as Moberg (1965) observed it is not possible at this time to determine the direction of this relationship, it is clear that older church members score high on tests of personal adjustment, maintain a healthier outlook on life, and express a greater degree of life satisfaction. Markides (1983) and Ortega and associates (1983), argue that the church serves as a focal point for individual and community integration of the elderly and that this is crucial to their sense of personal well-being.

THE ROLE OF THE AGED IN THE CHURCH

Harvey Lehman (1953) found that while new religious *cults* and *sects* are most often founded by people under the age of 50, the established churches are more often led by people over 50. Most commonly the founders of new cults and sects are in their 30s.[22] Beth Hess and Elizabeth Markson (1980) offer a reason for the older leadership of established churches:

> Formalized religions generally select spiritual leaders from among the most experienced and hence wiser, but who are also persons presumed to be removed from worldly temptations. Since tenure in priestly office depends upon holiness, a quality that does not deteriorate over time, religious hierarchies tend to become populated by the longest lived.[23]

Hess and Markson point out further that the very fact that religious knowledge is unchanging means that the old have had longer to know the truth, and this enhances their value for leadership roles in the church.

In preliterate societies the old almost always perform the most sacred religious duties. Jack Goody (1976) has given these reasons for the dominant role of the elders in the church:

1. They have lived longer and therefore have had time to accumulate a complete knowledge of religious affairs and practices.
2. Since they will soon enter the spirit world themselves they are the logical intermediaries between this world and the next and between the living and their ancestors.[24]

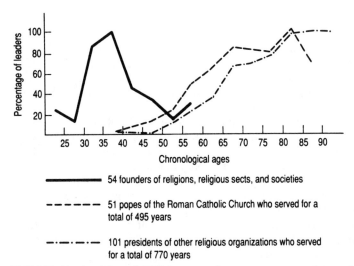

54 founders of religions, religious sects, and societies

------ 51 popes of the Roman Catholic Church who served for a
total of 495 years

—·—·—· 101 presidents of other religious organizations who served
for a total of 770 years

FIGURE 15–1   Ages of Religious Leaders versus Ages of Founders of Religions, Religious Sects, and Societies

Source: Harvey C. Lehman, *Age and Achievement* (Princeton, N.J.: Princeton University Press, 1953), p. 173.

David Fischer (1978) noted, similarly, that surviving to a very old age in preliterate societies was sufficiently uncommon to seem unnatural. Thus it was very easy to assume that the very old were endowed with supernatural properties.[25]

Lehman (1953) plotted the ages of a large number of popes, bishops, and presidents of religious organizations. He found that 97 percent of the popes were past the age of 52, with 65 percent being past 65. Ninety-three percent of the presidents of non-Catholic religious organizations were past 50, and 56 percent were 65 and older. Finally, out of 148 Protestant bishops, most were 70 to 74 years of age. (See Figure 15–1.) It may well be that by assuming the roles of religious leaders the elders of many societies were able to maintain dominant positions long after their physical abilities had waned.

Charles Longino and Gay Kitson (1976) believed that ministers would share the general negative view of old age that is so widespread in the United States. Therefore they assumed that ministers would not enjoy ministering to the needs of their elderly. But in surveying a national sample of Baptist ministers they did not find this to be the case. What was more crucial in a minister's willingness to serve the elderly was his perception of the role of ministers. Those ministers who felt that the ministerial role required them to be social activists attempting to change society did not enjoy the time they spent ministering to older church members. Those ministers who did not view social activism as a critical part of their role but rather saw themselves as counselors ministering to human problems seemed to enjoy the expressive contact involved in visiting with the older church members.[26] Thus while most of the Baptist ministers did not find ministering to aging parishioners their most desirable responsibility, those with an expressive orientation were most likely to enjoy the task.

CONCLUSION

The subject of religion and aging has not been one of the more widely researched areas in gerontology. Admittedly there may be a degree of scientific bias here, since scientists are somewhat less likely to be religious than the general public and may reflect the more secular attitudes of a society that is becoming more urbanized.

Although the studies of religion and aging are limited and sometimes dated some trends can be located. Church attendance hits a low point between 18 and 24, remains relatively stable between 25 and 54, rises slightly after 54, and drops slightly after the age of 80. Most researchers concluded that the drop in attendance after age 80 is a reflection of the declining health of older persons and the fact that many of them don't drive and frequently have no way of getting to church. For most of one's adult life up to age 80, then, church attendance is fairly stable with a slight rise in the later years. Glock et al. (1967) estimated that this pattern of church attendance may not remain true for future generations of old persons. He felt that the post–World War II generations were, on the whole, somewhat less likely to attend church than their elders had been. Blazer and Palmore (1976), in one of the few longitudinal studies of religious attitudes and participation, found that religious attitudes are fairly constant over time but that religious activities do decline with age (Figure 15–2).

In terms of belief in God, the research indicated that a majority of all age groups express a belief in God, but that the older people become, the more likely they are to do so. Similar patterns were found with regard to the importance of religion in a person's life, and a belief in immortality. Once again a majority of all age groups believe that religion is important in life and believe in immortality. A higher percentage of the older age groups believe that religion is important in one's life and believe in immortality. Since these studies of church attendance and religious beliefs have, for the most part, been cross-sectional, any interpretation of their results and any conclusions drawn from them must be made with considerable caution.

Glock et al. (1967) did not find that people became more orthodox and conservative in their religious beliefs as they aged. He felt that his most signifi-

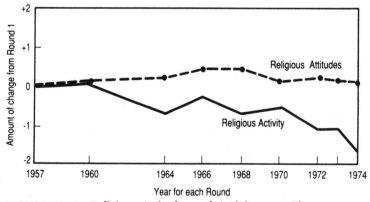

FIGURE 15–2 Religious Attitudes and Activity over Time
Source: Dan Blazer and Erdman Palmore, "Religion and Aging in a Longitudinal Panel," *Gerontologist*, 16, no. 1, pt. 1 (1976), 84.

cant finding was that the post–World War II generations were less likely to be orthodox.

Several studies found that older persons were more likely to engage in private devotions than younger age groups. Apparently the very old compensate for some of their decline in religious activity by engaging in private devotions. Perhaps the psychological studies that indicate a closure of personality and a turning inward by older persons can explain this increase in private devotionalism on their part.

All of the studies of religion and life satisfaction came to the same conclusions: Those persons who attend church experience greater life satisfaction and are better adjusted than the nonchurchgoer. This relationship may be explained in part by Crandall's (1980) observation that religious faith provides people with a philosophy of life as well as a series of attitudes, values, and beliefs that help them interpret and understand the world around them. Moreover, persons with strong religious beliefs are likely to attend church services and social functions whose participants share their beliefs and views of reality and thereby receive group support for their convictions. Markides (1983) and Ortega and her associates (1983) indicated that the church provides individuals a sense of social and community integration that is highly correlated with their sense of personal well-being. This integrative function of the church is very similar to Durkheim's discussion (1915) of the church as a moral community.

Religious activities tend to provide useful roles for older persons during their retirement years. They can become deacons, elders, or Sunday school teachers and thus assume leadership roles in religious activities that they may have been deprived of in work activities at their retirement. Since the work of the church in ministering to the needs of the community is a never-ending task, there are always a great variety of volunteer activities the older person can become involved in, from visiting the homebound to counseling to directing a recreational program for young people.

The church also provides its older members a wide range of social activities, which tend to pull them into contact with other people and to reduce the possibility of social isolation and loneliness. Regardless of the reasons, older church members tend to be happier and better adjusted than nonmembers.

While the founders of religious sects and cults tend to be in their 30s, the leaders of the established churches tend to be in their 60s and 70s. Church leaders, as a rule, are not required to retire and may serve until their death. Moreover, their age, experience, and wisdom are seen as valuable assets in their leadership roles.

KEY TERMS

cults
devotionalism
immortality
orthodox

religiosity
ritualism
sects
secularization

REFERENCES

AINLAY, STEPHEN C., and D. RANDALL SMITH, "Aging and Religious Participation," *Journal of Gerontology*, 39, no. 3 (1984), 357–63.

BAHR, HOWARD M., "Aging and Religious Disaffiliation," *Social Forces*, 49 (September 1970), 57–71.

BARRON, MILTON L., *The Aging American: An Introduction to Social Gerontology and Geriatrics.* New York: Thomas Y. Crowell, 1961.

BLAZER, DAN, and ERDMAN PALMORE, "Religion and Aging in a Longitudinal Panel," *Gerontologist,* 16, no. 1, pt. 1 (1976), 82–85.

COX, HAROLD, and ANDRÉ HAMMONDS, "Religion, Aging, and Life Satisfaction," *Journal of Religion and Aging,* 4, no. 3 (1988).

CRANDALL, RICHARD C., *Gerontology: A Behavioral Science Approach.* New York: Addison-Wesley, 1980.

DURKHEIM, E., *The Elementary Forms of Religious Life,* trans. J. W. Swain. New York: Macmillan, 1915.

EDWARDS, J. N., and D. L. KLEMMACK, "Correlates of Life Satisfaction: A Reexamination," *Journal of Gerontology,* 28 (1973), 497–502.

FICHTER, JOSEPH H., "The Profile of Catholic Religious Life," *American Journal of Sociology,* 58 (July 1952), 145–49.

FISCHER, DAVID H., *Growing Old in America.* New York: Oxford University Press, 1978.

GLOCK, CHARLES Y., ed., *Religion in Sociological Perspective: Essays in the Empirical Study of Religion.* Belmont, Calif.: Wadsworth, 1973.

GLOCK, CHARLES Y., BENJAMIN B. RINGER, and EARL BABBIE, *To Comfort and to Challenge: A Dilemma of the Contemporary Church.* Berkeley and Los Angeles: University of California Press, 1967.

GOODY, JACK, "Aging in Nonindustrial Societies," in *Handbook of the Aging and the Social Sciences,* ed. Robert H. Binstock and Ethel Shanas, pp. 117–28. New York: Van Nostrand Reinhold, 1976.

GORER, GEOFFRY, *Exploring English Character.* London: Cresset, 1955.

GUY, REBECCA FAITH, "Religion, Physical Disabilities, and Life Satisfaction in an Older Age Cohort," *International Journal of Aging and Human Development,* 15, no. 3 (1982), 225–32.

HAMMOND, PHILIP E., "Aging and the Ministry," in *Aging and Society, Volume 2: Aging and the Professions,* ed. Matilda White Riley, John W. Riley, Jr., and Marilyn E. Johnson, pp. 293–323. New York: Russell Sage, 1969.

HARRIS, LOUIS, and ASSOCIATES, *The Myth and Reality of Aging in America.* Washington, D.C.: National Council on the Aging, 1975.

HAVIGHURST, ROBERT J., and RUTH ALBRECHT, *Older People.* New York: Longmans, Green, 1953.

HESS, BETH, and ELIZABETH MARKSON, *Aging and Old Age.* New York: Macmillan, 1980.

LAZERWITZ, BERNARD, "Some Factors Associated with Variations in Church Attendance," *Social Forces,* 39 (1961), 301–9.

LEHMAN, EDWARD C., JR., and DONALD W. SHRIVER, JR., "Academic Discipline as Predictive of Faculty Religiosity," *Social Forces,* 47 (December 1968), 171–82.

LEHMAN, HARVEY C., *Age and Achievement.* Princeton, N.J.: Princeton University Press, 1953.

LONGINO, CHARLES F., JR., and GAY C. KITSON, "Parish Clergy and the Aged," *Journal of Gerontology,* 31, no. 3 (1976), 340–45.

MARKIDES, KYRIAKOS S., "Aging, Religiosity and Adjustment: A Longitudinal Analysis," *Journal of Gerontology,* 38 (1983), 621–25.

MINDEL, CHARLES H., and EDWIN C. VAUGHAN, "A Multidimensional Approach to Religiosity and Disengagement," *Journal of Gerontology,* 33, no. 1 (1978), 103–8.

MOBERG, DAVID O., "Religiosity in Old Age," *Gerontologist,* 5, no. 2 (1965), 80.

MOBERG, DAVID O., and MARVIN J. TAVES, "Church Participation and Adjustment in Old Age," in *Older People and Their Social World,* ed. Arnold M. Rose and Warren A. Peterson, pp. 113–24. Philadelphia: F. A. Davis, 1965.

ORTEGA, SUZANNE T., ROBERT D. CRUTCHFIELD, and WILLIAM A. RUSHING, "Race Differences in Elderly Personal Well-Being, Friendship, Family and Church," *Research on Aging,* 5, no. 1 (March 1983), 101–18.

PRATT, JAMES B., *The Religious Consciousness.* New York: Macmillan, 1928.

RILEY, MATILDA WHITE, ANNE FONER, and ASSOCIATES, *Aging and Society, Volume 1: An Inventory of Research Findings.* New York: Russell Sage, 1968.

SARASON, SEYMOUR, *Work, Aging and Social Change: Professionals and the One Life–One Career Imperative.* New York: Free Press, 1977.

SCHULZ, JAMES A., *The Economics of Aging* (4th ed.). Belmont, Calif.: Wadsworth, 1988.

SCHWARTZ, ARTHUR N., and JAMES A. PETERSON, *Introduction to Gerontology.* New York: Holt, Rinehart & Winston, 1979.

SPREITZER, ELMER, and EDDON E. SNYDER, "Correlates of Life Satisfaction Among the Aged," *Journal of Gerontology,* 29 (1974), 454–58.

STARK, RODNEY, "Age and Faith: A Changing Outlook or an Old Process?" in *Religion in Sociological Perspective: Essays in the Empirical Study of Religion,* ed. Charles Y. Glock, pp. 48–57. Belmont, Calif.: Wadsworth, 1973.

THALHEIMER, FRED, "Continuity and Change in Religiosity: A Study of Academicians," *Pacific Sociological Review,* 8 (Fall 1965), 101–8.

TIRST, ERIC, "Toward a Post-Industrial Culture," in *Handbook of Work, Organization and Society,* ed. Robert Dubin. Skokie, Ill.: Rand McNally, 1976.

TOBIN, SHELDON S., "Social and Health Services for the Future Aged," *Gerontologist,* 15, no. 1, pt. 2 (1975), 32–37.

WARD, RUSSELL, *The Aging Experience*. Philadelphia: Lippincott, 1979.

WINGROVE, C. RAY, and JON P. ALSTON, "Age and Church Attendance," *Gerontologist*, 4 (1971), 356–58.

WOLFF, KURT, "Group Psychotherapy with Geriatric Patients in a State Hospital Setting: Results of a

Three-Year Study," *Group Psychotherapy*, 12 (1959), 218–22.

YOUNG, GAY, and WINIFRED DOWLING, "Dimensions of Religiosity in Old Age: Accounting for Variation in Types of Participation," *Journal of Gerontology*, 42, no. 4 (1987), 376.

NOTES

1. Fred Thalheimer, "Continuity and Change in Religiosity: A Study of Academicians," *Pacific Sociological Review*, 8 (Fall 1965), 101–8.
2. Edward C. Lehman, Jr., and Donald W. Shriver, Jr., "Academic Discipline as Predictive of Faculty Religiosity," *Social Forces*, 47 (December 1968), 171–82.
3. See, for example, Joseph H. Fichter, "The Profile of Catholic Religious Life," *American Journal of Sociology*, 58 (July 1952), 145–49.
4. See, for instance, C. Ray Wingrove and Jon P. Alston, "Age and Church Attendance," *Gerontologist*, 4 (1971), 356–358.
5. Howard M. Bahr, "Aging and Religious Disaffiliation," *Social Forces*, 49 (September 1970), 57–71.
6. Dan Blazer and Erdman Palmore, "Religion and Aging in a Longitudinal Panel," *Gerontologist*, 16, no. 1, pt. 1 (1976), 82–85.
7. Robert J. Havighurst and Ruth Albrecht, *Older People* (New York: Longmans, Green, 1953), pp. 202–3.
8. Richard C. Crandall, *Gerontology: A Behavioral Science Approach* (New York: Addison-Wesley, 1980), p. 464.
9. Matilda White Riley, Anne Foner, and associates, *Aging and Society, Volume 1: An Inventory of Research Findings* (New York: Russell Sage, 1968), p. 492.
10. James B. Pratt, *The Religious Consciousness* (New York: Macmillan, 1928), p. 253.
11. Riley and Foner, *Aging and Society*, p. 493.
12. Charles Y. Glock, *Religion in Sociological Perspective: Essays in the Empirical Study of Religion* (Belmont, Calif.: Wadsworth, 1973), p. 51.
13. Wingrove and Alston, "Age and Church Attendance," p. 357.
14. Glock, *Religion in Sociological Perspective*, pp. 55–56.
15. Rodney Stark, "Age and Faith: A Changing Outlook or an Old Process?" in *Religion On Sociological Perspective: Essays in the Empirical Study of Religion*, edited by Charles Y. Glock (Belmont, Calif.: Wadsworth, 1973), p. 54.
16. Milton L. Barron, *The Aging American: An Introduction to Social Gerontology and Geriatrics* (New York: Thomas Y. Crowell, 1961), p. 166.
17. Kurt Wolff, "Group Psychotherapy with Geriatric Patients in a State Hospital Setting: Results of a Three-Year Study," *Group Psychotherapy*, 12 (1959), 218–22.
18. David O. Moberg and Marvin J. Taves, "Church Participation and Adjustment in Old Age," in *Older People and Their Social World*, ed. Arnold M. Rose and Warren A. Peterson (Philadelphia: F. A. Davis, 1965), pp. 113–24.
19. J. N. Edwards and D. L. Klemmack, "Correlates of Life Satisfaction: A Reexamination," *Journal of Gerontology*, 28 (1973), 497–502; Elmer Spreitzer and Eddon F. Snyder, "Correlates of Life Satisfaction Among the Aged," *Journal of Gerontology*, 29 (1974), 454–58.
20. Blazer and Palmore, "Religion and Aging," p. 85.
21. Suzanne T. Ortega, Robert D. Crutchfield, and William A. Rushing, "Race Differences in Elderly Personal Well-Being, Friendship, Family and Church," *Research on Aging*, 5, no. 1 (March 1983), 110–11.
22. Harvey C. Lehman, *Age and Achievement* (Princeton, N.J.: Princeton University Press, 1953), p. 173.
23. Beth Hess and Elizabeth Markson, *Aging and Old Age* (New York: Macmillan, 1980), pp. 292–93.
24. Jack Goody, "Aging in Nonindustrial Societies," in *Handbook of Aging and the Social Sciences*, ed. Robert H. Binstock and Ethel Shanas (New York: Van Nostrand Reinhold, 1976), pp. 127–28.
25. David H. Fischer, *Growing Old in America* (New York: Oxford University Press, 1978), p. 34.
26. Charles F. Longino, Jr., and Gay C. Kitson, "Parish Clergy and the Aged," *Journal of Gerontology*, 31, no. 3 (1976), 340–45.

16

Aging and the Aged: Future Prospects and Issues

Often the most learned, wise, and scholarly persons appear foolish when making long-range predictions about the future. This is particularly true if their predictions are widely known by others and examined over a prolonged period. The hazards are based on the fact that a large number of interrelated variables must be taken into account in making any projection. Each of these variables can move in any of a variety of directions, and therefore none is entirely predictable. Since no one can perfectly predict changes over time in any of these variables, to predict how the entire group is going to be altered is even more hazardous.

After recognizing the imprecision of many predictions and the foolhardiness of attempts to make them, most authors of textbooks reveal themselves to be more bold than wise and attempt in a concluding chapter to make some educated guesses regarding the future of their discipline. This author is no different.

Since predictions cannot immediately be reality-tested, they often range between extremes. Herman Kahn and Anthony Wiener (1968) have painted a picture of a utopia in the year 2000. They see technical innovations resulting in permanent undersea colonies, large-scale desalinization of sea water, and genetic control of plants and animals, as well as new drugs that will aid memory and learning. Others, however, paint a gloomy picture of the future that includes population explosions resulting in overpopulation, depletion of energy and food sources, and a battle between "rich" and "poor" nations for control of the remaining resources.

The future of aging can be seen from two perspectives: that of the individual experiencing old age and that of the scientist studying the aging process. Thus, what life will be like for the 65+ group in the year 2000 and what the critical issues and research questions will be for gerontologists studying the problems of aging in the year 2000 or beyond are two different questions. Both for the individual arriving at the later years and the scientists studying gerontology, the future can be seen either optimistically or pessimistically. Here, though, instead of a discussion of the glorious golden years or the gloom and doom of the future, a range of variables from family to health, from retirement to theories of aging, will be considered and an attempt made to determine possible future developments and issues.

GERONTOLOGY: THE FUTURE OF THE DISCIPLINE

Gerontology is a discipline whose time has arrived. The increasing public aware-ness of the problems of aging has resulted in pressure for political action, govern-ment services, scientific research, and practical solutions to those problems. Gerontology seems to be a discipline in ferment and perhaps one that is at the threshold of new discoveries and knowledge. As a result, gerontology is an excit-ing field for a scientist. There is much fertile soil for new research that needs to be carefully cultivated by those in the field.

The discipline will probably continue to command the interests of scientists from a variety of subject areas. Biologists, psychologists, sociologists, economists, political scientists, and psychiatrists will be conducting research in the field. This interdisciplinary nature of the field is likely to result in considerable cross-fertilization of ideas. Theoretical perspectives developed by sociologists may prove useful to psychologists, or the perspective of the biologists may be incorporated into the human developmental theories of both the psychologists and the sociolo-gists. The future directions and developments of new knowledge in the field should prove interesting as scientists attempt to integrate information from a variety of subject matters and theoretical perspectives.

The press to solve the immediate problems of older persons has resulted in research and findings that produce immediate results but may not be well grounded theoretically. Over time the discipline is likely to become much more sophisticated scientifically. Undoubtedly the future holds much in the way of theoretical developments that address the subject of human development and aging.

While the future of gerontology certainly appears promising, there may be problems. Much is expected of the discipline by the public, politicians, and government planners. Public attention and sensitivity to aging and its related problems have led leaders to expect a great deal in the way of new discoveries and expert advice. Will gerontologists be able to live up to these expectations? Only time will tell. It is certainly fair to say that never has any academic discipline been placed more in the public limelight.

In examining what we really know about aging, Antoinette Bosco and Jane Porcino (1977) outlined a number of paradoxes in the field:

1. While doctors spend about 60 percent of their time with the 40 percent of their patients who are over 65, geriatrics as a branch of medicine has been extremely slow in developing in the United States. In a congressional survey of all medical schools only 15 out of 20,000 faculty members identified aging as their specialty. Health needs of the elderly, it is felt, are often viewed as not worth the bother in medical schools.

2. The belief that older persons have been abandoned by their families appears not to be true. Often older family members move near their adult children during retirement and interact with them frequently. Moreover, a higher percentage of the sick elderly live with a family member rather than in a nursing home. At the same time, there is a strong sentiment among the general population to shift the responsibility for aging family members off themselves and onto the government.

3. Retirement is not a dreaded evil feared universally by older persons. A high proportion of older persons look forward to this stage of life and when retired become involved in a variety of creative activities.

4. Romance, love, and sexual fulfillment are not the exclusive province of the young. People 65 and older can and do maintain intimate personal relationships, fall in love, marry, and remain sexually active.

5. Old people are not sick and feeble. While older people do suffer more frequently from chronic health problems, most of these are not debilitating and many are no more serious than short sight and hay fever.

6. Older people are not often senile. Older persons are often misdiagnosed as senile when they are in fact suffering from depression or a treatable physical disorder.

7. Government services are not so tied up with bureaucratic red tape that most older persons don't want to become involved. In reality most government services do not involve a means tests and are relatively accessible for both the economically advantaged and disadvantaged older persons. While many older persons choose not to participate, this choice is rarely related to the red tape involved.

8. While the goal of the gerontologist and the service providers is to help the old remain independent and self-sufficient members of the community, transportation, shopping centers, public buildings and most community activities are structured for the healthy young adult.[1]

Undoubtedly as knowledge in gerontology becomes more widely distributed and the public more informed and sophisticated in their understanding of aging, many of these paradoxes will disappear.

THEORIES OF AGING

Initially the theories of aging, though therapeutic, were narrowly focused and philosophical in nature. Thus successful aging was best accomplished through disengagement, activity, continuity of lifestyles, and so on. These approaches sensitized persons to the problems of later life and told them how best to adjust.

Later theories emphasize developmental processes and are broader-based, connecting the individual to the larger social system and describing the relation of the individual's adjustment patterns to the norms, roles, and institutions of society. Stratification and symbolic interaction are two of the more recent theoretical developments that fit this pattern. The age stratification approach looks at the relative positions of different age groups and examines the possibility of conflict over scarce resources and the more prestigious roles in the social system. Intergenerational conflict, strain, and tension can be easily examined from this theoretical basis. Moreover, one can expect changing attitudes and values as one's age and thereby one's position in the social system change over time. Russell Ward (1979) observes that although age does have a leveling effect, the aging experience differs for men and women, blacks and whites, blue-collar and white-collar workers. These differences cannot entirely be accounted for by the age stratification approach.

Subgroup and subcultural experiences in aging could perhaps best be explained by the symbolic interaction approach. Symbolic interactionists maintain that in order to truly understand the aging experience we must be able to take the role of the other. We must be able to figuratively put ourselves in the shoes of the aging person and view aging from his or her point of view. This approach would help us to understand differences in the aging experience for men and women, blacks and whites, rich and poor, since each of these groups confronts aging from a different perspective. Role losses such as retirement, a move to the Sun Belt, and declining health can be seen from this perspective to alter the social world and status of older persons and thereby both how they are treated by significant others and how they in turn are expected to respond to these others. Deprived of past social groups' identities and roles, the older person does have the opportunity to adopt new roles, reference groups, and lifestyles. Depending on the reaction of the older person, the retirement years, according to Ward (1979), can bring new opportunities, personal growth and development, or stress, maladjustment, and unhappiness.

Both age stratification and symbolic interaction as theoretical approaches to aging recognize that one cannot understand the experiences of the later years without understanding what occurred before. Aging is viewed as a developmental process encompassing the entire life cycle. Ward (1979) explains:

> One cannot understand aging as a developmental period without looking at the whole of the life cycle, retirement without looking at work, widowhood without looking at marriage.[2]

Thus, the more recent theoretical thrusts of the discipline seem to be broader-based and to attempt to understand the aging experience in light of the entire life cycle and the particular society in which the experience took place. The bias of this text has been in the direction of symbolic interaction, but undoubtedly age stratification and other as yet undiscovered theoretical approaches to aging will all lead to a better understanding of aging and intriguing new research questions.

While many of the unanswered questions in gerontology will be addressed in the traditional cross-sectional studies, which examine attitudes and behavior at one point in time, the longitudinal studies, which follow a particular sample of cohorts over time, offer the greatest promise for explaining the developmental processes in aging. Unfortunately, longitudinal studies require extreme dedication and patience. To systematically study a sample of cohorts for the next 10, 20, 30, or 40 years requires a very highly motivated scientist who can delay the rewards of scientific recognition and accomplishment for long periods. Few scientists have such dedication and patience. Moreover, few funding agencies are willing to invest in such long-range projects. Nevertheless, the longitudinal studies offer the greatest hope for resolving many of the unanswered questions in gerontology.

HEALTH

Life span is not likely to be changed by the year 2000 or 2010, but life expectancy will. Bernice Neugarten and Robert Havighurst (1977) report that it was the consensus of a panel of medical specialists that medical discoveries would extend life expectancy from 5 to 10 years by the year 2000.[3] *Life span* refers to the maximum number of years *Homo sapiens* can survive. This currently appears to be somewhere between 110 and 120 years and is not likely to change in the near future. What we will see is a larger proportion of the total population living well into their 80s and remaining in good health throughout most of their later years. This will have the effect of extending life expectancy at birth.

Medical research will undoubtedly continue to examine the biological and organic changes that accompany aging. Research on cell division, the immune system, and the deterioration of the body's vital organs will undoubtedly lead to medical breakthroughs in the control of cancer and heart disease. Any major breakthrough that allows medicine to gain greater control over the body chemistry of older persons will undoubtedly extend their lives. Jon Hendricks and C. Davis Hendricks (1986) report that

> extensive research is already under way to investigate basic immunological systems perhaps involved in aging and the disruption of the body's internal communication processes that enable it to discriminate between inherent and foreign elements.[4]

The body's ability to distinguish between internal and external threats could lead to control of the crippling diseases, such as arthritis, in which the body reacts against itself.

The recognition in recent years that life expectancy can be affected by such things as housing, nutrition, sanitation, smoking, and alcoholism has led to a discussion of both preventive medicine and holistic medicine. Adults are now better educated and better informed on health problems. A sizable segment of the adult population are both knowledgeable and concerned about their health. These people watch their diet and have stopped smoking, developed a pattern of regular exercise, and adopted an attitude of maintenance and prevention about health care. Jogging, handball, tennis, and a great variety of other sports are participated in regularly by this ever-larger segment of the adult population. These are the people who will be entering their older years in the twenty-first century, and one can expect that they will be a healthier group than the current generation of retirees.

Charles Nelson (1981), reporting on the predictions of a futurologist regarding *biofeedback*, points out that people themselves may learn to control their body's internal chemistry through conscious effort and meditation. In the animal world stress triggers a biological reaction that allows the frightened animal to run farther and faster as it attempts to flee danger. Once the burst of energy is expended, the animal has usually escaped the danger and is able to return to a state of relaxation. Stress in humans is often produced not by attacks on life but rather by competition and conflict in families, in work, and in the community. Tension in human life is most often a result of conflict with significant others in the individual's environment. Modern society requires the individual, rather than fleeing threat, to remain outwardly calm and appear to be rational in reaction to whatever may have produced the stress. Thus, the individual's blood pressure rises, the heart pumps faster, and the body's chemistry is altered, but there is no immediate socially acceptable way to relieve this tension. Moreover, people, with their acquisition of language, have the ability to rethink the stressful situation, to relive the insult over and over again in the mind, thus recreating the stress many times over. Students of stress believe that if people are capable of creating stress by their own thoughts, by remembering insults and anxiety-arousing situations, they should equally well be able to recognize stress, alter their thought processes, and relax. Thus an individual may learn to recognize and react to the symptoms of rising blood pressure. Researchers have not really begun to investigate this biofeedback. Once this model of biological control is carefully examined it could lead to a variety of alterations in behavior patterns, lifestyles, and mechanisms of self-control that few of us can currently imagine.

Regardless of the direction medical research is now going in, the result is fairly predictable. There will be a stronger and healthier life for an ever-increasing proportion of the adult population. We may be entering a period in which most Americans can expect to live in good health well into their 80s.

Tobin (1976) sees three forms of future health services becoming more prevalent. First community-based organizations provide a range of health services to the elderly in order to delay institutionalization. Second, small local nursing facilities care for the elderly who need constant care. Tobin believes the smaller institutions can provide more personal care. Third, hospices will be established to care for and help the dying and to provide counseling for their families. Neighborhood health services and hospices may well become more common in the future, but small nursing homes are highly unlikely. A series of federal regulations requiring fire escapes, sprinkler systems, recreational therapists, just to name a few, while well intended, have had the effect of putting small nursing homes out of business since the regulations have made them too expensive to operate. The result is large nursing homes that are economically feasible and that will undoubtedly become the most common form of health service for those persons requiring institutionalization in the future.

RETIREMENT INCOME

While current retirees earn approximately half of what their income was when they were working, the future looks somewhat brighter. First, private pension and insurance programs have become more common and in the future will cover a larger proportion of retirees. Hendricks and Hendricks (1986) observe that the more than 5 million private pension plans in existence in 1975 covered 35 million workers, representing almost half the full-time workers in the country. An additional 40 million workers are either self-employed or employed where pension plans are not available. Hendricks and Hendricks believe that those covered by private pension programs will increase and the programs will become more solvent as a result of the Employee Retirement Security Act of 1974 (ERISA). This law encourages the establishment of private pension programs and insures the benefits of workers who participate in them. Eligibility for existing plans must be determined by age 25 and must grant the employee the right to half of the benefits after 10 years of service and an additional 10 percent for each year thereafter. This law also imposes restrictions on the investments and actions of trust officers for private pensions, thus insuring the soundness of the programs. Simultaneously the government established the Individual Retirement Account (IRA), which enabled those wanting to supplement social security to set aside 15 percent of their income in an annual *tax-sheltered annuity*. The IRA constitutes an income reduction: No taxes are paid on either the amount set aside or on the accumulated interest.[5] As was mentioned in Chapter 12, social security benefits, while lagging somewhat behind inflation, can be adjusted periodically by Congress to stay abreast of inflation.

All of these factors are likely to increase the retirement incomes of older persons. In addition, American workers are becoming increasingly aware of the problems of retirement income, and these are more frequently becoming items for collective bargaining during contract negotiations. Thus it seems clear that an ever-increasing proportion of future retirees will be covered by more than just their social security benefits and that their overall retirement income should rise.

Some would argue that government will have to keep increasing the social security tax on American workers in order to pay the benefits earned by an ever-increasing older population. It has been estimated that by the year 2030 there will be one social security beneficiary for every two workers paying social security taxes, instead of the current one beneficiary for every three workers. Many political analysts have predicted a tax revolt that would set the adult working population against the elderly. This does not seem likely, however, for two reasons: First, the adult population will themselves retire some day, and they do not want to see social security benefits attacked; second, most of them would prefer to see their older relatives receive social security benefits rather than be individually responsible for them economically. In short, a taxpayers' revolt against social security seems unlikely.

Moreover, it seems unlikely that Congress is going to do anything other than support the social security program since such a large group of voters are dependent on it for their economic survival. Bernice Neugarten (1975) has predicted that by the year 2000 industries will ask older workers to continue working, because of a shortage of young people entering the job market. If this prediction does not come to pass, we may see a struggle emerge between the federal government and the business community. Currently the government would like to do whatever it can to raise the age of retirement in order to keep the social security program from having to pay so many retirees over such a prolonged period. This has the effect of shifting some of the responsibility for the income of older persons off the government and onto their employers—the business community. Since older workers tend to rank high on the salary schedule and on the company's retirement and fringe benefit programs, the company is usually anxious for them to retire so they can be replaced by younger and less expensive workers. Thus the federal government's desire to keep the social security program financially solvent means that they would like to see older workers stay in the labor force longer. Business, on the other hand, wanting to keep their labor costs down, would like to see older workers retire sooner. The outcome of this struggle is impossible to determine at this time.

Most observers expect that the number of older persons with income below the poverty line will have decreased by the year 2000 and that the overall incomes of retirees will have increased. Schulz (1988) predicts an increase in retirement incomes due to the *demographic turnover*. That is, every day a large number of persons enter the 65 age group and a large number over 65 die. Those who die are usually poorer than those who have just become members of the aged population. The new aged often retire on pension incomes considerably higher than those of the previous generation of retirees.

FAMILY

As was pointed out in Chapter 8, approximately two thirds of all aged persons are husband–wife couples living alone, most of whom maintain their own household. These couples have for the most part had one fourth of their married life to live after the last child left home. Legitimate topics for future research on the family will undoubtedly include adjustment patterns of widows and widowers, second marriages, and alternative family forms during later life.

While the typical elderly couple today have often enjoyed a long-standing marriage lasting 30 or 40 years, some have projected that the high divorce rate, the greater tolerance of and acceptance of divorce, as well as more casual attitudes toward *cohabitation*, might result in many older persons in the future not being married. The Population Reference Bureau's 1978 article in *Inter-Change* does not indicate that this will be the case, however. There is evidence that the divorce rate has reached its peak and may even decline during the next few years. This seems to be related to the fact that fewer marriages are occurring among the very young and other groups that have traditionally been known to have high divorce rates. The U.S. Bureau of the Census data indicate that fewer Americans, especially women, are marrying in their teens and that couples are having fewer children and delaying the birth of their first child. All of these trends tend to improve the economic position of the family, which contributes to marital stability.[6] Simultaneously there will be fewer families broken up because of the death of a spouse.

Richard Clayton and Harwin Voss (1977) have suggested that "living together," along with delayed marriages, will lead to a more careful selection of a spouse and thus to a more enduring marriage in terms of the survival rate of the marriage. Table 16–1 illustrates the pattern of survival rates for marriage projected by Clayton and Voss (1977).

TABLE 16–1　How Long Do Marriages Last?

Wedding Anniversary, First Marriage	Chances of Reaching the Anniversary
5th	5 of every 6
10th	4 of every 5
20th	3 of every 4
30th	2 of every 3
35th	1 of every 2
40th	2 of every 5
45th	1 of every 3
50th	1 of every 5
55th	1 of every 10
60th	1 of every 20
65th	1 of every 50
70th	1 of every 100

Source:　Richard R. Clayton and Harwin L. Voss, "Shacking Up: Cohabitation in the 1970s," *Journal of Marriage and the Family*, 39, no. 2 (May 1977), 273–83. Copyright 1977 by the National Council on Family Relations. Reprinted by permission.

Thus, it may well be expected that probably just about as many couples arriving at age 65 in the twenty-first century will have lived together for a considerable proportion of their adult life as those now 65. They will probably have married a few years later than their parents and grandparents did and have had fewer children. Most of them, however, will have experienced marital stability throughout most of their adult lives.

Projections about the *sex ratio* in the year 2000 or 2010 are less consistent and depend on the point of view of the person making the projection. Bosco and Porcino (1977), for example, report that

> the elderly population of the future will be mostly female, and many of them will be widows. Of these 65 and older, there are now 69 males for every 100 females; whereas, 400 years ago the ratio was about even. By the year 2000, there will be an estimated 65 males for every 100 females of the same age.[7]

As pointed out in this text, there is evidence that more boys are conceived than girls; during the nine months of pregnancy, during childbirth, and at every age in life thereafter, boys are more likely to die than girls. The result has been that the older a group of cohorts become, the more imbalanced the sex ratio becomes in favor of women. Moreover, each new medical discovery has so far ended up saving more women's lives than men's, and the gap in the life expectancy of the two groups widens. Thus, it is easy to understand the reasons for Bosco and Porcino's (1977) projections.

There is, however, a counterargument being made by students of the feminist movement and the family: As women enter careers and strive for success and upward mobility with the same vigor that men have in the past, they will experience the same physiological stresses and strains and thereby come to approximate males in frequency of ulcers, heart attacks, and other stress-related illnesses and deaths. The result should be a narrowing of the gap in life expectancy between men and women and the narrowing of the differences in the number of men and women in the 65-and-over group. Actually, the 1980s was the first decade in this century to record a reduction in the gap between men's and women's life expectancy. Instead of the difference between the life expectancy of men and women increasing as it had since 1900, it actually decreased slightly. If the differential in life expectancy was to continue to gradually decrease over the next two or three decades we would undoubtedly find more equal numbers of older men and women in later life in the twenty-first century.

The best guesses about the older family in the twenty-first century might be that both husbands and wives will have been involved in occupational pursuits throughout most of their married life. They will have had small families of two or three children at most and will have more than one fourth of their married life to live after the last child leaves home. They will have had a marriage based on companionship and a sharing of child-rearing and household chores rather than on a complicated division of labor. They will have experienced more adequate and stable incomes during their adult years as a result of both partners working. Similarly, their retirement incomes will be more secure since they will be able to depend on two separate retirement incomes rather than one. Inevitably, one of the marital partners will precede the other in death and it will be crucial to the remaining partner that a proportion of the deceased partner's retirement income be transferred. While two cannot live as cheaply as one, together they can live cheaper than two separately. Rent, utilities, heat, and other bills continue whether there is one or two persons in the household. The retirement couples of the twenty-first century will probably enjoy their retirement more and have more common interests during the retirement years. Having had a marriage in which household duties as well as recreation and leisure interests were shared on a companionship basis rather than as a division of labor based primarily on sex, future retired couples should have many more common interests and shared values on which to build their retirement lives.

RESIDENTIAL LOCATION

In terms of migration patterns and shifts of the population, the elderly have in the past been the group least prone to move. Earlier, they were disproportionately represented in the rural areas, then they were left in the zones immediately surrounding the inner city as younger people moved to the suburbs. The next projected concentrations of the elderly might be in the suburbs as the current population in the suburbs ages and younger people move elsewhere. The relatively low crime rates and less expensive living costs of small towns across the country will probably continue to be attractive to older persons. Therefore, we would expect small towns in rural areas to have disproportionately larger numbers of older persons residing there.

The future generation of retirees will probably be even more likely than the past generation to move to the Sun Belt. First, their incomes are going to be better as retirement programs become more widespread and their benefits more secure. Second, as was just observed, there will be more couples with two retirement incomes. Given adequate incomes, more older persons will have more freedom to chose where they would like to live rather than being forced to live in their present location because they cannot afford to do anything else. Undoubtedly, many will choose to live a part or all of their retirement years in the warmer climates. Some older persons will follow the common pattern of wintering in Florida, Arizona, or California and spending their summers in other states in which their children are located, thus maintaining viable family relations. Others will choose to reside permanently in the Southern states, visiting their children periodically during vacations.

In all probability what one will find is that if the incomes of retirement couples improve, then their choices of residential location and lifestyle will become more diverse. Guaranteed adequate resources, they will become much like other age groups, whose values and personal choices lead them in a variety of directions. Economic deprivation often leaves few choices available to the current population of older Americans, and they tend to cling to their current homes and residential locations regardless of their appropriateness.

POSTINDUSTRIAL SOCIETY

Everett Hughes (1964), Daniel Bell (1973), and other social scientists have speculated on what life will be like in postindustrial society. The consensus of the social scientists seems to be that the postindustrial period will see a shift away from expansion in manufacturing and industry to the expansion of social services, entertainment, athletics, and recreation and leisure enterprises. The basic argument of the social scientists is that as the industrial development of a nation peaks and as an ever-efficient manufacturing technology emerges, less of the population will be required to produce the nation's goods. This will make surpluses of labor available; the service occupations, the entertainment industry, and industries catering to recreation and leisure activities will develop. Bell (1973) believes that postindustrial society may be characterized by a new elite based on professional expertise. He observes that the number of scientists and engineers doubled from 1900 to 1975 and predicts that by the year 2000 the technical and professional class will be the largest occupational group in the country. It will, he argues, form a pool of experts that government and industry can use to plan and organize for the future. The result is expected to be a tremendous growth of government employment and the expansion of social services. Simultaneously the reduced working hours, the advent of a four-day work week, and related trends will result in larger amounts of free time for the average citizen. This will mean greater opportunity for entertainment, athletic events, recreation, and other leisure pursuits as well as opportunity for education and cultural enrichment. Colleges and universities are more likely to find their student bodies composed of all age groups rather than just 18-to–25-year-olds, as the adult population has more free time to pursue its own interests and personal development.

VALUES

The values of the postindustrial period are expected to be slightly different from what we know today. It is thought that there will be a movement away from the Protestant ethic and toward emphasis on the quality of life, including considerable emphasis on individuality, self-expression, and personal development. There will be somewhat less pressure to shape oneself to fit the demands of industry by developing a narrow occupational skill. There may well emerge in the postindustrial period the belief that everyone should be guaranteed the right to work and that a job should be shaped to fit the individual as much as the individual should be shaped to fit the job.

According to Rhona and Robert Rapoport (1975), achievement, productivity, and independence may seem less important in the postindustrial period and be replaced by such values as the importance of congeniality, concern for the meaning of life, and the cultivation of satisfying human relationships. Eric Trist (1976) argues that the postindustrial period will be marked by value shifts from achievement to self-actualization, from self-control to self-expression, from independence to interdependence.

If the values of the twenty-first century shift along the lines suggested by the social scientists, we should expect an improvement in the status of older persons. Less emphasis on achievement and productivity, in which the young are always viewed as having the greatest potential for development, and greater concern with interpersonal relationships and the meaning and quality of life, in which the old may have the distinct advantage of breadth of experience and wisdom accumulated over a lifetime, should improve the status of older persons. Robert Butler (1975) argues that the "loosening up of life," in which we are not locked into lifelong careers and bound by decisions made early in life, may greatly benefit those in the middle and later years. Time for recreation and leisure activities throughout the entire life cycle is to be expected. For many, the opportunity for second and third careers in later life will become more common.

WORK AND LEISURE

As greater flexibility in work and leisure patterns emerges, and thereby greater flexibility in lifestyles, one would expect people to enter and exit from formal educational programs at different phases of the life cycle. Adults may be retrained after deciding to change careers in midlife. Sarason (1977) has written a book depicting the variety of midlife career changes experienced by a number of persons in very diverse occupations. Sarason asserts that the major reason for the frequent midcareer changes is self-expression. Over time people realize that the manner in which they are required to present themselves in their current occupation is inconsistent with their innermost view of self. They thus change jobs in order to assume a role in which their best self-image can be presented. Sarason's hypothesis is consistent with the symbolic interactionist view of personality development. To the degree that this pattern becomes more widespread, we would expect a greater number of the adult population to change careers more frequently and to enter formal educational training programs at different phases of the life cycle. This may make formal education a lifelong experience rather than the exclusive privilege of the young. Thus, older persons might be more inclined to return to colleges and universities after retiring as a means of cultural enrichment rather than for career preparation. The time available to the individual for recreational and leisure pursuits will undoubtedly grow.

POWER

If the trend of low birthrates that has prevailed since the mid-1960s continues, we can expect the mean age of the population to move upward and for the 65+ group to make up an even larger percentage of the total population. Instead of middle-aged persons maintaining a concentration of power in our society, we might expect middle-aged and older persons to share power. We have already seen the legal retirement age changed from 65 to 70. Ultimately, cases will be brought to court claiming reverse age discrimination in employment. One might expect that more semiprofessional and professional employees in the future will choose to work beyond age 65. These two groups in particular have been found to find greater satisfaction and meaning in their work than have many blue-collar workers. If they do work beyond age 65, these persons will often be found in key organizational positions, exercising considerable authority in decision making. In short, the power now concentrated in the hands of middle-aged adults may shift in the direction of older adults.

DEATH

Traditional attitudes and values surrounding death may be challenged more than any other of society's cherished beliefs. The capacity of medical technology to maintain and prolong life, even if only in a near-vegetable condition, will ultimately force society to address the issue of humankind's apparent control over life and death. One does not like to think of oneself as deciding either individually or for loved ones when the proper time to die shall be. We have generally viewed self-determination of death as suicide and maintained that suicide is an act of desperation or cowardice. In the future our values may shift so that we come to believe that it is a person's right to choose to die if life is maintained only by medical technology and there is no hope for an improvement. Euthanasia may be more acceptable in the next century than it is presently.

GOVERNMENT SERVICES

While there may be temporary setbacks and reversals, the long-range trend will be to increase government services for older Americans. This group will clearly be a large voting bloc capable of keeping political leaders informed of their more pressing problems. The political process in the United States tends to be strongly influenced by interest groups. Political leaders, faced with organized groups of older Americans, will no doubt favor legislation that would improve the welfare of this group of citizens. Harold Cox and Gurmeet Sekhon (1981) asked a sample of old, rural, and low-income Americans to rank their most pressing needs. These were perceived to be

1. Adequate income
2. Concern about physical health
3. Energy (fuel, gas, electric)
4. Transportation
5. Nutrition
6. National health insurance

Having a rural sample rank national health insurance as important to them when it is usually identified as a clearly liberal cause is somewhat surprising; rural Americans have generally been thought to be the most conservative politically. Apparently they are willing to endorse liberal programs that they believe will bring much-needed assistance to them. These results suggest that in both rural and urban America there will be growing pressure for an increasing number and variety of service programs for older Americans.

CONCLUSION

Older Americans in the future can be expected to be reasonably healthy into their 80s and to have greater economic security than the previous generation of older persons. The result will be more diverse and heterogeneous lifestyles for future retirees. Their increasing resources will allow them to choose more freely among geographic locations, housing, neighborhoods, communities, and social groups with which they would like to identify. In short, it would appear that future generations of older persons will have brighter prospects than the past generations for a healthy and productive later life, with greater reserves and freedom to choose among a wide range of lifestyles, roles, and activities.

KEY TERMS

biofeedback
cohabitation
demographic turnover

sex ratio
tax-sheltered annuity

REFERENCES

BELL, DANIEL, *The Coming of Post-Industrial Society.* New York: Basic Books, 1973.

BOSCO, ANTOINETTE, and JANE PORCINO, *What Do We Really Know About Aging.* Stony Brook: State University of New York at Stony Brook, 1977.

BUTLER, ROBERT, *Why Survive? Being Old in America.* New York: Harper & Row, 1975.

CLAYTON, RICHARD R., and HARWIN L. VOSS, "Shacking Up: Cohabitation in the 1970s," *Journal of Marriage and the Family,* 39, no. 2 (May 1977), 273–83.

COX, HAROLD, and GURMEET SEKHON, *Statistical Report—1981 White House Conference: Prioritizing the Needs of the Rural Elderly.* Washington, D.C.: National Green Thumb, 1981.

HENDRICKS, JON, and C. DAVIS HENDRICKS, *Aging in Mass Society.* Cambridge, Mass.: Winthrop, 1986.

HUGHES, EVERETT, *Men and Their Work.* New York: Free Press, 1964.

KAHN, HERMAN, and ANTHONY WIENER, "The Next Thirty-Three Years: A Framework for Speculation," in *Toward the Year 2000: Work in Progress,* ed. Daniel Bell. Boston: Houghton Mifflin, 1968.

NELSON, CHARLES, "Holistic Medicine." Lecture at Futures Forum, Indiana State University, 1981.

NEUGARTEN, BERNICE, "The Future and the Young–old," *Gerontologist,* 15, no. 1 (1975), 7.

NEUGARTEN, BERNICE, and ROBERT HAVIGHURST, eds., *Extending the Human Life Span: Social Policy and Social Ethics.* Washington, D.C.: U.S. Government Printing Office, 1977.

POPULATION REFERENCE BUREAU, *Inter-Change: Population Educators Newsletter* (ISSN: 0047-0465), 7, no. 1 (January 1978), 2.

RAPOPORT, RHONA, and ROBERT RAPOPORT, *Leisure and the Family Life Cycle.* London: Routledge & Kegan Paul, 1975.

SARASON, SEYMOUR, *Work, Aging and Social Change: Professionals and the One Life-One Career Imperative.* New York: Free Press, 1977.

SCHULZ, JAMES H., *The Economics of Aging* (4th ed.). Dover, Mass.: Auburn House, 1988.

TOBIN, SHELDON, *Effective Social Services for Older Americans.* University of Michigan/Wayne State: Institute of Gerontology, 1976.

TRIST, ERIC, "Toward a Post-Industrial Culture," in *Handbook of Work, Organization and Society,* ed. Robert Dubin. Skokie, Ill.: Rand McNally, 1976.

WARD, RUSSELL, *The Aging Experience.* New York: J.B. Lippincott, 1979.

NOTES

1. Antoinette Bosco and Jane Porcino, *What Do We Really Know About Aging* (Stony Brook: State University of New York at Stony Brook, 1977), pp. 75–78.
2. Russell Ward, *The Aging Experience* (Philadelphia: Lippincott, 1979), p. 502.
3. Bernice Neugarten and Robert Havighurst, eds., *Extending the Human Life Span: Social Policy and Social Ethics* (Washington, D.C.: U.S. Government Printing Office, 1977).
4. Jon Hendricks and C. Davis Hendricks, *Aging in Mass Society* (Cambridge, Mass.: Winthrop, 1986), p. 508.
5. Ibid., pp. 396–97.
6. Population Reference Bureau, *Inter-Change: Population Educators Newsletter* (ISSN: 0047-0465), 7, no. 1 (January 1978), 2.
7. Bosco and Porcino, *What Do We Really Know About Aging,* p. 77.

Index